Reginald Godfrey Marsden

**A Treatise on the Law of Collisions at Sea**

with an Appendix, containing extracts from the Merchant shipping acts, the

international regulations of 1863 and 1880 for preventing collisions at sea, and

local rules for the same purpose in force in the

Reginald Godfrey Marsden

**A Treatise on the Law of Collisions at Sea**
*with an Appendix, containing extracts from the Merchant shipping acts, the international regulations of 1863 and 1880 for preventing collisions at sea, and local rules for the same purpose in force in the*

ISBN/EAN: 9783337780289

Printed in Europe, USA, Canada, Australia, Japan

Cover: Foto ©Suzi / pixelio.de

More available books at **www.hansebooks.com**

A TREATISE ON

THE LAW OF

# COLLISIONS AT SEA,

WITH

## An Appendix,

CONTAINING

EXTRACTS FROM THE MERCHANT SHIPPING ACTS, THE INTER-
NATIONAL REGULATIONS (OF 1863 AND 1880) FOR PREVENTING
COLLISIONS AT SEA, AND LOCAL RULES FOR THE
SAME PURPOSE IN FORCE IN THE THAMES,
THE MERSEY, AND ELSEWHERE.

BY

## REGINALD G. MARSDEN,

OF THE INNER TEMPLE, ESQ., BARRISTER-AT-LAW.

*"Si navis tua impacta in meam scapham damnum mihi dederit quæsitum
est quæ actio mihi competeret."*
Dig. lib. ix., tit. ii., fr. 29, § 2.

LONDON:
STEVENS AND SONS, 119, CHANCERY LANE,
Law Publishers and Booksellers.
1880.

# PREFACE.

STATISTICS issued by Lloyd's show that in the year 1878 there were in collision 1790 sailing-ships and 836 steam-ships. About 15 per cent. of the steam-ships and 3.6 per cent. of the sailing-ships of the world (estimated as numbering respectively 5462 and 49,524) suffered loss from this one cause. Some idea of the amount of that loss may be formed from the fact that in the Admiralty Division of the High Court of Justice in this country there were instituted in the year ending 31st October, 1878, actions in which sums amounting to £985,550 were claimed for damage by collision. In the same year occurred the collision between the *Bywell Castle* and the *Princess Alice* in the River Thames, in which were lost upwards of 600 lives; also that between the *Grosser Kurfürst* and the *König Wilhelm*, off Folkestone, where 281 of the crew of the former ship perished. The importance of the subject treated of in the following pages is sufficiently shown by the above facts.

To seamen having the charge of ships this treatise is offered in the hope that by setting forth the exact requirements of the law it may enable them to navigate in accordance with the law, and possibly avert collision. To others interested in shipping, and to the legal profession, is is offered as containing a summary of the law and cases relating to collisions between ships. Its publication at the present moment is explained by the recent issue of new International Regulations for preventing collision at sea, which comes into force on the 1st of September next.

I am indebted to my friend, Mr. C. F. Jemmett, of Lincoln's Inn and the Inner Temple, for valuable suggestions and assistance in preparing the following sheets for the press. For errors of arrangement, commission and omission (for which I alone am responsible) I ask the indulgence of the reader.

5, NEW SQUARE, LINCOLN'S INN,
        March, 1880.

# TABLE OF CONTENTS.

## CHAPTER I.

# ADDENDA.

Page 26, note (o) ; see the judgment of the Court of Appeal delivered by
Brett, L.J., in *The Parlement Belge* (Court of Appeal, February
27, 1880 ; *Times*, February 28, 1880).

  „   29, note (e) ; see the observations of Brett, L.J., on *The Bold Buccleugh*
in *The Parlement Belge, ubi supra.*

  „   31, The nature of proceedings *in rem* was fully considered in *The
Parlement Belge, ubi supra.*

  „   33, note (h) ; opposed to the view that the "wrongdoing" ship is
liable in Admiralty without regard to her ownership is the judgment of the Court of Appeal in *The Parlement Belge, ubi supra.*
"The liability to compensate must be fixed not merely on the
property but on the owner through the property," *per* Brett, L.J.,
*ibid.* In the same case, it was held that the shipowner is, in fact,
impleaded in an Admiralty action *in rem*, and that the proceedings are not merely against the ship.

  „   64, note (y) ; *Lohre* v. *Aitchison* is reported on appeal, 4 App. Cas. 755.

  „   71, note (p) ; see *The Consett*, 28 W. R. 307 ; on app. 42 L. T., N. S., as
to the costs of cargo owners before the registrar and merchants.

  „   93, The decision of Sir R. Phillimore that *The Parlement Belge* was
liable to arrest, was reversed by the Court of Appeal upon the
following grounds :—(1) That the person and the property of a
foreign Sovereign are exempt from the jurisdiction of a British
Court upon the same grounds, namely, that the exercise of such
jurisdiction is incompatible with the absolute independence of the
Sovereign of every superior authority ; (2) That this principle
applies to an Admiralty action *in rem ;* (3) That a ship owned
and used by a State or Sovereign for public purposes is exempt
from arrest, whether process *in rem* is considered as a proceeding
against the ship or against the shipowner ; (4) That in an action
*in rem* the shipowner is indirectly impleaded. The question
whether the ship was exempt from arrest by virtue of the convention mentioned in the text (p. 93) was not considered ; *The
Parlement Belge, ubi supra.*

  „   158, 253, 259. It is intended by Order in Council to postpone the
coming into operation of Article 10 of the Regulations of 1880 as
to fishing boats' lights until the 1st of September, 1881.

  „   271—279. By an Order in Council, dated the 18th of March, 1880,
the bye-laws for the River Thames printed in the Appendix,
pp. 271—274 (except No. 15, p. 271), have been repealed. By
the same Order the rules and bye-laws printed in italics (pp.
274—279), and headed as "Proposed" rules, have been enacted in
their place. The Schedule to the Order in Council contains an
additional bye-law, No. 30, imposing a penalty of £5 for infringement of the bye-laws. The new bye-laws come into force on the
1st of June, 1880.

# TABLE OF CASES.

## A.

## C.

F.

## G.

b

## J.

## K.

Cases Decided by Courts of the United States of America are Cited from the
following Reports:—

| | |
|---|---|
| ABBOT, | Admiralty (District Court) Reports. |
| AMERICAN REPORTS (all the Courts of last resort). | |
| BENEDICT, | District Court Reports. |
| BLATCHFORD, | Circuit Court Reports. |
| BROWN, | Admiralty Reports. |
| GALLISON, | Circuit Court Reports. |
| HOWARD, | Supreme Court Reports. |
| NEWBERRY, | Admiralty (District Court) Reports. |
| OLCOTT, | Admiralty (District Court) Reports. |
| SPRAGUE, | Admiralty (District Court) Reports. |
| WARE, | District Court Reports. |
| WALLACE, | Supreme Court Reports. |
| WALLACE, Junior, | Circuit Court Reports. |

# THE

# LAW OF MARITIME COLLISION.

## CHAPTER I.

### GENERAL RULES.

For the purpose of determining by whom and in what shares the loss is to be borne, collisions between ships have been divided into four classes. "In the first place, it (collision) may happen without blame being imputable to either party, as where the loss is occasioned by a storm, or other *vis major*. In that case the misfortune must be borne by the party on whom it happens to light, the other not being responsible to him in any degree. Secondly, a misfortune of this kind may arise where both parties are to blame, where there has been want of due diligence or of skill on both sides; in such a case the rule of law is that the loss must be apportioned between them, as having been occasioned by the fault of both of them. Thirdly, it may happen by the misconduct of the suffering party only ; and then the rule is that the sufferer must bear his own burden. Lastly, it may have been the fault of the ship which ran the other down, and in this case the innocent party would be entitled to an entire compensation from the other " (a).

The four cases of collision.

(a) Per Lord Stowell in *The Woodrop*, Sims, 2 Dods. 83, 85. As to the meaning of "collision" in Admiralty see *The Maxey*, Abbot. Ad. 73.

B

Rule as to equal division of loss where both ships are in fault. The law "apportions" the loss where both ships are in fault by obliging each of them to pay half the loss of the other. Thus, if the loss on A. is £1000 and that on B. is £2000, A. can recover £500 against B., and B. can recover £1000 against A. The Courts make no attempt to administer distributive justice by apportioning the loss according to the degree of fault of which each ship is guilty (b). The rule as to equal division of loss where both ships are in fault now prevails in all the Courts. Until recently (c) it prevailed only in Admiralty proceedings; at Common Law neither ship could recover anything against the other where both were in fault (d).

Whether the rule of equal division of loss where the ships in collision are both in fault applies where there is a collision between two ships, A. and B., caused by the fault of one of them, B., and of a third ship, C., so as to entitle B. to recover half her loss from C., is not clear (e). It has been applied as between a ship being launched and another under way, where the fault of the former was committed on shore and consisted in being started at an improper moment (f).

What is negligence causing collision. The mere fact that a ship strikes, or goes foul of another, creates no liability against herself, her owners, or those in charge of her. Nor does it advance the case to assert that the one ship "ran down" the other, or "ran into" her (g). So that damages may be recovered fault must be proved for which the owners or persons on board the ship sued are responsible. What degree of fault entitles the plaintiff to recover it is difficult or impossible to define (h).

(b) *Hay* v. *Le Neve*, 2 Shaw's Scotch App. Cas. 395, and cases there cited ; *The Milan*, Lush. 388.

(c) The Judicature Act, 1873, altered the law ; 36 & 37 Vict. c. 66, s. 25, sub-s. 9.

(d) For some account of the law as to the incidence of loss where both ships are in fault in this an 1 other countries, see the note at the foot of this chapter, *infra*, p. 49.

(e) See *The Energy*, *infra*, p. 80 ; *The James Gray*, 21 Wall. 184.

(f) *The United States*, 12 L. T. N. S. 31.

(g) *The James Watt*, 2 W. Rob. 270, 278.

(h) Bynkershoek says : *præcipue eâ in re valet judicis arbitrium.*

Apart from the particular circumstances of each case the question does not admit of an answer. A collision can seldom or never be avoided at the moment of its occurrence. It is often inevitable for some moments before the ships come together. It is not enough for a ship to show that as soon as the necessity for taking measures to avoid a collision was perceived, all that could be done was done. When two ships are shown to have been in a position in which a collision was inevitable, the question is, by whose fault, if there was fault, did the vessels get into such a position (*i*). If there would have been no loss but for the vessels coming into contact, it is immaterial, upon the trial of the question, Who is to bear the loss, that its amount was increased by negligence, previous to, or at the time of, the collision, provided such negligence did not contribute to the collision (*j*). Thus, when a ship, A., was, by her own fault, in collision with another, B., that was negligently carrying her anchor a-cockbill in the Thames, and in consequence of the anchor being in that position its fluke was driven into B.'s side and she sank, it was held that B. was entitled to recover full damages against A. (*k*).

In a similar case, where the question was whether the damage was caused by the negligence of the pilot in navigating the vessel so as to come into collision, or by the negligence of the master and crew in carrying the anchor improperly, Dr. Lushington held that it was caused not by the improper position of the anchor, but by the ship being improperly steered and towed. It was held that the posi-

---

(*i*) *Maddox* v. *Fisher; The Independence*, 14 Moo. P. C. C. 103, 109; *The Despatch*, ibid. 83; *The Pennsylvania*, 3 Mar. Law Cas. O. S. 477; *The America*, 2 Otto. 432; and see below, p. 6.

(*j*) Negligence subsequent to the collision, by which the loss is increased, may be material upon the question of damages. See below, pp. 55, seq.

(*k*) *Sills* v. *Brown*, 9 Car. & P. 601. As to an act material only as regards the parts of the ships which are in contact, see *The Governor* and *The John McIntyre*, Holt's Rule of the Road, 184.

tion of the anchor was material only in case there would have been no damage but for its being carried where it was (*l*).

So if a vessel suffers more severely in a collision in consequence of her being in a weak or strained condition, she is not on that account prevented from recovering full damages (*m*). Nor is it any answer to an action for damages that the loss would not have occurred but for the negligence of a third ship, if the collision or loss was in fact caused partly by the fault of the vessel sued (*n*).

Though, at the time of the collision, a vessel is being navigated in an improper manner, she will not be held in fault for the collision, if it is proved that the particular act of imprudence or negligence did not cause or contribute to the collision. Though it be proved that her crew was insufficient, her speed too great, her condition unseaworthy, or her officers incapable, if the circumstance had no connection with the collision, it is altogether irrelevant (*o*). If the negligence of the party injured did not, in any degree, contribute to the immediate cause of the accident, that negligence ought not to be set up as an answer to the action (*p*).

If it is open for a vessel to adopt either of two courses, one of which is safe and the other hazardous, and she elects the latter, she is responsible for mischief which ensues. And she cannot, in such a case, insist upon the fact that she had a right to be where she was, or that she complied with the letter of the law. "If it be practicable to pursue a course which is safe, and you follow so closely upon the track of another that mischief may ensue, you are bound to adopt the safe course. This is the principle that is

(*l*) *The Gipsey King*, 5 Not. of Cas. 282.

(*m*) *The Egyptian*, 2 Mar. Law Cas. O. S. 56 ; *Luxford* v. *Large*, 5 C. & P. 421 ; *The Batavier*, 1 Sp. E. & A. 378 ; and see *infra*, Ch. 11.

(*n*) See p. 40, *infra*.

(*o*) *The Hope*, 1 W. Rob. 154 ; *The Lord Saumarez*, 6 Not. of Cas. 600.

(*p*) *Per* Pollock, C.B., *Greenland* v. *Chaplin*, 5 Ex. 243.

always acted upon in cases of injuries done to ships at sea " (q).

Where there is negligence on the part of both vessels, but one of them might, by the exercise of ordinary care, have avoided the collision, she will be held solely in fault (r), unless the negligence of the other consists in an infringement of one of the Statutory Regulations for preventing collision, which might, by possibility, have contributed to the collision. In that case, whether it did in fact contribute to the collision or not, both ships will be held to be in fault (s). And where negligence is proved on the part of the plaintiff, unless the Court is satisfied that it did not contribute to the accident, he can recover nothing, unless the other ship is also in fault (t).

Where there is negligence, but one ship might by ordinary care have avoided a collision.

As to the degree of skill and precaution which the law requires of seamen, Dr. Lushington described it as ordinary skill and ordinary diligence : " We are not to expect extraordinary skill or extraordinary diligence, but that degree of skill and that degree of diligence which is generally to be found in persons who discharge their duty " (u). A ship that is partially disabled, or navigating in an unusual manner, or otherwise especially dangerous to other vessels, must take more than ordinary care to avoid collision (x).

Degree of skill required.

Where two vessels are upon courses which will take them clear of each other, the one which, by unnecessarily altering her course, causes risk of collision, is in fault (y).

(q) Per Ellenborough, C.J., in Mayhew v. Boyce, 1 Stark. 423.

(r) Tuff v. Warnam, 2 C. B. N.S. 740 ; 5 C. B. N. S. 573 ; Dowell v. General Steam Navigation Co., 5 E. & B. 195 ; The Lord Saumarez, 6 Not. of Cas. 600 ; Radley v. London and N. W. Ry. Co., 1 Ap. Cas. 754, 759 ; Greenland v. Chaplin, 5 Ex. 243 (infra) ; Smith v. Voss, 2 H. & N. 97.

(s) 36 & 37 Vict. c. 85, s. 17 ; see below, p. 14, seq.

(t) Luxford v. Large, 5 C. & P. 421.

(u) The Thomas Powell and The Cuba, 2 Mar. Law Cas. O. S. 344, 345.

(x) See infra, Ch. VI., Art. 5 and Art. 23 ; The Eleanor and The Alma, 2 Mar. Law Cas. O. S. 240.

(y) The Velocity, L. R. 3 P. C. 44. See also The Esk and The Niord, ibid. 436.

A wrong step taken in the agony of the collision is not negligence.  If a vessel by her own fault makes a collision so imminent that it cannot be avoided except by the exercise of extraordinary skill or exertion on the part of the other ship, and a collision occurs, it will be held to have been occasioned by the former, and she will be liable for the entire loss. In such a case, and in every case where a ship by her own negligence places another in sudden peril, the latter will not be held in fault for omitting at the last moment to do something that would have averted the collision (z). And the rule is the same whether the emergency and sudden peril is caused by the fault of the other vessel or not. A vessel is not required to foresee and provide for every accident. The mere omission to do something that would have prevented the collision, or the doing something without which the collision would not have occurred, is not in every case negligence. The plaintiff can recover, although by taking steps other than those he did take he might have prevented the collision, provided he was not in fault for not taking such steps (a).

Where a steam-ship coming up the Thames at night passed a schooner, and when about 300 yards a-head of her took the ground and stopped, the schooner was held not in fault for a collision which followed, although, possibly, if she had at once let go her anchor she might have prevented the collision (b).

A steam-ship bound down the river Thames on a very

(z) The Nor, 2 Asp. Mar. Law Cas. 264 ; The C. M. Palmer and The Larnax, infra; The Pyrus and The Smalis, Holt 40 ; The Elizabeth and The Lotus, 2 Mar. Law Cas. O. S. 238 ; The Sisters, 1 P. D. 117 ; The Bywell Castle, 4 P. D. 219. The same rule prevails in the American courts, The Benefactor, 14 Blatchf. 254 ; The Byfoged Christiansen, 4 App. Cas. 669.
(a) The Jesmond and The Earl of Elgin, L. R. 4 P. C. 1, 7 ; The

Sisters, 1 P. D. 117 ; The Marpesia, L. R. 4 P. C. 212 ; Vennall v. Garner, 1 Cr. & M. 21 ; The City of Antwerp and The Friedrich, Inman v. Beck, L. R. 2 P. C. 25. Cf. per Ellenborough, C.J., in Jones v. Boyce, 1 Stark. 493, 495 : "If I place a man in such a situation that he must adopt a perilous alternative (as jumping off a coach), I am responsible for the consequences."
(b) The Elizabeth and The Adalia, 3 Mar. Law Cas. O. S. 345.

NEGLIGENCE CAUSING COLLISION.

dark night was rounding-to in Gravesend reach before coming to an anchor. While rounding-to she ran into and sank a vessel at anchor without a riding light up. The instant the latter vessel was seen the engines of the steamship were stopped and reversed, but her anchor was not let go. It was held that, even if the collision could have been averted by letting go the anchor, the master of the steam-ship was not guilty of negligence because, at the moment, it did not occur to him to let go his anchor (c).

But if a ship seeks to excuse herself for taking a wrong step which, in fact, caused or contributed to the collision, upon the ground of sudden peril, she must show clearly that she was in no way responsible for the sudden peril (d).

Upon the same principle, if a ship, by carrying wrong lights, or by navigating in an improper or unusual manner, misleads or embarrasses another, she cannot attribute as a fault to the latter any act which was the probable result of her own negligence (e). So where a ship is hailed from another to take a particular course, and she obeys the hail, the other ship cannot be heard to say that the course was wrong, although, in fact, it caused the collision and was in violation of the Regulations (f).

*Misleading lights, hailing, or other embarrassing acts.*

(c) *The C. M. Palmer* and *The Larnax*, 2 Asp. Mar. Law Cas. 94.
 (d) See *The Bywell Castle*, 4 P. D. 219, and the cases cited above. It has been repeatedly held by the Supreme Court of the United States that a vessel which by her own fault causes sudden peril to another cannot impute to the other as a fault a measure taken *in extremis*, although it was a wrong step, and but for it the collision would not have occurred. A mistake made in the agony of the collision is regarded as an error for which the vessel causing the peril is altogether responsible : *The Nichols*, 7 Wall. 656 ; *The Carroll*, 8 Wall. 302 ; *The City of Paris*, 9 Wall. 634 ; *The Lucile*, 15 Wall. 676 ; *The*

*Favorita*, 18 Wall. 598 ; *The Falcon*, 19 Wall. 75 ; *The Sea Gull*, 23 Wall. 165. There are decisions of the French courts to the same effect : Abordage Nautique (Caumont), § 134.
 (e) *The Rob Roy*, 3 W. Rob. 190 ; *The Scotia*, 14 Wall. 170; *The Mary Hounsell*, 40 L. T. N. S. 368.
 (f) See *The Carolus Rotchers*, 3 Hag. Ad. 343, note. In this case a ship close-hauled on the starboard tack hailed another close-hauled on the port tack to keep her luff. The latter did so, and a collision occurred. The first ship was held in fault. Notwithstanding 36 & 37 Vict. c. 85, s. 17, the rule would probably be the same at the present day. It would probably be held that, after

Ship unman-
ageable or
disabled.
If a ship is in an unmanageable state, and whilst in that
condition injures another, she will be held to be in fault
for the collision if her unmanageable condition was the
result of her own negligence, or of a previous collision for
which she was in fault (*g*). So if she has lost her lights by
her own fault, or in a collision for which she was in fault,
she would probably be held in fault for a second collision
caused, or which might have been caused, by the absence
of lights (*h*). If she gets ashore by her own negligence,
and in coming off unavoidably does damage, such damage
is held to be caused by her own negligence (*i*).

Both ships
must take
precautions.
Where there is risk of collision, and the Rule of the Road
requires both the ships to alter their courses, or to take
definite measures to avoid collision, it is negligence in
either ship not to take the prescribed step. She cannot
excuse herself for disobeying the law upon the ground that
there would have been no collision if the other had obeyed
the law. In such a case she would be prevented from
recovering more than half her loss by 36 & 37 Vict. c. 85,
s. 17 (*k*) ; and independently of the statute a vessel which,
by infringing the Regulations, or by negligence in any other
respect, contributes to a collision, is clearly in fault (*l*).
Failure to comply with the Statutory Regulations for preventing collisions is always negligence, and, as will be
seen below, it will in almost every case be held to be negligence contributing to the collision.

Negligence of
tug or salvor.
If a vessel which is engaged in rendering salvage service

such an intimation from the other
ship for her intended course, a departure from the Regulations was necessary to avoid immediate danger
(Art. 23). See also *The James Watt*,
2 W. Rob. 270 ; *The Independence*,
14 Moo. P. C. C. 103, 109 ; *The
Huntress*, 2 Sprague, 61.

(*g*) *Seccombe* v. *Wood*, 2 Moo. &
Rob. 290. See also *Brown* v. *Mallet*,
5 C. B. 599 ; *White* v. *Crisp*, 10 Ex.
312 ; *Lords, Bailiffs, &c., of Romney*

*Marsh* v. *Corporation of Trinity
House*, L. R. 5 Ex. 204 ; *ibid.* 7 Ex.
247 ; *Kidson* v. *McArthur*, 5 Sess.
Cas., 4th series, 936.

(*h*) See *The Kjobenhavn*, 2 Asp.
Mar. Law Cas. 213 ; 36 & 37 Vict.
c. 85, s. 17.

(*i*) *Lords, Bailiffs, &c., of Romney
Marsh* v. *Corporation of the Trinity
House, ubi supra.*

(*k*) See below, p. 14.

(*l*) See *The America*, 2 Otto. 432.

to another negligently runs into her, she is liable for the damage; but she does not thereby forfeit her right to a sum which has been previously agreed upon as remuneration for the salvage service, unless the negligence is very gross. In such cases the Court regards error or negligence in the salvor less severely than in ordinary cases of collision (*m*). If the salvor, without negligence on her own part, is injured by collision with the ship she is assisting, she can recover for her loss (*n*). The relative duties of a tug and her tow are considered in a subsequent chapter.

To recover damages for a collision, negligence must, except in the cases mentioned below, in all cases be proved (*o*) against the other ship. The plaintiff must at least make a *primâ facie* case. The burden of proof lies on him so far (*p*). But it does not at all follow that it lies

*Negligence must be proved.*

---

(*m*) *The C. S. Butler* and *The Baltic*, L. R. 4 A. & E. 178. See also *The Thetis*, 3 Mar. Law Cas. O. S. 357; *Stevens* v. *The S. W. Downs* and *The Storm*, Newb. Ad. 458.

(*n*) *The Mud Hopper*, 40 L.T.N.S. 462.

(*o*) 17 & 18 Vict. c. 104, ss. 282, 285, does not, it seems, make the official log evidence in collision actions where it is not admissible apart from the statute. As to the ship's log not being evidence, see *The Henry Coxon*, 3 P. D. 156. A verdict and judgment in a common law action cannot be pleaded or given in evidence in Admiralty proceedings. And the result of proceedings at a Board of Trade enquiry, or coroner's inquest, is not material: *The Mangerton*, Swab. Ad. 120; *The City of London*, ibid. 245. A protest may be used to contradict the master, but not as evidence for the ship: *Christian* v. *Coombe*, 2 Esp. 489; Abbot on Ship., 11th ed., 336; *The Ljudica*, 23 L. T. N. S. 474; *The Emma*, 2 W. Rob. 315. The same rule applies to depositions before receivers of

wreck: *The Little Lizzie*, L. R. 3 A. & E. 56; *Nothard* v. *Pepper*, 17 C. B. N. S. 39. The statements of seamen cannot be used as admissions against the owners: *The Lord Seaton*, 3 W. Rob. 391, 403; 4 Not. of Cas. 164; *The Foyle*, Lush. 10; and see *The Great Eastern*, Holt 169. In America statements by the master have been used as admissions against the owner: *The Potomac*, 8 Wall. 590; and under the old procedure were so received in the English Admiralty Court: *The Midlothian*, 15 Jur. 806; *The Manchester*, 1 W. Rob. 63; *The Europa*, 13 Jur. 856; *The Actæon*, 1 Sp. E. & A. 176. Evidence in a common law action for the same collision cannot, except by consent, be used in a subsequent action in Admiralty: *The Demetrius*, 41 L. J. Ad. 69; *The William Hutt*, Lush. 25. Statements by the pilot of the defendant ship at the time of the collision have been admitted in evidence as part of the *res gestæ*: *The Schwalbe*, Swab. Ad. 521.

(*p*) *The Bolina*, 3 Not. of Cas. 208, 210; *The Carron*, 1 Sp. E. & A. 91; *The London*, 11 Moo. P. C. C.

10 GENERAL RULES.

upon him throughout the whole case. Frequently, by
proving certain circumstances, the burden of proof is
thrown back on the defendant, and he is bound to make
out his case (*q*). Thus, where the ship is at anchor in a
proper berth, or in stays, or otherwise not under command
without negligence on her own part, the presumption is
that the other vessel is in fault (*r*).

A vessel under way is bound to keep clear of another at
anchor ; and in case of collision with a ship at anchor, the
vessel under way is *primâ facie* in fault. If the ship at
anchor shows that she was brought up in a proper place,
and that she was not guilty of negligence in respect of
her lights and other proper precautions, the burden
of proof lies on the ship under way to show that she was
not in fault (*s*). And the rule seems to be the same
in the case of collision with a fishing-boat fast to her
nets (*t*), or with a ship hove-to and unable to keep out
of the way (*u*).

And although a ship is brought up in an improper place,
another running into her may be held in fault. " It is the
bounden duty of a vessel under way, whether the vessel at
anchor be properly or improperly anchored, to avoid, if

307 ; *The Marpesia*, L. R. 4 P. C.
212 ; *The Benmore*, L. R. 4 A. & E.
132 ; *The Abraham*, 28 L. T. N. S.
775 ; *The Albert Edward*, 44 L. J.
Ad. 49.

(*q*) *The Ligo*, 2 Hag. Ad. 356,
360 ; *The Sisters*, 1 P. D. 117 ; *The
City of Antwerp* and *The Friedrich*,
L. R. 2 P. C. 25. See *Daniel* v.
*Metropolitan Railway*, L. R. 3 C. P.
216 ; *ibid.* 591, as to what is sufficient evidence of negligence.

(*r*) In some American cases it has
been said that where one ship is
required by the Regulations to keep
out of the way of the other, as in
the case of a steam-ship and a sailing-ship, upon proof that the latter
is not in fault, unless the former
proves that the collision was an in-

evitable accident, she will be held
to have been in fault: *The Carroll*,
8 Wall. 302, 304 ; *The Scotia*, 14
Wall. 170, 181 ; *New York, &c.,
Mail Co.* v. *Rumball*, 21 How. 372,
385.

(*s*) *The Bothnia*, Lush. 52 ; *The
Telegraph*, *Valentine* v. *Clough*. 1
Sp. E. & A. 427 ; *The Beaver*, 2
Bened. 118, and *The Baltic, ibid.*
452, are American cases to the same
effect.

(*t*) *The Columbus*, 1 Pritch. Ad.
Dig. 199 ; *The Two Sisters, ibid.*;
*The Bottle Imp*, 28 L. T. N. S. 286.

(*u*) *The Eleanor* and *The Alma*, 2
Mar. Law Cas. O. S. 240 ; but see
*The London*, 6 Not. of Cas. 29,
where a vessel hove-to was held in
fault.

it be possible with safety to herself, any collision whatever " (v).

Where a sailing-ship was lost with all hands in a collision with a steam-ship, the steam-ship was held in fault upon the facts stated in her own pleadings, and with no further proof on the part of the sailing-ship than the evidence of a person on board a third ship who had seen the sailing-ship's lights burning some time before the collision (x).

It is not enough to prove that the other ship omitted to do something that would have prevented the collision, or that she did something without which the collision would not have occurred. It must be proved that the omission or act complained of was negligent. If the plaintiff ship has herself infringed the Regulations, or has been guilty of negligence which might have contributed to the collision, the burden is on her to show that the collision was not caused entirely by her own fault.

When one ship alleges want of lights or of a proper look out, or insufficient moorings, or any such negligence on board the other as it is impossible or difficult for her to prove by direct evidence, the burden is on the latter, as it is peculiarly in her power, to prove that her lights were sufficient, or that there was no such negligence (y).

The mere fact that a ship strikes and damages another does not make her liable. The collision may be the result of inevitable accident; and in every case the burden is on

(v) Per Dr. Lushington in The Batavier, 2 W. Rob. 407; The Dura, 1 Pritch. Ad. Dig. 174; The Marcia Tribou, 2 Sprague, 17.

(x) The Aleppo, 35 L. J. Ad. 9. The French Courts adopt highly artificial presumptions as to which ship is in fault : see Les Codes Annotées (Sirey et Gilbert), Art. 407, C. C. By the German and Dutch Codes, if a ship sinks after collision before reaching port, the presump-

tion is that she was lost by the collision : see German Comm. Code, Art. 739; Comm. Code of Holland, Art. 539. By the Maritime Code of Riga, the presumption was against a ship without a light : 4 Black Book of the Admiralty (Sir T. Twiss' ed.), 373, note.

(y) The Swanland, 2 Sp. E. & A. 107; The John Harley and The William Tell, 13 L. T. N. S. 413.

the ship charging negligence to prove it. Where there is no *primâ fâcie* case of want of seamanship, the burden of proving it does not necessarily attach to the ship alleging inevitable accident (*z*).

**Identification of wrong-doing ship.**

It has occurred in some cases that the plaintiff has failed to identify the defendant ship as that with which he has been in collision. If he sues the wrong ship unjustifiably, he does so at the risk of costs (*a*).

**Statutory rules as to presumption of fault.**

There are two cases in which damages can be recovered against another ship apart from the question whether the collision was caused by her negligence or not. The first is where a ship neglects to "stand by" the other after the accident. Section 16 of 36 & 37 Vict. c. 85 is as follows:

**36 & 37 Vict. c. 85, s. 16: "Standing by" the other ship.**

" In every case of collision between two vessels it shall be the duty of the master or person in charge of each vessel, if and so far as he can do so without danger to his own vessel, crew and passengers (if any), to stay by the other vessel until he has ascertained that she has no need of further assistance, and to render to the other vessel, her master, crew and passengers (if any), such assistance as may be practicable and as may be necessary in order to save them from any danger caused by the collision ; and also to give to the master or person in charge of the other vessel the name of his own vessel, and of her port of registry, or of the port or place to which she belongs, and also the names of the ports and places from which and to which she is bound.

" If he fails so to do, and no reasonable cause for such failure is shown, the collision shall, in the absence of proof to the contrary, be deemed to have been caused by his wrongful act, neglect or default.

" Every master or person in charge of a British vessel who fails without reasonable cause to render such assistance or give such information as aforesaid shall be deemed guilty of a misdemeanor (*b*), and if he is a certificated officer an inquiry into his

---

(*z*) *The Bolina*, 3 Not. of Cas. 208; *The Marpesia*, L. R. 4 P. C. 212.
(*a*) See *infra*, p. 72.

(*b*) Punishable by fine of £100 or imprisonment for six months : 17 & 18 Vict. c. 104, s. 518.

conduct may be held and his certificate may be cancelled or suspended."

The temptation for a ship to run away from another with which she has been in collision by her own fault, in the hope of escaping detection, has been found in many cases stronger than the dictates of humanity. "Standing by" was first made a statutory duty by 25 & 26 Vict. c. 63, s. 33 (c). Previous to this Act, however, the duty of one ship to render assistance to the other was distinctly recognised by the Admiralty Court, and failure to stand by a ship injured in a collision was punished by compelling the defaulting ship to pay the costs of the suit, although she was free from blame in other respects, and successful in the suit (d).

However free from blame a ship may be in other respects, and however wanton the collision on the part of the other ship, the law requires each to stand by the other. If either ship fails to do so, in the absence of proof to the contrary (e), she will be held to be in fault for the collision, and will be unable to recover the whole of her loss.

The "person in charge" mentioned in s. 16 is the master, although at the time of the collision the ship is in charge of a pilot (f). If the master is below, the duty to stand by lies on the mate or other person in charge of the deck, until the master comes on deck; if life or property is still in danger, it is then transferred to the master (g). Where a collision occurred between a ship in tow and a third ship, it was said by Sir R. Phillimore that the Act of 1862 required the tug to stand by the ships in collision (h).

<hr/>

(c) It was introduced into the statute by Lord Kingsdown, see *The Hannibal* and *The Queen,* L. R. 2 A. & E. 53, 56.

(d) *The Celt,* 3 Hag. Ad. 321.

(e) In *The British Princess* and *The Sedim Duhrovacki,* Ad. Ct., March 11—14th, 1879, there was such "proof to the contrary," and a ship which left the other, with which

she had been in collision, recovered damages for the collision.

(f) *The Queen,* L. R. 2 A. & E. 354.

(g) *Ex parte Ferguson* and *Hutchinson,* L. R. 6 Q. B. 280.

(h) See *The Hannibal* and *The Queen,* L. R. 2 A. & E. 53; the three last mentioned cases were decided under 25 & 26 Vict. c. 63, s. 33.

The penalty for not "standing by" is strictly enforced. A ship must obey the law although there is some risk to herself, and the other appears to be in no danger. A steamship was held in fault for not standing by another with which she had been in collision, although, being in narrow waters, and herself of great length (450 feet), she could not do so without risk of going ashore, and although she had hailed another ship, better able to assist, to do so (*i*).

Although a vessel which fails to render assistance to another with which she has been in collision breaks the law, it appears that her right to salvage remuneration, where she renders assistance to a ship with which she has been in collision by no fault of her own, is not affected by 36 & 37 Vict. c. 85, s. 16. In a case under the Act of 1862 it was held that the right to salvage reward of a tug, whose tow was damaged in a collision with a third ship, for which the latter was in fault, was not affected by the statutory enactment as to standing by (*k*).

The "standing by" section of the Act of 1862 was held to apply in the case of a collision with an open fishing-boat (*l*).

The application of the statute in the case of collision with a foreign ship is considered below (*m*).

The other case in which damages can be recovered for a collision, without proof of negligence on the part of the defendant contributing to the collision, is as follows. By 36 & 37 Vict. c. 85, s. 17, it is enacted that :—

" If, in any case of collision, it is proved to the Court before which the case is tried that any of the Regulations for pre-

(*i*) *The Adriatic*, 3 Asp. Mar. Law Cas. 16. The present Act is more stringent than former Acts (25 & 26 Vict. c. 63, s. 33; 34 & 35 Vict. c. 110, s. 9). Other cases under the Act of 1862 are *The Lucia Jantina* and *The Mexican*, Holt 130; *The Queen of the Orwell*, 1 Mar. Law Cas. O. S. 300; *The Eliza* and *The Orinoco*, Holt 98.
(*k*) *The Hannibal* and *The Queen*, L. R. 2 A. & E. 53.
(*l*) *Ex parte Ferguson* and *Hutchinson*, L. R. 6 Q. B. 280.
(*m*) *Infra*, p. 91.

venting collision contained in or made under the Merchant Shipping Acts, 1854—1873, has been infringed, the ship by which such Regulation has been infringed shall be deemed to be in fault, unless it is shown to the satisfaction of the Court that the circumstances of the case made departure from the Regulation necessary."

The object of this section was to enforce the observance of the Regulations and to lessen the difficulty of deciding collision cases upon evidence which is often conflicting. Its effect is to exclude proof that an infringement of the Regulations, which might have contributed to the collision, did not, in fact, do so. The statute, therefore, imposes on the vessel guilty of an infringement the burden of proving not only that it did not, but that it could not, by possibility, have contributed to the collision (n).

If the Regulation which has been infringed is one which has no possible connection with the disaster, and which could not by any possibility have contributed to it, the section does not apply. If, for example, a vessel is run into by another approaching her from her port side, she will not be held in fault under s. 17 for having no light on her starboard side (o). In the case of *The Fanny M. Carvill* it was held that the other ship, *The Peru*, was not in fault under s. 17 because her screens were seven inches short of the statutory length (3 feet); it being proved that her lights were not in fact seen across her bow.

The application of s. 17 is not without difficulty. In a recent case in the Admiralty Court it was held that s. 17 did not prevent a vessel without the Regulation lights recovering full damages. *L'Etoile* was a French trawler, Difficulty of applying s. 17. Case of *The Englishman.*

---

(n) *The Hibernia*, 2 Asp. Mar. Law Cas. 454 ; *The Fanny M. Carvill, ibid.* 565. The law in America has been stated in almost precisely similar terms by the Supreme Court, although there is no enactment similar to 36 & 37 Vict. c. 85, s. 17 : see

*The Pennsylvania*, 19 Wall. 125, 136.

(o) *The Fanny M. Carvill*, L. R. 4 A. & E. 417, 422 ; S. C. affirmed on app., 2 Asp Mar. Law Cas. 565 ; see also *The Hibernia, ibid.* 454.

close-hauled on the port tack, and going two or three knots. The night being fairly clear, *The Englishman,* an English sailing-vessel, was seen coming towards her with the wind free. *L'Etoile* had a bright light at her mast-head; her side-lights were waved on deck, but failed to attract the other ship's notice. *The Englishman* came on and struck *L'Etoile* on the port side. On the part of *The Englishman* it was alleged that nothing was seen or heard of *L'Etoile* until she struck her. It was held by the Admiralty Court that there was no look-out on board *The Englishman,* and that the absence of lights on board *L'Etoile* could not have contributed to the collision; that s. 17, therefore, did not apply, and *The Englishman* was solely in fault (*p*).

*The Fanny M. Carvill* was before the Court in *The Englishman,* and the decision in the latter case was expressly stated by the Court to be in conformity with that of the Privy Council. It appears to have been considered by the Court that the admission by *The Englishman* that nothing was seen of *L'Etoile* until the moment of the collision was equivalent to an admission that the absence of side-lights on board the latter could not, by possibility, have contributed to the accident.

Ship in tow or towing another is responsible under s. 17 for the fault of the other.

Section 17 has been held to apply as against a ship towing another which had improper lights. A., sailing with her side-lights burning, had in tow a boat from which she had taken a pilot. The latter was carrying her mast-head light. The sailing-ship was, under s. 17, held in fault for a collision with a third ship (*q*). It will be seen below that a tug and her tow are in law for some purposes together treated as one ship (*r*).

History of the rule as to infringement of the Regulations.

The exact effect of s. 17 is, perhaps, best explained by a reference to previous enactments. By 14 & 15 Vict. c. 79, s. 28, and by 17 & 18 Vict. c. 104, s. 298, it was enacted,

---

(*p*) *The Englishman,* 3 P. D. 18.   N. S. 368.
(*q*) *The Mary Hounsell,* 40 L. T.   (*r*) See *infra,* p. 78.

in effect, that if a collision was occasioned by an infringement of the Regulations of those Acts, the vessel guilty of
such infringement should recover no part of her loss, either
in the Admiralty or any other Court.

The effect of these enactments was that she could recover
nothing, although the other ship was also in fault. An infringement of the Regulations was constituted negligence,
and the question had to be tried in every case, whether it
was negligence contributing to the collision or not (s).
By 25 & 26 Vict. c. 63, s. 29, the old Admiralty rule as to
the division of damages was applied to cases of statutory
negligence, and a vessel guilty of an infringement of the
Regulations which contributed to the collision was enabled
to recover half her loss in the Admiralty Court, if the other
vessel was also in fault. The question whether the infringement did, in fact, contribute to the collision or not,
had still to be tried in every case (t). The alteration in
the law effected by s. 17 of the Act now in force consists
in excluding evidence that an infringement that might by
possibility have contributed to the accident did not, in
fact, do so.

In a case under the Act of 1854 it was doubted by Dr.
Lushington whether the disabling section (s. 296) applied
if the helm was ported, but not sufficiently (u). Under the
present Act it could scarcely be contended that insufficient
porting, or an infringement, even to the smallest extent, of
any one of the Regulations which was material to the
collision, could not, by possibility, have contributed to the

---

(s) *The Panther,* 1 Sp. E. & A.
31 ; *The Aliwal, ibid.* 96 ; *The Fairy,*
*ibid.* 298 ; *The Telegraph, ibid.* 427 ;
*The Swanland,* 2 Sp. E. & A. 107 ;
*Tuff* v. *Warnam,* 2 C. B. N. S.
740 ; on app.. 5 C. B. N. S. 573 ;
*Morrison* v. *Gen. St. Nav. Co.,* 8 Ex.
733 ; *Dowell* v. *Gen. St. Nav. Co.,* 5
E. & B. 195; *The Virid,* 10 Moo. P.
C. C. 472 ; *The Renown* and *The*

*Rattler,* 2 Mar. Law. Cas. O. S. 243 ;
*Whittel* v. *Crawford,* 27 L. T. 223.
(t) *The Palestine,* 13 W. R. 111 ;
*The Bougainville* and *The James C.*
*Stevenson,* L. R. 5 P. C. 316 ; *The*
*Pyrus* and *The Smales,* 2 Mar. Law
Cas. O. S. 288 ; *The Pennsylvania,*
3 Mar. Law. Cas. O. S. 477.
(u) *The Bothnia,* Lush. 52.

disaster (*v*). In *The Tirzah* (*x*), a barque, with the wind free, was in collision with a brig close-hauled. The brig's side-lights had, so as to protect them from seas breaking over her, been shifted to the after-part of the vessel a few hours before the collision. In their position on the quarter they were not visible from right ahead to a point, or a point and a-half, on either bow. It was held, under s. 17, that the brig was in fault for the collision. Sir R. Phillimore considered that the question whether the partial obscuration of the side-lights could, by possibility, have contributed to the collision, was for the nautical assessors to advise the Court upon.

*Infringement of the Mersey rules involves the penalty of s. 17.*

It has been held that a ship which infringes the river Mersey sea channels Regulations (*y*) is to be deemed in fault for the collision under 36 & 37 Vict. c. 85, s. 17 (*z*). But where a foreign ship came into the Mersey without having on board a second riding-light, as required by the Mersey rules, and, the master having gone ashore to get one, the collision occurred before he returned, it was said that the circumstances made a departure from the Regulations necessary within the meaning of s. 17 (*a*).

*Bad seamanship or negligence, apart from the Regulations, is not within the penalty of s. 17.*

The object of s. 17 appears to be to enforce the observance of the Statutory Regulations, and not the rules of seamanship generally. Neglect to keep a look-out, or to observe any precaution required by the ordinary practice of seamen would not, it is submitted, bring a ship within the penalty of s. 17 (*b*). Nor would the infringement of one of the Regulations which could not by possibility have contributed to the collision, although it may have aug-

---

(*v*) In such a case s. 17 would prevent the application of the doctrine of *Davies* v. *Mann*, 10 M. & W. 546.

(*x*) 4 P. D. 33.

(*y*) Under 37 & 38 Vict. c. 52.

(*z*) *The Lady Downshire*, 4 P. D. 26.

(*a*) *The Calypso* and *The Missis-*

*sippi*, Ad. Ct., March 7th, 8th, and 9th, 1878 (Mitch. Mar. Reg.).

(*b*) By American Courts neglect of such precautions has been called an infringement of the Act of Congress embodying the Regulations : *The Farragut*, 10 Wall. 334 ; *The Atlas*, 10 Blatchf. 459, 466.

mented the damage (c), prevent a ship from recovering full damages.

It has not been decided whether an infringement of local Regulations, such as those in force in the Thames, which are not, by the local Act, specially incorporated with the General Regulations, brings a ship within the penalties of s. 17. It would probably be held that such local rules are not within the provisions of that section. This was the opinion of the Court of Appeal in a recent case, but it was not there necessary to decide the point; in the Court below the learned judge appears to have been of a contrary opinion (d). The same question arises as to rules made under 25 & 26 Vict. c. 63, s. 32.

The application of s. 17 to foreign ships is considered in a subsequent chapter (e).

*Whether infringement of local Regulations is within s. 17.*

---

(c) As in *The Governor* and *The John McIntyre*, Holt 184 ; *Greenland* v. *Chaplin*, 5 Ex. 243.

(d) *The Swansea* and *The Condor*, 4 P. D. 115.

(e) See *infra*, p. 91. There is no law in America corresponding to 36 & 37 Vict. c. 85, s. 17. The Supreme Court has declared that it will not " accept blindly an artificial rule which is to determine in all cases whether the navigator is liable to the charge of negligence in causing any damage that may happen :" *The Farragut*, 10 Wall. 334. But the burden is on a vessel which has infringed the Statutory Regulations to prove that the infringement did not contribute to the collision : *The Pennsylvania*, 19 Wall. 125 ; *The Ariadne*, 2 Bened. 472. If, however, such proof be forthcoming, a ship will recover full damages although she did not comply with the Regulations : 1 Parsons on Shipping (ed. 1869), 596, 597 ; *Chamberlain* v. *Ward*, 21 How. 548, 567 ; *The Gray Eagle*, 9 Wall. 505 ; *The Continental*, 14 Wall. 345 ; *The Sunnyside*, 1 Otto. 208 ; *The City of Washington*, 2 Otto. 31. And *Blanchard* v. *New Jersey Steamboat*

Co., 59 New York Rep. 292 ; and *Whitehall Transport Co.* v. *New Jersey, &c., Co.*, 51 N. Y. Rep. 369 ; and *Hoffman* v. *Union Ferry of Brooklyn*, 7 Amer. Rep. 435, are decisions of the State of New York Courts to the same effect. In *The Pennsylvania* a steam-ship and a sailing-ship were in collision. The latter was not sounding her foghorn, but was ringing a bell, though she was under way. The Supreme Court refused to admit evidence that the bell could be heard further than the horn, and held that the sailing-ship was in fault for the collision. The following passage, which occurs in the judgment of the Court, shows that the law in America as to the effect of an infringement of the Regulations is identical with that of this country : " Where a ship, at the time of collision, is in actual violation of a statutory rule intended to prevent collisions, it is no more than a reasonable presumption that the fault, if not the sole cause, was at least a contributory cause of the collision. In such a case the burden rests upon the ship of showing, not merely that her fault might not have been one of the causes, or that

C 2

Owner's liability as carrier.

Proof of negligence is not always necessary to enable the owner of cargo, or a passenger, to recover against the carrier. The ship-owner's liability as carrier, apart from the express stipulations of the contract of affreightment, is that of insurer, except as against the Queen's enemies and the act of God (*f*). Except where it is caused by the fault of the carrying ship, collision is a "peril of the sea" within the meaning of that term in a bill of lading (*g*). In the absence of a special contract restricting his liability it seems that the ship-owner is liable for loss or injury to the owners of cargo or passengers on board his ship, in the case of collision, whether his ship is in fault or not. Railway companies, carrying by sea, cannot, by notice, free themselves from liability to passengers and cargo owners for a collision caused by the fault of the carrying ship (*h*).

Case of "inscrutable fault."

By the law of this country every ship bears her own loss by collision, unless it is proved to have been caused by the negligence of the other ship (*i*). And this is so if the evidence does not satisfy the Court with whom the fault lies, although each ship alleges negligence against the other, and it is manifest that the collision was caused by fault somewhere. The English law as to the incidence of loss in this case differs from the general maritime law (*k*).

it probably was not, but that it could not have been." The same ship was, in this country, held free from fault: see *The Pennsylvania*, 3 Mar. Law Cas. O. S. 477.

(*f*) *Nugent v. Smith*, 1 C. P. D. 19. As to what is an "act of God," see *ibid.*, p. 34. Some cases of collision by "inevitable accident," as defined below, would not come within the exception of "acts of God."

(*g*) *Buller v. Fisher*, 3 Esp. 67 ; *Lloyd v. General Iron S. C. Co.*, 3 H. & C. 284 ; *Grill v. General Iron S. C. Co.*, L. R. 3 C. P. 476.

(*h*) *Doolan v. Midland Railway Co.*, 2 App. Cas. 792.

(*i*) *The Maid of Aukland*, 6 Not. of Cas. 240 ; *The Catherine of Dover*, 2 Hag. Ad. 154 ; *The Laconia*, 2 Moo. P. C. C. N. S. 161.

(*k*) See Bell's Commentaries on the Law of Scotland, 581. There is no express authority for this statement as to the peculiarity of English law beyond the cases cited above, and the fact that no case is to be found in the books in which damages have been recovered in a case of inscrutable fault, or in any case in which negligence has not been proved against the other ship. As to the Roman and foreign law on the point, see the note at the foot of this chapter.

Where a collision occurs without fault on the part span style="float:right">Case of inevi-<br>table accident.
of either ship, it is said to be the result of inevitable
accident. In this case each ship bears her own loss (*l*).
Inevitable accident is "where one vessel doing a lawful act
without any intention of harm, and using proper precautions to prevent danger, unfortunately happens to run into
another vessel" (*m*).  In another case it was thus defined:
"To constitute an inevitable accident it is necessary that
the occurrence should have taken place in such a manner
as not to have been capable of being prevented by ordinary
skill and ordinary prudence.  We are not to expect extraordinary skill or extraordinary diligence, but that degree
of skill and that degree of diligence which is generally to
be found in persons who discharge their duty" (*n*).

Elsewhere inevitable accident has been defined to be
"that which a party charged with an offence could not
possibly prevent by the exercise of ordinary care, caution,
and maritime skill" (*o*).

It is not enough to show that the collision was inevitable
at the moment of, or immediately previous to, its occurrence (*p*).  The question is what previous measures could
have been adopted to make its occurrence less probable.  If a
vessel is shown to have been proceeding at too great speed,
she cannot be heard to allege that the collision was an inevitable accident.  "Inevitable accident is not this: where
a man proceeds carelessly on his voyage, and afterwards
circumstances arise, and it is too late for him to do what is
fit and proper to be done" (*q*).

hr/>

(*l*) The law in America is the
same: *Steinbuck* v. *Rae*, 14 How.
532.  As to Roman, mediæval, and
foreign law on this point, see the
note at the foot of this chapter.

(*m*) Per Dr. Lushington in *The
Europa*, 14 Jur. 627, 629.

(*n*) *The Thomas Powell* and *The
Cuba*, 2 Mar. Law Cas. O. S. 344;
and see *The Plato* and *The Persever-
ance*, Holt 262.  For a definition by

the Supreme Court of the United
States, see *The Mayboy* and *The
Cooper*, 14 Wall. 204, 215.

(*o*) *The Virgil*, 2 W. Rob. 201,
cited by the P. C. in *The Marpesia*,
L. R. 4 P. C. 212, 220; and see *The
Lochibo*, 3 W. Rob. 310, 318.

(*p*) *The Uhla*, 3 Mar. Law Cas.
O. S. 148.

(*q*) Per Dr. Lushington, *The
Juliet Erskine*, 6 Not. of Cas. 633;

Burden of proving inevitable accident.   Where a collision is the result of inevitable accident the burden of proving that it was so does not in the first instance attach to the ship alleging it.  But where a *primâ facie* case of negligence is made out, then it lies on the ship alleging inevitable accident to prove it (*o*).

Vessel infringing the Regulations cannot plead inevitable accident.   It seems that a vessel in default for not having lights, or for not complying with the Regulations, cannot, at least where such non-compliance by possibility might have contributed to the collision, successfully plead inevitable accident (*p*).  But such a defence may be good where the circumstances of the case made a departure from the Regulations necessary, or where her inability to take the proper measures was caused by no fault of her own.

A collision may be an inevitable accident so far as the ship sued is concerned, although it was caused by fault elsewhere; as in the case of a ship which is thrown against another by the swell of a passing steam-ship, or by a third ship coming foul of her (*q*).

Disabled ship.   Where a ship is unable to take the proper measures to avoid a collision owing to her being disabled, or for some reason for which she is not responsible, it is the duty of the other ship to avoid her if she can.  But a collision occurring in consequence of her disabled state will be held to be an inevitable accident, if the other vessel was ignorant of it, and was not in fault for not being aware of it, or for not keeping out of the way (*r*).  *The Aimo*, close-hauled on the starboard tack, saw the red light of *The Amelia*, a vessel closed-hauled on the port tack, a little on her port bow.  *The Aimo* kept her course.  *The Amelia*, having lost her head-sails in a previous collision, was unable to

and see *The Merrimac*, 14 Wall. 199, 203.

(*o*) *The Bolina*, 3 Not. of Cas. 208; *The Marpesia*, L. R. 4 P. C. 212; and see above, p. 9.

(*p*) 36 & 37 Vict. c. 85, s. 17; see *supra*, p. 14, *seq.*

(*q*) See 1 Parsons on Ship. (ed. 1869), 533; *The Sisters*, 1 P. D. 117; *The Hibernia*, 4 Jur. N. S. 1244.

(*r*) *The John Buddle*, 5 Not. of Cas. 387.

bear up, and a collision occurred. It was held to be an inevitable accident (s).

In the following cases the Courts have held that the collisions occurred without fault in either ship, and that they were the result of inevitable accident.

A steamer rounding-to in the Thames on a dark night against a strong flood-tide under a starboard helm, with her head to the southward, was seen by a brig coming down. Notwithstanding that all that could be done was done by both vessels, a collision occurred. It was held to be a case of inevitable accident. The Court said that if the steamer had put her helm to starboard with a view to bring up after seeing the brig she would have been to blame (t).

A ship, which had made fast by order of the port authority to a private buoy, was held not to be in fault for a collision caused by the parting of the band round the buoy (u); and a collision caused by the parting of the band was held to be an inevitable accident.

In the absence of evidence of negligence on the part of the crew, the jamming of the cable round the windlass, when the anchor was let go, was held to be an inevitable accident (x).

The parting of a cable in a gale of wind (y), and of moorings in calm weather (z), has been held to be an inevitable accident. But if there is negligence in not letting go an anchor, or in not having an anchor ready to let go when the vessel is adrift, she cannot sustain the defence of inevitable accident (a).

Where a collision occurred in consequence of the break-

(s) *The Aimo* and *The Amelia*, 2 Asp. Mar. Law Cas. 96 ; and see *The Venus*, 1 Pritch. Ad. Dig. 129. As to a vessel disabled by her own fault, see *supra*, p. 8.

(t) *The Shannon*, 1 W. Rob. 463.

(u) *The William Lindsay*, L. R. 5 P. C. 338.

(x) *The William Lindsay, supra; The Peerless*, Lush. 30.

(y) *The London*, 1 Mar. Law Cas. O. S. 398.

(z) *The Ambassador*, Ad. Ct., Feb. 12th, 1875, cited in *The Pladda*, 2 P. D. 34, 37.

(a) *The Pladda*, 2 P. D. 34 ; *The Kepler, ibid.* 40. As to such a plea by a ship which has given another a foul berth, see *The Secret, infra*, p. 220.

ing of part of the steering gear, there being a latent defect
in the metal, it was held to be an inevitable accident (b).
But if the gear is manifestly insufficient or weak, the
defence of inevitable accident cannot be sustained (c).

Where a ship, A., at anchor in the Thames, was run into
by another, B., and was, without fault on her own part,
driven by B. against a third ship, C., it was held that, so
far as A. was concerned, the collision between her and C.
was an inevitable accident (d).

A ship which had been ashore on a sand, was driving over
it and came into collision with another brought up in deep
water to leeward of the sand.   To have let go her anchor
before she was clear of the sand would have been dangerous
to herself, and without letting go while on the sand she
could not keep clear of the ship at anchor.   A collision
which followed was held to be inevitable (e).

A dumb barge in the Thames, driving with the tide,
came into collision with a steamer going up against the
ebb at the rate of two knots.   There was evidence that
the barge could not have been seen sooner than she was
seen.   In the absence of evidence of negligence on the part
of the steamer, the collision was held to be an inevitable
accident (f).

Where two ships, by no fault of their own, suddenly find
themselves in a position in which a collision is imminent,
and one of them omits to execute a manœuvre which
possibly might have averted the collision, she will not
necessarily be held in fault for not having taken the
measure suggested.   Where two large sailing-ships, one in
the act of going about, and the other going free, sighted
each other in a dense fog at a distance of less than 300

(b) The Virgo, 3 Asp. Mar. Law
Cas. 285.
(c) The M. M. Caleb, 10 Blatchf.
467.
(d) The Hibernia, 4 Jur. N. S.

1244.
(e) The Thornley, 7 Jur. 659.
(f) The Swallow, 3 Asp. Mar.
Law Cas. 371

yards, and a collision occurred in less than a minute, it was held that the ship in stays was not in fault for not having hauled aft her head-sheets to assist her helm, although if she had done so the collision might have been averted. The collision was held to be a case of inevitable accident (g).

In the following American cases the defence of inevitable American cases. accident has been sustained.

A vessel in the open sea overtook another at night, the darkness being so great that she could not see the vessel ahead in time to avoid her (h). A sailing-ship in a narrow channel being suddenly compelled to let go her anchor to save herself from going ashore, in consequence of the wind failing, a steam-ship close astern unavoidably ran into her (i).

A large steamer was entering a harbour by a course that was not the usual one, but which was a course she had a right to go. As she was rounding the stern of a hulk she suddenly saw and ran into a schooner which the hulk had prevented her seeing before. The schooner, which had just cast off from her tug, was setting her sails and drifting with the tide in a helpless condition. The collision was held by the Supreme Court to have been inevitable (k).

But where a schooner in a leaky condition, in order to avoid sinking in deep water, cast off from a wharf alongside which she was lying, and, before she was got under command, drove against another vessel, it was held that the collision was not an inevitable accident (l). A ship improperly attempting to pass another ashore in a narrow channel failed to sustain the defence of inevitable accident; and it was held that in attempting to pass clear of the ship ashore she did so at her own peril (m). In this country it

(g) The Marpesia, L. R. 4 P. C. 212.
(h) The Morning Light, 2 Wall. 550, 557.
(i) The Electra, 6 Bened. 189.
(k) The Java, 14 Wall. 189.
(l) Sherman v. Mott, 5 Bened. 372.
(m) The Merrimac, 14 Wall. 199.

was held recently that a ship driven from her moorings by
another which came foul of her in a gale of wind could not
escape liability to a third ship, against which she drove, on
the ground of inevitable accident, because she omitted to
let go another anchor (*n*).

Parties liable.   Where fault is established against a ship, a further
"The wrong-
doer."           question frequently arises as to who is liable for damages.
It is not in every case where a ship is injured in a collision
caused by the negligence of those on board the other ship
that damages can be recovered against the owners of the
latter, either personally, or indirectly by proceedings *in
rem* against the ship. In many cases there is difficulty in
determining on whom the liability for damages falls, as
well as who is the actual wrong-doer. This question is
distinct from that already considered as to which ship is in
fault. The custom of speaking of the ships themselves as
being in fault, or wrong-doers, though convenient, is sometimes misleading. "In cases like the present, where
damages are claimed for tortious collisions, a chattel, such
as a ship or carriage, may be, and frequently is, spoken of
as the wrong-doer; but it is obvious that although redress
may be sometimes obtained by means of the seizure and
sale of the ship or carriage, the chattel itself is only the
instrument by the improper use of which the injury is
inflicted by the real wrong-doer (*o*).

Owners of        In most cases it is sought to make the owners of the
the ship in
fault are        wrong-doing ship liable, either personally in an action at
*primâ facie*     law, or indirectly by Admiralty proceedings *in rem* against
liable.
the ship herself. *Primâ facie* the registered owners of a
ship are liable for the negligence of those in charge of her.
If the actual owner is a different person from the registered
owner, or if it is shown that the latter is not the employer

---

(*n*) *The Pladda*, 2 P. D. 34.        107, 111; *Simpson* v. *Thompson*, 3
(*o*) *Per* Selwyn, L.J., in *The*     Ap. Cas. 279, as to the necessity of
*Halley*, L. R. 2 P. C. 193, 201.      determining who is "the actual
And see *The M. Moxham*, 1 P. D.       wrong-doer."

of the crew or person causing the collision, the presumption is otherwise. It has been held that, in the absence of proof to the contrary, those in charge of a ship are presumed to be in the employment of the owners (*p*). So far as the liability of the owners is concerned, it makes no difference that the collision occurs whilst the ship is in dock, or the master ashore, or when, for any other reason, the ship is in charge of the mate or some one of the crew (*q*).

Owners are liable at common law only where the person, by whose wrongful act the collision is caused, is their agent or servant, and he is acting within the scope of his employment (*r*). Where a ship is being worked by a charterer or hirer, who appoints and pays the officers and crew, under a charter-party or agreement, which amounts to a demise of the vessel, the owner is not liable at law for damage she may do while in the possession of the charterer. But if the owner remains in possession of the ship, either by himself or his agents, he is liable, though she is under charter to another. Where a ship was chartered to J. D. for six months at £20 a week for the carriage of passengers and goods as he should direct—J. D. paying all disbursements and the wages of officers and crew, but the owners keeping the ship in repair—it was held that the owners were liable for a collision caused by the fault of their ship (*s*).

In *Dalyell* v. *Tyrer* (*t*), H., the lessee of a ferry, hired a tug with her master and crew to assist in working the ferry for a day. A person who had contracted with H. for a season ticket was injured whilst on board the tug by the negligence of her crew, who were the owners' servants.

*Owner's liability at common law.*

(*p*) *Joyce* v. *Capel*, 8 C. & P. 370; *Hibbs* v. *Ross*, L. R. 1 Q. B. 534, and cases there cited.
(*q*) *The Northampton*, 1 Sp. E. & A. 152; *Hibbs* v. *Ross*, *ubi supra*; *The Kepler*, 2 P. D. 40.
(*r*) See *per* Lord Blackburn in *Simpson* v. *Thompson*, 3 App. Cas. 279, 293; *River Wear Commissioners*

v. *Adamson*, 2 Ap. Cas. 743, 751.
(*s*) *Fenton* v. *Dublin Steam Packet Co.*, 8 Ad. & Ell. 835. The decision went upon the words of the charter-party; but it was proved that the owners had appointed and had power to dismiss the crew and officers.
(*t*) Ell. Bl. & Ell. 899.

It was held that he could recover against the owners, and
that his right against them for the negligence of their crew
was independent of his right against H. upon the contract.

In *Steel* v. *Lester* (*x*), the actual owner, who was also
registered as managing owner (*y*), had agreed with the
skipper that the vessel should be worked entirely by him,
the owner having no control over her, the crew to be
engaged and the voyages to be determined at the absolute
discretion of the skipper. The owner was to receive one
third of the ship's net profits. It was held by the
Common Pleas Division that the owner was liable for a
collision caused by the fault of his ship. Whether the
skipper was the owner's servant, or his partner (*z*) in the
adventure, navigating the ship for the joint benefit of himself and the owner, it was held that the owner's liability
was the same.

It has been doubted whether the owners of a ship which
is manned by a master and crew who are the owners' servants, but who, by the charter-party, are bound to obey the
orders of a third party who is not the owners' servant, are
liable at law for damage done by the ship while acting
under the immediate orders of such third party. Upon
principle it is difficult to see why the owners, by placing
their servants under the control and orders of a third party,
should escape liability for their wrongful acts. And in
*Fletcher* v. *Braddick* (*a*) Sir J. Mansfield held the owners
liable in such a case.

But where a vessel was one of a fleet of transports engaged in the service of the Government upon an expedition
of war, it was held by Cockburn, C.J., that it was an incident to such an employment that all the vessels should obey
the orders of those in command of the expedition ; and
that if one of them damaged another of the fleet, whilst

(*x*) 3 C. P. D. 121.
(*y*) Under 38 & 39 Vict. c. 88.
(*z*) But see *contra*, *Burnard* v.
*Aaron*, 31 L. J. C. P. 334 ; *The
Phebe*, Ware's Rep. 263.

(*a*) 2 N. R. 182. This case is
stated by the editor of Abbot on
Shipping (11th ed.), p. 44, to be
unsatisfactory.

acting in strict obedience to such orders, her owners would not be liable (b).

Where a Thames barge was lent by her owner to a person who navigated her with his own men, it was considered clear by Best, J., that the owners were not liable for damage done by her (c).

Where a ship in the course of her employment for the owner's benefit, by the fault of those on board, does injury by collision with another ship, a charge for the amount of the loss attaches to her in favour of the injured party. *Admiralty action in rem. Maritime lien for damage.* This charge or privilege, called a maritime lien, may be enforced against the ship in an action on the Admiralty side of the Probate and Admiralty Division of the High Court of Justice, or in a County Court or other inferior Court having Admiralty jurisdiction (d). Proceedings in such an action are against the ship herself, and are said to be *in rem*. They commence with the arrest of the ship, which, thereupon, with her gear and tackle, and the freight she is earning at the time of the collision, become security to the plaintiff for any damages he may recover in the action (e). The privilege or right of the injured party against the ship is inchoate from the moment of collision, and cannot be displaced even by a subsequent sale to a *bonâ fide* purchaser without notice (e) ; or by a sale under the order of a foreign Court where the proceedings are not *in rem* (f). The injured party must, however, sue within a reasonable time, or he will lose the benefit of the lien (g).

(b) *Hodgkinson* v. *Fernie*, 2 C. B. N. S. 415 ; this statement of the law was approved by the Court.

(c) *Scott* v. *Scott*, 2 Stark. 438.

(d) As to the Admiralty jurisdiction of the County Courts see Roscoe's Admiralty Law and Practice, pp. 65, *seq.*

(e) *The Bold Buccleugh*, *Harmer* v. *Bell*, 7 Moo. P. C. C. 267 ; *The Nymph*, Swab. Ad. 86 ; *The Mellona*, 3 W. Rob. 16 ; or, it seems, by the owner's bankruptcy; *The Young Mechanic*, 2 Curtis, 404 (Amer. case).

(f) *The Charles Amalia*, L. R. 2 A. & E. 330. The doctrine of the lien following the ship into the hands of a purchaser may be compared with the *noxa caput sequitur* of the civil law.

(g) In *The Europa*, 2 Moo. P. C. C. N. S. 1, the lien was held to be existing three years after the collision.

If between the collision and the arrest the ship has been repaired, and her value increased, the plaintiff, in an action for damage, does not get the benefit of such increase in value (*h*).

Cargo on board the ship arrested forms no part of the *res* to which the lien attaches; but it is subject to arrest, in order to compel the payment into Court of freight due to the ship-owner (*i*). Such freight is part of the *res*, although the cargo in respect of which it is payable was not on board at the time of the collision, if the vessel arrested was in fact then engaged in earning it. Thus, where a ship was in collision on her outward voyage with a cargo on board for the owner's benefit, it was held that the cargo which she was then under charter to bring home from the foreign port was liable to arrest (*k*). But where the freight had been paid, and the ship was subsequently, and before arrest, sold, it was held that the new owner was not liable beyond the value of the ship (*l*).

A plaintiff who obtains judgment against a ship is entitled to enforce his lien to the exclusion of another claimant for damage who institutes his action after judgment, even on the same day (*m*). And the lien for damage takes precedence of other charges on the ship, such as mortgages and bottomry bonds, though prior in date to the collision (*n*), liens for wages (*o*), pilotage and towage (*p*), and the possessory lien of a shipwright for repairs (*q*), though, probably, not to a lien for salvage (*r*). In the case of a

(*h*) *The St. Olaf*, L. R. 2 A. & E. 360; and see *The Aline*, 1 W. Rob. 111.

(*i*) *The Victor*, Lush. 72; *The Leo*, Lush. 444; *The Roceliff*, L. R. 2 A. & E. 363; *The Flora*, L. R. 1 A. & E. 45; *Nixon* v. *Roberts*, 1 J. & H. 739.

(*k*) *The Orpheus*, L. R. 3 A. & E. 308.

(*l*) *The Mellona*, 3 W. Rob. 16, 25.

(*m*) *The Saracen*, 6 Moo. P. C. C.

56; and see *The Markland*, L. R. 3 A. & E. 340.

(*n*) *The Aline*, 1 W. Rob. 111.

(*o*) *The Benares*, 7 Not. of Cas. Suppl. p. 50; *The Linda Flor*, Swab. Ad. 309, where, however, the ship was foreign.

(*p*) Abbot on Sh., 11th ed., 619.

(*q*) It was so held of the lien for salvage: *The Gustaf*, Lush. 506; but see *The Aline*, 1 W. Rob. 111.

(*r*) See *The Selina*, 2 Not. of Cas. 18.

ship owned by a company in liquidation, the lien may be enforced in priority to the claims of general creditors (s). The assignee of a lien for repairs is entitled to enforce his right against the ship, notwithstanding a composition deed executed by the assignor after the arrest of the ship; and although at the date of the assignment the ship was not under arrest, and the right of the assignor was inchoate only (t). It seems that the right of an assignee of a lien for damage would be the same.

Barges, and craft propelled by oars only, are subject to arrest, wherever the collision occurs on a tideway (u), except, perhaps, where the injury is to a dumb barge and the collision occurs within the body of a county (v). But a ship injuring a barge is liable to arrest (x); and a foreign ship, detained under 17 & 18 Vict. c. 104, s. 527, was, after an absolute appearance by her owners in Admiralty, held liable *in rem* for injury to a barge within the body of a county (y).

The nature of proceedings *in rem* is discussed by Dr. Lushington in *The Mellona* (z). He there states that Nature of proceedings *in rem*.

(s) *In re Rio Grande do Sul Steamship Co.*, 5 Ch. D. 282; and see *In re Australian Direct Steam Nav. Co.*, L. R. 20 Eq. 325.
(t) *The Wasp*, L. R. 1 A. & E. 367.
(u) *The Sarah*, Lush. 549; *Purkis v. Flower*, L. R. 9 Q. B. 114; *The Emily*, Times, July 14th, 1879.
(v) *Everard v. Kendall*, L. R. 5 C. P. 428.
(x) *The Malvina*, Lush. 493; Br. & Lush. 57.
(y) *The Bilboa*, Lush. 149.
(z) 3 W. Rob. 16, 20. See further on proceedings *in rem The Aline*, 1 W. Rob.111; *The Orient*,3 Mar. Law Cas. O. S. 321; L. R. 3 P. C. 696; *The Bold Buccleugh*, 7 Moo. P. C. C. 267; *The Two Ellens*, L. R. 4 P. C. 161; *Taylor v. Carryl*, 20 How. 584. In *The Bold Buccleugh* arrest in Admiralty was compared with the practice of foreign attachment in the Lord Mayor's Court. Arrest of a defendant's property or person, to compel him to appear, *licet in jure civili*

*nullum habet fundamentum*, was a practice which formerly extensively prevailed on the continent of Europe — *res totâ Europâ usitatissima:* Huberi Positiones, juris, ii., 4; Hub. Prælectiones, jur. civ., vol. 2, 88, seq. In Brown's Adm. Law, 143, it is stated that it is agreeable to the practice of Roman law. The shipowner's liability for damage by collision under the Roman law is not altogether clear. The law on the subject appears to come under the heads of *lex Aquilia, Exercitoria actio,* and *Edictum de nautis, cauponibus, et stabulariis:* see D. 4, 9; D. 14, 1; D. 9, 2; D. 44, 7, 5; D. 45, 2, 3,1; D. 47, 5, 1; J. 4, 3; and see Gaius, 3, 218, 219. The liability of the owner (*dominus*) was not always the same as that of the charterer (*exercitor*)—the person for whose benefit the ship was worked, and who received her earnings. The latter, when not the general owner, was, as *pro hâc vice* owner, generally liable

the main object of arresting a vessel in a cause of damage
is to cause an appearance on the part of her owners to
answer for damage to the plaintiff's ship; and that the process of the Court can be enforced against a ship without
reference to the question whether her owners at the time
of her arrest were or were not her owners when the
collision occurred.

Proceedings against the ship in Admiralty provide the
sufferer by collision with a remedy in many cases where he
would otherwise be without redress; as where the owners
of the wrong-doing ship are resident abroad, or for other
reasons cannot be sued personally.

Whether the
ship may be
liable where
the owner is
not.

The question has arisen in several cases whether the ship
may be liable in proceedings *in rem* where the collision is
not caused by the fault of the owner or his agents, and
where, consequently, he could not be made liable at law.
In some recent cases the liability of the ship and the
responsibility of the owners have been spoken of by the
Privy Council as if they were always concurrent (*a*).   But

for the acts of the master (*propositus,*
*magister*), though not always for the
acts of the crew. Where the *exer-*
*citor* and the general owner (*dominus*)
were not the same, the latter was
free from liability: 3 Kent's Comm.
161, note.  Bynkershoek contends
that the *exercitor* was not liable in
the *exercitoria actio* for damage to
another ship by the fault of the
master: *ei autem mandatum non*
*est aliorum naves obruere; quod si*
*fecisset, ipse (magister), quod dedit,*
*luat, non magister.*  But see contra
Voet ad Pandect. 14, 1, 7: *quod*
*si obliquerat (magister) si quidem in*
*ipso officio cui erat propositus, dum*
*forte datâ operâ, vel culpâ atque im-*
*prudentiâ manifestâ in narigium*
*alienum impegit suum . . . exercitor*
*ex quasi delicto teneri debebit;* and
see Huberi Prælect., jur. civ., 14, 1,
8, to the same effect.  By some
authorities it is stated generally that
the owner was liable for the obligations of the master arising *ex delicto:*
3 Kent's Comm. 161, note; and *per*

Ware, J., in *The Rebecca*, Ware's
Rep. 188; and *The Phebe, ibid.* 263,
268.  For injury to cargo or passengers on board his own ship the
owner or *exercitor* was liable under
the *edict. de nautis*, &c., D. 4, 9;
where there were several owners,
each to the extent of his share only:
D. 4, 9, 7, 5.  In the *exercitoria*
*actio* owners were liable *in solido* for
the acts of the master; but if they
contracted in their own names (*per*
*se exerceut*), only in proportion to
their respective shares in the ship:
D. 14, 1, 4.  By the Aquilian law
the owners were not liable for the
negligence of the master or crew,
the only remedy being against the actual wrong-doer: Bynkershoek, Ob-
serv. jur. Rom. l iv., c. 16; D. 9, 2,
29, 4.

(*a*) *The Diana, Stuart v. Ise-*
*monger,* 4 Moo. P. C. 11, 19; *The*
*Amalia,* 1 Moo. P. C. C. N. S. 471,
484; *The Halley,* L. R. 2 P. C. 193;
*The Orient,* 3 P. C. 696, 702; *The*
*M. Moxham,* 1 P. D. 107.

this is not always the case.  There are several decisions of
the Admiralty Court holding the ship liable where the
owner could not be sued at law (*b*).

Where a yacht was placed by her owners in the hands of
an agent for sale, and whilst in his possession, and owing
to his negligence in not striking her top gear she drove
from her moorings and injured another ship, it was held
that the yacht was liable.  The proceedings being *in rem*,
Dr. Lushington said that the common law doctrine as to
the non-liability of her owner for the negligence of an independent contractor had no application (*c*).

Where a vessel was chartered to the French Govern- Ships under
ment, and whilst in tow of a steam-ship, which the charter.
charterers ordered her to employ, by the fault of the
steam-ship, went foul of a third vessel, Dr. Lushington
held that, the proceedings being *in rem*, the maritime lien
for damage attached, notwithstanding any prior contract
between the owner and a third party.  "It is impossible,"
he said, "that because a person has entered into a volun-
tary contract by which he is finally led into mischief, that

(*b*) Besides the cases mentioned
below, it was so held in *The Neptune
the Second*, 1 Dods. Ad. 467 ; and
*The Girolamo*, 3 Hag. Ad. 169,
where the vessel was condemned for
the fault of a compulsory pilot.
These decisions were, however, not
followed in subsequent cases : see
*The Protector*, 1 W. Rob. 45 ; *The
Maria, ibid.* 95. In *The Druid*, 1
W. Rob. 391, Dr. Lushington said
that the liability of the ship, and
the responsibility of the owners,
were convertible terms.  In the case
of one who charters or hires a vessel,
and works her with his own crew,
this dictum must be taken to refer
to the charterer, in his character of
*pro hâc vice* owner, and not to the
actual owner.  In America it has
been held that the liability of the
ship arises without regard to the
ownership : see *The China*, 7 Wall.
53 ; *The R. B. Forbes*, 1 Sprague,
328 ; and *The Cumberland*, Stuart's

Vice. Ad. Rep., Lower Canada,
(1858), 75.  In Ireland the same has
been held by Townsend, J. : see *The
Mullingar*, 26 L. T. N. S. 326.  Under
the Act incorporating the company
owning a ship sued in Admiralty,
the company could not be sued without notice.  It was held by Townsend, J., that notice to the company,
in proceedings against their ship in
Admiralty, was not necessary.  He
said that in Admiralty it is the *res*
against which the suit is instituted ;
this was shown by the old forms
of procedure in which the ship was
always called "the party impug-
nant or proceeded against in the
suit."  "In Admiralty," he said,
the owners could not be said to be
liable except in a loose and popular
sense ; Cf. 10 Amer. Law Rep. 432,
as to the personification of the ship.
(*c*) *The Ruby Queen*, Lush. 266 ;
*The Orient*, L. R. 3 P. C. 696.

D

that can relieve him from making good the mischief which
he has done." And he said that this was the case though
the ship has been demised by the owner to another who
has the appointment of the master and crew (*d*).

The case anticipated by Dr. Lushington in *The
Ticonderoga* recently came before Sir R. Phillimore, and
was decided in accordance with the opinion of Dr. Lushington expressed in *The Ticonderoga*. In *The Lemington* (*e*) the vessel was chartered by her owners to a person
upon terms by which the charterer had the sole and
absolute management of her, and the appointment of her
crew. The charterer was to pay all expenses connected
with the ship, and her owners were to receive one-fifth of
her gross earnings. It was held by Sir R. Phillimore that
the ship was liable in proceedings *in rem*. In this case
Sir R. Phillimore said:—

"A vessel placed by its real owners wholly in the
control of charterers or hirers, and employed by the latter
for the lawful purposes of the hiring, is held by the
charterers as *pro hâc vice* owners. Damage wrongfully
done by the *res* while in possession of the charterers is
therefore damage done by the owners or their servants,
although those owners may be only temporary. Vessels
suffering damage from a chartered ship are entitled, *primâ
facie*, to a maritime lien upon that ship, and look to the
*res* as a security for the restitution. I cannot see how the
owners of the *res* can take away that security by having
temporarily transferred the possession to third parties. A
maritime lien attaches to a ship for damage done through
the negligence of those in charge of her, in whoseso-
ever possession she may be, if that damage is inflicted
by her whilst in the course of her ordinary and lawful
employment, authorised by her owners. Whether the

(*d*) *The Ticonderoga*, Swab. Ad.
215. The liability of the ship as
opposed to that of the owner is
strongly marked in French law; see
*infra*, p. 77.
(*e*) 2 Asp. Mar. Law Cas. 475.

damage is done through the default of the servants of the
actual owners, or of the servants of the chartered owners,
the *res* is equally responsible, provided that the servant
making default is not acting unlawfully or out of the scope
of his authority " (*f*).

In a recent case it was held that a tug, towing a ship in
charge of a compulsory pilot, was liable for a collision between
the tow and a third ship caused entirely by the tug acting
in obedience to the orders of the pilot, and without negligence on her own part or on the part of the ship in
tow (*g*).

It has not been expressly decided whether the lien for
damage attaches in cases where the Admiralty Court has
jurisdiction only under the recent statutes, 3 & 4 Vict.
c. 65 and 24 Vict. c. 10. If the collision occurs within
the body of a county, or if one ship is injured by the
negligence of those in charge of another ship, without
actually being in contact with the latter (*h*), the wrong-
doing ship may be sued in Admiralty *in rem*, and there
are strong grounds for holding that in these, as in other
cases of damage, the lien attaches (*i*). But it is not in

(*f*) See also *The Emily, ubi sup.*,
p. 31, where a barge, worked by the
hirer's servants, was held subject to
arrest ; Cf. also *The Phebe*, Ware,
263. The charterer of a ship in
the situation of *The Lemington*,
*supra*, p. 34, is held to be entitled to
owner's salvage reward : *The Scout*,
L. R. 3 A. & E. 512 ; but the actual
owner is entitled to owner's salvage,
where, notwithstanding the charter, the ship remains in his, or his
agent's, possession : *The Collier*,
L. R. 1 A. & E. 83 ; *The Waterloo*,
2 Dods. Adm. 433. In France it
seems that a ship in the position of
*The Lemington* is liable to the
sufferer by collision as "guarantie
speciale :" Manuel de Droit Commercial, par P. Bravard Veyrières,
7th ed., par Ch. Demangeat, p. 343.
In America the ship is liable by
Act of Congress of 3rd March,

1851 ; and the charterer who "mans,
victuals and navigates" her is
deemed to be *pro hâc vice* owner.
Upon the question whether the
owners of the chartered ship are
liable in Admiralty proceedings *in
rem* for "torts committed by the
ship" the Supreme Court was
equally divided : *Thorp v. Hammond*, 12 Wall. 408 : and see *The
Clarita* and *The Clara*, 23 Wall. 1.

(*g*) *The Mary*, 41 L. T. N. S. 351.
In this case the tug was in fact guilty
of contributory negligence ; so that
the statement of the law as to her
liability for the fault of the compulsory pilot was not necessary for
the decision of the case.

(*h*) As in *The Industrie*, L. R.
3 A. & E. 303 ; *The Energy, ibid.* 48.

(*i*) *The Two Ellens*, L. R. 4 P. C.
161, 167. In America it has been
held that a ship may recover in

every case in which the ship may be sued *in rem* that
the lien attaches (*k*); and there are cases in which the
Admiralty Court has statutory jurisdiction, as in the case
of damage by a ship to a pier (*l*), and certain collisions
within a county (*m*), in which it does not appear to have
been expressly decided whether the lien attaches (*n*).

**Common law action may be supplemented by action *in rem*, and *vice versâ*.** Where proceedings have been taken *in rem* in Admiralty,
and the amount realised by the sale of the ship is not
sufficient to recompense the sufferer, he may bring his
action at law for the residue of his loss (*o*); and, *vice versâ*,
an action may be brought *in rem* for damages which,
owing to the defendant's insolvency, were not recovered at
law (*p*). If the owner of the ship arrested appears and
defends the action, he may be compelled to pay costs (*q*),
beyond the value of the ship and freight, or the amount
of his bail bond. Whether an excess of damages can be
so recovered is doubtful (*r*). But to an action *in rem*

Admiralty the value of an anchor
and chain from which she had to
slip to avoid another ship driving
towards her: *The Perkins*, 2 Mar.
Law Cas. O. S. Dig. 548; and that
no lien attaches to a ship for damage
to a bridge: 1 Parsons on Sh., ed.
1869, p. 532; but the owner of a
pier improperly built in a fairway
was sued in Admiralty for damage
to a ship sunk by collision with it,
no question being raised as to jurisdiction: *Atlee* v. *The Packet Co.*,
21 Wall. 389. In another case a
ship was sued in Admiralty for
injury caused by her warp, which
was negligently stretched across a
river: *McCord* v. *The Steamboat
Tiber*, 6 Bissel, 409. As to Admiralty jurisdiction in case of collision
between a raft and a ship, see *The
W. T. Clark*, 5 Bissel, 295. By the
Supreme Court it was held that the
owners of a ship from which fire
had been communicated to a ware-
house on shore could not be sued in
Admiralty: *The Plymouth*, 3 Wall.
20. The Royal Court of Jersey
has held that personal injury caused

by the breaking of a ship's warp by
improper straining is not within
Admiralty jurisdiction: *The Cygnus*,
2 L. T. N. S. 196.

(*k*) See *The Picve Superiore*, L. R.
5 P. C. 482.

(*l*) As in *The Uhla*, 3 Mar. Law
Cas. O. S. 148; *The Excelsior*, L. R.
2 A. & E. 268; *The Albert Edward*,
44 L. J. Ad. 49; *The Maid of
the Mist*, 21 W. R. 310, decided
under the Court of Admiralty (Ireland) Act, 1867, s. 29.

(*m*) See above, p. 31.

(*n*) See *The Two Ellens*, L. R. 4
P. C. 161.

(*o*) *Nelson* v. *Couch*, 15 C. B. N. S.
99; *The Bold Buccleugh*, 7 Moo.
P. C. C. 267; *The Orient*, L. R.
3 P. C. 696, 702; *The Pet*, 20
L. T. N. S. 961.

(*p*) *The John and Mary*, Swab.
Ad. 471; *The Bengal*, *ibid.* 468;
*The Demetrius*, 41 L. J. Ad. 69.

(*q*) *The John Dunn*, 1 W. Rob. 159;
*The Freedom*, L. R. 3 A. & E. 495.

(*r*) See *The Kalamazoo*, 15 Jur.
885; *The Zephyr*, 2 Mar. Law Cas.
O. S. 146; *The Hero*, Lush. 447.

proceedings *in personam* for the like purpose cannot be engrafted (*s*).

A verdict and judgment at law that one of two ships, Judgment at law cannot be pleaded in Admiralty. B., is in fault for the collision, and that her owners are liable to the owners of the other ship, A., for their loss, is no bar to subsequent proceedings *in rem* against A. by the owners of B.; nor can they be pleaded or given in evidence in the Admiralty action (*t*). But a plaintiff who has been unsuccessful on the merits at law (*u*), or who has obtained payment of the sum for which he obtained judgment (*x*), cannot afterwards proceed against the ship in Admiralty for the same collision; nor would he be allowed to sue in Admiralty and at law at the same time for the same collision (*y*).

In Admiralty a plaintiff can recover the whole of his No set off in Admiralty. loss without regard to any right of set-off to which the defendant would elsewhere be entitled (*z*).

Owners are not liable for damage caused by acts of the Owners not liable for wilful or criminal acts of master or crew. master or crew not within the scope of their employment (*a*); as where they wilfully drive their ship against another (*b*); or cut another adrift (*c*). But for damage caused by non-observance by the master or crew of the Statutory Regulations for preventing collisions owners are

---

(*s*) *The Hope*, 1 W. Rob. 154.

(*t*) *The Clarence*, 1 Sp. E. & A. 206 ; *The Friends*, 4 Moo. P. C. C. 314, 321 ; *The Velocity*, L. R. 3 P. C. 44 ; *The Calypso*, Swab. Ad. 28.

(*u*) See *The Griefswald*, Swab. Ad. 430, 435.

(*x*) *The Orient*, L. R. 3 P. C. 696.

(*y*) *The John and Mary*, Swab. Ad. 471. But if the remedy at law is insufficient, he may proceed in both actions ; and an action *in personam* cannot be pleaded in bar of an action *in rem*: *The Bold Bucclcugh*, 7 Moo. P. C. C. 267, 286 ; *The Orient*, L. R. 3 P. C. 696. An ordinary mortgagee may

pursue all his remedies at once : Fisher on Mortgages, 3rd ed., 321.

(*z*) *The Don Francisco*, Lush. 468. See below, Ch. II., as to the decree where both ships are in fault.

(*a*) Cf. 1 Parsons on Shipping (ed. 1869), 106 ; *Bowcher* v. *Noidstrom*, 1 Taunt. 568. As to what acts are within the scope of the servant's employment, see 1 Smith's L. C., 8th ed., 383 ; as to the owner's liability by Roman and general maritime law, see *supra*, p. 31, note (*z*) ; Bynk. Quæst. jur. priv. iv., c. 20—23.

(*b*) *The Druid*, 1 W. Rob. 391 ; *Macmanus* v. *Cricket*, 1 East 106.

(*c*) *The Ida*, Lush. 6.

liable, although under 25 & 26 Vict. c. 63 such non-observance is a misdemeanour, and damage caused thereby is deemed to have been caused by the wilful default of the person in charge of the deck (*d*). And damages may be recovered against the owners although the negligence of their servants which caused the collision was criminal and amounted to manslaughter (*e*).

Where a master, without any instructions from his owner as to assisting disabled ships, offered to tow a disabled ship to port, and whilst attempting to get her in tow negligently ran into her, it was held that he was acting within the scope of his employment, and the owner was held liable (*f*).

Collision caused by compulsory pilot or other person placed in charge by the law.When a ship is being navigated under the orders of a person empowered by the Legislature to take charge of her, as when a compulsory pilot, dock, or harbour-master is in charge, the owner is not liable, provided there is no negligence on the part of the ship's officers or crew in carrying out the orders of the person in charge, or in performing the ordinary duties of the ship (*g*). In such cases it seems that the pilot or harbour-master is alone responsible. Attempts to make the harbour or pilotage authority liable for the negligence of a harbour-master or pilot, appointed or licensed by them, have been made without success (*h*).

Liability of part owners and joint wrong-doers.Part owners of a ship in fault for a collision are at law severally liable as joint wrong-doers, or joint employers of the actual wrong-doer. One of them may be sued alone (*i*);

---

(*d*) It was so held under the corresponding provisions of a former Act: *The Seine*, Swab. Ad. 411. Cf. *Poulton* v. *London & S. W. Ry. Co.*, L. R. 2 Q. B. 534; and see *Grill* v. *General Iron Screw Collier Co.*, L. R. 3 C. P. 476.

(*e*) *The Franconia*, 2 P. D. 8, 163; *Reg.* v. *Keyn*, 2 Ex. D. 63.

(*f*) *The Thetis*, 3 Mar. Law Cas. O. S. 357.

(*g*) See below, Ch. V.

(*h*) *Dudman & Brown* v. *Dublin Port & Docks Board*, Ir. Rep. 7 C. L. 518; *Metcalf* v. *Herington*, 24 L. J. N.S., Ex. 314; but see *The Excelsior*, L. R. 2 A. & E. 268.

(*i*) *Mitchell* v. *Tarbutt*, 5 T. R. 649. As to the liability of part owners by the civil law, see *supra*, p. 31, note (*z*). By the maritime law of the middle ages a part owner was

but if judgment is recovered against one part owner, it seems that no action can be brought against the others, though the judgment is unsatisfied (k).

Where a part owner, without the knowledge of his co-owner, entered into a bond to obtain the release of his ship from arrest in a collision cause in the Admiralty Court, and subsequently became bankrupt, it was held that a surety who had been compelled to pay the amount of the bond could recover against the co-owner (l).

A part owner who has been compelled to pay the whole of the damages can recover in an action for contribution against his co-owners. And money so paid for damages, where the owner's liability is limited, may be brought into account as money disbursed for the use of the ship (m).

If a collision occurs between two ships belonging to the same owner, the only remedy is against the actual wrong-doer. And the case seems to be the same, both at law and in Admiralty, where the two ships have one or more part owners in common. But the owners of cargo, or passengers, on board either ship, can recover against either ship, if she is in fault (n). As to the rights of underwriters in such a case, see below, p 42.

*Collision between owned wholly or in part by the same persons.*

If a collision occurs between two ships, A. and B., by the fault of one of them, and A., or B., or both of them, whilst in collision, or in consequence of the collision, drive against

*Collision where three or more ships are implicated.*

liable only to the extent of his interest in the ship: Emerigon Contr. à la grosse, Ch. IV., s. 11; Grotius de jur. belli et pacis, lib. 2, Ch. 11, s. 13. And this appears to be the law in France: Codes Annotées, Sirey et Gilbert, Art. 216, C. C.

(k) *Brinsmead* v. *Harrison*, L. R. 7 C. P. 547. As to the several liability where two ships are sued in Admiralty, see *The Atlas*, 3 Otto. 302; *The Juniata*, ibid. 337; *The Alabama* and *The Gamecock*, 2 Otto. 695; but see note (p), infra.

(l) *Barker* v. *Highley*, 11 W. R.

968.

(m) See 1 Smith's Lead. Cas. (8th ed.), 169; and 17 & 18 Vict. c. 104, s. 515.

(n) See *Simpson* v. *Thompson*, 3 App. Cas. 279. The question whether in the latter case a lien for damage attaches to the wrong-doing ship does not appear to have been decided. In *The Glengaber*, L. R. 3 A & E. 534, it was held that a ship was entitled to salvage, notwithstanding the fact that some of her owners were owners of the tug which had caused the mischief.

and injure a third ship, C., C. can recover against the ship in fault for the first collision. But the ship that comes into her is not liable, unless she was in fault either for the first or the second collision (o). It will, however, be seen in a subsequent chapter (Ch. III.), that a ship in tow is generally responsible for the fault of her tug; she will, therefore, be liable for a collision between her tug and a third ship, or between herself and a third ship, though she was herself not in fault.

If two ships, A. and B, are both in fault for a collision between one of them and a third ship, C., C. can proceed in Admiralty against either A. or B., or against both of them. And, it seems, that she can recover the whole of her loss in an action against one of them (p). But if C. is in tow of A. or B., the rule is different (q).

Where, by the negligent navigation of one ship, a collision occurs between two others, or another ship is damaged, either by collision or in any other way, the first ship is liable, and not the less so because she escaped collision herself (r).

If a vessel engaged in towing another, or in rendering to her salvage service, negligently damages her by collision or in any other way, the tug or salvor cannot recover for the towage or salvage service. Nor can a tug recover salvage reward for assistance rendered to a ship with which her tow has been in collision by the fault of herself, the tug. But a salvor (s) damaged, without negligence on her

---

(o) *The Venus, infra; The Hibernia,* 4 Jur. N. S. 1244; *The Sisters,* 1 P. D. 117; *The Moxey,* Abbot Adm. 73 (Amer. case).

(p) *The Lyra* and *The Venus,* 2 Mar. Law Cas. O. S. Dig. 522; S. C. nom. *The Venus,* 1 Pritch. Ad. Dig. 129. See, however, *The Milan,* Lush. 388, where it was held that the owners of cargo on board one of two ships, which were both in fault for the

collision, could recover only one half their loss against the other ship. As to the liability of joint wrong-doers at law, see above, p. 38.

(q) As to the liability where a tug or tow is in collision, see below, Ch. III.

(r) *The Industrie,* L. R. 3 A. & E. 303; *The Ivanhoe* and *The Martha M. Heath,* 7 Bened. 213. See *infra,* p. 55.

(s) See pp. 46, 47, *infra.*

own part, by collision with the vessel she is assisting, is entitled to recover against the latter.

Owners are not liable for damage caused by a ship which they have abandoned, if the abandonment was justifiable. But if the abandonment, though necessary for the safety of those on board, was the result of negligence for which the owner is responsible, it seems that he remains liable notwithstanding the abandonment (*t*). So long as a ship remains in the owner's possession he is liable for damage to another ship striking her, though she is sunk or ashore, if such damage was caused by the absence of proper lights or precautions on her part. In Scotland it has been held that in such a case no liability attaches to the river or harbour authorities (*u*) having statutory powers to remove wreck and obstructions. It is the duty of those in charge of a vessel sunk in a fairway to mark her position with a buoy (*x*). In America it has been held that no liability attached to a tug for damage caused to a third ship by her tow, which had been sunk without fault on the part of the tug (*y*).

*Liability for damage by a ship ashore, or sunk, or abandoned.*

Besides the owners, all persons by whose personal negligence (*z*), or by the negligence of whose agents, a collision occurs, are liable for damages. The officer in charge, the pilot (*a*), or crew, and in some cases, it seems, the charterers as well as the owners (*b*), may be responsible. The master is under a special liability to passengers and cargo owners, as well for acts of negligence as misfeasance on the part of himself or his crew (*c*). Against a pilot (*d*), and against

*Persons liable other than owners.*

(*t*) *Brown* v. *Mallet*, 5 C. B. 599; *White* v. *Crisp*, 10 Ex. 312 ; *Rex* v. *Watts*, 2 Esp. 675.

(*u*) *Kidson* v. *McArthur*, 5 Sess. Cases, 4th Series, 936.

(*x*) *Harmond* v. *Pearson*, 1 Camp. 515; *Hancock* v. *York, &c., Railway Co.*, 10 C. B. 348.

(*y*) *The Swan*, 3 Blatchf. 285.
(*z*) Cf. Code de Commerce, Art. 221 ; German C. C., Art. 736; Span-

ish C. C., Art. 676.
(*a*) *Smith* v. *Voss*, 2 H. & N. 97, was an action against a pilot.
(*b*) See Abbot on Sh., 11th ed., 46.
(*c*) Story on Agency, § 314—316 ; *Morse* v. *Slue*, 1 Ventris, 238.
(*d*) *The Alexandria*, L. R. 3 A. & E. 574 ; *The Urania*, 1 Mar. Law Cas. O. S. 156 ; 10 W. R. 97.

owners resident abroad (*d*), where the collision occurred
beyond British jurisdiction, and service of the writ cannot
be effected within the jurisdiction, the Admiralty Court
has refused to entertain a personal action for damages.

It has been said that the master is liable for the negligent
and wrongful acts of the crew, as well as for his own acts (*e*).
His liability as carrier, unless specially limited, may extend
so far; but it does not appear to have been held in any
case decided in this country that he is liable to the owners
of another ship for damage by collision for which he was
himself free from blame (*f*). For wilful injury by the
pilot or crew to another ship he is clearly not liable (*g*).

The ship-owners, or employers of the master or actual
wrong-doer, by whose fault a collision occurs, can recover
against him any damages which they have been compelled
to pay, or any loss which they have suffered by his
negligence (*h*).

Underwriters;<br>their rights<br>and liabilities. Loss by collision is a loss by peril of the sea within the
meaning of that term in the ordinary marine policy of
insurance (*i*). Whether the collision is by inevitable accident, by the fault of both ships, or by the fault of the one
or the other of them, the insurers are liable (*k*). Where
the collision is by the fault of the insured ship alone, there
has been no direct decision as to the underwriters' liability;
but there is little doubt that they are liable as for a loss
caused either by barratry or by peril of the sea (*l*).

(*d*) *The Vivar*, 2 P. D. 29; *Re
Smith*, 1 P. D. 300; *Harris* v.
*Owners of the Franconia*, 2 C. P. D.
173.

(*e*) Story on Agency, § 314—317;
Molloy II., c. 3, s. 13.

(*f*) See *Aldrich* v. *Simmonds*, 1
Stark. 214. It has been held in
America that the master is liable in
such a case: Story on Agency, § 316,
note; *Denison* v. *Seymour*, 9 Wen-
del, 9; 3 Kent's Comm., 218.

(*g*) *Bowcher* v. *Noidstrom*, 1 Taunt.
568.

(*h*) Addison on Torts, 4th ed., 26.

(*i*) As to a bill of lading, see *supra*,
p. 20.

(*k*) Park on Insurance, 8th ed.,
139; *Smith* v. *Scott*, 4 Taunt. 126.

(*l*) Arnould on Insurance, 5th ed.
744—746; Phillips on Insurance, §
1417—1420; and see *Simpson* v.
*Thompson*, 3 Ap. Cas. 279. Cf. French
Commercial Code, Art. 350 and 353;
Spanish C. C., Art. 861; Dutch C.
C., Art. 637; German C. C., Art. 824
and 825. By the two first codes, only
*abordages fortuits*, by the others, all
collisions are at the insurer's risk.

Where both ships are in fault, and the insured ship is sued and made liable for damages which exceed the amount of her own loss, the underwriters on her are not liable under the ordinary policy for such excess (m). *De Vaux v. Salvador*, the case by which this was decided, was formerly dissented from in America by the Supreme Court; but is now recognised by that Court as binding (n). It has produced the "collision clause" in a Lloyd's policy, by which the underwriters insure three-fourths of the damages which the insured ship may be compelled to pay for collision with another. The remaining fourth may be covered by insurance elsewhere. The collision clause does not cover costs which the insured may incur in defending an action by the other ship (o). Where it was expressed to cover damages which the assured ship should be compelled to pay for running down and damaging another ship, it was held that it did not include damages recovered against the insured ship by the representatives of persons on board the other ship who lost their lives in the collision (p).

A ship, M., was insured in a policy containing a running down clause by which the insurers undertook to bear three-fourths of any sum, not exceeding the value of the ship and freight, which the assured should become liable to pay, and should pay, for collision with another ship. The ship insured was sold in an Admiralty damage suit for less than her value. It was held that the underwriters were liable for no more than three-fourths of the sum for which the ship was sold (q).

Underwriters can recover against the wrong-doer in the collision damages for the collision which under their policy

(m) *De Vaux v. Salvador*, 4 Ad. & El. 420. *Aliter* by French law: Caumont Dict. de Droit Mar. tit. Abordage ; and by German law : German C. C., Art. 824.

(n) *General Mutual Insurance Co. v. Sherwood*, 14 How. 352.

(o) *Xenos v. Fox*, L. R. 4 C. P.

665.

(p) *Taylor v. Dewar*, 5 B. & S. 58 ; but the contrary has been held in Scotland, *Cuey v. Smith*, 22 Court of Session Cases, 955 ; *Excelsior Co. v. Smith*, 2 L. T. N. S. 90.

(q) *Thompson v. Reynolds*, 7 E. & B. 172.

they were bound to pay, and have paid to the insured, provided the insured could himself have sued for and recovered them, but not otherwise (*q*).  They have no right of action apart from him, and they must sue in his name (*r*).  If the insured has received the amount of his loss from the underwriters, he is a trustee for them of any damages he may recover in respect of the collision (*s*).  But the fact that he has been compensated by them is no answer to his claim for damages against the wrong-doer (*t*).

**Rights of underwriters in case of collision between ships of the same owner.** Where a collision occurred between two ships belonging to the same owner, and one of them, with cargo on board not belonging to the ship-owner, was sunk by the fault of the other ship, the ship-owner paid into Court, under the Merchant Shipping Acts, the amount to which his liability, as owner of the wrong-doing ship, was limited.  It was held, that as against the cargo owners, underwriters upon the innocent ship, who had paid the insurance upon her, were entitled to no part of the money paid into Court (*u*).  The decision would, it seems, be the same in the case of a collision between two ships owned in part by the same persons.

In *Simpson* v. *Thompson*, Lords Cairns, Penzance, and Blackburn declined to express an opinion whether the ordinary marine policy covers a loss by collision with another ship belonging to the assured.

**Cargo owners not liable.** The owners of cargo on board a ship in fault for a collision are not liable for damage done by the ship (*x*); but the cargo may be arrested in order to secure the payment of unpaid freight due to the ship-owner (*y*).

---

(*q*) *Yates* v. *Whyte*, 4 Bing. N. C. 272, 283 ; 5 Scott 640 ; *The John Bellamy*, 22 L. T. N. S. 244.

(*r*) *Simpson* v. *Thompson*, 3 App. Cas. 279 ; *Regina del Marc*, Lush. 315.

(*s*) *Yates* v. *Whyte*, *ubi supra*.

(*t*) *Taylor* v. *Dewar*, 4 B. & S. 58.

(*u*) *Simpson* v. *Thompson*, 3 App.

Cas. 279.  In this case the rights and liabilities of underwriters in case of collision were fully discussed by the House of Lords.

(*x*) *The Victor*, Lush. 72, 76 ; *The Flora*, L. R. 1 A. & E. 45. Cf. German C. C., Art. 736.

(*y*) See above, p. 30.

Her Majesty's ships, and ships of war of a foreign State, Liability for are not subject to arrest (z). In the case of a collision by the fault of the fault of a Queen's ship, the legal responsibility attaches to the actual wrong-doer (a). If the ship is properly in charge of an inferior officer, the captain is not responsible in a civil action. The appointment of all officers being with the Government, the superior officer is not in such a case answerable for the acts of his subordinate (b).

collision by the fault of a Queen's ship or foreign ship of war.

Whether vessels belonging to a department of the Government, and employed for the special purposes of the department, are entitled to the immunity from arrest enjoyed by ships of war belonging to Her Majesty, seems doubtful (c).

The liability of owners resident abroad; in respect of a collision abroad; and in case of collision where one of the ships is a tug or in tow, is considered in subsequent chapters (d).

Foreign owners; collision abroad; tug and tow.

Beyond incurring the civil liability for damages, the person guilty of reckless or negligent navigation, whereby a collision occurs in which life is lost, or bodily injury (e) suffered, may be prosecuted criminally. "Those who navigate (the Thames) improperly, either by too much speed, or by negligent conduct, are as much liable, if death ensues, as those who cause it on a public highway, either by furious driving or negligent conduct" (f). The criminal liability attaches only to those by whose personal miscon-

Criminal liability for a collision.

---

(z) As to ships of a foreign Sovereign which are engaged in trade, see below, p. 93. In America Government ships are subject to Admiralty process: *The Siren*, 7 Wall. 152.

(a) *The Mentor*, 1 C. Rob. 179. For the practise in case of an action against a Queen's ship, see Williams and Bruce Ad. Practice, p. 68. *The Athol*, 1 W. Rob. 374; *The Volcano*, 2 W. Rob. 337; *The Birkenhead*, 3 W. Rob. 75; and *The Bellerophon*, 3 Asp. Mar. Law Cas. 58, are in-

stances of actions against Queen's ships.

(b) *Nicholson* v. *Mounsey*, 15 East 384.

(c) See *The Cybele*, 3 P. D. 8.

(d) As to foreign ships and collisions abroad, see Ch. IV.; as to tug and tow, Ch. III., *infra*.

(e) As to bodily injury, see Mr. Justice Stephen's Digest of Criminal Law, Art. 211.

(f) *Per* Parke, B., in *Reg.* v. *Taylor* 9 C. & P. 672, 674.

duct or negligence the collision occurs (g). But where a foreign ship, in charge of an English pilot in the Thames, ran down a boat and drowned a man, and the collision was caused by the man at the helm, a foreigner, not understanding and carrying out the pilot's orders, it was held that the pilot was guilty of manslaughter, if by his own negligence he failed to make his orders understood (h).

The criminal liability of the offender in a collision where one or both the ships is foreign, or the offender himself a foreigner, or where the collision occurs out of British waters, is considered in a subsequent chapter (i).

The master, pilot, or any seaman of a British ship, who wilfully or negligently endangers the life of any person on board such ship, or endangers the ship herself, is guilty of a misdemeanour (k).

**Board of Trade certificate may be cancelled.** If a collision involving loss of life, or serious damage to either ship, is caused by the wrongful act or default of an officer holding a Board of Trade certificate, his certificate may be cancelled or suspended at a Board of Trade enquiry (l).

**Tug or salvor in collision with the ship she is assisting.** One of the consequences of negligence causing collision is that the wrong-doer cannot claim salvage for service rendered to the ship with which he has been in collision, although the latter is also in fault for the collision (m). But a vessel engaged in a salvage service to another does not forfeit her right to salvage by going into collision with the other (n). And an innocent ship may recover salvage

(g) Rex v. Allen, 7 C. & P. 153; Rex v. Green, ibid. 156; and see Oakley v. Speedy, 40 L. T. N. S. 881.

(h) Reg. v. Spence, 1 Cox. C. C. 352.

(i) See p. 98, infra.

(k) 17 & 18 Vict. c. 104, ss. 239, 366. This Act is more lenient than some of the mediæval codes. Decapitation at the windlass, or keelhauling, was the punishment pro-

vided for negligent and incompetent pilots.

(l) See 17 & 18 Vict. c. 104, s. 242; 25 & 26 Vict. c. 63, s. 23.

(m) Cargo ex Capella, L. R. 1 A. & E. 356; and see The Glengaber, L. R. 3 A. & E. 534. The rule is the same in America: The Clarita, 23 Wall. 1; The Sampson, 4 Blatchf. 28.

(n) The C. S. Butler and The Baltic, L. R. 4 A. & E. 178.

for services rendered to another which has negligently run
into her.  The law which makes it the duty of a ship
which has been in collision with another to stand by her,
and render assistance, does not prevent her from recovering
salvage reward for assistance so given (o).  A salvor damaged,
without negligence on her own part, by collision with the
vessel she is assisting, may recover against the latter (p).
But a tug cannot recover salvage reward for assistance
rendered to a ship with which her tow has been in collision
by the fault of herself, the tug (q); nor, after a collision
between the tow and her tug by the fault of the latter, can
the tug recover upon towage contract (r).

All persons injured in their persons or property in a Persons
collision caused by the fault of one or both ships are entitled to
recover.
entitled to recover damages.  Such persons may be owners
of the injured ship (except where she is alone in fault),
whether they be registered owners or not (s); owners,
consignees, bailees, and other persons having a special
property in, or temporary possession of, cargo on board
either ship (t), indorsees of bills of lading (u), persons
entitled under Lord Campbell's Act to recover damages
for relatives killed (v), or persons on board either ship who
are hurt in the collision.

There is some doubt whether a person on board a ship Whether per-
which is herself in fault can recover at common law (x). sons on board
a ship herself
The better opinion is that such a person is not prevented in fault can
recover.
by the fault of his own ship from recovering from the
owners of the other (y).  In the Admiralty Court there

(o) *The Retriever* and *The Queen*,
2 Mar. Law Cas. O. S. 555.
(p) *The Mud Hopper*, 40 L. T.
N. S. 462.
(q) *The Glengaber*, ubi supra.
(r) *Infra*, p. 63.  As to tug and
tow generally, see Ch. III.
(s) *The Ilos*, Swab. Ad. 100.
(t) Addison on Torts, 4th ed., 919.
(u) *The Marathon*, 40 L. T. N. S.

163.
(x) 9 & 10 Vict. c. 93 ; see below,
p. 64.  An unborn child may recover for the loss of its father : *The
George and Richard*, L. R. 3 A. & E.
466.
(x) *Thorogood* v. *Brian*, 8 C. B.
115; *Catllin* v. *Hills*, ibid.
(y) Smith's Lead Cas., 7th ed., 300.

seems no doubt that he could recover; and it has been expressly held that owners of cargo on board a ship in fault can recover against the other, if she is also in fault (z).

**Bailee of ship; indorsee of bill of lading; consignee of cargo.** The indorsee of a bill of lading, even though the cargo has been sold (a); bailees, and other persons having a special property in the ship or cargo, can recover in Admiralty (b) as well as at law. The consignee or assignee of a bill of lading can, where no owner or part owner of the ship is domiciled in England or Wales at the time of the action being instituted, proceed against the ship in Admiralty for damage to the cargo by the fault of the master or crew (c). In such an action it seems he could recover for loss of cargo in a collision for which the carrying ship was wholly or partly in fault. To enable him to maintain the action it is not necessary that the property in the goods should have passed to him (d).

The holder of a bottomry bond on freight of a ship, A., is entitled, in an action for limitation of liability by the owner of another ship, B., which has negligently damaged A. by collision, to a rateable share with the owners of A. of the amount payable by the owner of B. (e).

**Actions by part owners; consolidation of actions.** It seems that part owners of the injured ship might recover damages for their respective losses in successive actions (f). But the defendant would be entitled to have the other co-owners added as plaintiffs, so that he should not be vexed by more than one action. If a part owner dies after the collision and before action brought, the right

(z) *The Milan*, Lush. 388; *The City of Manchester*, 40 L. T. N. S. 591.
(a) *The Marathon*, 40 L. T. N. S. 163.
(b) *The Minna*, L. R. 2 A. & E. 97. In an American case full damages were recovered for a collision, although all interest in the injured ship had been transferred to a foreigner, whereby the ship was forfeited to the State : *The Nabob*,

Brown Ad. 115.
(c) 24 Vict. c. 10, s. 6 ; 36 & 37 Vict. c. 66, s. 16.
(d) See *The Figlia Maggiore*, L. R. 2 A. & E. 106; *The Nepoter, ibid.* 375; *The Pieve Superiore*, L. R. 5 P. C. 482.
(e) *The Empusa*, 48 L. J. Ad. 36.
(f) *Addison* v. *Overend*, 6 T. R. 766; *Sedgworth* v. *Overend*, 7 T. R. 280.

of action survives to the other part owners (*g*). Where
two or more actions are brought by different plaintiffs in
respect of the same collision, the actions may be consolidated. But it appears that the present practice of the
Admiralty Division is not to force consolidation upon unwilling plaintiffs (*h*).

A servant cannot recover against his employer for in- Doctrine of
jury sustained in the course of his employment through common employment.
the negligence of a fellow servant (*i*). It seems, therefore,
that the ship's officers and crew cannot recover against the
ship-owner for injury suffered in a collision caused by one
of themselves (*k*), except, perhaps, where the wrong-doer is
the captain (*l*). But a compulsory pilot is not a servant
of the ship-owner, and the rule above stated does not
prevent him from recovering against the owner (*m*).

Where there are several claimants for damages in Order of
several actions *in rem* in respect of the same collision, they claimants in several actions
rank in the order of their judgments (*n*). A plaintiff who *in rem.*
institutes his action after another has been instituted, but
before judgment, is entitled to damages rateably with the
plaintiff in the previous action (*o*).

## NOTE.

*History of the Law as to Division of Loss where both Ships are in Fault.*

The history of the rule as to equal division of loss where both
ships are in fault is curious. It is at least as old in the Admiralty Court of this country as the reign of Queen Anne : *The
Petersfield* and *The Judith Randolph*, cited by Lord Gifford in

(*g*) See Maude and Pollock on
Shipping, 2nd ed., 67, 68.
(*h*) See *The William Hutt*, Lush.
25; Rules of Supr. Court, Ord. LI.,
r. 4; *The Jacob Landstrom*, 4 P. D.
191.
(*i*) *Priestly* v. *Fowler*, 3 M. & W.
1; Chitty on Contr., 10th ed., 537.
(*k*) *Leddy* v. *Gibson*, 11 Sess. Cas.

3rd ser. 304 (Scotch).
(*l*) *Ramsay* v. *Quinn*, Ir. Rep.
8 C. L. 322.
(*m*) *Smith* v. *Steele*, L. R. 10 Q. B.
125.
(*n*) *The Saracen*, 6 Moo. P. C. C.
56.
(*o*) *The Clara*, Swab. Ad. 1; see
*infra*, pp. 65, 68, 89.

E

# 50

hr.

*Hay* v. *Le Neve*, 2 Shaw's Scotch App. Cas. 395 ; and see *The Lord Melville* cited in the same case.  It is opposed to the rule of the common law, that a person cannot recover for a loss caused in part by his own negligence; and in the common law Courts it has been much abused.  In *De Vaux* v. *Salvador*, 4 Ad. & El. 420, Denman, C.J., says of it : " It is an arbitrary provision in the law of nations, not dictated by natural justice, nor, possibly, quite consistent with it."  Though recognised by foreign jurists as part of the law maritime, it meets with little approbation at their hands.  Bynkershoek disapproves of it : *quia in pari causâ melior est conditio possidentis . . . . parem autem causam facit utriusque culpa; nam simul ac accesserit omnem actionem excludit.* Quæst. Jur. Priv. l. IV., c. 22.

By the Laws of Oleron, a maritime code attributed by Pardessus to the twelfth century, it was provided that where a ship at anchor is injured by another under way, " the mayster of the shyp that hyt the other must swere on a boke, and hys marchaunts with hym, that he dyd it not with hys wyll," and thereupon the loss shall be equally divided between the ships.  The reason for the rule is stated to be " that an olde shyp wyllyngly lyeth not in the waye of a better, so fer forth as it knoweth not to domage it by grevyng, but whan it knoweth wel that it must part by halfe it wyll pass by out of the way."  (English translation of the Laws of Oleron, Black Book of the Admiralty, Sir Travers Twiss' Ed. Vol I., p. 109.  Cleirac (Us et Coustumes de la Mer, Ed. 1661, Bordeaux, p. 68), in his observations upon this article, agrees with the framers of the Laws of Oleron in their low estimate of maritime morality : " est considerable que les gens de mer sont ordinairement enclins au mal et à la baraterie."  He approves of the singular law which deprived ship-owners and merchants of their natural right to receive full compensation for their loss, but only upon the questionable ground above stated, that facilities must not be given for getting ships wilfully run down.  He illustrates the principle of the rule by citing the Book of Exodus, Ch. xxi., ver. 35.  That he had not a high opinion of the justice of the rule is apparent : " les juris consultes nomment et qualifient cette decision par moitié *judicium rusticorum . . . .* et se prattique ordinairement par les arbitres, arbitrateurs, et amiables compositeurs, lors et quand l'interieur des parties, ou le motif de la question n'est pas à desconvert et connen ; ou bien quand il y a de la coulpe de part et d'autre—*aut quando sunt diversæ judicium opiniones hinc inde probabil.* Boer dec. 42, n. 39—tel fut le jugement reconnen tant juridic du sage Roy Salomon qu'il donna sur la question naturele entre deux mers" (*sic*). Chancellor Kent (Kent's Comm., § 231), follows Cleirac in stigmatizing the rule as *judicium rusticum.* The rule probably had its origin, partly in the disposition of the mediæval Courts to treat all collisions as perils of the sea, for which seamen and ship-owners could not properly be held responsible ; and partly in their recognition of the extreme difficulty of ascertaining the facts necessary to enable them to arrive at a just decision in each case. So the rule of dividing the loss came to be adopted—*ob culpæ probandæ difficultatem,* Grotius, *De Jure Belli et Pacis,* l. 2, c. 17, s. 21. It has by some writers been said that the rule is desirable upon grounds of public policy, in order to make the masters of large ships more careful of smaller craft : see Bell's Comm. 581.

The rule of equal division of loss where both ships are in fault forms no part of the Roman law. It is not to be found in the Laws of Oleron or any other mediæval code of maritime law. There can, however, be little doubt that it had its origin in the provision above quoted of the Laws of Oleron. If its policy or justice can be supported at the present day, it must be upon grounds other than those suggested by Cleirac for the analogous rule of the Laws of Oleron. It narrowly escaped abolition at the time of the passing of the Judicature Act, 1873 ; but under that Act, as finally passed, it has become the law of England, and is now administered by common law, as well as by the Admiralty Courts. By the Judicature Act, as originally drawn, the Admiralty rule was abolished, and gave place to the common law rule, that he who is the author of his own loss can recover nothing ; but in consequence, it seems, of a letter addressed to the Lord Chancellor by H. C. Rothery, Esq., the then Registrar of the Admiralty Court, the Admiralty rule was reinstated, and, in the result, has superseded the common law rule in all the Courts.

A provision similar to that of the Laws of Oleron as to the

E 2

division of loss where the collision is not wilful is contained in several of the mediæval codes. See Sir Travers Twiss' Ed. of the Black Book of the Admiralty, I., 36, 39, 108, 109 ; II., 229, 449 ; III., 21 ; IV., 87, 88, 271, 373, 435. By some of these codes the loss was not necessarily divided in equal shares; it appears to have been apportioned between the ships in proportion to their values, or their fault; *ibid.* Vol. III., 287 ; IV., 435 ; Danish Code of 1683, 1. IV., c. 3, s. 4. But Bynkershoek was unable to persuade the Superior Court of Holland to adopt any other than the rule of division in equal shares : *memini me senatore et de geometricâ proportione perorante, reliquos senatores obstupuisse, atque si Jovis ignibus icti essent ;* Bynk. Quæst. Jur. Priv. IV., 20.

The rule of division of damages does not appear to have been applied by the Admiralty Court of this country except where both ships have been found to be in fault for the collision. By the general maritime law it was not confined to this case. It was applied in the case of inevitable accident, and also in the case of inscrutable fault : see Bell's Commentaries on the Law of Scotland, p. 581. Valin, Sur l'Ordonnance, 1. III., tit. 7, Art. 11, says of it : " par la difficulté de reconnoitre de quel côté est la faute, et juger même si la faute est de nature à mériter que celui, à qui elle est imputée, supporte le dommage en entier, il arrive presque toujours que le dommage reçu de part et d'autre est jugé avarie commune, ce qu'approuve Grotius, &c."

Although, by the maritime law, the loss was divided between the two ships in the case of inscrutable fault, and the rule is so applied in the Courts of France and other countries, it has never been adopted in the Admiralty of this country. In *The Maid of Auckland,* 6 Not. of Cas. 240, where, if such a rule had existed, it would have been applicable, or at least mentioned, Dr. Lushington dismissed both suits upon the ground of *deficit probatio.*

The rule has been applied, in some cases, so as to prevent an innocent sufferer by collision from recovering more than half his loss against a wrong-doer : *The Milan,* Lush. 388 ; Comm. Code of Holland, Art. 540 ; Bynk. Quæst. Priv. Jur. IV., c. 21.

In America the rule as to the incidence of loss by collision is the same as that of this country; except, perhaps, in the case of inscrutable fault. In this case, according to some writers, the loss is divided : *The Tracy J. Bronson*, 3 Bened. 341 ; and see 1 Parsons on Sh. (Ed. 1869) 527 ; Story on Bailments, § 609 ; 3 Kent's Comm., § 231 ; Sedgwick on Damages (6th Ed.) 577, note ; but in a recent case before the District Court of New York, it was held that neither ship could recover : *The Breeze*, 6 Bened. 14.

Art. 407 of the French Commercial Code is as follows : En cas d'abordage de navires si l'événement a été purement fortuit, le dommage est supporté, sans répétition, par celui des navires qui l'a éprouvé. Si l'abordage a été fait par la faute de l'un des capitaines, le dommage est payé par celui qui l'a causé. S'il y a doute dans les causes de l'abordage, le dommage est réparé à frais communs, et par égale portion, par les navires qui l'ont fait et souffert. Dans ces deux derniers cas, l'estimation du dommage est faite par experts. The case of inscrutable fault is that described in Art. 407—"s'il y a doute, &c."—that is, "lorsqu' il est impossible de préciser par la faute de qui le dommage est arrivé." In this case the French differs from the English law in dividing the loss equally—Abordage Nautique, Caumont, § 151. But the French law agrees with our own in requiring proof of negligence to enable the cargo owner to recover in such a case, *ibid.* § 154, 155. Where both ships are in fault, but not to the same extent, the damages are apportioned according to the degree of each ship's fault ; but as between ship-owners and third parties, the former are severally liable for the whole of the damages, subject to the right of each to free himself by abandonment of his interest in the ship and freight : *ibid.* § 12, 108, 152. Where both ships have been guilty of an infringement of the Rule of the Road (manœuvres réglementaires), it seems that neither can recover : *ibid.* § 109. The case of inevitable accident is complicated by attempts to attribute the collision partly to " force majeure," and partly to negligence : *ibid.* § 94.

The Belgian Commercial Code (Art. 407) contains the same provisions as to the incidence of loss as the French Code.

The law in Germany as to the incidence of loss in the four cases of collision seems to be the same as that of this country ;

except that where both ships are in fault, neither can recover. See German Commercial Code, Arts. 736—741.

By the Dutch Code, where both ships are in fault, and also when the collision occurs without fault in either ship, each bears her own loss. If there is doubt whether the collision was caused by the fault of one or both ships, or not, the aggregate loss upon both ships and cargoes is made good by a general average contribution between the owners of ships and cargoes. Where a ship under way goes foul of another at anchor, even if the collision is an inevitable accident, the ship under way has to pay half the loss. But these rules apply only to seagoing ships, and not to inland navigation. See the Commercial Code of Holland, Arts. 534—540, 756.

The Spanish Commercial Code contains no provision as to the division of the loss where both ships are in fault, or any other case. It distinguishes between collisions caused by the fault of one or both ships, and those caused by inevitable accident. In the first case it seems that the captain, or the actual wrong-doer, is alone responsible; in the other case each ship bears her own loss, unless insured. *Abordaje casual*, which, besides cases of inevitable accident, includes collisions by the fault of one or both ships, where fault is not proved, is a particular average, and is at the risk of insurers. See Código de Comercio, Arts. 624, 676, 682, 861, 935, § 7.

Art. 516 of the Italian Comm. Code, and Arts. 1567—1570 of the Portuguese Comm. Code, are to the same effect as Art. 407 of the French Code, *supra*. Art. 1581 of the Portuguese Code requires a ship under way damaging another at anchor to pay half the loss. This code is identical with the Dutch Code in many of its provisions, and goes into considerable detail: see Port. Code, Arts. 1567—1581.

The Russian Code is not clear as to the incidence of loss. Where the collision is an inevitable accident, and where both ships are in fault, it seems that the loss rests where it falls: Arts. 835, 845. But in some cases the total loss on the ships, though not on cargo, is borne by the two rateably: Art. 847. See Russian Code, Arts. 835—848.

# CHAPTER II.

## DAMAGES.

OWNERS, and other persons answerable for damage caused by the negligent navigation of a ship, are liable for all the reasonable consequences of their negligence (*a*). This is the rule whether the negligence causes a collision or not. In a case where, in order to avoid a collision with a ship, A., made imminent by A.'s own fault, a tug, B., was compelled to cast off her tow, C., and C. went ashore and was damaged, it was held that C. could recover against A. (*b*). Where, in order to avoid A., lying ashore in a fairway without a light up, B. was obliged to put herself ashore, and received injury, it was held that B. could recover against A. (*c*). The value of an anchor and chain slipped to avoid collision was recovered in an American Admiralty Court (*d*).

If the negligence of one ship causes a collision between two others, the damage received by both of them can be recovered against the first. And if a vessel is in an unmanageable state, or has lost her lights, by her own

*The wrong-doer is liable for all the reasonable consequences of his negligence, whether there is a collision or not.*

(*a*) Mayne on Damages (3rd ed.), 39. As to damages for collision generally, see Sedgwick on Damages (6th ed.), 576.

(*b*) The *Wheatsheaf* and The *Intrepide*, 2 Mar. Law Cas. O. S. 292. The Admiralty Court has jurisdiction where a ship has done or received damage, though there is no

collision : The *Industrie*, L. R. 3 A. & E. 303 ; The *Energy*, ibid. 48 ; and it seems that so far as it decides the contrary The *Robert Pow*, Br. & L. 99, would not now be followed.

(*c*) The *Industrie*, ubi supra.

(*d*) The *Perkins*, 2 Mar. Law Cas. O. S. Dig. 548.

negligence, any damage she does while in that state would
probably be held to be the result of her own negligence (e).
So if a vessel sinks another by her swell raised by going
at too great speed, she is liable for the loss (f).

**Loss of injured ship after collision presumed to be caused by the collision.** Where a ship is lost, or receives further injury after a
collision, the presumption is that the loss or damage is
caused by the collision; and the burden is on the other
vessel, if proved to be in fault for the collision, to show
that the subsequent loss or damage was not caused by her
negligence. Where a ship was partially disabled in a collision for which she was not in fault, and subsequently drove
ashore in consequence of the parting of her cable, it was held
that the ship in fault for the collision was liable for the loss
by the stranding of the other ship (g). In this case Dr.
Lushington said : " It is admitted that *The Peusher* is to
blame for the collision, and the consequence of this is,
that all the damage arising from the collision must be
borne by *The Peusher*, unless it can be shown by clear
and positive evidence that any part of that subsequent
damage arose from gross negligence or great want of skill
on the part of those on board the vessel damaged."

In another case (h), *The Mellona*, a ship claiming
damages against the ship with which she had been in
collision, had gone ashore after the collision, in consequence of having been disabled in the collision, and was
totally lost. For the other ship it was contended that
*The Mellona* need not have gone ashore if she had been
hove-to, and proper skill had been shown by those on
board. It was held that *primâ facie* the loss was
attributable to the collision. Dr. Lushington said that
where one vessel is found in fault for a collision, and the
other is subsequently lost, the presumption of law is that

(e) See *supra*, p. 8.
(f) *The Batavier*, 1 Sp. E. & A.
378 ; 9 Moo. P. C. C. 286 ; *Luxford
v. Large*, 5 C. & P. 421.

(g) *The Peusher*, Swab. Adm. 211,
213.
(h) *The Mellona*, 3 W. Rob. 7, 13.

the latter was lost in consequence of the collision. "In all questions of this description that is the *primâ facie* presumption; and great, indeed, would be the inconvenience, and still greater the difficulty, if, in all cases of this kind when the vessel did not go down immediately, but was subsequently lost, the Court had to enter into an investigation whether all the measures adopted on board the damaged vessel were right, or whether, if other measures had been pursued, the vessel might not have been saved" (*i*).

In another case a ship was run into whilst brought up and riding with two anchors down. One cable having parted in the collision, the other failed to hold her, and she drove ashore. It was held that the loss from her going ashore was recoverable as damages by the collision (*k*).

So where, bad weather having come on, the injured ship went ashore twenty-one hours after the collision, the representatives of some of the crew who were drowned, but who might have been saved if they had gone on board other vessels which offered assistance after the collision, were held entitled to recover against the wrong-doing ship (*l*).

But the fact of a ship being injured by the negligence of another does not justify those on board in neglecting to take all reasonable measures to save the ship, and lessen the effects of the collision. They must exhibit ordinary courage in standing by their vessel, and show proper skill and seamanship according to the circumstances of the case. The Court, however, will make reasonable allowance for the excitement which usually attends a collision, and those on board will not be expected

*Those on board the injured ship must exhibit ordinary skill and courage in standing by her.*

---

(*i*) See also *The Linda*, Swab. Ad. 306; 30 L. T. 234; 4 Jur. N. S. 146.
(*k*) *The Despatch*, 14 Moo. P. C. C.

83.
(*l*) *The George* and *The Richard*, L. R. 3 A. & E. 466.

to be so acute in their judgment, or to act with the same skill and coolness as if there had been no collision (m).

**They must take assistance, if necessary.**

Where the injured ship went ashore, and those in charge wilfully refused assistance to get her off, it was held that her owners could not recover for loss arising from the obstinacy of those on board (n).

**If they abandon her unjustifiably, damages cannot be recovered as for a loss caused by the collision.**

If the injured vessel is abandoned unjustifiably, the other vessel, if in fault for the collision, is not liable for a total loss, but only for the actual damage done in the collision (o).

The question whether the abandonment of a ship injured by collision was justifiable is for the Court to decide upon the particular circumstances of each case. In considering it the Court will not be exacting in requiring those on board to stand by her. In *The Blenheim* (p) Dr. Lushington said :

" When a collision takes place on a dark night, particularly at a tempestuous period of the year, and when the vessel producing the collision is of greater burden than the one struck, I cannot possibly settle with satisfaction to my own mind, or security to justice, what ought to be the reasonable extent of fear and apprehension to the crew of the vessel so struck. It is impossible for any Court of justice to say, with any degree of certainty, what are the precise circumstances that would justify the abandonment of a vessel. If there be any reasonable prospect that the lives of the crew are endangered, I have determined, and I will do so, until I am overruled, that they are justified in quitting the vessel, and the consequences most fall on the wrong-doer " (q).

**Salvage ex-**

If a ship is improperly abandoned after a collision, her

(m) *The Hannah Park* and *The Lena*, 2 Mar. Law. Cas. O. S. 345 ; *The Thuringia*, 1 Asp. Mar. Law Cas. 283.

(n) *The Flying Fish*, Br. & Lush. 436 ; 2 Mar. Law Cas. O. S. 221.

(o) *The Thuringia*, *ubi supra*.

(p) 1 Spinks E. & A. 285, 289.

(q) See also *The Linda*, 30 L. T. 234; *The Hope* and *The Chili*, 2 Mar. Law Cas. O. S. Dig. 546 ; *The Lindsay*, Ir. Rep. Ad. 1 Eq. 259.

owner will not be entitled to recover, as damage caused penses not recoverable if abandonment unjustifiable.
by the collision, either the value of the ship or salvage
expenses payable upon her being brought into port (*r*).

*The Thuringia*, a steam-ship which had been run down
by the fault of another vessel, was improperly abandoned,
and subsequently sank. It was held that she could recover
no more than the expense which would have been incurred
in making good the damage caused by the collision (*s*).
The collision in that case occurred sixteen or eighteen
miles from Heligoland in fine weather. The ship remained afloat three hours after the collision, and might
have been taken to Heligoland.

In another case (*t*) no attempt was made to repair the Loss through neglect to repair injury received in the collision not recoverable as damages caused by its collision.
damage received in the collision, such damage consisting
in a small hole which might easily have been stopped. In
consequence of the hole being left unstopped the cargo
was injured by water. It was held that the cargo owner
could not recover damages against the other ship, although
she was in fault for the collision. The duty of the master
of the injured ship to take proper steps to preserve and
under some circumstances to sell an injured cargo has been
considered in several cases (*u*). It was held negligence in
a master not to have discharged a cargo of beans which
were wetted in a collision (*v*).

But where a ship is sunk at sea by collision, there is no Where the ship is sunk.
obligation upon the owner to raise her, even if it would
be possible to do so (*w*). If he elects to raise her, and it
turns out, upon a survey, that she is not worth repairing,
he is entitled to recover as damages the expense of raising
and docking her, less her value in the dock (*x*). If he
repairs her at a cost exceeding her value before collision,

(*r*) *The Linda*, Swab. Ad. 306.
(*s*) *The Thuringia*, 1 Asp. Mar. Law Cas. 283.
(*t*) *The Eolides*, 3 Hag. 367.
(*u*) See Cargo ex *Argos*, L. R. 5 P. C. 134, 165, and cases there cited.
(*v*) *Notara* v. *Henderson*, L. R. 7 Q. B. 225.
(*w*) *The Columbus*, 3 W. Rob. 158. The principles of abandonment as applied in insurance cases do not apply in collision cases : *ibid.* 165.
(*x*) *The Empress Eugenie*, Lush. 138.

he cannot recover the cost of repairs beyond such value; nor anything in the nature of demurrage (*y*).

If, acting as a prudent owner, he elects not to repair, and sells her, he is entitled to recover her value at the time of collision, less the proceeds of sale, together with interest from the date of the collision (*z*).

**Difficulty of determining whether damage consequent on collision is caused by the collision.** There is difficulty, in some cases, in determining whether the damage is caused by the collision or not. A passenger on board *The Bachelor* was injured by an anchor on board that vessel which was caused to fall on him by a collision for which *The Sons of the Thames* was in fault. In an action by the passenger against the owners of *The Sons of the Thames*, Pollock, C.B., left it to the jury to say whether there was negligence on the part of the crew of *The Bachelor* in stowing the anchor so that it fell on the plaintiff, and whether there was negligence on the plaintiff's part in being in the part of the ship where the anchor was stowed. The verdict was for the plaintiff; the jury finding that there was no negligence on his part, or on part of the crew of *The Bachelor*. A rule *nisi* for a new trial which was obtained on the ground that the verdict was against the weight of the evidence was discharged. In discharging the rule, Pollock, C.B., said, with regard to the general law, that if the negligence of the plaintiff did not in any degree contribute to the immediate cause of the accident, that negligence ought not to be set up as a defence to the action. And he doubted whether a person, who is guilty of negligence, is responsible for all the consequences which might under any circumstances arise, and in respect of mischief which could, by no possibility, have been foreseen, and which no reasonable person would have anticipated (*a*).

(*y*) *The Empress Eugenie*, Lush. 138.
(*z*) *The South Sea*, Swab. Ad. 141.
(*a*) *Greenland* v. *Chaplin*, 5 Ex.
243; see also *The Gipsey King*, 5 Not. of Cas. 282 ; *Sills* v. *Brown*, 9 C. & P. 601 ; *Lynch* v. *Nurdin*, 1 Q. B. 29; *Byrne* v. *Wilson*, 15 Ir. Com. Law, 332.

Damage occurring during or after the collision, but caused by negligence other than that which caused the collision, cannot be recovered as resulting from the collision. Where, whilst two ships were in collision, the damage was increased by those on board the plaintiff's ship omitting to cut a lanyard which held the ships together, it was said by the Court to be negligence on their part not to have cut it (b).

If the damage received in a collision is greater because of the weak condition of one of the vessels, the other is liable for the entire loss, if she is in fault for the collision. The principle is, that if a part of the damage was clearly attributable to the wrong-doer, and it is impossible to draw the line with precision, and to say how much, the wrong-doer must make good the whole loss (c).

Consequential damages are in some cases recoverable. Where a smack was run down while performing a salvage service, it was held that she was entitled to recover what she would have earned if she had not been prevented from completing the salvage service (d). In another case, where a ship was run down whilst on a voyage to Norway to bring home a cargo of lobsters, and another ship was taken up for the purpose, it was held that the freight of the lobsters was recoverable as consequential damages (e).

If the injured ship sinks in consequence of the collision, the expenses of raising and docking her (f), and salvage expenses generally, are recoverable as damages, if they are properly incurred, and in consequence of injury received in the collision (g). In an American case the expense of

*Consequential damages recoverable; loss of salvage, freight, or charter-party; demurrage; salvage expenses; interest; diminished market value of injured ship.*

(b) The Massachusetts, 1 W. Rob. 371 ; see also The Flying Fish, Br. & Lush. 436 ; Grill v. General Iron Screw Collier Co., L. R. 1 C. P. 600 ; ibid. 3 C. P. 476.

(c) The Egyptian, 2 Mar. Law Cas. O. S. 56 ; The Sam Gaty, 5 Bissel, 190.

(d) The Betsy Caines, 2 Hag. Ad.

28.

(e) The Yorkshireman, 2 Hag. Ad. 30, note.

(f) The Empress Eugenie, Lush. 138.

(g) The Linda, 30 L. T. 234. For decisions of French Courts to the same effect, see Abordage Nautique (Caumont), § 11.

detaining the crew after the collision, and of attempts to save cargo was allowed (*h*).

Where it was proved that the market value of a yacht sunk in a collision was diminished, it was held that in addition to the sum required for repairs, the difference between her market value before and after the collision was recoverable as damages (*i*).

Where the owners suffer loss by the enforced idleness of their ship which has been injured in a collision, demurrage is allowed by way of damages whilst the necessary repairs are being effected. And demurrage runs whilst the ship is detained for the transaction of business connected with the collision, such as making a protest, and obtaining the necessary official documents (*k*).

Where, in consequence of the collision, a vessel lost the benefit of a charter-party, damages were allowed for the loss of the charter-party in addition to demurrage (*l*).

A fishing smack recovered, besides the value of her nets and gear which she was obliged to cut adrift, the amount she might reasonably have been expected to earn during the rest of the fishing season (*m*).

Where the innocent ship was sunk by the collision, and her owners recovered for a total loss, the master and crew, in a subsequent action, recovered the value of their clothes and effects (*n*).

If the injured ship is in the course of earning freight, and is prevented by the collision from completing the voyage, the amount of freight, less the charges which would have been incurred in earning it, together with interest

(*h*) *Hoffman* v. *Union Ferry of Brooklyn*, 68 New York Rep. 385.

(*i*) *The Georgiana* and *The Anglican* (Irish case), 21 W. R. 280.

(*k*) *The City of Buenos Ayres*, 1 Asp. Mar. Law Cas. 169; *The Clarence*, 3 W. Rob. 283. As to demurrage where the injured ship is one of a line advertised to sail at

fixed intervals, see *The Black Prince*, Lush. 568.

(*l*) *The Star of India*, 1 P. D. 466.

(*m*) *The Gleaner*, 3 Asp. Mar. Law Cas. 582.

(*n*) *The Cumberland*, 5 L. T. N. S. 496. The master and crew are usually co-plaintiffs with the owners in such a case.

from the probable termination of the voyage, is recoverable (o). If she is lost, and was not engaged in earning freight, interest upon her value at the time of the collision from the date of the collision to the time of payment is in all cases allowed (p).

Where damages are estimated upon the footing of a total loss, although, in fact, the ship was subsequently saved and repaired, with the exceptions mentioned above, no more than the ship's value at the time of the collision can be recovered. In such a case nothing will be allowed for, or or in the nature of, demurrage (q).

Damages which, although consequent upon the collision, do not immediately or necessarily flow from it, cannot be recovered against the ship in fault for the collision (r). Where the master and part owner of a vessel lost by collision claimed his probable future earnings as master, and profits as part owner, it was held that he was entitled to nothing more, by way of damages, than the value of the ship at the time of the collision (s).

It has never been the practice to give damages for loss of market for cargo on board a ship injured by collision (t).

The rule as to the measure of damages is that the injured party is entitled to full compensation. His right against the wrong-doer is to be placed by him in the position in which he would have been if the collision had not occurred (u). The owner of the injured ship is entitled to have her fully and completely repaired; and if the necessary

*Remoteness of damage.*

*Measure of damages: "restitutio in integrum."*

(o) *The Canada,* Lush. 586.
(p) See *infra,* p. 64.
(q) See *The Columbus,* 3 W. Rob. 158.
(r) As to remoteness of damage, see Mayne on Damages, 3rd ed., 40, *seq.;* 2 Smith's L. C., 8th ed., 566, *seq.*
(s) *The Columbus,* 3 W. Rob. 158; and see *The Clarence, ibid.* 283. In France the probable catch of a fish-

ing voyage has been recovered as damages : Abordage Nautique, Caumont, § 148.
(t) *Per* Mellish, L.J., in *The Parana,* 2 P. D. 118, 124 ; *Smith* v. *Condry,* 1 How. 28 ; *The Jos. W. Dyer* v. *National Steamship Co.,* 14 Blatchf., p. 483.
(u) " *Restitutio in integrum* " is the phrase used in many of the cases to describe the injured party's right.

consequence of this is, that the value of the ship is increased, so that the owner receives more than an indemnity for his loss, he is entitled to that benefit. No deduction is made from the damages recoverable on account of the increased value of the ship, or the substitution of new for old materials (*x*). In this respect the owner of a ship injured by collision is in a different position from an owner claiming his indemnity under the ordinary marine policy of insurance (*y*).

If the ship is totally lost the owner is entitled to recover her market value at the time of the collision (*z*), with interest from the day of the collision if the ship was not earning freight. If she was earning freight he is entitled to the estimated value of the ship at the end of her voyage, with the freight she would have earned, less the costs of completing the voyage, and interest on the whole from the probable end of the voyage. If payment is made before that time an allowance is made for discount. If, however, the plaintiff's loss exceeds the amount of the owner's statutory liability, interest runs from the date of the collision, whether freight was being earned or not (*a*).

**Damages for loss of life.** Damages for loss of life are recoverable under Lord Campbell's Act (*b*) by the relatives or representatives of persons killed by collision. It has been held by the Admiralty Court that such damages may be recovered in proceedings *in rem;* there is, however, considerable doubt as to the jurisdiction of the Admiralty Court in such cases, the decisions upon the subject being conflicting (*c*).

---

(*x*) *The Pactolus,* Swab. 173; *The Gazelle,* 2 W. Rob. 279; and see *The Star of India,* 1 P. D. 466, 471.

(*y*) As to the rule of "one-third new for old" in insurance cases, see *Lohre* v. *Aitchison,* 3 Q. B. D. 558; on app., 28 W. R. 1.

(*z*) *The Clyde,* Swab. Ad. 23; *The Ironmaster, ibid.* 441.

(*a*) For a full statement by Sir

R. Phillimore of the principle upon which compensation to the injured party is made in cases of collision, see *The Northumbria,* L. R. 3 A. & E. 6, 12.

(*b*) 9 & 10 Vict. c. 93; and see 27 & 28 Vict. c. 95.

(*c*) *The Sylph,* L. R. 2 A. & E. 24; *The Guldfaxe, ibid.* 325; *The Beta,* L. R. 2 P. C. 447; *The Boro-*

Under the Merchant Shipping Act, 1854, the Board of Trade has power to institute proceedings for the recovery of damages for loss of life or personal injury. Damages recovered in such proceedings are assessed at £30 for each case of death or injury, and are payable in priority to other claims. This, however, is not the limit of the owner's liability. The full amount to which he is liable under 25 & 26 Vict. c. 63, s. 54, can be recovered in proceedings, either by the Board of Trade or by any person dissatisfied with the amount recovered in the Board of Trade proceedings. If the amount of the owner's statutory liability is insufficient to provide damages at the rate of £30 for each claimant, the claims abate rateably (d).

If a vessel wilfully or negligently injures a light-ship, in addition to her liability for damages, she incurs a penalty of £50 (e). Notwithstanding the words of the Act, the liability for damages is probably limited to the statutory amount, in this as in other cases. Penalty for injuring a light-ship.

Even where the other ship can be proved to have been in fault for the collision, the whole loss cannot in all cases be recovered. Where both ships are in fault, as has been already stated (pp. 1, 49, *supra*), the rule is that the aggregate loss must be borne by the two ships in equal shares. In this case, therefore, no more than half her loss can be recovered by either ship against the other (f). Nor can the owner of cargo on board either ship recover against the other ship more than half his loss (g). If part has been recovered against the owner of the carrying ship, the difference, up to one-half the loss, may be recovered against The whole loss by collision cannot be recovered against the wrong-doing ship (1) where both ships are in fault.

*dino,* 5 L. T. N. S. 291 ; and *contra, Smith* v. *Brown,* L. R. 6 Q. B. 729 ; *Simpson* v. *Blues,* L. R. 7 C. P. 290. In *The Franconia,* 2 P. D. 163, the Court of Appeal was equally divided ; see also *Taylor* v. *Dewar,* 5 B. & S. 58.

(d) See 17 & 18 Vict. c. 104, ss. 507—516 ; 25 & 26 Vict. c. 63, s.

56 ; *Glaholm* v. *Barker,* L. R. 2 Eq. 598 ; S. C., L. R. 1 Ch. 223; see also *The Franconia,* 2 P. D. 163, 166. Proceedings under this Act are rarely, if ever, taken.

(e) 17 & 18 Vict. c. 104, s. 414.

(f) See *The Sapphire,* 18 Wall. 51.

(g) *The Milan,* Lush. 388.

the other ship (*g*).  But the owner of the carrying ship, and,
if the cargo is carried into any port in England or Wales and
all the owners are domiciled elsewhere, it seems the ship
herself is liable to the cargo owner for the whole loss (*h*).

(2) Where the      The other case in which the whole loss cannot be
loss exceeds
the defendant   recovered against the wrong-doing ship or her owners is
ship-owner's    where the loss exceeds a sum to which the Legislature has
statutory
liability.      limited the ship-owner's liability.  By 25 & 26 Vict. c. 63,
s. 54, it is enacted that in cases where there is no actual
fault or privity on the part of the owner or master of a
British or foreign ship, the liability of the owner or master
for loss of life, personal injury, and damage to another ship,
or to cargo on board his own or another ship, is limited to
an amount which varies with the tonnage of his ship (*i*).
Where there is loss of life, or personal injury, his liability
is calculated at the rate of £15 per ton of his ship's
registered tonnage (*k*).   For damage to ship or cargo,
whether accompanied by loss of life or personal injury or
not, his liability is at the rate of £8 per ton.   This Act
applies in every case of collision, whether the ships are
both British, or both foreign, or one British and one foreign;

(*g*) *The Demetrius*, L. R. 3 A. & E.
523 ; 41 L. J. Ad. 69.
   (*h*) *Chapman* v. *The Royal Nether-*
*lands Steam Navigation Co.*, 4 P. D.
157 ; see *per* Jessel, M.R., p. 165 ;
24 Vict. c. 10, s. 6.  *The Milan, ubi*
*supra*, so far as it decides that the
innocent cargo owner can recover no
more than half his loss against the
other ship, has not been followed
in America.  It has been held by
the Supreme Court that the innocent
cargo owner is entitled to a decree
for the whole of his loss against
either of the wrong-doing ships if
one only is sued ; if both are sued
he is entitled to a decree for half
his loss against each ; and if a
moiety of his loss exceeds in amount
the statutory liability of either of
them, or if, for any other reason, he
fails to obtain half his total loss from

either of them, be is entitled to a
further decree against the other for
the difference ; see *The Alabama*
and *The Gamecock*, 2 Otto. 695 ;
*The Juniata*, 3 Otto. 337 ; *The*
*Atlas*, *ibid.* 302 ; *The Virginia*
*Ehrman*, 7 Otto. 309 ; *The City of*
*Hartford* and *The Unit, ibid.* 323 ;
*The City of Paris*, 14 Blatchf. 531.
   (*i*) See Appendix, p. 244.
   (*k*) In the case of a steam-ship,
the tonnage, for the purpose of
calculating liability, is the registered
tonnage, *plus* engine-room and crew
spaces :  *The Franconia, Hamburg,*
*&c., Gesellschaft* v. *Burrell*, 3 P. D.
164 ; in which case *Burrell* v.
*Simpson*, 4 Sess. Cas., 4th series,
177, was not followed as to crew
spaces.  As to the tonnage measurement of foreign ships, see 25 & 26
Vict. c 63, s. 60.

whether the collision occurs in British or foreign waters, or on the high seas (*l*); and whether the action is in one of the Common Law Divisions at law or in the Admiralty Division.

But the owners of a ship which is British, in so far that her owners are British, and that she is British built, are not entitled under the Act of 1862 to limitation of their liability if their vessel was unregistered at the time the damage was done.   Thus, where a ship, which, by the negligence of those in charge, as she was being launched from the builder's slip on the Mersey, ran into and damaged another, her owners, who were British, were held liable for the entire loss (*m*).   It does not appear to have been decided what is a "ship" within the meaning of the enactment (25 & 26 Vict. c. 63, s. 54) by which liability is limited (*n*). *Liability in respect of an unregistered ship of a British owner.*

In an action for damages by *The Vesuvius* against *The Savernake*, and upon a counterclaim by *The Savernake*, it was held that both ships were in fault for the collision. *The Vesuvius*, with cargo on board, sank, and was totally lost.   Her value, apart from her cargo, was £28,000. *The Savernake* was injured to the extent of £4000.   The owners of *The Savernake*, under an order made in a subsequent action for limitation of their liability, paid into Court £5212 3s. 5d., the amount for which they were declared liable under the statute.   A contest arose in the limitation action as to the rights and liabilities of the owners of the two ships and the owners of the cargo on board *The Vesuvius*.   It was held by the Court of Appeal that the owners of *The Vesuvius*, and the owners of cargo on board her, were entitled to the £5212 3s. 5d. rateably, in proportion to their respective losses; and that the owners of *The Savernake* were entitled to be paid £2000 *Amount payable where both ships are found in fault upon a claim and counterclaim.*

---

(*l*)  *The Amalia*, 1 Moo. P. C. C. N. S. 471; Br. & Lush. 151.

(*m*)  *The Andalusian*, 3 P. D. 182; see 17 & 18 Vict. c. 104, ss. 19, 516.

(*n*)  The word "seagoing" which occurs in 17 & 18 Vict. c. 104, s. 504, is omitted in 25 & 26 Vict. c. 63, s. 54.   As to inland craft under a former Act, see *Hunter* v. *M'Gowan*, 1 Bligh. 571.

in full by the owners of *The Vesuvius*.  It was contended
before Jessel, M.R., in the limitation action, that the
owners of cargo were entitled to be paid out of the
£5212 3s. 5d., in priority to the owners of *The Vesuvius*;
but Jessel, M.R., held that ship-owners and cargo owners
were entitled to be paid *pari passu*.  It was also contended
by the owners of *The Vesuvius*, that they were entitled to
deduct, or set off, the £2000 in which they were condemned
upon the counterclaim in the collision action from the
£14,000 in which the owners of *The Savernake* were
condemned in that action; and that they were entitled,
without paying anything to the owners of *The Savernake*, to
prove against the fund in Court for £12,000, the difference.
It was held by Jessel, M.R., in the Court below, and by
Brett, L.J., in the Court of Appeal, that such was their
right; but the majority of the Court of Appeal held that
they were liable to pay the £2000 in full (o).

*Limit of
owner's lia-
bility for loss
of life.*

Lord Campbell's Act, enabling the representatives of
persons killed by negligence to recover damages, is not
repealed or affected by the Merchant Shipping Acts,
except so far as those Acts limit the extent (p) of the
ship-owner's liability.  It has been already stated that
although the damages for loss of life recoverable in
proceedings taken by the Board of Trade are assessed
at £30 for each life, that is not the limit of the owner's
responsibility (q).

*Liability
limited for
breach of con-
tract as well
as for tort.*

An injury done to the vessel in tow by her tug, during
the performance of the towage contract, is "improper
navigation" within the meaning of 25 & 26 Vict. c. 63,
s. 54; and the tug-owner's liability is limited (r).  And

(o) *Chapman* v. *The Royal Nether-
land Steam Nav. Co.*, 4 P. D. 157. In
a similar case in Holland, Byuker-
shoek, Quæst. Jur. Priv., l. IV. c.
21, states that the decree went for
the difference between the losses on
the two ships.  See also *The Sapphire*, 18 Wall. 51.

(p) *Glaholm* v. *Barker*, L. R. 1
Ch. 223; and see *ibid.*, 2 Eq. 598.
(q) See *supra*, p. 64.
(r) *Wahlberg* v. *Young*, 24 W.
R. 847; 4 Asp. Mar. Law Cas. 27,
note.  As to collisions generally,
where one ship is in tow, see Ch.
III.

owners are entitled to the benefit of the Act in respect of a breach of contract as well as in respect of a mere tort. Thus, carriers by sea, or partly by land and partly by sea, were held to be entitled to limitation of liability as against passengers and owners of cargo on board their ship, which was in collision and sunk by her own negligence (s).

The liability of a railway company under a contract for the carriage of persons, animals, or goods by sea, is probably limited by 34 & 35 Vict. c. 78, s. 12, in cases where the carrying ship is not owned by the company, and is not navigated by their servants (t). {.sidenote}Liability of railway company where the carrying ship does not belong to the company.

Where by the same act, and at the same time, a ship damages two others, the owners are not liable beyond the statutory limit, which is the same whether the collision is with one or more ships. Where a steam-ship ran into a tug and the ship to which she was passing her tow line, it was held that the amount for which the steam-ship was liable was to be calculated as upon one collision, and not on two (u). In another case, where one steam-ship was towing another, and both ran into and damaged a third ship by the negligence of the towing ship, it was held that the towing ship alone was liable. And the owners of the tug and tow being the same, their liability was calculated at £8 per ton on the tonnage of the towing ship (x). {.sidenote}Liability where two ships are damaged by a third. Or where two ships run into and damage a third.

It seems that the fact of the master of the wrong-doing ship being a part owner will not deprive his co-owners of the benefit of the statute, although he is personally in fault (y). And an owner in fact is entitled to limitation of liability, although he is not the registered owner (z). If it is intended to make a master, who is also owner, liable {.sidenote}Liability where master is also owner; "fault or privity."

(s) London & South Western Rail. Co. v. James, L. R. 8 Ch. 241 ; The Normanby, L. R. 3 A. & E. 152.

(t) But see Doolan v. Midland Railway Co., 2 App. Cas. 792, 809.

(u) The Rajah, L. R. 3 A. & E. 539.

(x) Union Steamship Co. v. Owners

of The Aracan, The American, and The Syria, L. R. 6 P. C. 127.

(y) The Spirit of the Ocean, Br. & Lush. 336 ; and see Wilson v. Dickson, 2 B. & Ald. 2.

(z) The Spirit of the Ocean, ubi supra ; and see Steel v. Lester, 3 C. P. D. 121.

beyond the statutory limit, as for a collision caused by his fault or privity, he must be sued as master in the first instance (a). It is not clear what constitutes "fault or privity" depriving a master or owner of the benefit of the statute. Where the master, who was also part owner, was on board but not on deck at the time of the collision, and the ship was properly in charge of the mate and pilot, it was held that there was no " fault or privity " on the part of the master (b).

**The statute limiting owners' liability is construed strictly.** The law by which ship-owners' liability is limited has been said to take away a remedy—the natural right of the sufferer to a full compensation—and it is therefore construed strictly (c). It applies only where the injury is to a ship, or to cargo or persons on board a ship (d), and then only when the injury is caused by improper navigation. Owners and masters of ships alone can claim the benefit of the Act. The liability of pilots, harbour and dock-masters, and of any other person, not being the owner or master, who takes charge of a ship, is not touched by the Act. Nor does the Act affect the liability, under a contract to carry, of a person (not being a railway company) who carries in a ship not belonging to himself (e).

**Action for limitation of liability.** Where several claims are made against a ship in respect of a collision, her owners may institute an action in Chancery, and when the ship or the proceeds thereof are under arrest ( f ), in Admiralty, for the purpose of determining the amount of their liability, and for the distribution

(a) The Volant, 1 W. Rob. 383 ; and see 17 & 18 Vict. c. 104, s. 516.
(b) The Obey, L. R. 1 A. & E. 102 ; and see Kidson v. McArthur, 5 Sess. Cas., 4th series (Renuie), 936.
(c) Gale v. Laurie, 5 B. & C. 156, 164 ; and see The Northumbria, L. R. 3 A. & E. 6, 13 ; and per Brett, L..J., in Chapman v. Royal Netherlands Steam Nav. Co., 4 P. D. 157, 184 ; The Andalusian, 3 P. D. 182, 190.

(d) For injury to a pier, owners are liable to the full extent of the damages : 10 & 11 Vict. c. 27, s. 74.
(e) See per Lord Blackburn in Doolan v. Midland Railway Co., 2 App. Cas. 792, 808 ; as to railway companies, see S. C. and supra, p. 20.
( f ) See James v. London & South Western Ry. Co., L. R. 7 Ex. 187 ; on app., ibid. 287.

of that sum, in case their ship is held to be in fault for the collision, amongst the claimants (*g*). It has been held in Chancery that before instituting an action for limitation of liability, the plaintiff (the owner of the defendant ship in the collision action) must admit his liability for damages (*h*); but this seems doubtful, and it has been held in the Admiralty Court that liability need not be admitted (*i*).

In Scotland it has been held that where the ship-owner has settled out of Court some of the claims in respect of a collision for which his ship was in fault, he is entitled, upon a petition for limitation of his liability, to take into account the sums previously paid in respect of such claims; and that the other claimants are not entitled to any more than they would have recovered if none of the claims had been settled (*k*).

The liability to arrest cargo in order to compel payment of freight is not affected by 25 & 26 Vict. c. 63, s. 54 (*l*).

Beyond the sum to which the ship-owner's liability is limited by statute, he is liable for interest on the damages (*m*), and for the costs of the action (*n*). The general rules as to costs are as follows. Where both ships are in fault each bears her own costs (*o*); but an owner of cargo on board one ship suing the other ship, is entitled to costs, though both ships are in fault (*p*); in other cases,

(*g*) 17 & 18 Vict. c. 104, s. 514; 24 Vict. c. 10, s. 13.

(*h*) *Hill* v. *Audus*, 1 K. & J. 263.

(*i*) *The Amalia*, Br. & Lush. 151; *The Sisters*, 2 Asp. Mar. Law Cas. 589; see also *James* v. *London & South Western Ry. Co.*, L. R. 7 Ex. 287.

(*k*) *Rankine* v. *Raschen*, 4 Sess. Cas., 4th series, 725.

(*l*) *The Orpheus*, L. R. 3 A. & E. 308.

(*m*) *The Amalia*, 34 L. J. Ad. 21; *The Northumbria*, L. R. 3 A. & E. 6; *Smith* v. *Kirby*, 1 Q. B. D. 131, and

see generally *supra*, p. 62.

(*n*) Under former Acts, costs were recoverable beyond the value of the ship and freight: *The Dundee*, 2 Hag. Ad. 137; *Ex parte Rayne*, 1 Gale & Dav. 374. In America costs are recoverable beyond the statutory limit: *The Wanata*, 5 Otto. 600.

(*o*) *The Agra* and *The Elizabeth Jenkins*, L. R. 1 P. C. 501.

(*p*) *The City of Manchester*, 40 L. T. N. S. 591, not following *The Hibernia*, 31 L. T. N. S. 805.

the general rule, except, perhaps, in the Admiralty Division,
is that costs follow the event of the action (q).   In the
Privy Council and formerly in Admiralty the rules as to
costs were somewhat different; and it seems these rules
have, since the Judicature Acts, been followed in the
Admiralty Division.  Where the collision was the result
of inevitable accident, and the plaintiff had no means of
knowing this; or where the defendant fails upon the
merits, but succeeds upon the defence of compulsory
pilotage, it was formerly the practice in Admiralty and
in the Privy Council to give the plaintiff no costs (r).
And this practice was followed in a recent case in the
Admiralty Division by Sir R. Phillimore (s).   But the
defendant in such a case will not be ordered to pay costs (t).
A plaintiff who, without negligence, sued the wrong ship,
has escaped paying costs (u) ; and violence on the part of
the crew of the plaintiff ship against those on board the
other ship at the time of the collision has deprived her of
her right to costs (x).   A defendant who admits that his
ship was in fault, but raises and succeeds upon the defence
of compulsory pilotage, will obtain his costs (y).   Though
no order as to costs can be made against a Queen's ship,
costs may be recovered if the Queen's ship is found to be
in fault (z).   Co-plaintiffs are severally liable for costs (a).

Liability of
Trinity House
pilot.
      The liability of a London Trinity House pilot is limited
to £100, the amount of his bond, and his pilotage fee (b).

(q) *The Swansea* and *The Condor*,
4 P. D. 115 (in which case the pre-
vious decisions in *The Daioz*, 3 Asp.
Mar. Law. Cas. 477 ; *The City of
Cambridge*, 35 L. T. N. S. 781 ; *The
Corinna, ibid.*, were not followed) ;
*The General Steam Navigation Co.* v.
*The London and Edinburgh Shipping
Co.*, 2 Ex. D. 467.
(r) *The Juno*, 1 P. D. 135 ; *The
Royal Charter*, L. R. 2 A. & E. 362 ;
*The Princeton*, 3 P. D. 90 ; *The In-
nisfail*, 35 L. T. N. S. 819.
(s) *The Matthew Cay*, W. N. 1879,
p. 190.

(t) *The Schwann*, L. R. 4 A. & E.
187.
(u) *The Evangelismos*, Swab. Ad.
378 ; 12 Moo. P. C. C. 352 ; *The
Active*, 5 L. T. N. S. 773.
(x) *The Catalina*, 2 Sp. E. & A.
23.
(y) *The Schwann, ubi supra.*
(z) *H.M.S. Swallow*, Swab. Ad.
30 ; *The Leda*, Br. & Lush. 19.
(a) *The Leda, ubi supra.*
(b) The pilot cannot be sued in
Admiralty : *The Alexandria*, L. R. 3
A. & E. 574 ; *The Urania*, 10 W. R.
97 ; *Flower* v. *Bradley*, 44 L. J. Ex. 1.

Ship-owners' liability for damage to a wharf or pier is unlimited. But they are not liable where the damage is the result of an act of God or inevitable accident (c). They are liable whether the damage is done by the ship whilst in charge of their own servants or not; but not where the damage is done by a compulsory pilot (d).

Liability for damage to a wharf or pier.

## NOTE.

*Limitation of Ship-owners' Liability.*

The history of the singular legislation which enables the owners and masters to do mischief with ships at a cheaper rate than is permitted to other people, or with other instruments, is as follows. Until the year 1734, by the common law of England, and by the maritime law as administered in the Admiralty Court, the liability of ship-owners was unlimited. In that year an Act was passed (7 Geo. II. c. 15) limiting owners' liability for loss of cargo by the theft of the master or crew to the value of the ship and freight. Subsequently, by 26 Geo. III. c. 86, the same privilege was extended to owners in case of theft by any person, and in case of loss by fire. By 53 Geo. III. c. 159, the same limit was fixed for liability in case of damage to other ships, or to cargo on board either of two ships in collision. It was held under this Act that owners were liable in respect of freight which had been paid before the collision: *Wilson* v. *Dickson*, 2 B. & Ald. 2. By 17 & 18 Vict. c. 104, the limitation was extended to damages for loss of life or personal injury, with a provision that in such cases the value of the ship should not be taken at less than £15 per ton: see *Nixon* v. *Roberts*, 1 J. & H. 739; *Leycester* v. *Logan*, 4 K. & J. 725. Under all these Acts

History of the law as to limitation of ship-owners' liability.

(c) Notwithstanding the words of 10 & 11 Vict. c. 27, ss. 25, 74 : see *River Wear Commissioners* v. *Adamson*, 1 Q. B. D. 547 ; 2 App. Cas. 743 ; overruling *The Merle*, 31 L. T. N. S. 447, and *Dennis* v. *Tovell*, L. R. 8 Q. B. 10. In these cases there is jurisdiction in Admiralty : *The Chla*, 3 Mar. Law. Cas. O. S. 148 ; *The Sylph*, L. R. 2 A. & E. 24 ; *The Clara Killam*, L. R. 3 A. & E. 161.

(d) *River Wear Commissioners* v. *Adamson, ubi supra.*

the value of the ship and freight at, or shortly before, the time of the collision had to be ascertained, *Dobree* v. *Schroder*, 2 M. & Cr. 489 ; *Wilson* v. *Dickson*, *ubi supra; Brown* v. *Wilkinson*, 15 M. & W. 391; *African Steamship Co.* v. *Swanzy*, 2 K. & J. 660, often a matter of expense and difficulty. To obviate this, by 25 & 26 Vict. c. 63, a rough average value for all ships was struck, and the limit of the owner's liability fixed at £8 or £15 per ton on their ship's tonnage, as described in the Act.

The limitation of owners' liability in this country depends entirely upon statute law. According to some writers the owner's liability by the maritime law for the wrongs committed by the master, as well as upon contracts entered into by him, in his character as master, was limited to the value of the ship and freight : see Kent's Comm., § 218 ; 4 Phillimore's International Law, 2nd ed. 628 ; Valin sur l'Ordonnance de la Marine, l. 2, tit. 8, Art. 2; Cours de Droit Comm. Mar., Boulay-Paty, Vol. I., 263—298 ; Pardessus Droit Commercial, Part 4, tit. 2, c. 3, s. 2 ; Emerigon Cont. à la Grosse, ch. 4, s. 11 ; and see *per* Bradley, J., in *The Jos. W. Dyer* v. *The National Steamship Co.*, 14 Blatchf. 483, 487 ; and *per* Ware J., in *The Rebecca*, Ware's Rep. 188, 195, 198. Whether such was the rule of the maritime law or not (if, indeed, any such law ever existed, as to which see *per* Willes, J., in *Lloyd* v. *Guibert*, L. R. 1 Q. B. 115, 124), it was never applied in this country, either by the Admiralty Court or elsewhere. By the general or common law of nations, as administered in this country, the liability for damages was unlimited : see *per* Lord Stowell, in *The Dundee*, Hag. Ad. 109, 120 ; *The Carl Johann*, referred to 3 Hag. Ad. 186 ; *The Aline*, 1 W. Rob. 111 ; *The Volant, ibid.* 283 ; *The Mellona*, 3 W. Rob. 16, 20 ; *The Wild Ranger*, Lush. 553, 564 ; *Wilson* v. *Dickson*, 2 B. & Ald. 2 ; *Gale* v. *Laurie*, 5 B. & C. 156, 164 ; *Cope* v. *Doherty*, 4 K. & J. 367, 378.

By the civil law the liability of owners was co-extensive with the damage or loss : see *supra*, p. 31, note (*z*). Nor is there any trace in the maritime codes of the middle ages of any limitation of owners' liability for damage done to other ships : see Twiss' Black Book of the Admiralty, I., 37, 108 ; II., 229, 449 ; III., 283, 285, 291 ; IV., 273, 284, 373, 435. Bynkershoek compares the right of the ship-owner to be free upon abandonment of ship and freight to the provisions of the civil law with regard to *noxæ deditio, actio de pauperie*, and *damnum ab ædibus ruinosis datum :* Quæst. Priv. Jur. iv. 20; Cf. 10 Amer. Law Rev. 432.

In the case of damage done by a ship owned by foreigners resident abroad, the damages recoverable are, in most cases, practically limited to the value of the ship and freight, which, by arrest in Admiralty, is made available as a compensation to the sufferer. The statutory limit is probably connected with this fact ; although arrest of the ship was, in the first instance, adopted to compel the owners to appear, and not because their liability was limited to the value of the ship: *The Bold Buccleugh*, 7 Moo. P. C. C. 267, 283.

The doctrine of limited liability probably had its origin in the contract of *commande*, or joint adventure of ship and cargo owners, which is referred to in the Consolato del Mare, and was in general use in the middle ages, and particularly in the countries bordering upon the Mediterranean—see Pardessus, Lois Maritimes, Index, tit. Commande. With the contract of *commande* corresponds the Société en Commandite, or limited partnership of modern times, in which each member is liable only for the sum which he risks in the adventure. The doctrine that the master cannot bind the owners by his contracts beyond the value of the ship and freight has prevailed in the maritime codes of almost every country except England. It is spoken of by Grotius, *De Jur. Bell. et Pac.*, l. 2, ch. 11, s. 13, as consonant with natural justice, and necessary for the encouragement of ship-owners—*absterrentur enim homines ab exercendis navibus si metuant ne ex facto magistri quasi in infinitum teneantur.* And the preamble of 7 Geo. II. c. 15, shows that similar motives of public policy lead to the statutory limitation of owners' liability in this country. At the present day it is applied almost exclusively in collision cases, so as to preclude the innocent sufferer by reckless or careless navigation from recovering full compensation, and in favour of the wrong-doer or his servant. It has frequently been stigmatised in the Courts as productive of injustice : see cases cited *supra*, p. 70, note (*c*). Whether natural justice requires that owners should be answerable for a collision caused by the fault of other persons seems doubtful : see *per* James, L.J., in *The M. Moxham*, 1 P. D. 107,110; *The Halley*, L. R. 2 P. C. 193; Grotius, *De Jure Belli et Pacis*, II. 17,20,2. Although by English law employers are liable, to the full extent, for wrongs done by their servants acting within the scope of their employment, this is so rather upon grounds of expediency than upon any principle of natural justice. Whether upon the same ground of expediency it is not desirable that ship-owners should be under the ordinary obligation to ensure that their ships are navigated with care, so as not to run down others, may well be doubted. So far as the law limiting their liability departs from the ordinary rule—*respondeat superior*—it affords a direct encouragement to reckless navigation.

It appears that ship-owners' liability is limited in most, if not all, foreign countries. In the United States of America owners are not liable in the Federal Courts for loss or damage beyond the amount of their interest in the ship and freight at the time of the collision. But there is no limitation of liability for damages by a vessel wholly engaged in inland navigation : *The War Eagle*, 6 Bissel 364. If the wrong-doing ship is herself sunk, it seems that the owners are altogether discharged : 2 Parsons on Sh. (ed. 1869) 120—140; 9 U.S. Stat. at Large, 635; *Norwich Steamboat Co. v. Wright*, 13 Wall. 104 (in this country the loss of their own ship never discharged the owners : *Brown v. Wilkinson*, 15 M. & W. 391). But certain formalities must be gone through, and the ship must be surrendered, or the owners will not be entitled to the benefit of the Act of Congress limiting their liability : see *The Jos. W. Dyer v. National Steamship Co.*, 14 Blatchf. 483. In some of the States' Courts it has been doubted whether the owner's liability is limited; but it appears that where one of the ships is foreign the States' Courts have not jurisdiction, and that the foreign ship has the benefit of the Act of Congress : see a letter from Mr. Thornton to Lord Tenterden, of 25th Nov., 1872.

Upon the Continent of Europe the rule that abandonment of the ship discharges the owners is almost, if not quite, universal. Art. 216 of the French Code de Commerce is as follows :—

"Tout propriétaire de navire est civilement responsable des

faits du capitaine, et tenu des engagements contractés par ce dernier pour ce qui est relatif au navire et à l'expédition. Il peut dans tous les cas s'affranchir des obligations ci-dessus par l'abandon du navire et du fret. Toutefois la faculté de faire abandon n'est point accordée a celui qui est en même temps capitaine et propriétaire ou co-propriétaire du navire. Lorsque le capitaine ne sera que co-propriétaire, il ne sera responsable des engagements contractés par lui, pour ce qui est relatif au navire et à l'expédition, que dans la proportion de son intérêt."

Arts. 451, 452 of the German Commercial Code; Art. 321 of that of Holland; Art. 216 of the Belgian Code; Art. 311 of the Italian; Art. 649 of the Russian; Art. 1345 of the Portuguese; and Arts. 621, 622 of the Spanish Codes, are to the same effect. In France the rule of the law by which the ship-owner's liability is limited to the value of the ship and freight has no application in the case of a collision between craft engaged in inland navigation. A distinction is drawn between collisions "maritimes" and "non-maritimes." In the one case the owner's liability is limited, in the other not. "Comme dans l'un, c'est la chose, autrement dit le navire qui répond plutôt le dommage, et dans l'autre, la personne :" Jurisprudence et Doctrine en Matière d'Abordage, par M. Sibille, pp. 7, 8.

78

# CHAPTER III.

## TUG AND TOW.

A tug and her tow are in law one ship, the tug being the servant of the tow.

WHERE one vessel is in tow of another the two ships are, by intendment of law, one, the motive power being with the tug, and the command or governing power being with the tow. This is the general rule as regards obedience to the Rule of the Road. There is ground for the opinion that in Admiralty the same or a similar rule that the tug is the servant of the tow applies so as to make the tug and her tow mutually liable to a third ship for a collision caused by the fault of either (*a*). Thus, a ship in tow has been held responsible for a collision caused by the neglect of the tug to carry side lights (*b*); and a vessel towing the boat from which she had just taken her pilot was held liable for a collision caused by the pilot boat carrying improper lights (*c*). But the liability of a ship that has not herself been in collision is not clear. Elsewhere than in Admiralty the owners of a ship in tow would not be liable for a collision caused entirely by the fault of the crew of the tug, who were not their servants or agents.

(*a*) *The Kingston-by-the-Sea*, 3 W. Rob. 152; *The Cleadon*, Lush. 158; *The American* and *The Syria*, L. R. 6 P. C. 127, 132; *The Unity*, Swab. Ad. 101; *The Glengaber*, L. R. 3 A. & E. 534; *The Energy*, ibid. 48. See also the cases cited *supra*, p. 55, and *The Mary*, *infra*, p. 81. As to the law in the United States of America with regard to the duties and liability of tug and tow, see the note at the foot of this chapter.

(*b*) *The Giraffe*, 1 Pr. Ad. Dig. 153; and see *The U. S. Grant* and *The Tally Ho*, 7 Bened. 195, 208.

(*c*) *The Mary Hounsell*, 4 P. D. 204; 40 L. T. N. S. 368.

If a vessel has another in tow in performance of a sal- *Except where the command* vage service, the command, or governing power, as well as *as well as the* the motive power, is usually in the towing vessel. In such *motive power is with the* a case the tug is not the servant of the ship in tow, and the *tug.* rule that the two ships are, in intendment of law, one, does not apply.

One steam-ship, *The American*, while towing another, *The Syria*, which she had picked up in a disabled condition, negligently ran into *The Aracan*. *The Syria*, without negligence on her part, ranged up alongside *The American*, and also damaged *The Aracan*. It was held that no liability attached to *The Syria*, and that *The American* was alone liable (*d*).

The Rule of the Road applies to a tug with one or more *Application* ships in tow equally with other steam-ships. For this pur- *of the Regulations to tug* pose also the law considers a tug and her tow as one ship, *and tow.* and that a steam-ship (*e*). But it is obvious that a tug with a ship in tow has not the same facility of movement as if she were unencumbered. She is not, in anything like the same degree, mistress of her own movements. She cannot, by stopping or reversing her engines, at once stop or back the ship in tow. In taking measures to avoid a third vessel she has to consider her tow; and a step that would be right, and take her clear, if she were unincumbered, may bring about a collision between her tow and the ship which she herself has avoided (*f*). Although, therefore, it is the duty of a tug with a ship in tow to comply, so far as is possible, with the Regulations for preventing collisions, it is also the duty of a third ship to make allowance for the encumbered and comparatively

(*d*) *The American* and *The Syria*, L. R. 6 P. C. 127.

(*e*) *The Warrior*, L. R. 3 A. & E. 553 ; *The American* and *The Syria*, *ubi supra*. The same has been held in America: *New York, &c., Co.* v. *Philadelphia, &c., Co.*, 22 How. 461 ;

*The Ivanhoe* v. *The Martha M. Heath*, 7 Bened. 213 ; *The Cirilla* and *The Restless*, 6 Bened. 309.

(*f*) See *The Arthur Gordon* and *The Independence*, Lush. 270 ; *The Kingston-by-the-Sea*, 3 W. Rob. 152.

disabled state of a tug, and to take additional care in
approaching her (g).

**Tug alone liable in some cases.**
In some cases the tug alone is liable for damage done by
herself or by the ship in tow. Where the service she is
performing is not ordinary towage, but a salvage service,
as where she has picked up a derelict, or where the ship
in tow is entirely under the charge of the towing ship,
those on board taking no part in her navigation, it seems
that the tug alone is liable. Where both the towing ship
and the ship in tow belonged to the same owners, and both
came into collision with a third ship, by the fault of those
on board the towing ship, it was held that the liability of
the owners was limited to the statutory amount, calculated
upon the tonnage of the towing ship (h).

**The contract of towage; its terms and performance.**
It is an implied term in the contract of towage that the
tug shall implicitly obey the orders of the ship in tow (i).
If no orders are given by the latter, it is the duty of the
tug to take such a course as will carry herself and her tow
clear of collision and other dangers. If she fails to do so,
she cannot recover, against the ship in tow, damage she
may herself suffer by collision with a third ship. If, however, such damage was in consequence of improper orders
from the tow she could probably recover. But if no orders
are given by the tow as to avoiding a third ship, and, by
the fault of the tug, a collision occurs between the tow and
the third ship, the tow is herself in fault for giving no
orders, and cannot recover from the tug either for injury
which she has herself received or damages which she has
been compelled to pay to the third ship (k).

(g) The American and The Syria,
ubi supra; The La Plata, Swab. Ad.
220; on app., ibid. 298.
(h) The American and The Syria,
ubi supra; and see per Sir R.
Collier, ibid., p. 133, as to the liability of the tug alone.
(i) The Christina, 3 W. Rob. 27;

6 Moo. P. C. C. 371; Smith v. St.
Lawrence Tow Boat Co., L. R. 5
P. C. 308.
(k) The Energy, L. R.3 A.&E. 48;
Smith v. St. Lawrence Tow Boat Co.,
ubi supra; The Robert Dixon, 40 L. T.
N. S. 333.

Although the tug is usually bound to obey the orders of the tow, there is doubt whether she is exempt from liability to a third ship for a collision caused entirely by her acting in obedience to the orders of a compulsory pilot in charge of the ship in tow. In a recent case (*l*) it was held by Sir R. Phillimore that the statutory exemption from liability does not apply to the tug; and, upon this and other grounds, the tug was held liable. The point, however, was not expressly decided, as the tug was, in fact, guilty of contributory negligence. It was held by Dr. Lushington in several cases that the tug is free from liability in such a case (*m*); and although these decisions were under a former Act, the reasons upon which they were founded seem to be equally cogent at the present day as regards the liability of the tug-owners by the general law.

The reason for the rule that, under ordinary circumstances, the tug must obey the orders of the ship in tow is, that there may be no divided responsibility or double command. It is considered necessary for the safety of both that they should be under the supreme command of one person. "I am well aware," said Dr. Lushington, "that mischief may in some instances arise from pilots (in charge of the tow) having entire control over steam tugs, and giving directions contrary to the judgment and experience of the masters of steam tugs, conversant, as they are, with every part of the waters in which they are employed. At the same time, I feel still greater difficulties would be occasioned by two conflicting and independent authorities being exercised in the navigation of one and the same vessel" (*n*).

(*l*) *The Mary. infra*, p. 109.
(*m*) *The Duke of Sussex*, 1 W. Rob. 270, 273 ; *The Christina*, 3 W. Rob. 27 ; and see *The Ocean Wave*, L. R. 3 P. C. 205; *The Gipsey King*, 5 Not. of Cas. 282, 288.

(*n*) *The Christina*, 3 W. Rob. 27, 33 : in *The Duke of Sussex*, *ubi supra*, the decision was to the same effect and upon similar grounds : see *infra*, p. 83.

Although it is the duty of the tug to obey the orders
from the ship in tow, her duty does not end here.  It has
been already stated that, in the absence of orders from the
tow, she is bound to show proper care and skill in the
course she takes and in the performance of the towage
service.  And if the orders she gets from the ship in tow
are manifestly wrong, it is her duty, even if the orders are
given by a pilot in charge of the tow, to warn the tow of
her danger.  " The vessel and the lives of the crew are not
to be risked because there is a law which imposes the
ordinary responsibility upon one individual. . . . . It
is not for the steamer (the tug), knowing the danger, to
maintain, as it were, a sulky silence, and make herself, as
it were, instrumental in the destruction of life and property" (o).  But except in case of manifest incapacity or
error on the part of the pilot, it would seem that it is not
the duty of the tug to exercise a discretion as to carrying
out the pilot's orders ; nor would she be justified in disobeying them, although there may be risk of collision in
carrying them out (p).

The responsibility for the employment of a tug, in
ordinary cases, rests with the master, whether the ship is
in charge of a pilot or not.  But if the employment of the
tug is necessary for the safety of the ship there is some
doubt whether the responsibility does not rest with the
pilot (q).

Collision be-
tween tug
and tow.

Although the tug is, for some purposes, held to be the
servant of the tow, the doctrine of common employment
(*Priestly* v. *Fowler*, 3 M. & W. 1) does not apply as between
a tug and her tow, so as to prevent the tug from recovering
from the tow damages for a collision caused by the fault of
the crew of the tow (r).

(o) *The Duke of Manchester*, 4
Not. of Cas. 575, 582 ; 5 Not. of
Cas. 470.  The tug was, in this case,
performing a salvage service.  See
*The Robert Dixon*, 40 L. T. N. S.

333, as to the responsibility of the
tug for the sufficiency of the hawser.
(p) *The Christina*, 3 W. Rob. 27.
(q) *The Julia*. Lush. 224, 226.
(r) *The Julia*, ubi supra.

Where the ship in tow is herself in fault for a collision
with a third ship, she cannot recover damages against her
tug, although the tug is also in fault. Nor, in such a case,
could the tug recover against the ship in tow. A barque
in charge of a compulsory pilot was being towed up the
Thames. She fell in with a brig working up the river
against a head wind. The pilot gave no orders to the tug,
and the tug improperly attempted to cross the bows of the
brig. The barque cast off her tow line and attempted to
go under the brig's stern, but failed to clear her. The
collision might have been avoided if the tug had cast off
the tow line. The pilot gave no orders throughout. The
barque was sued by the brig, and damages were recovered
against her. In an action brought by the barque against
the tug, it was held that she could not recover these
damages, being herself partly in fault for the collision (s).

In the towage contract each party engages to use proper
skill and diligence. If a collision occurs between the tug
and her tow in consequence of improper orders given by
the tow, the tow will be held to be solely in fault. Thus,
where a ship, having engaged a tug off Dungeness to take
her to Gravesend, ordered her to take the tow line on
board at a time when the state of the weather made it unnecessary and dangerous for her to do so, it was held that the
ship in tow was liable for a collision which occurred whilst
the line was being passed from the one ship to the
other (t).

If a tug is compelled to cast off her tow in order to
save herself from a collision, it is her duty to pick the tow
up again as quickly as possible (u).

Where the tug, in performance of a towage or salvage
service, negligently damages her tow by collision, or in any

(s) *The Energy*, L. R. 3 A. & E.
48 ; and see *Smith v. St. Lawrence
Tow Boat Co.*, L. R. 5 P. C. 308.

(t) *The Julia*, L. R. 2 P. C. 1.
see *The Energy* and *The Golden
Light*, L. R. ...

other way, she forfeits her right to towage or salvage remuneration (x).

The steam-ship *Thetis* fell in with *The Sardis* in a disabled state. The master of *The Thetis* agreed to tow the latter to port. He had received no instructions from his owner as to offering towage or salvage service to other ships, but the policy of insurance effected upon *The Thetis*, and her bills of lading, contained provisions as to her performing such services. In attempting to take *The Sardis* in tow, *The Thetis* negligently ran into and sank her. It was held that the master of *The Thetis* was acting within the scope of his employment in undertaking to tow *The Sardis*, and her owners were held liable for the collision (y).

The liability of the owner of the tug for damage done to the tow by the tug in the performance of the towage contract is limited by the statute in this as in other cases (z).

Jurisdiction of Admiralty Courts in case of negligent towage.

The tug can be sued in Courts of Admiralty for damage to the ship in tow received in a collision caused by negligent towage; whether such damage is sustained by the tow in a collision with a third ship, or with the tug (a). And the tug may be sued in the same Courts for damages which the tow has been compelled to pay to a third ship for a collision caused by the fault of the tug (b).

Two or more ships in tow of the same tug.

Where two or more ships are in tow of the same tug,

(x) *The Christina*, 3 W. Rob. 27, as to the towage contract not being performed; *The Duke of Manchester*, ubi supra, as to salvage. But see *The Sweepstakes*, Brown Ad. 509, where a set-off was allowed.

(y) *The Thetis*, 3 Mar. Law Cas. O. S. 357.

(z) *Wahlberg v. Young*, 24 W. R. 847 ; 45 L. J. C. P. 783.

(a) *The Nightwatch*, Lush. 542 ; *The Julia*, ib. 224.

(b) *The Energy*, L. R. 3 A. & E. 48. As to the mode of trying the ques-

tion of negligence as between the tug, tow, and third ship, see *The Cartsburn*, 5 P. D. 35 ; on app., 41 L. T. N. S. 710. It seems that Admiralty Courts have jurisdiction in a claim for damage caused by negligent towage, whether such damage is received in a collision or not : see supra, p. 55, note (b). The Admiralty jurisdiction of the United States Courts includes all claims arising out of towage contracts : 2 Parsons on Ship. (ed. 1869), 176, 188 ; *The Webb*, 14 Wall. 406.

and no agreement has been come to between them and the tug as to which ship is to have the command, it has not been decided with whom the command rests (c). But it has been held in such a case that one of the ships in tow could not recover against the tug for damage caused by being under way in a thick fog when they ought all to have brought up. It was assumed by the Court that it was the duty of the ship in tow to give the order to bring up (d). Where two vessels were in tow of the same tug, without objection on the part of that one of them which was nearest the tug, and the leading vessel took the ground and was run into by the other astern, it was held that she could not recover against the vessel that ran into her (e).

## NOTE.

*American Cases as to the Duties and Liabilities of a Tug and Ship in Tow.*

The decisions of the Courts of the United States of America as to the duties and liabilities of a tug and her tow are very numerous. They are not altogether consistent with the English cases upon the subject. The different character of much of the towage service in American waters, where large fleets of barges are constantly being navigated in charge of a single tug, probably accounts for the somewhat different view of the law taken by the American Courts. In *Sturges* v. *Boyer*, 24 How. 110, the law as to the liability of tow and tug was thus stated by the Supreme Court : " Cases arise, undoubtedly, where both the tow and tug are jointly liable for the consequences of a collision ; as where those in charge of the respective vessels jointly participate in their control and management, and the master and crew of both vessels are either deficient in skill, omit to take due care, or are guilty of negligence in their navigation. Other cases may well be imagined where the tow alone would be responsible ; as

American law as to tug and tow.

(c) *The Gipsey King*, 5 Not. of Cas. 282.

(d) *Smith* v. *St. Lawrence Tow*

*Boat Co.*, L. R. 5 P. C. 308.

(e) *Harris* v. *Anderson*, 14 C. B. N. S. 499.

where the tug is employed by the master or owners of the tow as
the mere motive power to propel their vessel from one point to
another, and both vessels are exclusively under the control and
direction and management of the master and crew of the tow . . . .
But whenever th : tug under the charge of her own master and
crew, and in the usual and ordinary course of such an employment,
undertakes to transport another vessel which, for the time being,
has neither her master nor crew on board, from one point to
another over waters where such accessory power is necessarily or
usually employed, she must be held responsible for the proper
navigation of both vessels . . . . Assuming that the tug is a
suitable vessel, properly manned and equipped for the undertaking, so that no degree of negligence can attach to the owners
of the tow on the ground that the motive power employed by
them was in an unseaworthy condition, the tow, under the
circumstances supposed, is no more responsible for the collision
than so much freight. And it is not perceived that it can make
any difference in that behalf that a part or even the whole officers
and crew of the tow are on board, provided it clearly appears that
the tug was a seaworthy vessel properly manned and equipped for
the enterprise." In *The Alabama* and *The Gamecock*, 2 Otto,
695, it was said by the Supreme Court that a ship in tow bears
the same relation to the collision as cargo on board either of the
ships. In *The Coleman* and *The Foster*, Brown Adm. Rep. 456,
and *The Maybey* and *The Cooper*, 14 Wall. 204, both tug and
tow were held liable ; in *The R. B. Forbes*, 1 Sprague, 328, and
*The Rescue*, 2 Sprague, 16, the tug was held liable for collision
between a tow, lashed alongside, and a third ship ; in *Smith* v.
*The Creole* and *The Sampson*, 2 Wall. C. C. Rep. 485, the tow
alone was held liable ; and in *The Cambridge*, *The Underhill*,
and *The Chase*, 4 Bened. 366, *Cushing* v. *The Owners of the
John Fraser*, 21 How. 184, *The Clarita* and *The Clara*, 23
Wall. 1, and *The Galatea*, 2 Otto, 439, the tug alone was held
liable. In several recent cases, *The Virginia Ehrman* and *The
Agnese*, 7 Otto, 309, *The City of Hartford* and *The Unit*, 7
Otto, 323, *The Atlas*, 3 Otto, 302, *The Juniata*, *ibid.* 337,
decrees have been made in Admiralty proceedings instituted by
the owners of ships and cargo sunk by a tug with ships in tow

against both the tug and tow ; the decrees being against each of them for half the damages, with recourse against the other for any part of the moiety of the damages which the first failed to pay. A tug with a fleet of barges or canal boats in tow is generally held liable for damage done by, as well as to, the barges in tow : 1 Parsons on Ship. (ed. 1869) 536; *The Quickstep*, 9 Wall. 665 ; although she is not an insurer of the barges or cargo on board them : *The Stranger*, Brown Ad. 281; *The Margaret*, 4 Otto, 494. It is the tug's duty to arrange and make up her tow, to see that the tow lines are sufficient and properly made fast, and generally to superintend and navigate the tow, so that other ships are not injured by it, and so that the barges themselves do not injure each other : *The Quickstep, ubi supra; The Stranger, ubi supra; The Cayuga*, 16 Wall. 177; *The Francis King*, 7 Bened. 11 ; *The Syracuse*, 12 Wall. 167. In the case of tugs towing other vessels, considerable responsibility is thrown on the tug. Thus it has been held that it is the duty of the tug to be acquainted with the waters she navigates, and to keep her tow clear of local dangers : *The Lady Pike*, 21 Wall. 1 ; *The Webb*, 14 Wall. 406 ; *The Margaret*, 4 Otto, 494. Where the tow line was furnished by the ship in tow, it has been held that the tug is not responsible for its insufficiency : *The Echo*, 7 Bened. 70; *The A. R. Wetmore* and *The Epsilon*, 5 Bened. 147. The duty of the ship in tow to follow in the wake of the tug has been the subject of decision : *The Stranger, ubi supra; The Maria Martin*, 12 Wall. 31. As to the liability of tug and tow generally, see 1 Parsons on Ship. (ed. 1869) 534, note.

Where a tug, A., was in fault for a collision between her tow, B., and a third ship, C., and C. was also in fault for having an improper light, it was held by the Supreme Court of the United States that the rule of equal division of loss applied as between C. and A.: *The James Gray* and *The John Fraser*, 21 How. 184.

In France it has been held that the tug, as being the governing power, is *primâ facie* liable for a collision with her tow : Abordage Nautique (Caumont), § 226. But see *ibid.* § 216, *seq.*

French law as to tug and tow.

# CHAPTER IV.

## FOREIGN SHIPS—FOREIGN LAW.

Law applicable to foreign ships.

In collision cases where one or both the ships are foreign, questions frequently arise as to the law applicable to the case, and particularly as to the application of British statutes to foreign ships. The general rule is that municipal laws are binding upon the subjects of the state by which they are enacted everywhere, but upon foreigners only when they are within its jurisdiction (a).

The principle which governs questions of jurisdiction and remedies has been thus stated: "In regard to the merits and rights involved in actions, the law of the place where they originated is to govern . . . . but the forms of remedies, and the order of judicial proceedings, are to be according to the law of the place where the action is instituted, without any regard to the domicil of the parties, the origin of the right or the country of the act" (b).

Where one or both the ships in collision were foreign, questions of difficulty have arisen whether the British or the foreign law as to the Rule of the Road, the extent of owners' liability, the presumption of fault, the liability of

(a) As to the limits of the jurisdiction, see *The Saxonia* and *The Eclipse*, Lush. 410 ; *The Annapolis* and *The Johanna Stoll*, Lush. 295 ; *Regina* v. *Keyn*, *The Franconia*, 2 Ex. D. 63. As to Admiralty jurisdiction, *supra*, p. 97.

(b) Story's Conflict of Laws, Ch.

14, § 558, 7th ed. p. 702 ; and see *Donn* v. *Lippman*, 5 Cl. & Fin. 1. So a foreigner in France suing for a collision is subject to the disabilities (*fin de non recevoir*) of the Code de Commerce, Arts. 435, 436 ; Abordage Nautique, Caumont, § 82, 83.

the ship or her owners for the fault of those in charge of her, or as to the order in which claims against the ship should rank, should be applied. By the Act mentioned below it is provided, with regard to some of these subjects, that in the Courts of this country foreign as well as British ships shall be subject to British law. Where there is no express provision by statute, the question in each case is whether the law sought to be applied relates to the rights and merits of the question, or whether it is a *lex fori*, relating only to remedies and procedure. Thus it has been held, where there are several claims against a ship, that they must rank and be paid according to British law, the matter being governed by the *lex fori* (c).

Order of claims against a ship is *lex fori.*

In a former chapter it has been stated that the general or natural right of a sufferer by collision to obtain from the wrongdoer a full recompense has, from time to time, been considerably modified by British statutes. Until the passing of 25 & 26 Vict. c. 63, the Act now in force, there was frequently great difficulty, in cases where one or both the ships in collision were foreign, in determining whether the municipal law limiting owners' liability was, or was not, applicable (d). Under the Act above mentioned no such difficulty can arise. Whether the ships are both British or both foreign, or one British and one foreign, and whether the collision occurs in British waters or on the high seas, the limit of owners' liability is the same. In all cases it is fixed by 25 & 26 Vict. c. 63.

Extent of owner's liability the same for foreign and British ships.

(c) *The Union,* 3 L. T. N. S. 280.
(d) The provisions of the M. S. Act, 1854, did not, in terms, apply to foreigners. Under this Act it was held that the liability of the owners of a British ship in collision with a foreigner, within three miles of the shores of the United Kingdom, was limited: *General Iron Screw Collier Co.* v. *Schurmanns,* 1 J. & H. 180 ; that the liability of the owners of two foreign ships in collision on the high seas, beyond that distance from the United Kingdom, was unlimited : *Cope* v. *Doherty,* 4 K. & J. 367 ; on app. 2 De G. & J. 614 ; and that the liability of the owners of a foreign ship in collision with a British ship, beyond the three-mile limit, was unlimited : *The Wild Ranger,* Lush. 553 ; even although the foreign ship's liability by the municipal law of her own state were the same as that of the British ship by British law : *The Wild Ranger, ubi supra.*

In *The Amalia* (*e*) it was held that the liability of the
owners of a British ship in collision with a foreign ship on
the high seas (in the Mediterranean) is limited by the Act
of 1862. It was contended that the Legislature had no
power to alter the rights of foreigners in the case of a
collision on the high seas, or to limit the amount of the
damages to which by the maritime law they were entitled.
It was, however, held by the Privy Council (affirming the
decision of Dr. Lushington) that there is no breach of
international law in such legislation; and it was said
by Lord Chelmsford in the course of the judgment, and
the decision in the case went upon the principle, that
the owners of a foreign ship in a similar case would be
entitled to the benefit of the Act—that, in all cases, the
liability of the owners of a foreign ship is limited in the
same way, and to the same extent, as that of owners of a
British ship (*f*).

Rule of the
Road for
foreign ships.

The Regulations to prevent collision contained in Acts
previous to that of 1862 were held not to apply in the
case of a collision between two foreign ships, or a British
and a foreign ship, on the high seas. The question of
negligence in such cases was tried by the general maritime
law, under which the Rule of the Road did not always agree
with that of the British statute. A ship, therefore, meeting another on the high seas, had to obey one rule if both
were British, and another, and a different rule, if one were
not British (*g*). This state of things, which could not fail
to be productive of collisions, led to the adoption of the

(e) Br. and Lush. 151.

(f) It seems that the law limiting
owners' liability is not a *lex fori*.
Such was the opinion of Wood, V.-C.,
in *Cope* v. *Doherty*, 4 K. & J. 367,
384 ; and in *The General Iron Screw
Collier Co.* v. *Schurmanns*, 1 J. &
H. 180, 197. In *The Amalia* the
Privy Council expressed no opinion
upon the point, but Dr. Lushington

(Lush. p. 153) was of the same
opinion as Wood, V.-C., in the cases
above mentioned. Cf. also *per* Lord
Stowell, in *The Carl Johan*, mentioned in *The Girolamo*, 3 Hag. Ad.
169, 186.

(g) *The Dumfries*, Swab. Ad. 63 ;
*The Saxonia* and *The Eclipse*, Lush.
410 ; *The Zollverein*, Swab. Ad. 96 ;
*The Elizabeth*, 3 L. T. N. S. 159.

existing International Regulations. No question as to the Rule of the Road, or the law applicable to the particular case, such as arose in the cases (*supra*, note (*y*)) decided under former Acts, can now be raised. Nearly all maritime nations having adopted the Regulations, and the Courts of this country being required by the municipal law to apply the Regulations to the ships of all nations that have adopted them, the Rule of the Road is the same for all ships, and the same Rule is recognised alike by international, municipal, and maritime law.

Foreign ships, equally with British ships, are bound to know and observe local Regulations for preventing collisions in force in various rivers and harbours of this country (*h*). *Foreign ships bound to comply with local Regulations.*

The law by which the owners of a ship which has been in collision are, upon proof of certain circumstances as to infringement of the Regulations, or not standing by to assist the other ship, made liable for the collision, without further proof of negligence upon the part of their ship, has been considered in a former chapter (*i*). There seems to be no doubt that this enactment applies to foreign ships (*k*). · In two cases recently before the Admiralty Division, it was assumed that it applied to a British ship in collision with a foreigner on the high seas (*l*). The wording of 36 & 37 Vict. c. 85, s. 16, favours the contention that that part of it which relates to presumption of fault applies to foreign as well as British ships. Both sections, moreover, would probably be held to be rules of *Application to foreign ships of 36 & 37 Vict. c. 85, ss. 16 and 17.*

(*h*) 25 & 26 Vict. c. 63, ss. 32, 57; see *The Fyenoord*, Swab. Ad. 374; *The Seine*, *ibid.* 411, as to the law on this subject under the M. S. Act, 1854; and see *The Michelimo* and *The Dacca*, Mitch. Mar. Reg. 1877, as to the application to British ships of local Regulations abroad.

(*i*) 36 & 37 Vict. c. 85, ss. 16 and 17; see above, pp. 12, *seq.*

(*k*) *The Magnet*, L. R. 4 A. & E. 417. See *per* Sir R. Phillimore in *Reg.* v. *Keyn*, 2 Ex. D. 63, 85. The doubt expressed by the Privy Council in *The P. M. Carvill*, 2 Asp. Mar. Law Cas. 565, 569, appears to be not well founded.

(*l*) *The British Princess* and *The Sedmi Dubrovacki*, Ad. Ct. March, 1878; *The Englishman*, 3 P. D. 18.

evidence, or otherwise applicable to foreign ships as *lex fori* (*m*).

Defence of "compulsory pilotage" available for foreign ships.

The defence of "compulsory pilotage" is available for a foreign as well as for a British ship (*n*). The statutory exemption of owners from liability for damage done by a ship when in charge of a compulsory pilot probably applies to foreign ships; and, independently of the statute, foreign as well as British owners are not liable for the acts of a person placed in charge of their ship by the state (*o*). The employment of a pilot may be made compulsory on a foreign ship by a British statute beyond three miles from the shores of the United Kingdom (*p*).

(*m*) It was held by Dr. Lushington in *The Zollverein*, Swab. Ad. 96, that s. 298 of 17 & 18 Vict. c. 104 was a *lex fori* relating to remedies. In that case the section was held not to apply in the case of a collision between a British and a foreign ship on the high seas, so as to prevent the British ship from recovering against the foreigner. The ground of the decision was that the previous section (s. 296), containing the rule of the road, was a municipal law not applicable to foreign ships on the high seas, and that therefore s. 298, which depended on s. 296, had no application to the foreign ship. Since, therefore, the foreigner was not prevented by s. 298 from recovering against a British ship that to which by the maritime law he would be entitled, it was held to be unfair to allow the foreigner to avail himself of a breach by the British ship of the municipal law as a defence. The existing Regulations being international, it is submitted that the decision in *The Zollverein*, as to the application of s. 298 of the Act of 1854, affords no ground for contending that s. 17 of the Act of 1873 does not apply to foreign ships. In *The Nevada*, 1 Asp. Mar. Law Cas. 477, however, the Vice-Admiralty Court of N. S. Wales held that

s. 33 of the Act of 1862 did not apply to an American ship. In *The Germania*, 3 Mar. Law Cas. O. S. 140, s. 29 of 25 & 26 Vict. c. 63 was applied to a foreign ship; but in the same case on appeal (*ibid.* 269) Lord Romilly appears to have considered that s. 33 of that Act (as to "standing by") applied only to British ships. In *The Thuringia*, 1 Asp. Mar. Law Cas. 283, nothing was said as to the application of that section to a foreign ship on the high seas. As the effect of ss. 57 and 58 of the same Act, see the observations of Lord Chelmsford in *The Amalia*, 1 Moo. P. C. C. N. S. 471, 485.

(*n*) As to compulsory pilotage generally, see Ch. V.

(*o*) 17 & 18 Vict. c. 104, s. 388; *The Maria*, 1 W. Rob. 95, 106. In *The Girolamo*, 3 Mar. Ad. 169, and other cases under 6 Geo. IV. c. 125, it was held that the statutory exemption of owners from liability for the fault of a compulsory pilot did not apply so as to exempt the owners of a foreign ship in proceedings *in rem*. In *The Vernon*, 1 W. Rob. 316, Dr. Lushington appears to have considered that the statutory exemption of owners was *lex fori*.

(*p*) *The Annapolis* and *The Johanna Stoll*, Lush. 295.

It is a principle of international law that a sovereign Damage by
prince or state cannot be sued in a foreign Court. And it ship of a
foreign
seems that this principle applies in the case of proceedings sovereign;
proceedings
*in rem* against the public ship of a foreign sovereign (*q*). in rem.
But it has been said by Sir R. Phillimore that if a ship of
a foreign sovereign engages in trade, she is liable to arrest,
and the sovereign must be taken to have waived the
privilege of immunity from arrest which attaches to a
public ship of a foreign state (*r*). It has also been held
that it is not in the power of the Crown, without the
consent of Parliament, to exempt the trading ship of a
foreign sovereign from arrest (*s*).

A frigate of the United States was stranded on the
south coast of England, and received salvage services from
an English tug. She had on board, under an Act of Congress, and for public purposes, cargo owned by American
citizens. The tug-owner sought to arrest the frigate and
her cargo in a claim for salvage. It was held that no
warrant for arrest could issue either in respect of ship or
cargo (*t*).

*The Parlement Belge*, a vessel belonging to the King
of the Belgians, commanded and manned by officers and
men commissioned and paid by him, was engaged in carrying mails in connection with the British Post Office,
together with passengers and cargo. On her voyage from
Ostend to Dover, when close to Dover pier, she ran into a
British ship at anchor. Notwithstanding the fact that a
convention had been entered into between Her Majesty
and the King of the Belgians declaring that the mail
boats, of which *The Parlement Belge* was one, should be
deemed to be ships of war, and should not be liable to arrest,
it was held by Sir R. Phillimore that she was liable to

(*q*) *The Constitution*, 4 P. D. 39.    decision of the case : *The Swift*, ]
See, however, *The Charkieh*, L. R. 4    Dods. Adm. 320, 339.
A. & E. 59 ; *ibid.* 8 Q. B. 197.      (*s*) *The Parlement Belge*, 4 P. D.
(*r*) *The Charkieh, supra* ; but the    129.
dictum was not necessary to the      (*t*) *The Constitution*, 4 P. D. 39.

proceedings *in rem* at the suit of the owner of the injured vessel (*u*).

A foreign ship that has injured a British ship, or property of a British subject, in any part of the world, may be detained if found within three miles of the coasts of the United Kingdom (*x*). But owners resident abroad can seldom be sued personally in respect of a collision on the high seas below low-water mark of the shores of the United Kingdom (*y*).

It has been held by Sir R. Phillimore that the representatives of foreigners killed in a collision on the high seas on board a foreign ship can recover damages under Lord Campbell's Act in the Courts of this country (*z*); and under the same Act a foreign ship has been made liable, in proceedings *in rem*, for loss of life on the high seas caused by her negligent navigation (*a*).

The liability for damage done by a vessel depends, in some cases, upon the law of the place where the collision occurs, and of the country to which the ship belongs. If it occurs in the territorial waters of a country by the law of which an owner is not liable for the wrongful acts of his officers or crew, it seems that he would not be liable in the Courts of this country. Nor is he liable, in this country, for a collision in a foreign country, unless the negligence causing the collision is that of a person for whose acts he is responsible by the law of England. "No action can be maintained in the Courts of this country on account of a wrongful act either to a person or to personal property committed within the jurisdiction of a foreign country, unless the act is wrongful by the law of the

(*u*) *The Parlement Belge*, 4 P. D. 129; see Addenda.

(*x*) 17 & 18 Vict. c. 104, s. 527.

(*y*) *Harris* v. *Owners of The Franconia*, 2 C. P. D. 173; and see *infra*, p. 98.

(*z*) *The Explorer*, L. R. 3 A. & E.

289; and see *infra*, p. 98.

(*a*) *The Guldfaxe*, L. R. 2 A. & E. 325. There is, however, doubt whether it is competent to proceed *in rem* for damages under Lord Campbell's Act see above, p. 64.

country where it is committed, and also by the law of this country "(b).

In *The M. Moxham*, an English company, possessed of a pier in Spain, instituted an action in the Admiralty Court against a British ship for negligently injuring the pier. The ship-owners, by their answer, pleaded that by the law of Spain they were not liable for the negligence of the crew in the navigation of the ship. The Court of Appeal held that, assuming the Court had jurisdiction, the law of Spain was applicable, and that the plea was good (c).

The owners of a British ship, which had been in col- Compulsory
lision with a foreign ship in the Scheldt, were sued by the pilotage
abroad.
foreign ship in this country. The British ship alleged that the collision was caused entirely by the negligence of the pilot, whom, by the Belgian law in force in the Scheldt, she was compelled to take. By the Belgian law owners are liable for the acts of a compulsory pilot. It was held by the Privy Council (reversing the decision of Court below) that the Belgian law, which imposed a liability upon owners to which they were not subject, either by the law of this country or by any principle of justice, had no application, and that the British owners were not liable (d).

In an action in a Common Law Court by the owners of a British ship against a French subject for a collision with a French ship on the high seas, it was pleaded that the injury complained of happened out of British jurisdiction, and that it was not committed by the defendant personally, but by the master of the French ship; that the defendant was a French subject; that by the law of France he was not liable for the acts of the master; and that by the same law a French corporation, who were the proprietors

---

(b) *Per* Mellish, L.J., in *The M. Moxham*, 1 P. D. 107, 111.
(c) *The M. Moxham*, 1 P. D. 107.

(d) *The Halley*, L. R. 2 P. C. 193; in the Court below, *ibid.* 2 A. & E. 3.

of the ship, and the master's employers, were alone liable. The plea was held good (e).

*Res judicata: effect of foreign judgment.* The judgment of a competent foreign Court upon the merits of a collision, given in the presence of both parties, is a bar to an action in this country between the same parties for the same collision (f). If the parties are not the same, as where the ship-owners sue in one country and the cargo-owners in the other (g), or if the foreign tribunal had not jurisdiction (h), or if the plaintiffs in this country were not subjects of, nor resident, nor present in the foreign country, and did not as plaintiffs abroad select the foreign tribunal (i), or if the foreign judgment went by default (j), it is not a bar to an action here, and is immaterial.

*Foreign judgment in rem enforced by the Admiralty Court of this country.* It has been held, in a recent case, by Sir R. Phillimore, that a foreign judgment, condemning a ship for collision, may be enforced against the ship by Admiralty proceedings *in rem* in this country. *The City of Mecca,* a British steam-ship, was in collision on the high seas with a Portuguese ship. *The City of Mecca* was arrested in Portugal and found by the Portuguese Court to be in fault for the collision. Owing to some informality she was released from arrest by the Portuguese authorities, and came to England, the foreign judgment remaining unsatisfied. She was arrested in England by the plaintiffs in the Portuguese action; and it was held that international comity required that the English Admiralty Court should enforce the decree of the Portuguese Court (k).

---

(e) *The General Steam Navigation Co.* v. *Gillou,* 11 M. & W. 877, 895.

(f) See Phillimore's Internat. Law, 2nd. ed. IV. 733, *seq.;* Westlake's Private International Law, 376.

(g) Cf. *The Pennsylvania,* 19 Wall. 125; *The Pennsylvania,* 3 Mar. Law Cas. O. S. 477. As to the effect of a foreign judgment *in rem,* see *Castrique* v. *Imrie,* L. R. 4 H. L. 414.

(h) *The Greifswald,* Swab. Ad. 430; *Havelock* v. *Rockwood,* 8 T. R. 268.

(i) *General Steam Navigation Co.* v. *Gillou,* 11 M. & W. 877, 894.

(j) *The Delta* and *The Erminia Foscolo,* 1 P. D. 393.

(k) *The City of Mecca,* 5 P. D. 28. It was held that the Judicature Acts did not interfere with the ancient jurisdiction of the Court in such a case; this case is under appeal.

Foreign municipal regulations as to ships' lights, and rules to be observed in navigating foreign waters, may, as evidence of negligence, be material in determining, in the courts of this country, the liability for a collision in such waters; although foreign municipal law is not binding on our Courts. *Foreign local rules for navigating foreign waters.*

Actions for collision are said to be *communis juris;* and the Admiralty Court has never refused to entertain an action because the owners of both ships are foreigners, or because the collision did not occur within British jurisdiction (*l*). A British subject injured by a foreign ship abroad may cause her to be arrested wherever she is found within British jurisdiction (*m*). The ancient jurisdiction of the Admiralty extended over all waters where the tide ebbs and flows; and although the Admiralty Court was for many years restrained by prohibition from exercising its jurisdiction in cases of collision occurring within the body of a county, by a recent statute its jurisdiction over such waters has been restored. Under the same Act the Admiralty Court has jurisdiction in all cases of collision, whether the collision occurs within the ebb and flow of the tide or not, and whether in British or foreign waters, or on the high seas (*n*). *Jurisdiction in case of collision abroad, or between foreign ships.*

In the case of a collision in foreign waters between foreign ships, if it is clear that an action is pending in a foreign court in respect of the same matter, the Admiralty Court will stay its proceedings (*o*). In a case of wilful damage by the master of one foreign ship to another

(*l*) The *Johann Friedrich*, 1 W. Rob. 35 ; *In re Smith*, 1 P. D. 300 ; *The Greifswald*, Swab. Ad. 430; *The Vivar*, 2 P. D. 29 ; and see *per* Story, J., in *The Invincible*, 2 Gall. 29.

(*m*) 17 & 18 Vict. c. 104, s. 527.

(*n*) 24 Vict. c. 10 ; *The Diana*,

Lush. 539 ; *The Courier, ibid.* 541 ; *The Mali Ivo*, L. R. 2 A. & E. 356 ; as to colonial waters. *The Peerless*, Lush. 30. As to Admiralty jurisdiction generally, see *per* Story, J., in *De Lovio* v. *Boit*, 2 Gall. 398.

(*o*) *The Mali Ivo, ubi supra ; The Catterina Chiazzare*, 1 P. D. 368.

H

foreign ship in foreign waters, the Court refused to entertain the action (*p*).

The common law courts have jurisdiction, whether the
ships are British or foreign, and whether the collision occurs
in foreign waters, or elsewhere. " The right of all persons,
whether British subjects or aliens, to sue in the English
courts for damages in respect of torts committed in
foreign countries, has long since been established ; and, as
is observed in the note to *Mostyn* v. *Fabrigas* (*q*), there
seems to be no reason why aliens should not sue in
England for personal injuries done to them by other aliens
abroad, when such injuries are actionable both by the law
of England, and also by that of the country where they
are committed ; and the impression which had prevailed to
the contrary seems erroneous (*r*)."

*Liability of owners resident abroad.* Unless the writ can be served within the jurisdiction,
owners resident abroad cannot be sued personally for
a collision occurring on the high seas below low-water
mark of the shores of the United Kingdom (*s*). But their
ship is liable in proceedings *in rem*, and in some cases
may be detained if found within three miles of the United
Kingdom, so as to compel the owner to abide the event of
any action for damage caused by her (*t*). But the ship
cannot be detained in respect of personal injury received
in a collision for which she was in fault (*u*).

*Criminal liability where the ship or the offender* In the case of a collision caused by the criminal fault of
a foreigner, or where the collision occurs abroad, if it is
sought to punish the offender in this country, questions of

(*p*) *The Ida*, Lush. 6. This case
was decided before 24 Vict. c. 10,
came into operation. In America
the Admiralty jurisdiction of the
U.S. Courts extends to inland
waters.

(*q*) 1 Smith's Leading Cases, 8th
ed. 652.

(*r*) *Per* Selwyn, L.J., in *The
Halley*, L. R. 2 P. C. 193, 202, 203.

(*s*) *Harris* v. *Owners of The Franconia*, 2 C. P. D. 173 ; *Re Smith*, 1

P. D. 300 ; *The Virar*, 2 P. D. 29.

(*t*) 17 & 18 Vict. c. 104, s. 527.
As to an action *in rem*, see *The
Bilbao*, Lush. 149. In America any
property of the owners of the ship
sued which is found within the
jurisdiction of the Court may be
seized ; 2 Parsons on Ship. (ed.
1869), 390.

(*u*) *Harris* v. *Owners of The Franconia*, 2 C. P. D. 173 ; and see *supra*,
p. 64.

difficulty arise as to his liability to the criminal law of is foreign, or<br>the collision<br>occurs abroad. England, and the jurisdiction of our courts (*x*). The liability and jurisdiction depend upon (1) the offender's nationality; (2) the flag of the ship on board which the offence was committed; and (3) the place of collision. In the case of a person killed or injured on board one ship in a collision caused by the fault of a person on board another, the offence, if intentional, would probably be held to have been committed on board the latter; if not intentional, as where it consists in negligence, on board the former (*y*). The criminal liability for reckless or negligent navigation seems to be as follows. If the ship is British, the offender is liable whether a British subject or a foreigner, and wherever the collision occurs (*z*). If it occurs in the United Kingdom, or in British territory or waters, he is liable, whether a British subject or a foreigner, and whether the ship is British or foreign (*a*); if he is a British subject, and probably also if he is a foreigner (*b*) and the ship British, or if within three months of the offence he has been employed on board a British ship, he is liable wherever the collision occurs (*c*); if he is a British subject, and the ship British, he is liable if the collision occurs in a foreign port or harbour (*d*); if he is a foreigner, and the ship British, he is liable if the collision occurs on the high seas; if he is a British subject, and the ship British or foreign, and also, perhaps, if he is foreigner, and the ship British, he is liable if the collision occurs out of, and the

(*x*) As to criminal negligence causing collision, see *supra*, p. 45.

(*y*) See the judgment of Cockburn, C.J., in *Reg.* v. *Keyn*, 2 Ex. D. 63, 232, *seq.* But see also the judgments of Denman, J., and Lord Coleridge, C.J., *ibid.* pp. 101, 158.

(*z*) *Reg.* v. *Sattler*, D. & B. C. C. 525; *Reg.* v. *Anderson*, L. R. 1 C. C. R. 161. As to what is sufficient

evidence of the ship being British, see *Reg.* v. *Sven Seburg*, 22 L. T. N. S. 523.

(*a*) *Cunningham's Case*, Bell's C. C. 220, 234; 4 Phillimore's International Law, 2nd ed. 767.

(*b*) See *Reg.* v. *Anderson*, *ubi supra*; *Reg.* v. *Menham*, 1 F. & F. 369.

(*c*) 17 & 18 Vict c. 104, s. 267.

(*d*) 18 & 19 Vict. c. 91, s. 21.

H 2

injured person dies within, England or Ireland (*e*) ; if he
is a British subject, and the ship a foreign ship to which
he does not belong, he is liable if the collision occurs elsewhere than in the Queen's dominions (*f*) ; and, lastly, if
he is a foreigner and the ship foreign, he is liable if the
collision occurs within three miles of low-water mark on
the shores of the United Kingdom (*g*).

(*e*) 24 & 25 Vict. c. 100, s. 10.
This Act does not apply to foreigners
on board foreign ships ; see *Reg. v.
Lewis*, 1 D. & B. C. C. 182, decided
upon 9 Geo. IV. c. 31 ; and *per*

Cockburn, C.J., in *Reg.* v. *Keyn*, 2
Ex. D. 63, 171.
(*f*) 30 & 31 Vict. c. 124, s. 11.
(*g*) 40 & 41 Vict. c. 73.

# CHAPTER V.

## COMPULSORY PILOTAGE.

A PILOT, whether licensed or not, whom the owners are not compelled or required by any penalty or direction of law to employ, is their servant; and they are answerable for a collision caused by his fault or negligence (*a*). *Owners liable for the negligence of a pilot employed voluntarily.*

The master is not responsible for the acts of a pilot properly placed in charge, either civilly in damages (*b*) or at a Board of Trade inquiry in respect of his certificate (*c*). Nor is he liable in such a case for penalties imposed by law for improper navigation of the ship (*d*). *But not the master.*

In some waters the law requires a ship to be navigated by a qualified or licensed pilot; and not to take a pilot is a statutory offence punishable by a penalty. A pilot taken under these circumstances is called a " compulsory " pilot. He is not the owners' servant, and they are not responsible *Owners not liable for the negligence of a pilot placed in charge by the law.*

(*a*) *The Maria*, 1 W. Rob. 95, 108; *The Eden*, 2 W. Rob. 442 ; and see the cases cited below. Under 6 Geo. IV. c. 125, and former Pilot Acts, it was held that where the pilot was employed in pursuance of the Acts, but without compulsion, the statutory exemption of owners from liability applied : *Lucey* v. *Ingram*, 6 M. & W. 302 ; *The Fama*, 2 W. Rob. 184. Under the Act now in force there is no exemption except where the employment of the pilot is compulsory.

(*b*) See 3 Kent's Comm. § 176. In *The Portsmouth*, 6 C. Rob. 317, note,

the non-liability of those in charge of a prize for the fault of a pilot is expressly recognised by Sir W. Scott.

(*c*) See *The Vesta* and *The City of London*, before the Wreck Commissioner, Times, Sep. 15th, 1879. But see also *The Ostrich* and *The Benbow*, Mitch. Mar. Reg. 1878, where it was held that the master was in fault for the ship's speed.

(*d*) *Oakley* v. *Speedy*, 40 L. T. N.S. 881. As to the relative positions of the pilot and captain on board a Queen's ship, and in foreign ships, see below, p. 110, note (*u*).

for his negligence. For a collision caused entirely by the fault of a compulsory pilot, the pilot alone is responsible.

Pilotage is held to be compulsory, so as to exempt owners from liability for the acts of the pilot, in all waters, and for all ships, in and for which the employment of the pilot is enforced by penalty, or where the pilotage charge can be recovered against the ship or her owners, whether the pilot is employed or not (e).

Where a ship is navigated by her own master having a pilotage certificate, her owners are not exempt from liability, although, except for the master's certificate, pilotage is compulsory for the ship (f).

Owners are exempt from liability for the negligence of a compulsory pilot by Statute, as well as by the Common Law. Section 388 of 17 & 18 Vict. c. 104, is as follows:—

"No owner of or master of any ship shall be answerable to any person whatever for any loss or damage occasioned by the fault or incapacity of any qualified pilot acting in charge of such ship within any district where the employment of such pilot is compulsory by law."

Independently of the statute, owners are not liable at common law for the acts of a compulsory pilot who is placed in charge of the ship by the law, and who is not their servant (g). It seems doubtful whether the statute has any effect except as declaratory of the common law (h). In *The Maria* (i) Dr. Lushington said, "The leading principle of the Legislature in exonerating owners from any liability for damage occasioned by their vessels having pilots on board is this: that the masters are compellable

(e) *Carruthers* v. *Sidebotham*, 4 M. & S. 77 ; *The Maria*, 1 W. Rob. 95, 109 ; *The Arbutus*, 2 Mar. Law Cas. O. S. 136 ; *The Hibernian*, L. R. 4 P. C. 511.

(f) 17 & 18 Vict. c. 104, ss. 340-344, 355 ; *The Killarney*, Lush. 202; *The Beta*, 2 Mar. Law Cas. O. S. 165.

(g) *The Maria*, 1 W. Rob. 95 ; *The Halley*, L. R. 2 P. C. 193 ; *The Annapolis* and *The Johanna Stoll*, Lush. 295.

(h) See *General Steam Nav. Co.* v. *British & Colonial Steam Nav. Co.*, L. R. 4 Ex. 238.

(i) 1 W. Rob. 95, 99.

to take pilots on board, and the owners are not responsible for the acts of the persons to whom they are thus forced to commit the management of their property, and over whom they have no control. This, I apprehend, is a rule founded upon a great principle of justice and equity."

The rule has been applied even in the case of a collision in the territorial waters of a country by the law of which owners are expressly made liable for the negligence of a compulsory pilot (k). Whether the compulsion is by the law of this country, or by the law of the place where the collision occurs, the owner is equally free from liability (l). Damage by compulsory pilot abroad.

By the Thames Conservancy Act, 1857, (m) it is enacted that owners of vessels navigating the Thames shall be liable for damage to property of the Conservators caused by persons belonging to or employed in their vessels. It has been held that this Act does not affect sect. 388 of the Merchant Shipping Act, 1854, and that the owners of a vessel in the Thames in charge of a compulsory pilot are not liable for damage done by the fault of the pilot to a vessel or other property belonging to the Conservators (n). Damage to property of Thames Conservancy by compulsory pilot.

Although the ship-owner is, under the Harbours, Docks and Piers Clauses Act, 1847, liable for damage to a pier or harbour works, even when such damage is caused by his ship when in the possession and control of persons for whose acts he would not be responsible at law, it is expressly provided that he shall not be liable under the Act when his ship is in charge of a compulsory pilot (o). Damage to pier, dock or harbour works caused by compulsory pilot.

The fact that the compulsory pilot is selected by the Damage by compulsory

(k) The Halley, L. R. 2 P. C. 193. See also Smith v. Condry. 1 How. 28, in which it was held by the Supreme Court of the United States that an American ship was not liable for a collision in British waters caused by the fault of a compulsory pilot.
(l) The Hibernian, L. R. 4 P. C. 511 ; The Peerless, Lush. 30 ; The

Halley, ubi sup.
(m) 20 & 21 Vict. c. 147 (Local), s. 96.
(n) Conservators of the River Thames v. Hall, 3 Mar. Law Cas. O. S. 73.
(o) 10 & 11 Vict. c. 27, s. 74 ; see River Wear Commissioners v. Adamson, 1 Q. B. D. 546 ; 2 Ap. Cas. 743.

<table>
<tr><td>

pilot in owner's constant employment.

</td><td>

owners, and in their regular employment, does not prevent the application of the rule exempting the owners for damage caused entirely by his negligence (*p*).

</td></tr>
<tr><td>

Where, at the time of the collision, the pilot is on board and in charge, but not by compulsion of law.

</td><td>

The presence on board of a pilot whose employment, in the first instance, was compulsory, but whose duty as a pilot is at an end, and who is no longer in charge of the ship by compulsion of law, or otherwise than by the owner's or master's choice, does not discharge the owners. A vessel in charge of a compulsory pilot was brought up in the Mersey in an improper berth, and lay there from the 27th to the 29th of October, the pilot remaining on board. On the night of the 29th she was in collision with another ship to which she had given a foul berth. It was held that it was the master's duty to have shifted his berth between the 27th and the 29th, and that the owners were liable (*q*).

</td></tr>
<tr><td>

Owners held exempt where at the place of collision there was no compulsion to take a pilot.

</td><td>

Owners are exempt from liability in some cases where the collision is caused by a qualified pilot in charge of the ship, although at the spot where the collision occurs there is no compulsion to take a pilot on board. A vessel bound to London took a London pilot off Dungeness, where his employment was compulsory. A collision occurred by the pilot's fault on the voyage up the river at a spot within the port of London but short of the ship's destination. It was held, assuming that the ship, which belonged to the port of London, could not have been compelled to take on board a pilot at the place where the collision occurred, that the owners were not liable for the collision. The engagement of the pilot having been, in the first instance, compulsory, and the right and duty of the pilot under that

</td></tr>
</table>

(*p*) *The Batavier*, 2 W. Rob. 407 ; *The Hibernian*, L. R. 4 P. C. 511.

(*q*) *The Woburn Abbey*, 3 Mar. Law Cas. O. S. 240. This case was decided upon the words of the Local Act. In *The Christiana*, 7 Moo. P.C.C. 160 (under 6 Geo. IV. c. 125, s. 55), it was said by the Privy Council (though the dictum was not necessary for the decision of the

case) that a pilot on board under somewhat similar circumstances remained in charge of the ship. See also the case next stated in the text. In America (*The Lotty*, Olcott. Adm. 329) it was held that the owners were liable for improper moorings twelve hours after the pilot had brought the ship up.

engagement being to navigate the ship to her destination, it was held that the relation of master and servant never arose between the owners and the pilot so as to make the owners liable for the pilot's acts (r).

A ship, being obliged by law to be navigated by a pilot when "proceeding to sea," left the Liverpool docks in charge of a pilot. Owing to unfavourable weather she was brought-up in the river. It was held that the owners were not liable for a collision caused by the pilot's negligence whilst the ship was lying in the river (s). *Collision whilst the ship is lying in the river with pilot on board.*

A vessel, inward bound, was brought-up in the river Mersey by a compulsory pilot preparatory to docking. The pilot remained on board, and in charge, receiving daily wages under the Local Pilotage Act. It was held that the owners were not liable for damage done by her whilst so lying at anchor (s).

In every case of collision it is the duty of the master of each ship to "stand by" and assist the other ; and not the less so because at the time of the collision his ship is in charge of a compulsory pilot. The law is express that, if he fails to do so, his ship "shall be deemed to be in fault." But, notwithstanding the terms of the statute, it seems that the owners would not be liable for the collision, if it were, in fact, caused entirely by the compulsory pilot (t). *The defence of compulsory pilotage is good notwithstanding 36 & 37 Vict. c. 85, s. 17.*

Where a collision occurred when the pilot was unavoidably below for a few minutes, after he had given the course, and left the deck in charge of one of the ship's officers, it *Collision while pilot below.*

---

(r) *General Steam Navigation Co. v. British & Colonial Steam Nav. Co.*, L. R. 3 Ex. 330 ; on app., *ibid.* 4 Ex. 238. In *The Hankow*, 40 L. T. N. S. 335, the decision in the case in the text that pilotage is not compulsory for a London ship in the port of London was not followed by Sir R. Phillimore in the Admiralty Division.

(s) *The City of Cambridge*, *Wood v. Smith*, L. R. 4 A. & E. 161 ;

*ibid.* 5 P. C. 451; *The Princeton*, 3 P. D. 90. These decisions were under the Local (Liverpool) Act. For other decisions under this Act, see below, p. 126.

(t) See *The Queen*, L. R. 2 A. & E. 354. This case was decided under 25 & 26 Vict. c. 63, s. 33. The decision would, it is submitted, be the same in a similar case under the present Act, 36 & 37 Vict. c. 85, s. 16 ; see *supra*, p. 12.

was held that the owners were liable for a collision for which the ship was in fault (u).

*Proof required that the negligence causing the loss was the negligence of the pilot.* To make the defence of " compulsory pilot " good, it must be proved that the negligence causing the collision was the negligence of the pilot (x). Where a collision was caused by the helm being improperly put to starboard, it was held that, to relieve the owners from liability, it must be proved that the order to put the helm to starboard was given by the pilot (y).

In *The Carrier Dove* (z), a ship in the Mersey was getting her anchor in heavy weather with the assistance of a tug a-head. She was struck by a squall, and driven on a ship at anchor. It was held by the Privy Council that the state of the weather, and other circumstances, made it imprudent and dangerous for her to get under way. The ship was in charge of a compulsory pilot; but, in the absence of proof that she was got under way by his orders, the owners were held liable.

A vessel was being towed from one dock to another at night when it was imprudent for her to be under way. The owners were held liable, notwithstanding the presence on board of a licensed pilot. It was said by the Court that the case differed from that of a ship in tow in broad daylight, when the tug is bound to obey the orders of the pilot (a).

*Owners not exempt from liability where there is contributory negligence on the part of the ship's crew.* It is only where the collision was caused *entirely* by the fault of the pilot that owners are exempt from liability. If any fault or negligence on the part of the owners or their servants or crew has contributed to the loss, they, as well as the pilot, are responsible (b). And the owners are

(u) *The Mobile,* Swab. Adm. 69 ; on app. *ibid.* 127. As to the duty of the master to be on deck, see *The Obey,* L. R. 1 A. & E. 102.

(x) *Clyde Navigation Co.* v. *Barclay,* 1 App. Cas. 790.

(y) *The Schwalbe,* Lush. 239.

(z) Brown. & Lush. 113.

(a) *The Borussia,* Swab. Adm.

94. It is not clear whether the Court considered the pilotage compulsory. From *The Maria,* L. R. 1 A. & E. 358, it seems that under the Local Act the employment of the pilot was not compulsory.

(b) *The Mobile,* Swab. Adm. 127 ; *The Diana,* 1 W. Rob. 131 ; 4 Moo. P. C. C. 11.

responsible for the whole of the loss, though caused in part
by the fault of the pilot (c).

There has been some confusion as to the burden of proof Burden of proof as to negligence.
in such cases; and until quite recently the law has been
unsettled. It was at one time held that where a compulsory pilot was in charge, or even on board, the owners were
*primâ facie* exempted from liability (d). Then it was held
that, in order to make good his claim to exemption, the
owner must prove, not only that the collision was caused
by the pilot's fault, but that there was no contributory
negligence on the part of the crew (e). It is now settled
that the owners are not required to prove absence of contributory negligence, but that, under certain circumstances,
it will be presumed. If the owners prove fault on the part
of the pilot sufficient to cause, and in fact causing, the
collision, in the absence of proof of contributory negligence
on the part of the crew, it is held that they have satisfied
the condition upon which their exemption depends, and
they will not be called on to adduce further proof of a
negative character to exclude the mere possibility of contributory fault. But if it appears that the owners, or their
servants, have committed acts, or been guilty of omissions,
which might have contributed to the collision, then it lies
on them to prove that those acts or omissions did not in
any degree contribute to the collision (f).

A qualified pilot is empowered by law, in pilotage waters, Qualified pilot superseding unqualified pilot.
to supersede an unqualified pilot in charge of a ship,
whether she is subject to compulsory pilotage, or not (g).
It has not been decided whether the owners are liable for a

(c) See *The Diana*, *Stuart* v. *Ire-
monger*, 4 Moo. P. C. C. 11.
  (d) *The Vernon*, 1 W. Rob. 316;
*Bennet* v. *Moita*, 7 Taunt. 258; *The
Christiana*, 2 Hag. Ad. 183.
  (e) *The Iona*, L. R. 1 P. C. 426.
  (f) *Clyde Nav. Co.* v. *Barclay*, 1
App. Cas. 790, in which case the
rule laid down in *The Iona*, L. R. 1

P. C. 426, was dissented from; *The
Marathon*, 48 L. J. Ad. 17.
  (g) 17 & 16 Vict. c. 104, s. 360.
It seems that the master of a tug
employed to tow only, and not to
pilot the ship, could not be superseded by a qualified pilot under this
Act; see *Beilby* v. *Scott*, 7 M. & W.
93, decided under 6 Geo. IV. c. 125.

collision caused by the fault of a qualified pilot who has
superseded an unqualified pilot, in the case of a ship for
which pilotage is not compulsory. The statutory exemption (17 & 18 Vict. c. 104, sect. 388) probably does not
apply to such a case ; but, apart from the statute, it seems
doubtful whether owners could be held liable for the acts
of a pilot who takes charge of their ship under the authority of the law, not by their choice, and not as their
servant.

**Exemption of owners in case of compulsory pilotage will not be extended.**    The rule that owners are not liable for damage done by
their ship when in charge of a compulsory pilot, and by his
fault, has been said to take away a remedy from the
sufferer, and it will not be extended (*h*). Where the
master of a French ship in the Thames, at the pilot's
request, engaged a waterman to take the helm, and a collision occurred by the fault of the waterman in not carrying
out the pilot's orders, it was held that the waterman was
in the employment of the owners, and that they were
liable (*i*). And in Admiralty it is held that a defendant
who succeeds only upon the defence of compulsory pilotage
must bear his own costs (*k*).

**Compulsory pilot in charge of a ship in tow.**    Where a ship in tow is in charge of a compulsory pilot,
there is doubt whether the tug and her owners are free
from liability for a collision between a third ship and the
tug or her tow caused entirely by the fault of the pilot.
The ship in tow, and her owners, are clearly free from
liability in such a case (*l*). In a case decided under
6 Geo. IV. c. 125, Dr. Lushington said : "If a licensed
pilot is on board (a vessel in tow), and his orders are
obeyed, the owners are absolved from responsibility for

(*h*) In *The Halley*, L. R. 2 A. &
E. 3, 15, Sir R. Phillimore said that
the law, by which owners of a wrong-
doing ship are not liable for the
fault of a compulsory pilot, is " fruitful in injustice ;" but see the observations of the L.JJ., S. C. on app.

L. R. 2 P. C. 193.
(*i*) *The General de Caen*, Swab.
Ad. 9.
(*k*) See *supra*, p. 72.
(*l*) *The Ocean Ware*, L. R. 3 P. C.
205.

damage occasioned by such vessel. But if the pilot was to be deprived of his authority, and the (tug) steamer was not bound to follow his directions, and a collision ensued, the (tug) steamer would be the agent of the owners of the vessel in tow, and the owners of that vessel would no longer be protected by the Act of Parliament" (m). These observations seem applicable at the present day as regards the liability of the ship in tow when a pilot is on board and in charge by compulsion of law. And there would seem to be difficulty in holding the owners of a tug to be liable for acts of her crew for which the compulsory pilot is responsible, and which are negligent only so far as they are in pursuance of his orders. In a recent case, however, it was considered by Sir R. Phillimore that in Admiralty the tug would be liable in such a case (n).

If a ship is deficient in hull or equipment, and a colli- Owners liable for deficiency sion occurs in consequence, her owners are liable although of ship or their ship is in charge of a compulsory pilot (o). Thus equipment. owners have been held liable for the insufficiency of ground tackle (p). So if the vessel will not steer (q), or if the crew is insufficient or incapable (r), or if the tug employed by the master is not of sufficient power (s), "compulsory pilotage" would be no defence.

But it is not necessary that the ship should be perfect in every respect, provided that, with ordinary care, she can be navigated with safety to other vessels. Where a vessel in collision with another was not in the best of trim, it was argued that the owners were liable, although she was

(m) The Duke of Sussex, 1 W. Rob. 270, 273.
(n) The Mary, 5 P. D. 14; and see supra, p. 81. And see generally as to Tug & Tow, Ch. III.
(o) The Christiana, Hammond v. Rogers, 7 Moo. P. C. C. 160.
(p) The Massachusetts, 1 W. Rob. 371.
(q) The Livia, 1 Asp. Mar. Law

Cas. 204; The Peru, 1 Pritch. Ad. Dig. 440.
(r) The General de Caen, Swab. Ad. 9; The Hope, 1 W. Rob. 154; and see below, p. 218.
(s) The Ocean Wave, Marshall v. Moran, L. R. 3 P. C. 205; The Belgic, 2 P. D. 57, note; and see The Julia, Lush. 224.

in charge of a compulsory pilot. It was held by Dr.
Lushington that the owners were relieved from liability (t).
He said: "If she was in ordinary safe trim, then,
although she might be in handier trim, and although the
trim of the ship in fact contributed to the collision, they
(the owners) are not responsible."

**Pilot supersedes the master in command.**
The pilot supersedes the master in all matters connected
with the command and navigation of the ship. His
authority is supreme, his orders must be implicitly obeyed,
and any negligence in carrying them out, or interference
with him in his duties, will make the owners liable in
case of collision. "The duties of the master and the
pilot are in many respects clearly defined. Although the
pilot has charge of the ship, the owners are most clearly
responsible to third persons for the sufficiency of the ship
and her equipments, the competency of the master and
crew, and their obedience to the orders of the pilot in
everything that concerns his duty; and under ordinary
circumstances we think that his commands are to be
implicitly obeyed. To him belongs the whole conduct of
the navigation of the ship, to the safety of which it is
important that the chief direction should be vested in one
only " (u).

(t) *The Argo*, Swab. Adm. 462.
(u) *Per* Parke, B., in *The Christiana*, *Hammond* v. *Rogers*, 7 Moo.
P. C. C. 160, 171 ; approved in *The
City of Cambridge*, *Wood* v. *Smith*,
L. R. 5 P. C. 451, 457. The Queen's
Regulations for the Navy of 1879,
following the language of previous
Regulations of 1808, 1833, and 1862,
contain a description of the duties
and responsibilities in Her Majesty's
Service of the captain, navigating
officer, and pilot. Art. 940 is as
follows : " The captain is to order
everything that relates to the navigation of the ship to be performed
as the pilot shall require ; but nevertheless he, and the navigating officer,
are to attend particularly to his conduct ; and if from his own or the
navigating officer's observations he
shall have reason to believe the pilot
not qualified to conduct the ship, or
that he is running her into danger,
the captain is to remove him from
charge, and take all necessary measures for the safety of the ship, noting the time of the pilot being so
removed in the ship's logbook ; and
if the ship be at any time damaged
through the ignorance or negligence
of the pilot when a common degree
of attention on the part of the captain and navigating officer would
have prevented the disaster, those
officers will be deemed to have neglected their duty. This Article is
equally applicable to the case of a

It is the exclusive duty of the pilot to give the orders Pilot's duties.
to the helm (v); to decide upon the proper time and place
of bringing up (x); and as to the proper mode of carrying
the anchor, before letting go (y); to see that the ship
rides with a proper scope of cable out; to tend her whilst
swinging; to let go a second anchor if necessary; and to
manœuvre her if she parts from her anchor (z).    He
decides as to the rate of speed, and the canvas to carry (a);
whether to run through a crowded roadstead at night, or
to bring up (b).  When brought up, he must keep an eye
on the weather, and be ready for a change without relying
upon the look-out for a report (c).

It is for the pilot to decide upon the time, place, and
manner of turning a ship, when docking (d).   The omission
to set some head sail to help the ship round was held by
the Privy Council to be the fault of the pilot, and not of
the master or crew (e).   It is the duty of the pilot to employ
a tug, where the safety of the ship requires it (f).  And
it seems that the pilot is responsible if the ship is got

ship in the charge of a Queen's
Harbour Master or the Master Attendant of a Dockyard." Under this
Article it seems that if a ship gets
ashore in consequence of an obviously wrong course given by the
pilot, the captain is held responsible.
The Spanish Commercial Code
(Art. 676, 691, and 693) places the
pilot in the position of adviser to
the captain, and the ultimate authority and responsibility of the
latter is expressly preserved. In
America, pilots of passenger ships
have a special authority; 10 Stat.
at Large, Ch. 66, s. 28. In the
Suez Canal, where pilotage is compulsory, the responsibility, as regards
the management of the ship, devolves solely on the captain; see
Regulations of 1st July, 1878. The
effect of this regulation on owners'
liability is not clear.

(v) *The Schwalbe*, Lush. 239.
(x) *The Agricola*, 2 W. Rob. 10;

*The George*, 4 Not. of Cas. 161; *The
Christiana*, 7 Moo. P. C. C. 160,
172; *The Lochibo, ibid.* 427; 3 W.
Rob. 310.
(y) *The Gipsey King*, 2 W. Rob.
537; but see *infra*, p. 112, as to the
duty of the crew to see that the
anchor is clear.
(z) *The City of Cambridge*, Wood
v. *Smith*, L. R. 5 P. C. 451; *The
Northampton*, 1 Sp. E. & A. 152;
*The Princeton*, 3 P. D. 90.
(a) *The Calabar*, L. R. 2 P. C.
238; *The Maria*, 1 W. Rob. 95,
110; *The Julia*, Lush. 224; *The
Batavier*, 1 Sp. E. & A. 378, 383;
9 Moo. P. C. C. 286; *The Lochibo,
ubi supra*.
(b) *The Lochibo, ubi supra*.
(c) *The Princeton*, 3 P. D. 90.
(d) *The Ocean Wave, Marshall* v.
*Moran*, L. R. 3 P. C. 205.
(e) *The Ocean Wave, ubi supra*.
(f) *The Julia*, Lush. 224; and see
*The Peerless*, 13 Moo. P. C. C. 484.

under way in weather when it is imprudent to move (g). This however is not clear, for, in some cases, it has been said that the master is responsible for being under way in improper weather (h).

**Duties of master and crew.**

Although the pilot's authority is paramount, the master is not free from responsibility. In *The Batavier* (i) Dr. Lushington said : "There are many cases in which I should hold that, notwithstanding the pilot has charge, it is the duty of the master to prevent accident, and not to abandon the vessel entirely to the pilot ; but that there are certain duties he has to discharge, notwithstanding there is a pilot on board, for the benefit of the owners."

The following are duties of the master and crew for which the owners are held responsible, notwithstanding the presence on board of a compulsory pilot. The master and crew must keep a good look-out, and keep the pilot informed of the position, movements of and possible danger to other ships (k) ; they must have the anchor clear, and ready to let go, when the pilot gives the order (l) ; the master is responsible for the sufficiency and power of a tug employed for ordinary towage service (m) ; and although not bound to be always on deck (n), he is generally responsible for the ordinary work of the ship being properly carried on, and usual precautions being taken without express order from the pilot (o).

A ship was in collision with another coming out of dock.

(g) *The Carrier Dove,* Br. and Lush. 113 ; *The Lochibo,* 7 Moo. P. C. C. 427.

(h) See *The Ocean Wave, ubi supra; The Girolamo,* 3 Hag. Ad. 169, *infra,* p. 115 ; *The Borussia,* Swab. Ad. 94.

(i) 1 Sp. E. & A. 378, 383 ; S. C. on App. Nom. *Netherlands Steamboat Co.* v. *Styles,* 9 Moo. P. C. C. 286.

(k) *The Batavier, ubi supra ; The Diana,* 1 W. Rob. 131 ; 4 Moo. P.

C. C. 11 ; *The Velasquez,* L. R. 1 P. C. 494 ; *The Julia,* Lush. 224 ; *The Atlas,* 2 W. Rob. 502.

(l) *The General Parkhill* and *The Centurion,* 1 Pritch. Ad. Dig. 172 ; and see *The Peerless,*13 Moo. P. C. C. 484.

(m) *The Ocean Wave, ubi supra ; The Julia, ubi supra.*

(n) See *The Obey,* L. R. 1 A. & E. 102.

(o) *The Christiana, infra ;* and see cases cited *infra,* p. 117.

The latter had not been reported by the look-out. It was held that, the duty of the look-out being to watch for and report vessels in the river, it was not negligence in them not to have reported the vessel in dock, and the vessel being in charge of a compulsory pilot, the owners were held free from liability (*p*).

A ship in charge of a compulsory pilot, having been in collision with another, drove on board a third. It was held that the owners were liable in consequence of the negligence of the master and crew in the following particulars: in not veering out more chain to bring the ship up; in not bending a line on to a tow rope, so as to enable a tug, which came alongside the ship sued, to keep her clear of the other ship; and in not getting sail on the ship (*q*).

A ship in charge of a compulsory pilot was riding in the Downs in heavy weather, and drove from her anchors on board another ship. If some of her gear aloft had been sent down, she might have ridden in safety and escaped collision. It was held by the Privy Council that there was contributory negligence on the part of the master in not sending down the yards, and that the owners were liable. Parke, B., in delivering the judgment of the Court, said: " The step being one which every master, according to ordinary rules of navigation, ought to have taken in every open roadstead, where many vessels were lying, and in blowing weather, that duty was not exclusively the pilot's, but that of the master also. And if the pilot had given express orders to the master not to send down topmasts, &c., we do not say that the owners might not have been excused from responsibility for the consequences of that omission " (*r*).

The owners are responsible for the pilot's orders being

(*p*) *The Calabar*, L. R. 2 P. C. 238.
(*q*) *The Annapolis* and *The Golden*
*Light*, 1 Mar. Law. Cas. O. S. 183.
(*r*) *The Christiana, Hammond v. Rogers*, 7 Moo. P. C. C. 160, 173.

I

promptly and efficiently carried out. If the helm is not
shifted (s), the anchor let go (t), or the engines stopped (u)
promptly at the pilot's order, and a collision ensues, the
owners are liable.  It is the master's duty to repeat
the pilot's orders (x), and to see that they are carried
out.  If, in carrying them out, ordinary prudence and
seamanship require a particular precaution to be taken,
it will be held to be negligence in the master if the
precaution is omitted.  Thus the omission to run out a
warp or check line when docking (y), or to cut a lanyard
which holds two ships together when in collision (z), is held
negligence in the master or crew.

Interference
by master
with the pilot.
In case of the pilot's intoxication, or manifest incapacity,
it is the duty of the master to take charge of the ship (a).
And if an emergency or sudden danger arises, when the
pilot is not at hand, or which he does not foresee, the master
would be justified in giving an order necessary for the ship's
safety (b).  But interference with the pilot's duties is
justified only by urgent necessity (c).  Care must be taken
not to interfere with the pilot unnecessarily; for if a
collision occurs in consequence of improper interference
with the pilot, the owners will be liable.  " It would be a
most dangerous doctrine to hold, except under the most
extraordinary circumstances, that the master could be
justified in interfering with the pilot in his proper vocation.
If the two authorities could so clash, the danger would be
materially augmented, and the interests of the owner, which
are now protected by the general principles of law, and

<hr>

(s) *The Lochibo*, 4 Moo. P. C. C.
427 ; *The Julia*, Lush. 224.
(t) *The Atlas*, 2 W. Rob. 502 ; *The
Peerless*, 13 Moo. P. C. C. 484.
(u) *The Ripon*, 6 Not. of Cas.
245.
(x) *The Admiral Boxer*, Swab. Ad.
193 ; *The Lochibo*, 3 W. Rob. 310,
328.
(y) *The Cynthia*, 2 P. D. 52.
(z) *The Massachusetts*, 1 W. Rob.

371.
(a) *The Christiana*, Hammond v.
*Rogers*, 7 Moo. P. C. C. 160, 172;
*The Lochibo, Pollok* v. *McAlpin, ibid.*
427; *The Hibernia*, 4 Jur. N. S.
1244.
(b) *The City of Cambridge*, *Wood*
v. *Smith*, L. R. 5 P. C. 451, 459 ;
*The Argo*, Swab. Ad. 462.
(c) *The Argo, ubi sup.*

specific enactments, from liability for the acts of the pilot, would be most severely prejudiced " (d).

In *The Girolamo* (e), a ship, with a pilot on board, was under way in the Thames in a fog so dense that she could not proceed without danger to other craft. Sir J. Nicholl expressed an opinion that, under such circumstances, it was the duty of the master to take the charge of the ship out of the pilot's hands, and to bring her up. In subsequent cases, however, it has been doubted whether the master would be justified in exercising his own discretion in such a case; and the better opinion seems to be that the pilot is alone responsible for bringing the ship up when necessary (f).

It has been held that when the pilot was taking a ship on the wrong side of the river, in direct violation of the law, the master was not in fault for not interfering, and that he would not have been justified in doing so (g). In *The Julia*, Lord Kingsdown said that for a master to give to the man at the wheel a different order from that given by the pilot, while a tug was coming alongside to take the tow line on board, was " misconduct in the master and disobedience to the orders of the pilot " (h).

It is not improper interference on the part of the master to make suggestions to the pilot or to offer him advice (i). And, in case of a manifest danger, it is the duty of the master to interfere to this extent. In a salvage case, where a ship in charge of a pilot was in tow, and the course given to the tug by the pilot was clearly dangerous and wrong, Lord Campbell, in delivering the opinion of the Privy

(d) *Per* Dr. Lushington in *The Maria*, 1 W. Rob. 95, 110. See also *The Hibernia*, 4 Jur. N. S. 1244 ; *The Duke of Sussex*, *supra*, p. 109, and the cases cited, *supra*, p. 81, as to the danger of clashing authorities.

(e) 3 Hag. Ad. 169.

(f) *The North American* and *The*

*Wild Rose*, 2 Mar. Law Cas. O. S. 319 ; *The Lochibo*, 3 W. Rob. 310, 320 ; 7 Moo. P. C. 427, and see *supra*, p. 111.

(g) *The Argo*, Swab. Ad. 462.

(h) Lush. 224 ; and see *The Lochibo, ubi supra.*

(i) *The Lochibo, ubi supra.*

Council, said : " The master of the tug, watching the course
the licensed pilot pursues, if he finds that this course will
lead the vessel into danger, is bound to interfere and make
a communication to the master of the ship, instead of
making himself instrumental to the destruction of life and
property " (k).

In *The Lochibo* (l), Dr. Lushington discusses at some length
the question what amount of interference with the pilot in
the performance of his duties will make the owners liable.
An order given by the master or crew to the helm, even
though repeated unthinkingly by the pilot, constitutes
" illegal interference ;" but mere suggestion to, or consulta-
tion with, the pilot is not interference.   Where there is
any peculiarity of the ship which makes her difficult for a
stranger to handle, it is clearly the duty of the master to
offer his experience and advice to a pilot who is a stranger
to her.

Dock or har-
bour-master
in charge.
In many ports the harbour or dock-master has power,
by Act of Parliament, to regulate the movements, mooring,
and berthing of ships.  When a vessel is acting under
the orders of such a person, her owners are, as regards
liability for damage done by her, to some extent in
the same position as when she is in charge of a compulsory pilot.  Thus it was held that a ship, which was
damaged by another falling over against her at low water,
was not entitled to recover damages against the other, the
latter having been berthed under the directions of the
dock-master (m).

But in a place where vessels are required to take up
their berths under the orders of a harbour-master, if, without any directions from him, a ship takes up a berth, at

---

(k) *The Duke of Manchester,*      7 Moo. P. C. C. 427.
*Shersby* v. *Hibbert,* 5 Not. of Cas.        (m) *The Economy,* 1 Pritch. Ad.
470, 476.                                      Dig. 177.
   (l) 3 W. Rob. 310 ; affd. on app.

which she is afterwards injured by another properly berthed, she cannot recover against the latter (*n*).

If ordered to do so by the dock authorities, a ship must send down her yards; and she must shift her berth, even after she has been properly moored by their order, and though she is safer where she is (*o*).

If, in carrying out the orders of the dock-master, ordinary prudence would suggest that a particular precaution should be taken, a vessel neglecting to take that precaution will be held to be in fault. Thus when a ship was being moved under the orders of a dock-master, and negligently omitted to use a check rope, her owners were held liable for damage she did to other craft in consequence (*p*).

A ship going out of dock under the orders of a dock-master was offered, and accepted, the services of the dock company's tug. Through want of power in the tug a collision occurred. The owners were held liable, there being no obligation upon them to accept the services of the tug, or on the company to supply one (*q*).

Barges in certain parts of the river Thames are required Owners liable for negligence by law to be navigated by licensed watermen; but the of licensed 'owners of a barge, which does damage whilst in charge of watermen in the Thames. a licensed waterman, are not relieved from liability (*r*).

Compulsory pilotage (*s*) exists only in waters within the Compulsory pilotage;

(*n*) *The Jacob*, *ibid.* 178.

(*o*) *The Excelsior*, L. R. 2 A. & E. 268.

(*p*) *The Cynthia*, 2 P. D. 52: see also *The Excelsior*, L. R. 2 A. & E. 268.

(*q*) *The Belgic*, 2 P. D. 59, note.

(*r*) *Martin* v. *Temperley*, 4 Q. B. 298; see 7 & 8 Geo. IV. c. 74 (local).

(*s*) Compulsory pilotage exists in many foreign countries, including the United States of America, France, Germany, Belgium, Holland, Spain, Portugal, Austria, and the Argentine Republic. But, except in

Germany (see Allgemeines Deutsches Handelsgesetzbuch, Art. 740), the law that owners are not responsible for the fault of a compulsory pilot does not prevail abroad; see, as to America, *The China*, 7 Wall. 53; *The Merrimac*, 14 Wall. 199; *Smith* v. *The Creole*, 2 Wall. Junr. C. C. Rep. 485; 2 Parsons on Shipping, ed. 1869, p. 117; *Smith* v. *Condry*, 1 How. 28. As to France, see Abordage Maritime, Caumont, § 191—194; Codes Annotées, par Sirey et Gilbert, C. C. Art. 216, § 9; Jurisprudence, &c., d'Abordage, Sibille, 280. As to Spain, see Codigo de Com-

where it exists.

jurisdiction of a duly constituted pilotage authority, and for certain classes of ships upon particular voyages. Some of the principal pilotage authorities, such as the London, Hull, Newcastle, and Leith Trinity Houses, were originally constituted by charter; but these, as well as various other authorities existing around the shores of the United Kingdom, are now regulated by Act of Parliament. The Acts relating to pilotage are general and local. The general law as to pilotage is contained in the Merchant Shipping Acts, 1854–1876 (*t*). The local Acts are stated below, in connection with the places to which they relate. The Acts authorize bye-laws to be made for the regulation of pilotage, which in some cases are required to be approved by Her Majesty in Council.

To ascertain whether, in a particular case, pilotage is compulsory or not, it is necessary to consider the combined effect of the general and local Acts, and of the bye-laws for the time being in force under them. The question is frequently one of considerable difficulty.

General Pilotage Acts.

By 17 & 18 Vict. c. 104, s. 353, compulsory pilotage was continued in all districts and for all vessels in and for which pilotage was compulsory on the 1st of May, 1855, the date of that Act coming into operation. The extent to which pilotage is compulsory under the general Act of 1854 can therefore be ascertained only by reference to the general and local Acts relating to pilotage in operation on

mercio, Art. 676, 691, 693. As to Belgium, see *The Halley*, L. R. 2 P. C. 193; and, generally, as to foreign law on the subject, see the report of the Pilotage Committee, 1870. In the Suez Canal pilotage is compulsory, but "the responsibility as regards the management of the ship devolves solely on the captain;" see the Regulations of 1st July, 1878.

The Canadian Pilotage Act, 36 Vict. c. 54 (Canada), makes the pay-

ment of pilotage dues compulsory, but expressly provides that no ship need be placed in charge of a pilot (ss. 56, 69); and that nothing in the Act shall be deemed to exempt owners from liability for the fault of a licensed pilot (s. 69).

(*t*) 17 & 18 Vict. c. 104, Part V.; 25 & 26 Vict. c. 63, ss. 40—42; 35 & 36 Vict. c. 73, ss. 9—11; 36 & 37 Vict. c. 85, ss. 19, 20. As to Cinque Port pilots, see the unrepealed sections of 16 & 17 Vict. c. 129.

the 1st of May, 1855. The general Act of that date was 6 George IV. c. 125 (*u*). By the same section of the M. S. Act, 1854 (s. 353), it was provided that all exemptions from compulsory pilotage in force on the 1st of May, 1855, should be continued. It has been held that this provision is general, and that its operation is not restricted by subsequent parts of the same Act which relate exclusively to the London Trinity House (*x*).

The following section (s. 354), however, restricts the operation of s. 353. It imposes compulsory pilotage on all vessels carrying passengers between places situated in the United Kingdom, Jersey, Guernsey, Alderney, Sark, or Man. So far as s. 354 is inconsistent with s. 353, the former section prevails. Pilotage, therefore, is compulsory for vessels carrying passengers between the places mentioned above (*y*), although they were exempt under 6 George IV. c. 125 (*z*).

*Ships carrying passengers between places in the United Kingdom.*

The following decisions illustrate the effect of the above sections. Notwithstanding the words of s. 379 purporting to exempt certain classes of ships in the London Trinity House district, "when not carrying passengers," those ships, if exempt under the Act of George IV., are not required to

---

(*u*) There is some doubt as to how far the Act of Geo. IV. is general, and how far it relates only to the London Trinity House pilotage. The preamble and some of its provisions appear to confine its operation to the London Trinity House pilotage : see *The Eden*, 2 W. Rob. 442 ; *Attorney-General* v. *Case*, 3 Price, 302 ; *The Maria*, 1 W. Rob. 95 ; *Tyne Improvement Commissioners* v. *General Steam Navigation Co.*, L. R. 2 Q. B. 65 ; but in *The Killarney*, Lush. 427, it was held to apply to Hull pilotage ; and some of its sections appear to be of general operation : see *Beilby* v. *Scott*, 7 M. & W. 93 ; *Carruthers* v. *Sidebotham*, 4 M. & S. 77 ; *The Hankow*, 40

L. T. N. S. 335.

(*x*) See *infra*, p. 126.

(*y*) A vessel must have at least one passenger on board to come within the operation of s. 354 : *The Hanna*, L. R. 1 A. & E. 283 ; *The Lion*, L. R. 2 A. & E. 102 ; on app. *ib.* 2 P. C. 525. The marginal note to s. 354 in the M. S. Act, 1854, which describes that section as relating to "home trade passenger ships," seems incorrect ; see s. 2 of the same Act.

(*z*) *The Temora*, Lush. 17. *The Queen of the Bay, Mumford* v. *Crocker*, Ship. Gazette, 14th June, 1878, seems inconsistent with *The Temora*.

take pilots, though carrying passengers, unless they are
plying between places in the United Kingdom or the
islands mentioned above. Thus a vessel on a voyage from
London to the Baltic, with passengers on board, is not
required to take a pilot in the Thames (*a*). But a vessel
navigating within her home port (*b*), an Irish trader in the
Thames (*c*), and a coaster (*d*) (some, if not all, of which were
exempt by the Act of George IV.), must take a pilot if
carrying passengers.

*The Marmion*, a steam-ship with passengers on board,
on a voyage from Leith to London, was in collision, by her
own fault, in the Thames above Gravesend, within the
port of London. Her master had a pilotage certificate
from Orfordness to Gravesend. At the time of the collision the ship was in charge of a Trinity pilot. The defence
of compulsory pilotage being set up, it was contended that
the ship was exempt as being a coaster within 16 George
IV. c. 125, s. 59. It was held that she was not exempt;
and that, being in charge of a compulsory pilot, her
owners were not liable (*e*).

*The Hankow*, a steam-ship with passengers on board,
and belonging to the port of London, on her voyage from
Australia to London, was in collision in the port of London,
whilst in charge of a Trinity river pilot taken on board at
Gravesend. It was held that pilotage was compulsory, and
that her owners were not liable (*f*). The Charter of James

(*a*) *Reg.* v. *Stanton*, 8 Ell. & B.
445 ; and see *The Earl of Aukland*,
Lush. 164 ; *The Moselle*, 32 L.
T. N. S. 570.
(*b*) *Dublin Port and Docks Board*
v. *Shannon*, Ir. Rep. 7 C. L. 116 ;
21 W. R. Dig. 233. There is some
doubt whether the Act of 6 Geo. IV.
c. 125, applied to Ireland : see *The
Eden*, 2 W. Rob. 442.
(*c*) *The Temora*, Lush. 17.
(*d*) *The Marmion, London Steam
Navigation Co.* v. *London and Edinburgh Ship. Co.*, Mitch. Mer. Reg.,
1st June, 1877.

(*c*) *The Marmion, ubi supra.*
(*f*) 40 L. T. N. S. 335. The
learned judge considered that the
case was governed by *The Killarney*,
Lush. 202, and that *The Stettin*, Br.
and Lush. 199, was not to be followed. The question as to the construction of the Act of Geo. IV. was
decided in accordance with *The
Stettin, ubi supra*, in *The General
Steam Navigation Co.* v. *The British
and Colonial Steam Navigation Co.*,
L. R. 3 Ex. 330 ; on app. *ibid.* 4
Ex. 238 (see *supra*, p. 104).

II. to the London Trinity House being produced to the Court, it was held that the port of London was a place for which "particular provision" as to pilotage had been made, within the meaning of 6 George IV. c. 125, s. 59; and, consequently, that there was no exemption from liability.

Pilotage is not compulsory for ships in distress, ships unable to obtain a qualified pilot, ships docking or changing moorings in port (*g*), or foreign ships under sixty tons, exempted by order in Council under 4 George IV. c. 77, s. 5, or 6 George IV. c. 125, s. 60. General exemptions from compulsory pilotage.

Another general exemption from compulsory pilotage is created by 25 & 26 Vict. c. 63, s. 41, which is as follows:—

"The masters and owners of ships passing through the limits of any pilotage district in the United Kingdom on their voyages between two places both situate out of such districts shall be exempted from any obligation to employ a pilot within such district, or to pay pilotage rates when not employing a pilot within such district: provided that the exemption contained in this section shall not apply to ships loading or discharging at any place situate within such district, or any place situate above such district, on the same river, or its tributaries" (*h*).

It is not clear whether a vessel arriving from abroad and calling at a place in the United Kingdom for orders would be exempt under this section. It would, probably, be held that she is not exempt. And (probably) the section does not apply so as to exempt ships, with passengers on board, plying between places in the United Kingdom or Channel Islands (*i*).

Ships, of which the master or mate has a pilotage certificate, are exempt (*k*).

(*g*) 17 & 18 Vict. c. 104, s. 362; as to this exemption, see *The Victoria*, Ir. Rep. 1 Eq. 336 ; and as to a similar exemption under the Act of Geo. IV., *McIntosh* v. *Slade*, 6 B. & C. 657.

(*h*) An exemption similar to this

is in force within the London Trinity House districts under a bye-law approved by Order in Council of 18th February, 1854, *infra*, p. 127.

(*i*) See *supra*, p. 119.

(*k*) 17 & 18 Vict. c. 104, ss. 340—344, 355. As to these certificates,

The policy of the law, which seems formerly to have inclined towards compulsory pilotage for the supposed benefit of commerce and safety of seamen's lives (*m*), is now in favour of restricting compulsory pilotage within as narrow limits as possible. The Acts of 1854 and 1862 enable pilotage authorities to make bye-laws to regulate pilotage, and to exempt ships. It has been held that, under these powers, pilotage can, in no case, be made compulsory for ships which were exempt at the time of the passing of the Act of 1854 (*n*).

*Places at which compulsory pilotage exists.*

The places at which, and the Acts, bye-laws, and Orders in Council, under which compulsory pilotage exists at various ports in the United Kingdom are as follows:—

*Aberavon :* See *Port Talbot.*

*Aberdeen :* Pilotage is compulsory for inward bound vessels; 31 & 32 Vict. c. 138 (Local), ss. 135, *seq.;* for bye-laws see Parl. Pap. No. 232 of 1873; Ord. in Council of 25th June, 1872.

*Aberdovey:* See *London Trinity House.*

*Arundel :* Pilotage is compulsory for all vessels of 30 tons and upwards; 33 Geo. III. c. 100 (Local); for bye-laws see Parl. Pap. No. 269 of 1877.

*Ayr :* Pilotage is compulsory for vessels inward and outward bound; 18 & 19 Vict. c. 119 (Local), s. 51; except vessels under 40 tons; see Parl. Pap. No. 408 of 1867; for bye-laws see Parl. Pap. No. 408 of 1867.

*Ballina :* Pilotage is compulsory for inward bound vessels; 23 & 24 Vict. c. 165 (Local), ss. 42, 43.

*Beaumaris :* See *London Trinity House.*

*Belfast :* Pilotage is compulsory for vessels inwards and outwards, except ships in ballast and ships coming in from stress of weather and whilst within the limits of the out-pilot ground;

<hr/>

see *The Killarney*, Lush. 202 ; *The Beta*, 2 Mar. Law Cas. O. S. 165 ; *The Earl of Aukland*, Lush. 164 ; on app. *ib.* 387.

(*m*) *Lucey v. Ingram*, 6 M. & W.

302 ; *The Fama*, 2 W. Rob. 184.

(*n*) Cf. *The Earl of Aukland*, Lush. 164 ; *Reg. v. Stanton*, 8 E.&B. 445 ; 25 & 26 Vict. c. 63, s. 40.

10 & 11 Vict. c. 52 (Local), ss. 98—106; for bye-laws see Parl.
Pap. No. 408 of 1867 (*o*).

*Blakeney* or *Cley:* Pilotage is compulsory for all vessels,
except coasters of 50 tons and upwards, entering or leaving the
harbour; 57 Geo. III. c. 70 (Local); for bye-laws see Parl.
Paper, No. 268 of 1879.

*Boston:* Pilotage is compulsory inwards and outwards for
vessels over 30 tons; 16 Geo. III. c. 23 (Local); for bye-laws
see Parl. Paper, No. 268 of 1879; see also 32 Geo. III. c. 79
(Local).

*Bridgwater:* See *London Trinity House.*

*Bristol:* Pilotage is compulsory for all vessels navigating the
Bristol Channel eastward of Lundy Island, except coasters, Irish
traders, and vessels bound to or from Cardiff, Newport, or
Gloucester; 47 Geo. III. (Sess. 2) c. 33 (Local), ss. 9—27; 24
& 25 Vict. c. 236 (Local), s. 4; for bye-laws see Parl. Papers,
No. 408 of 1867, and No. 268 of 1879; Order in Council of
19th July, 1862.

*Caernarvon, Carlisle:* See *London Trinity House.*

*Chester:* Pilotage is compulsory for inward bound vessels,
except coasters and Irish traders; 16 Geo. III. c. 61 (Local);
for bye-laws see Parl. Papers, No. 276 of 1875, and No. 268 of
1879.

*Clyde:* See *Glasgow.*

*Colchester,* and *Dartmouth:* See *London Trinity House.*

*Drogheda:* Pilotage is compulsory inwards and outwards for
all vessels except steam-ships; 5 Vict. Sess. 2, c. 56 (Local), ss.
200—205; and vessels under 30 tons; see bye-laws, Parl.
Paper, No. 268 of 1879.

*Dublin:* Pilotage is compulsory for all vessels inwards and
outwards of the port of Dublin or the harbour of Kingstown,
except coasters under 50 tons, vessels in ballast, and coasters
laden with fish in bulk, or potatoes; 32 & 33 Vict. c. 100
(Local), ss. 20, *seq.;* for bye-laws see Parl. Paper, No. 292 of
1876.

_____

(*o*) *The De Brus,* Ir. Rep. A. 1 Eq. 72; *The Arbutus,* 2 Mar. Law Cas.
O. S. 136.

*Dundalk :* Pilotage is compulsory for all vessels, in and out, except vessels under 30 tons, and vessels coming in from stress of weather; 18 & 19 Vict. c. 189 (Local), ss. 91, *seq.*

*Elgin :* See *Lossiemouth.*

*Exeter, Falmouth, Fleetwood,* and *Fowey :* See *London Trinity House.*

*Fraserburgh :* Pilotage is compulsory for all vessels inward bound; 2 & 3 Vict. c. 65 (Local), s. 82 ; for bye-laws see Parl. Paper, No. 232 of 1873.

*Gainsborough :* See *Kingston-upon-Hull.*

*Galway :* Pilotage is compulsory inwards and outwards from the roadstead to the docks for all vessels of and over 50 tons, and vessels coming in from stress of weather or contrary winds; 16 & 17 Vict. c. 207 (Local), ss. 62, *seq. ;* and see 23 & 24 Vict. c. 202 (Local).

*Glasgow :* Pilotage is regulated in the Clyde by 21 & 22 Vict. c. 149 (Local), s. 134, *seq.* It is compulsory for vessels over 60 tons navigating the Clyde between Hutchinsontown Bridge and a straight line drawn from the east end of Newark Castle to Cardross Burn, except vessels under 100 tons in tow of a tug whose master has a pilotage certificate ; see Order in Council of 12th September, 1863. The bye-laws are in Parl. Papers, No. 408 of 1867, and No. 268 of 1879.

*Goole :* See *Kingston-upon-Hull.*

*Greenock :* See *Glasgow.*

*Grimsby :* See *Kingston-upon-Hull,* and 12 & 13 Vict. c. 81 (Local).

*Harwich,* and *Holyhead :* See *London Trinity House.*

*Hull,* and *Humber :* See *Kingston-upon-Hull.*

*Ipswich,* and *Isle of Wight :* See *London Trinity House.*

*King's Lynn :* Pilotage is compulsory in and out for all vessels, except vessels under 30 tons ; 13 Geo. III. c. 30 (Local); and except vessels arriving within the Marsh Cut banks without falling in with a pilot ; for bye-laws see Parl. Paper, No. 204 of 1874, and Orders in Council of 1st March, 1864 ; 14th April, 1869 ; 21st February, 1874 ; and 26th March, 1878.

*Kingston-upon-Hull, Trinity House of :* The Trinity House of Hull was incorporated by charters of 23rd Elizabeth and 13th

Charles II. (*p*). Its jurisdiction (*q*) includes the river Humber, Hull, Goole, Selby, Grimsby, Gainsborough, Spalding, and Wisbeach. It is now regulated by 2 & 3 Will. IV. c. 105 (Local). Under that Act pilotage, outwards and inwards, is compulsory for all vessels except British coasters, British vessels drawing less than 6 feet of water, vessels putting in for shelter or provisions, and vessels under 100 tons drawing 10 feet, or less than 10 feet, of water and navigating between Goole and Hull Roads; see bye-law approved by Order in Council of 20th November, 1873; Parl. Papers, No. 204 of 1874, and No. 408 of 1867. See also for other bye-laws Parl. Papers, No. 178 of 1869, and No. 232 of 1873; and Orders in Council of 31st July (Gazette, 13th August), 1858, 11th January, 1859, 12th September, 1863, 10th May, 1872, and (as to Spalding) 25th June, 1857.

It has been held that under the Local Act (ss. 22, 89) pilotage is not compulsory for a vessel being towed from one part of the port of Hull to another (*r*).

In *The Killarney* (*s*) it was held that pilotage is compulsory for a Goole vessel inward bound to Goole. The compulsion is by virtue of 17 & 18 Vict. c. 104, s. 353, which continues 6 Geo. IV. c. 125, by which (s. 58) pilotage is compulsory in licensed waters, except (s. 59) (amongst other exceptions) where a ship is in her home port, being a port for which no "particular provision" as to pilotage had been made by Act or charter. The exception of s. 59 does not include Hull, for which provision was made by 52 Geo. III. c. 39.

Pilotage certificates are granted to the masters of foreign ships by the Trinity House of Hull (*t*).

By the original charters the Hull Trinity House was enabled to grant licenses to pilot vessels outward bound only. It was doubted by Dr. Lushington, in *The Killarney*, whether the

(*p*) See *The Killarney*, Lush. 427, 436.
(*q*) For the limits of the jurisdiction, see *The Killarney*, *ubi supra*; *Beilby* v. *Raper*, 3 B. & Ad. 284; *Dock Company of Hull* v. *Browne*, 2 B. & Ad. 43.
(*r*) *The Maria*, L. R. 1 A. & E.
358.
(*s*) Lush. 427. It seems, however, doubtful whether 6 Geo. IV. c. 125, ss. 58, 59, applies to Hull pilotage; see *supra*, p. 119, note (*u*).
(*t*) Report of Pilotage Committee, 1870, p. 24.

charters were valid to make pilotage compulsory under penalty, although they purported to do so. But by 52 Geo. III. c. 39, s. 21, provision was made for granting licenses for piloting vessels bound inwards.

*Kirkcaldy :* Pilotage is compulsory for vessels inward bound under 12 & 13 Vict. c. 30 (Local), s. 31.

*Lancaster :* Pilotage is compulsory in and out, 47 Geo. III. sess. 2, c. 37 (Local) ; for bye-laws see Parl. Pap. No. 408, of 1867.

*Littlehampton :* See *Arundel.*

*Liverpool :* Pilotage is compulsory inwards and outwards, except for coasting vessels in ballast, coasting vessels under 100 tons, and, perhaps, coasting steam-ships outward bound (*u*), 21 & 22 Vict. c. 92 (Local); for bye-laws see Parl. Pap. No. 408, of 1867, and Orders in Council of 9th May, 1866, and 30th Jan. 1854 (*v*). As to the meaning of "coasting vessels," see bye-law No. 148. The effect of the Act appears to be that vessels under 100 tons, not being coasters, are not exempt ; see ss. 130—141.

*London :* The principal pilotage authority in the United Kingdom is the London Trinity House, or the Trinity House of Deptford Strond. Its jurisdiction includes three districts, or classes of districts (*x*). They are—(1) The London District, extending from Orfordness, on the north, to Dungeness, on the south, and comprising the Thames and Medway up to London and Rochester Bridges ; (2) The English Channel District, extending from Dungeness to the Isle of Wight ; (3) The Trinity Outport Districts, comprising any pilotage district for the appointment of pilots within which no particular provision is made by any Act of Parliament or charter (*x*).

At Bridgwater, Ipswich, and Neath, the London Trinity House

---

(*u*) This exemption is not expressly repealed by the Local Act, and seems to be still in force under 17 & 18 Vict. c. 104, s. 353.

(*v*) For decisions under the Liverpool Act, see *The Princeton,* 3 P. D. 90 ; *The City of Cambridge,* L. R. 4 A. & E. 161 ; on app. *ib.* 5 P. C. 451 ; *The Ocean Wave,* L. R. 3 P. C. 205 ; *The Annapolis* and *The Johanna*

*Stoll,* Lush. 295 ; and under the former Liverpool Act, *Carruthers* v. *Sidebotham,* 4 M. & S. 77 ; *Attorney-General* v. *Case,* 3 Price 302 ; *Rodriguez* v. *Melhuish,* 10 Ex. 110 ; *The Northampton,* 1 Sp. E. & A. 152 ; *The Agricola,* 2 W. Rob. 10.

(*x*) See 17 & 18 Vict. c. 104, s. 370.

is the pilotage authority, and compulsory pilotage is established by special Acts (*y*). Between Orfordness and the Nore the jurisdiction of the London Trinity House is exclusive. The Leith Trinity House, notwithstanding the terms of its charter, and of 1 Geo. IV. c. 37, has no authority to grant pilotage licenses for that district (*z*).

The bye-laws of the London Trinity House are set out in Parl. Paper, No. 260 of 1872.

The names of the Trinity Outport Districts are : Aberdovey, Beaumaris, Bridgwater (*a*), Bridport, Caernarvon, Carlisle, Colchester, Dartmouth (*b*), Exeter (*c*), Falmouth (*d*), Fleetwood and Barrow, Fowey, Harwich, Holyhead, Ipswich (*e*), Isle of Wight, Maldon, Milford, Neath (*f*), Newhaven, Padstow, Penzance, Plymouth, Poole, Portmadoc, Rochester, Rye, St. Ives (Hayle), Scilly, Shoreham, Southampton, Teignmouth, Wells, Weymouth (*g*), Woodbridge, and Yarmouth. Their limits are defined in Parliamentary Paper, No. 516 of 1854—5. The production of evidence that the Trinity House was accustomed to license pilots for the district at and previous to the passing of 17 & 18 Vict. c. 104 is sufficient proof that the district is an outport district within s. 370 of the same Act (*h*).

Orders in Council approving bye-laws of the London Trinity House, by which various classes of ships are exempt from compulsory pilotage, and providing for the granting of pilotage certificates to masters and mates, are of the following dates : 18th Feb. 1854 ; 1st May, 1855 ; 21st Nov. 1855 ; two of the 16th July, 1857 ; 25th July, 1861 ; 21st Dec. 1871 ; two of 5th Feb. 1873 ; and 20th Nov. 1873.

In the London District and the Outport Districts, pilotage is expressly made compulsory by 17 & 18 Vict. c. 104, s. 376. In the English Channel District, it is free. There are, however,

---

(*y*) These Acts are specified in connection with the places to which they belong.

(*z*) *Hossack* v. *Gray*, 12 L. T. N. S. 701.

(*a*) See Ord. in Council of 17th May, 1867 ; 8 & 9 Vict. c. 89 (Local).

(*b*) See Ord. in Council of 12th Aug. 1859.

(*c*) See Ord. in Council of 4th

Nov. 1857.

(*d*) See *The Juno*, 1 P. D. 135.

(*e*) 15 Vict. c. 116 (Local), under which coasters under 50 tons are exempt; and see *Hadgraft* v. *Hewith*, L. R. 10 Q. B. 359.

(*f*) 6 & 7 Vict. c. 71 (Local).

(*g*) See Ord. in Council of 6th June, 1859.

(*h*) *The Juno*, 1 P. D. 135.

large classes of ships for which pilotage is free in the compulsory districts. Besides the ships free under the general exemptions mentioned above, the following are exempt in all the London Trinity House Districts:—Foreign ships coming up the Thames by the south channels, on their inward voyage from the Cattegat or White Sea, or any place in or between them; British ships on like voyages, inwards or outwards, and whether using the north or south channels of the Thames; ships trading to or from ports between Boulogne (inclusive) and the Baltic, but, as to foreign ships inward bound, only if entering the Thames by the south channels; ships passing through any pilotage district, except, it seems, when carrying passengers between places situated in the United Kingdom, Jersey, Guernsey, Alderney, Sark, or Man; ships sailing from Dover, Deal, or the Isle of Thanet, up or down the Thames or Medway or into or out of any place within the jurisdiction of the Cinque Ports, and owned wholly or in part by master or mate residing in Dover, Deal, or the Isle of Thanet. All these are exempt under 17 & 18 Vict. c. 104, s. 353, which continues 6 Geo. IV. c. 125, ss. 59, 62, and an Order in Council of the 18th of Feb., 1854 (*k*).

The following ships are also exempt when not carrying passengers (*l*) between places in the United Kingdom or the islands mentioned above: (A) coasters, ships of and under 60 tons, stone ships from the Channel Islands, ships navigating within their home ports; (B) ships in ballast, on a voyage between places in the United Kingdom; (C) ships trading between Great Britain, the Channel Islands, or the Isle of Man, and any place in Europe north of the Baltic, or between Brest (inclusive) and Boulogne; (D) ships passing through the limits of any pilotage district, not being bound to any place in such district, or anchoring therein (*m*).

---

(*k*) See *Reg.* v. *Stanton*, 8 E. & B. 445; *The Earl of Aukland*, Lush. 164; *The Moselle*, 2 Asp. Mar. Law Cas. 586; *The Wesley*, Lush. 268; *The Hanna*, L. R. 1 A. & E. 283. The last case establishes the distinction, stated in the text, between British and foreign ships. As to 24 & 25 Vict. c. 47, see *infra*, p. 131, note (*e*). As to the last class

of ships mentioned in the text, see *Williams* v. *Newton*, 14 M. & W. 747; *Peake* v. *Scrutch*, 7 Q. B. 603. The Act 16 & 17 Vict. c. 129 does not appear to have repealed 6 Geo. IV. c. 125, s. 62.

(*l*) *The Temora*, Lush. 17.

(*m*) As to (A), see 17 & 18 Vict. c. 104, s. 379. As to coasters, see *The Sea Queen* or *The Lloyds*, Lush.

*Londonderry :* Pilotage is compulsory on all vessels, inwards and outwards, except vessels of and under 60 tons in ballast; 48 Geo. III. c. 136 (Local), s. 23 ; 17 & 18 Vict. c. 177 (Local), ss. 68, *seq.* ; for bye-laws see Parl. Paper, No. 408 of 1867.

*Lossiemouth :* Pilotage is compulsory inwards and outwards for all vessels over 40 tons ; 19 & 20 Vict. c. 67 (Local), s. 57 ; 31 & 32 Vict. c. 47 (Local).

*Lowestoft, Maldon, Milford, Neath, Newhaven, Padstock,* and *Penzance :* See *London Trinity House.*

*Newcastle :* See *infra,* p. 131, as to foreign ships.

*Peterhead :* Pilotage is compulsory under 36 & 37 Vict. c. 157 (Local), ss. 77, *seq.,* for all vessels of 30 tons and upwards, bound in and out, except steam-tugs for the use of vessels frequenting the harbour.

*Plymouth,* and *Poole :* See *London Trinity House.*

*Port Talbot* (formerly *Aberavon*) : Pilotage is compulsory under 4 Will. IV. c. 43 (Local), s. 73, on all vessels inwards and outwards (*n*).

*Portmadoc, Rye, Scilly,* and *Shoreham :* See *London Trinity House.*

*Pulteney :* Pilotage is compulsory for vessels over 40 tons in and out ; 20 & 21 Vict. c. 93 (Local), s. 52, 54. See also *Wick.*

*Sligo :* Pilotage is compulsory for inward bound ships of 20 tons and upwards, except vessels reaching Oyster Island without being boarded ; 40 Vict. c. 35 (Local).

*Spalding :* See *Kingston-upon-Hull.*

*Swansea :* Pilotage is compulsory for vessels of 100 tons and upwards bound in or out ; 17 & 18 Vict. c. 126 (Local) ; for bye-laws see Parl. Pap. No. 178 of 1871 ; and Orders in

197 ; *The Agricola,* 2 W. Rob. 10. As to ships within their home port, where the port is London, *The Stettin,* Br. & Lush.199, and *General Steam Nav. Co. v. British & Colonial Steam Nav. Co.,* L. R. 3 Ex. 330 ; *ibid.* 4 Ex. 238, are in conflict with *The Hankow,* 40 L. T. N. S. 335. It is submitted that the decisions in the earlier of these cases are correct. See also, as to ships in their home

port, *The Killarney,* Lush. 427. As to the class (B), see Orders in Council of 21st Nov. 1855, and 25th July, 1861. As to (C), Order in Council of 21st Dec. 1871. As to (D), Order in Council of 18th Feb. 1854, and 17 & 18 Vict. c. 104, s. 379.

(*n*) From the Board of Trade returns it does not appear that any pilots are licensed under this Act.

Council of 22nd Feb. 1860, 4th Feb. 1861, and 7th Jan.
1864.

*Southampton :* See *London Trinity House.*

*Southwold :* Pilotage is compulsory, inwards and outwards, for
vessels of 40 tons and upwards ; 11 Geo. IV. c. 48 (Local) ; for
bye-laws see Parl. Pap. No. 204 of 1874.

*St. Ives (Hayle), Teignmouth, Thames,* and *Wells :* See *London
Trinity House.*

*Waterford :* Pilotage is compulsory in and out; 9 & 10 Vict.
c. 292 (Local) ; 37 & 38 Vict. c. 116, ss. 12, *seq.,* except for
vessels drawing less than 6 feet; for bye-laws see Parl. Pap.
No. 178 of 1871 (*a*).

*Westport :* Pilotage is compulsory for all vessels, in or out,
except within the limits of the out pilot grounds, or when
the master is licensed ; 16 & 17 Vict. c. 185 (Local), ss. 23,
*seq.*

*Wexford :* Pilotage is compulsory for all vessels, in or out,
with cargo or passengers ; 37 & 38 Vict. c. 40 (Local), ss. 73,
*seq. ;* see also 25 & 26 Vict. c. 122 (Local), and bye-laws
approved by Ord. in Council, 26th Oct. 1875.

*Weymouth :* See *London Trinity House.*

*Wick :* Pilotage is compulsory for vessels over 20 tons, entering
and leaving the harbour, except frequent traders whose masters
or mates have pilotage certificates (*b*) ; 25 & 26 Vict. c. 180
(Local), ss. 10, 22, 23, 24 ; see also 20 & 21 Vict. c. 93.

*Wicklow :* Pilotage is compulsory in and out, except for
steamships in certain cases; 5 & 6 Vict. c. 111 (Local), ss. 134,
*seq. ;* and see 14 & 15 Vict. c. 121 (Local).

*Wisbeach :* See *Kingston-upon-Hull ;* and see 50 Geo. III.
c. 206 (Local).

*Woodbridge, Yarmouth :* See *London Trinity House.*

Places at
which bye-
laws are in
existence
purporting to
make pilotage
compulsory.
At *Aberbrothwick* or *Arbroath, Irvine, Limerick, Llanelly,
Macduff, New Ross, Newry,* and *Tralee,* it is not clear whether
compulsory pilotage exists, or not.　In some cases bye-laws
purporting to make it compulsory have been made.　The Acts
have been made the local Acts ; but their language is not clear.

(*a*) As to Waterford, see *The
Victoria,* Ir. Rep. A. 1 Eq. 336.

(*b*) This seems to be the effect of

by which the pilotage authorities at these places are regulated are as follows :—

*Aberbrothwick*, or *Arbroath :* 2 & 3 Vict. c. 16 (Local); for bye-laws see Parl. Pap. No. 204 of 1874 ; *Irvine :* 7 Geo. IV. c. 107 (Local) ; see Parl. Pap. No. 232 of 1873 for bye-laws ; *Limerick :* 4 Geo. IV. c. 94 (Local), and Parl. Pap. No. 266 of 1878 ; *Llanelly :* 6 & 7 Vict. c. 88 (Local), 27 & 28 Vict. c. 203 (Local), Parl. Pap. No. 25 of 1868 and No. 88 of 1870; *Macduff :* 10 & 11 Vict. c. 127 (Local) ; *New Ross :* 24 & 25 Vict. c. 140 (Local) ; *Newry :* 10 Geo. IV. c. 126 (Local) ; *Tralee :* 9 Geo. IV. c. 118 (Local).

Pilotage authorities exist at the following places, but at all Places which pilotage is free. of them, except for foreign ships in the Newcastle Trinity House jurisdiction, pilotage is free. The Pilotage Acts are as follows :—

*Berwick :* 48 Geo. III. c. 104 (Local); 25 Vict. c. 31 (Local) ; *Buckie* (Cluny): 37 & 38 Vict. c. 185 (Local) ; *Cardiff,* including *Penarth :* 24 & 25 Vict. c. 236 (Local) ; *Carlingford Lough :* 27 & 28 Vict. c. 93, Ord. in Council of 16th May, 1878 ; *Cork* (c): 1 Geo. IV. c. 52 (Local), and see Parl. Papers, No. 408 of 1867 and No. 232 of 1873 ; *Douglas* (Isle of Man): 35 & 36 Vict. c. 23 ; *Dundee :* 38 & 39 Vict. c. 150 (Local) ; *Eyemouth :* 37 & 38 Vict. c. 185 (Local) ; *Gardenstown :* 39 & 40 Vict. c. 40 (Local) ; *Gloucester :* 24 & 25 Vict. c. 236 (Local); *Hartlepool :* 27 & 28 Vict. c. 58 ; *Hastings :* 25 & 26 Vict. c. 51 ; *Leith Harbour and Docks :* 28 Geo. III. c. 58 (Local) ; 38 & 39 Vict. c. 160 (Local), Ord. in Council of 30th June, 1860 ; *Leith Trinity House* (d): 1 Geo. IV. c. 37 ; *Newcastle-upon-Tyne :* the jurisdiction of the Newcastle Trinity House includes *Middlesbrough, Blyth, Seaham, Holy Island, Whitby, Warkworth Amble* and *North Sunderland.* Under 41 Geo. III. c. 86 (Local), pilotage is compulsory for foreign ships. It seems that it is now free, differential dues having been abolished by 24 & 25 Vict. c. 47 (e). The Tyne Pilotage Commissioners are

(c) See *The Eden,* 2 W. Rob. 442.
(d) The Leith Trinity House was incorporated by charter of 27th July, 1797. As to the limits of its jurisdiction, see *Hossack* v. *Gray,* 12 L. T. N. S. 701.

(e) It was held in *The Hanna,* L. R. 1 A. & E. 283, that compulsory pilotage is not a charge on ships ; and it seems that 24 & 25 Vict. c. 47 does not abolish differential pilotage dues. That Act

K 2

tho pilotago authority in tho Tyno : 28 & 29 Vict. c. 44 ; see Orders in Council of 19th July, 1862, and 5th February, 1872 ; *Newport* (Monmouth): 24 & 25 Vict. c. 236 (Local) ; *Penarth :* see *Cardiff ; Portcawl :* 18 Vict. c. 50 (Local), Parl. Pap. No. 268 of 1879, and Ord. in Council of 6th May, 1857 ; *Rosehearty :* 26 & 27 Vict. c. 104 ; *Sandhaven :* 36 & 37 Vict. c. 63 (Local), Ord. in Council of 20th March, 1877 ; *Sunderland, North :* 28 & 29 Vict. c. 59 (Local) ; and see *Newcastle.*

was not before the Court in *The Hanna.* The following cases have been decided under the Newcastle Pilotage Acts: *Dodds* v. *Embleton,* 9 D. & R. 27; *Tyne Improvement Commissioners* v. *General Steam Nav. Co.,* L. R. 2 Q. B. 65.

# CHAPTER VI.

### THE REGULATIONS FOR PREVENTING COLLISIONS.

MANY years before the Rule of the Road at sea was Legislation as
to the Rule of
regulated by Act of Parliament, the practice of seamen the Road.
had established rules to enable approaching ships to keep
clear of each other (*a*). These rules, which are the foun-
dation of those now in force, were well established by custom,
and formed part of the general maritime law administered
by the Admiralty Court. In the year 1840 a rule as to
the side on which steam-ships were to pass each other was
promulgated by the London Trinity House, and enforced
by the Admiralty Court. In 1846 the subject was first
dealt with by the Legislature, and since that year the law
has been altered or added to (*b*) by three successive Acts
of Parliament. The only Act now in force is 25 & 26 Vict.
c. 63.

By that Act power is given to Her Majesty, on the joint Enactment of
the existing
recommendation of the Admiralty and the Board of Trade, Regulations.
to make regulations for preventing collisions. Under this
power the Regulations in force at the present date (January,
1880) were made by Orders in Council of 9th January,
1863, and 30th July, 1868. Other Regulations coming
into force on the 1st of September, 1880, in substitution

---

(*a*) A Rule of the Road for ships
on opposite tacks existed in the
Navy at least as early as the latter
part of the last century. It was to
the effect that the ships on the larboard tack should bear up for those
on the starboard tack. This rule

appears in Admiralty Regulations of
the above-mentioned period.

(*b*) As several cases decided under
former Acts are referred to in this
and other chapters, the repealed
Acts as to the Rule of the Road are
set out in the Appendix; *infra*, p. 241.

134  THE REGULATIONS FOR PREVENTING COLLISIONS.

for those of 1863, were made by Order in Council of 14th
August, 1879 (c).

**In what waters they apply.** The Regulations are headed "for preventing collisions
*at sea*," and appear to be expressly binding only on ships
at sea (d). But, except in waters where local rules are in
force, it would probably be held that vessels are required
to navigate in accordance with them in rivers and harbours,
as well as at sea. Many cases have been decided upon
the assumption that they apply in rivers (e). The words
of Article 25 of the new Regulations seem to imply that,
except in the cases mentioned in that article, they apply
everywhere. On the sea, everywhere, except where local rules
apply, they are directly applicable (f). Their application in
winding rivers and in waters where local rules are in force
is considered below under Articles 21 and 25.

**To what ships they apply.** The Regulations apply to all ships and craft whose business it is to go to sea, whether large or small, and whether
propelled by oars or not (g). Whether they apply in rivers
and harbours to craft never intended to go to sea, as hulks
and barges, seems doubtful (h). As to their application to
Queen's ships, see Article 26, below.

(c) See the *London Gazette* of 19th
Aug. 1879. These as well as the
Regulations of 1863 are set out in
the Appendix; *infra*, p. 246.
(d) See *per* Brett, L.J., in *The
Franconia*, 2 P. D. 8. The *dictum*
of the Lord Justice, in this case, to
the effect that the Regulations of
1863 are inapplicable in a winding
river, cannot mean that they are
never applicable in such waters. It
must be taken to mean that they
are not always applicable in a winding river to ships in such positions
that they would be bound by them
if at sea. The Admiralty Rules of
1851 as to ships' lights were held to
apply in the Thames; *Morrison* v.
*General St. Nav. Co.*, 8 Ex. 733.
(e) *The Velocity*, L. R. 3 P. C. 44;
*The Cologne & The Ranger, ibid.* 4
P.C. 519; and see *The Fyenoord*,

Swab. Ad. 374. In America the
Act of Congress embodying the
Regulations of 1863 is expressed to
be for preventing collisions "on
water." By the Canadian Statute
31 Vict. c. 58 the Regulations are applicable over all the inland and other
navigable waters of the Dominion.
(f) See *The Saxonia*, Lush. 410,
as to the application of a former
Act to foreign ships in the Solent.
(g) *Ex parte Ferguson & Hutchinson*, L. R. 6 Q. B. 280; and see 25
& 26 Vict. c. 63, ss. 25, 27, and 28,
where the Regulations, including
those for fishing boats, are spoken of
as regulations for *ships*.
(h) Such a hulk was held not to
be a ship within 17 & 18 Vict. c.
104, s. 55; *European, &c., Mail Co.*
v. *P. & O. St. Nav. Co.*, 14 L. T.
N. S. 704.

The Regulations apply to British ships everywhere. To foreign ships within British jurisdiction they apply directly as forming part of the municipal law of the country (*i*). They are also applicable to foreign ships out of British jurisdiction, and, in the case of a collision on the high sea, or in foreign waters, are applied to such ships by British Courts by virtue of a special provision of the Act of 1862. Under that Act Her Majesty has power by Order in Council to direct that the Regulations shall be applied by British Courts to the ships of foreign countries which have adopted them (*k*). The regulations of 1863 were adopted by, and by various Orders in Council have been declared applicable to the ships of, the Argentine Republic, Austria, Belgium, Brazil, Chili, Denmark, France, Germany, Greece, the Hawaian Islands, Hayti, Italy, Morocco, the Netherlands, Norway, Peru, Portugal, the Republic of the Equator, Russia, Spain, Sweden, Turkey, Uruguay, and to the ships of the United States of America, both at sea and on the inland waters of America.

The Regulations of 1880 are, by Order in Council of the 14th of August, 1879, declared applicable to the ships of the above-named countries, except the Argentine Republic, Brazil, Morocco, Peru, the Republic of the Equator, Turkey, and Uruguay.

The Regulations of 1863 form part of the municipal law Their inter-of this country, of many foreign countries (*l*), and also of national character. Canada (*m*). In the United States, it has been held by the Supreme Court that, having been adopted by all maritime nations, they are of universal application, and are part of international or general maritime law (*n*).

---

(*i*) And expressly by 25 & 26 Vict. c. 63, s. 57.

(*k*) See 25 & 26 Vict. c. 63, s. 58.

(*l*) Amongst others, the United States, Act of Congress of 29th Ap. 1864, c. 69 ; France, Décrets of 25th Oct. 1862, 26th May, 1869, and 28th Oct. 1873 ; Germany, Penal Code, art. 145, Reichsgesetzbuch, 127.

(*m*) 31 Vict. c. 58 (Canada).

(*n*) *The Scotia* and *The Berkshire*, 14 Wall. 170. There being no law in the United States corresponding to 25 & 26 Vict. c. 63, s. 58, the

Their international character and the safety of navigation require that they should be understood by the seamen of different nations in the same sense.  It is therefore
of importance that the construction placed upon them by
the Courts of different countries should be uniform.  This
has been distinctly recognised in America.  The following
observations occur in a judgment of a Circuit Court of
the United States : "The paramount importance of having
international rules, which are intended to become part of
the law of nations, understood alike by all maritime powers,
is manifest ; and the adoption of any reasonable construc-
truction of them by the maritime powers named affords
sufficient ground for the adoption of a similar construction
of our statute by the Courts of this country " (o).

They furnish
the rule for
determining
which ship is
in fault, ex-
cept where
special circum-
stances make
them inappli-
cable.

Where no special circumstances exist to make the
Regulations inapplicable, they furnish the paramount rule
for the decision of the question as to which ship is in fault
in every case of collision.  " Public policy, as well as the
best interest of all concerned, requires that they should be
enforced in all cases to which they apply " (p).  Departure
from them is justifiable only in one event ; namely, where
it is necessary in order to avoid immediate danger.  If a
ship cannot take the step required by the Regulations
without going ashore, or endangering herself or other
vessels, the Regulations do not apply ; and in such a case
the question which ship is in fault is tried, without regard
to the Regulations, by the ordinary rules of seamanship.
Provided they are not inconsistent with the Regulations,
the rules or practice of seamen, although they have not the

question arose in this case whether
the Regulations as to lights applied
in the case of a collision between an
American and a British ship on the
high seas.  It was held that they did
apply, and that the American ship
was in fault for having shown a
light other than that required by
the Regulations.

(o) Per Benedict, J., in The

Sylvester Hale, 6 Bened. 523 ; and a
similar opinion was expressed by
the Court in The Free State, Brown
Ad. 251, 261.

(p) New York & Liverpool U.S.
Mail Steamship Co. v. Rumball, 21
How. 372, 383; and see The Byfoged
Christensen, 4 App. Cas. 669, infra,
p. 209.

force of law, are equally binding with the Regulations, and upon British and foreign ships alike (*q*).

The Regulations concerning the manœuvres to be taken to avoid collision are applicable only when ships are approaching each other so as to involve risk of collision. They apply only where there is risk of collision. What constitutes risk of collision so as to make it the duty of each of two approaching vessels to take the steps required by the law, it is difficult to define. "It was What constitutes "risk of collision." utterly impossible for the Legislature to have determined, or described, what should constitute risk of a collision ; for that must always be decided according to the circumstances of each case, by men of nautical experience" (*r*). It has been described as a "chance," a "probability;" a "strong," or a "reasonable" (*s*) probability of collision ; and distinguished from a "possibility" of collision (*t*). In a case under 14 & 15 Vict. c. 79, Dr. Lushington said : "This chance of collision is not to be scanned by a point or two. We have held over and over again that, if there be a reasonable chance of collision, it is quite sufficient . . . We have never got to this, and I hope never shall, that it (the rule) applies where two vessels are sailing properly, and there is no chance of a collision" (*u*).

In another case the same learned judge said : "The whole evidence shows that it was the duty of *The Colonia* with the wind free to have made certain of avoiding *The Susan*. She did not do so, but kept her course till she was at so short a distance of a cable-and-a-half's length in the hope that the vessels might pass each other. Now it never can

(*q*) In the Court of Appeal, and in the Admiralty Division of the High Court, nautical assessors advise the Court upon questions of seamanship. Other Divisions of the High Court may call in assessors if they think fit ; 36 & 37 Vict. c. 66, s. 56 ; but the rules of seamanship may be proved by experts. In Admiralty such evidence is not admissible ; *The Gazelle*, 1 W. Rob. 471.

(*r*) *Per* Dr. Lushington, in *The Mangerton*, Swab. Ad. 120.
(*s*) *The Cleopatra, ibid.* 135 ; *The Ericsson, ibid.*, 38 ; *The Duke of Sussex*, 1 W. Rob. 276 ; *The Dumfries*, Swab. Ad. 63, 65 ; with reference to the same expression in 17 & 18 Vict. c. 104, s. 296.
(*t*) *The Ericsson, ubi supra.*
(*u*) *The Sylph*, 2 Sp. E. & A. 75, 82.

be allowed to a vessel to enter into nice calculations of this
kind, which must be attended with some risk, whilst it has
the power to adopt, long before the collision, measures
which would render it impossible " (x).

Again, the same learned judge said as to risk of collision :
" So long as the green light is seen broad on the starboard
bow, there is no danger of collision.   It was never intended
that, when a vessel sees another at the distance of two miles,
she is to begin to change her course because there is a
possibility of collision.   The intention of the statute (17 &
18 Vict. c. 104) is, that when two vessels are approaching
each other, and are within such a distance that there is a
strong probability of a collision if both keep their courses,
in that case," the ships are to take the steps required by
the law (y).

In other cases it seems to have been held that the
measures required by the law must be taken where there
is a possibility of collision, however distant.   In addressing
the jury in a collision case, Pollock, C.B., said : " Whatever
be the distance, if there is any danger of a collision, no
man can be wrong " who takes the steps required by the
law where there is risk of collision (z).

American cases as to the meaning of " risk of collision."   The difficulty of defining the moment at which these
Regulations become applicable has been recognised by the
American Courts (a).   The following passage from a judgment of the Supreme Court of the United States expresses
the general rule as to the time at which and during which
they become and remain applicable :—" Rules of navigation,
such as have been mentioned (as to the duties of two vessels
approaching each other), are obligatory upon such vessels
when approaching each other from the time the necessity
for precaution begins ; and they continue to be applicable
as the vessels advance so long as the means and opportunity

(x)  *The Colonia*, 3 Not. of Cas. 13,
note.
(y)  *The Ericsson*, Swab. Ad. 38.

(z)  *General Steam Nav. Co.* v.
*Mann*, 14 C. B. 127, 132.
(a)  *The Nicholls*, 7 Wall. 656.

to avoid the danger remain. They do not apply to a vessel required to keep her course after the approach is so near that the collision is inevitable, and are equally inapplicable to vessels of every description while they are yet so distant from each other that measures of precaution have not become necessary to avoid a collision " (b).

In *The Milwaukee* (c) it was said by the same Court that where vessels are meeting or passing in a crooked and narrow channel there is always risk of collision.

The distance, rate of sailing, and course of another vessel, and the direction of the wind, are never known exactly. There is often great difficulty in determining the moment at which, and the manner in which, the Regulations are to be applied. In judging of the course and probable movements of a strange vessel, it must be assumed, under ordinary circumstances, that she can, and will, comply with the Regulations (d). Where there is no risk of collision, a vessel that improperly alters her helm so as to bring about a collision will be held to be in fault (e).

If a vessel is disabled, or slow in answering her helm, it is her duty to be prompt in taking the measures required by the Regulations (f).

If a ship sees another in a position that may involve risk of collision, but is unable to make out what course the other is on, she should keep her course, and not alter her

<hr/>

(b) *The Wenona*, 19 Wall. 41, 52. The same or similar words occur in the judgments in *The Nicholls*, 7 Wall. 656 ; *The Johnson*, 9 Wall. 146 ; and *The Dexter*, 23 Wall. 69.

(c) Brown Ad. 313.

(d) *The Jesmond* and *The Earl of Elgin*, L. R. 4 P. C. 1 ; see also *The Free State*, 1 Otto, 200, for a decision of the Supreme Court of the United States to the same effect. An erroneous view seems to have been taken in some American cases, in which it has been held that precautions should be taken, and the helm

altered, before any risk is incurred, if the courses are such that, if continued, there would be risk ; see *The Milwaukee*, Brown, Adm. 313, 331. In the same case, it was held that the chance of the other vessel disobeying the Regulations must be taken into account. This seems clearly wrong.

(e) *The Kezia* and *The Eliza*, Holt, 67 ; *The Dapper* and *The Lady Normanby*, ibid. 79 ; *The Esk* and *The Niord*, L. R. 3 P. C. 436 ; *The Inflexible*, Swab. Ad. 32.

(f) *The Test*, 5 Not. of Cas. 276.

helm, or take any decisive step until she has ascertained the other ship's course (g). "The mere discovery of a strange light does not, necessarily, immediately bind a person in charge of a vessel to follow any particular rule ; but as soon as he has opportunity of ascertaining, by reasonable care and skill, what the strange vessel is, and what course she is pursuing, then the rule which is· applicable to the circumstances at once becomes binding on him " (h).

An alteration of the helm made for greater safety when there is no risk of collision will not be held to be a fault. A sailing-ship (in 1856) seeing a green light from two to four points on her starboard bow, and distant about a mile and a half, put her helm to starboard, and subsequently came into collision with the other ship. It was held that she was not in fault for starboarding (i).

Cases in which there was "risk of col-lision." It has been held that the vessels were approaching " so as to involve risk of collision" in the following cases:—Two steam-ships meeting on nearly opposite courses at a joint speed of eighteen or nineteen knots, and distant a mile and a half (k) ; a steam-ship and a sailing-ship, distant two or three miles, and meeting at a joint speed of seventeen knots, the steam-ship not being able to make out the course of the sailing-ship, but knowing that it was probably nearly opposite to her own (l). Where two sailing-vessels were approaching each other on courses only half a point from being directly opposite, at a joint speed of twelve knots, and distant from each other two or three miles, it was held by the Supreme Court of the United States that there was risk of collision (m).

(g) The Rona and The Ava, 2 Asp. Mar. Law Cas. 182; The James Watt, 2 W. Rob. 270 ; The Moderation, 1 Mar. Law Cas. O. S. 413 ; The Bongainville and The James C. Stevenson, L. R. 5 P. C. 316, 321.
(h) Per Dr. Lushington, The Great Eastern, 2 Mar. Law Cas. O. S. 97.
(i) The Sylph, Swab. Adm. 233.
(k) The Jesmond and The Earl of Elgin, L. R. 4 P. C. 1.
(l) The Bongainville and The Jas. C. Stevenson, L. R. 5 P. C. 316.
(m) The Nicholls, 7 Wall. 656 ; and see The Cayuga, 14 Wall. 270.

When two ships are approaching each other with risk of collision, the Rule of the Road applies once and for all to take them clear. A ship is never required by the Regulations, after having sighted another, to alter her course first to starboard and then to port; or first to keep her course and then to keep out of the way; or *vice versâ*. In the case, for example, of steam-ships meeting end on or nearly so, each is required by Article 15 to alter her course to starboard. If, while under the port-helm, the relative positions and heading of the ships are changed, so that from meeting ships they become crossing ships, the meeting rule (Article 15) does not cease to operate, or give place to the " crossing " rule (Article 16). The manœuvre of porting must be persisted in until the risk of collision is determined. If porting will not take the ships clear, Article 18 or Article 23 may apply, and the engines may be stopped, or any other step taken which is necessary to avert collision; but the ships cannot afterwards, and whilst the risk continues, become crossing ships. If once a ship is within the "meeting" rule, or any other rule requiring her to take or keep a definite course, or requiring her to keep out of the way, she cannot, whilst the risk continues, come within the operation of the " crossing " rule, or any other rule requiring her to adopt a different manœuvre. The object of the Rule of the Road and of the Regulations would be entirely frustrated if it were possible for a ship to be thrown from one rule to another; if, whilst in the act of obeying one article, she were suddenly to come within the operation of another article requiring her, perhaps, to take an exactly opposite course, and so making the previous manœuvre of no effect.

The precautions required by the law to be taken where there is risk of collision must be taken in time to determine that risk (n). An alteration of the helm, or other step

*Marginal notes:* When the "meeting" or "crossing" rule applies, it continues applicable until the risk is determined.

*The Regulations must be complied with promptly and effectually.*

(n) *The Trident,* 1 Sp. E. & A. 217, 222.

taken in pursuance of the Regulations, is no defence, unless
it is shown that such precaution was taken at the proper
time.  To be effectual, precautions must be seasonable.  If
taken at an improper time, they are not a compliance with
the Regulations, and are no defence.  " If you adopt a
measure at an improper time, it does not take away the
culpability of not having done it before and preventing
the accident"(o).

A vessel is not justified in delaying to take precautions
until the last moment; or in trusting to being able to
"shave" clear of the other (p).  If by doing so she frightens
the other into taking a wrong step, and a collision occurs,
she will be responsible for the entire loss (q).  By a prompt
compliance with the Regulations, where a vessel is required
to alter her course to avoid another, she apprises the latter
of her ability and intention to comply with the Regulations,
whereas by delaying to take the required step she may
lead the other vessel to suppose that she is unable to comply
with them, and cause her to take a step which may make
a collision inevitable.  Where a ship, in order to show that
she is free from blame, is required to prove that she altered
her course at the proper time, it is not enough for her to
show that her helm was altered at that time, she must
prove that she answered her helm (r) in time.

Practice of
seamen, or
alleged cus-
tom, incon-
sistent with
the Regula-
tions cannot be
good.

No alleged practice of seamen of avoiding other ships
by taking measures other than, and inconsistent with,
those required by the Regulations is recognized by the law.
A defendant cannot be heard to allege such a practice as
an excuse for a violation of the Regulations (s).  Where a

(o) Per Dr. Lushington in The
Stadacona, 5 Not. of Cas. 371, 374.
The view taken by the Courts of the
United States is the same : The
Johnson, 9 Wall. 146 ; The Vander-
bilt, 6 Wall. 225 ; The Syracuse, 12
Wall. 167 ; The Sunnyside, 1 Otto,
208 ; The America, 2 Otto, 432.
    (p) The John Brotherick, 8 Jur.
276 ; The Benefactor, 14 Blatchf.

254.
    (q) See above, p. 6.
    (r) The La Plata, Swab. Adm.
220.
    (s) The Sylph, 2 Sp. E. & A. 75 ;
The Unity, Swab. Ad. 101 ; The
Hand of Providence, ibid. 107 ; The
Araxes and The Black Prince, 15
Moo. P. C. C. 122 ; The Velocity, L.
C. 3 P. C. 44, 50.

custom was set up that merchant ships should keep out of
the way of Queen's ships coming out of Devonport harbour by the deep water channel, it was held that it was not
binding in law (*t*). So, under former Acts requiring ships
to navigate on the starboard side of a river, it was held
that it was no excuse for a vessel on her wrong side that
she was keeping out of the strength of the tide (*u*).

Wilful infringement of the Regulations by a master or
owner is a misdemeanour punishable by fine or imprisonment. In case of damage arising from such infringement,
the person in charge of the deck is liable to these penalties,
unless it is proved that departure from the Regulations
was necessary (*v*). And although the master, or person in
charge of the ship, is liable criminally, the owner is answerable civilly for damage caused by his officer's negligence (*x*).

Consequences<br>of infringing<br>the Regula-<br>tions.

The penalties attached to non-observance of the Regulations by the enactments which require the Court to hold
a vessel infringing them in fault for the collision have
been considered in a former chapter (*y*).

---

## THE REGULATIONS.

The Regula-<br>tions of 1880.

The following are the Regulations coming into force
upon the 1st of September, 1880. They are, in substance,
the same as those in force at the present date (January,
1880). There are, however, some differences which are noted
in the text below. The Regulations of 1863, as well as

(*t*) *The Promise* and *H.M.S. Topaz,*
2 Mar. Law Cas. O. S. 38.

(*u*) See below, p. 195.

(*v*) 25 & 26 Vict. c. 63, ss. 27 and
28 ; 17 & 18 Vict. c. 104, s. 513. As
to the meaning of "master" and
"owner," see s. 2 and s. 100 of the
Act of 1854. As to whether an infringement of local regulations is
within the penalty of these Acts,

see *The Lady Downshire*, 4 P. D.
26 ; *The Swansea* and *The Condor*,
4 P. D. 115 ; *supra*, p. 19.

(*x*) See *Grill* v. *General Iron
Screw Collier Co.*, L. R. 3 C. P. 476,
where it was held that wilful infringement of the Regulations was
not barratry within the meaning of
a bill of lading.

(*y*) *Supra*, pp. 12—20.

those of 1880, are set out at length in the Appendix (z).
The cases cited below in illustration of the Regulations
were, for the most part, decided under the Regulations of
1863, but will, it is submitted, be found to be equally
applicable under the Regulations of 1880.

### ARTICLE 1.

**Art. 1.**

Definitions:
" Sailing-
ship ";
" steam-ship."

*In the following rules, every steam-ship which is under
sail and not under steam is to be considered a sailing-
ship; and every steam-ship which is under steam, whether
under sail or not, is to be considered a ship under steam.*

This Article is identical with Article 1 of the Regulations
of 1863.

" Under
steam ":
Meaning of
the term.

A steam-tug lying-to under sail, with her engines idle
and her fires banked up, is " under steam " within the
meaning of Article 1, and must keep out of the way of a
sailing-ship (a).

### ARTICLE 2.

**Art. 2.**

Lights.

*The lights mentioned in the following Articles, numbered
3, 4, 5, 6, 7, 8, 9, 10, and 11, and no others, shall be carried
in all weathers from sunset to sunrise.*

Importance of
observing the
rules as to
lights.

This Article corresponds with Article 2 of the Regulations
of 1863. The observations of Dr. Lushington in *The Rob
Roy* (b) with regard to the old Admiralty rules as to lights
apply with equal force to the existing Regulations. He said:
" If these regulations of the Admiralty are to be followed

(z) *Infra*, pp. 247—258.
(a) *The Jennie S. Barker* and *The
Spindrift*, 3 Asp. Mar. Law Cas. 42.
*The Sunnyside*, 1 Otto, 208, is a
similar decision by the Supreme
Court of the U. S.
(b) 3 W. Rob. 190, 198. By the
maritime law there was no obligation on a ship to carry a light at
night. It depended upon the darkness of the night and other circumstances, whether a light was necessary or not. *The Victoria*, 3 W.
Rob. 49; *The Iron Duke*, 4 Not. of
Cas. 94; *The Londonderry*, *ibid.*
Suppl. xxxi.

out, and vessels are to be guided by them, it is of the last
importance that those on board steamers should see that
the three lights are burning. For it is perfectly clear that,
unless this precaution is taken, and the three lights are kept
burning, other misfortunes of this nature will most probably
occur." In that case a collision which occurred in consequence of a steamer being misled by the improper lights
of another was held to be caused by the fault of the
latter.

The effect of this Article, when read together with A tug is a
Article 4 and the following Articles, is to place a steam- steam-ship
ship towing another vessel in the same category, generally meaning of
speaking, with other steam-ships; that is to say, the fact tions.
that she is engaged in towing does not exempt her from
the obligations otherwise imposed on her by the Regulations (c).

Notwithstanding the express prohibition contained in Circumstances
this Article against carrying lights other than the Regula- under which a
tion lights, a ship may, and it is her duty to, exhibit such a lights other
light under exceptional circumstances, when it is necessary lation lights.
to warn an approaching ship that does not see her danger.

A ship ashore in a navigable channel (d), or casting off
from her moorings (e), or being overtaken at night by a
vessel that appears not to see her, so that there is risk of
collision, must keep a good look-out astern, and warn the
other ship of her danger. Showing a white or flare-up Showing light
light astern to an overtaking ship is expressly made lawful to overtaking
by a subsequent Article (Article 11) (f).

The Regulation lights should be exhibited in the Lights must
positions required by the law, although there are circum- be carried in
the positions

(c) The American and The Syria, & E. 500.
L. R. 4 A. & E. 226; S. C. on app., (f) See infra, p. 160. Before that
ibid. 6 P. C. 127; The Warrior, L. Article was promulgated, a ship was
R. 3 A. & E. 553. held not to be in fault for showing
(d) The Industrie, L. R. 3 A. & E. one of her side lights over her stern:
303; The Thomas Lea, 3 Asp. Mar. The Anglo Indian, 3 Asp. Mar. Law
Law. Cas. 260. Cas. 1.
(e) The John Fenwick, L. R. 3 A.

Art. 2.

required by
the law.

stances which would make it appear desirable to exhibit them elsewhere. When there is a haze on the water which obscures the riding light at the elevation required by the Regulations, it seems to be doubtful whether a ship is, for that reason, required to exhibit the riding light elsewhere (*f*).

If lost must be replaced.

It is the duty of a ship that has lost her lights by bad weather or other accident, to replace them as soon as possible. A collision caused by their absence will be held to have been caused by her fault (*g*).

No excuse for absence of lights that they were being trimmed.

It is no excuse for not carrying the Regulation lights that they were being trimmed, or that they went out by accident (*h*).

Misleading lights.

A wrong and misleading light will almost certainly cause the ship carrying it to be held in fault if a collision occurs (*i*).

Spare lights.

Notwithstanding the express terms of the Regulations that the lights shall be carried, it seems that a ship will not necessarily be held in fault for a collision caused by the absence of lights, or by improper lights, if the Regulation lights have been destroyed, and there are no spare ones on board. The point, however, has not been expressly decided. A steam-ship at anchor, with her mast-head light up instead of her proper riding light, was held free from blame. Her riding light had been broken shortly before the collision in a previous collision for which she was not in fault (*k*).

(*f*) The *Michelimo* and The *Ducca*, Mitch. Mar. Reg., May 25, 1877. In this case it was alleged that there existed at Rangoon a local rule as to riding lights inconsistent with the general Regulations.

(*g*) The *Saxonia* and The *Eclipse*, Lush. 410, 422 ; The *Aurora* and The *Robert Ingram*, ibid. 327 ; The *Gray Eagle*, 1 Bissel, 476 ; 2 Bissel, 25.

(*h*) The *C. M. Palmer* and The *Larnax*, 2 Asp. Mar. Law. Cas. 94 ;

The *Flora Macdonald* and The *Palestine*, Holt, 52 ; The *Eclipse* and The *Saxonia*, *supra* ; The *Victoria*, 3 W. Rob. 49 ; The *Sylph*, 2 Sp. E. & A. 75, 85.

(*i*) The *Scotia* and The *Berkshire*, 7 Blatchf. 308 ; 14 Wall. 170 ; The *Rob Roy*, 3 W. Rob. 190 ; The *Mary Hounsell*, 40 L. T. N. S. 368.

(*k*) The *Kjobenhavn*, 2 Asp. Mar. Law Cas. 213.

The Regulation lights must not be obscured in any way. **Art. 2.**
A flare-up must not be burnt so as to make them in- Obscuration
distinct (*l*).  If a steam-ship has the wind aft, so as to blow of lights.
her smoke ahead and thereby obscure her lights, it is her
duty to slacken and not go at full speed (*m*).  Where a
ship carried a bright light in her cabin, which showed on
deck and obscured her side lights, and the other ship
alleged that she mistook it for a riding light, the former
was held in fault for the collision (*n*).

The fact that it is only a short time after sunset, and Lights to be
fine and clear weather, does not excuse an omission to alwayscarried.
carry lights (*o*).  Under the Admiralty Regulations as to
lights it was held that " it is not to be said that because it
was a bright night it was not necessary to obey the Act of
Parliament" (*p*).  By the Regulations (Article 2) vessels are
expressly required to carry them in all weathers.  When,
on account of bad weather, it is not possible to carry them
fixed, Article 7 may apply, and proper lights must be
exhibited from the deck (*q*).

Special lights are required to be exhibited by dumb Special lights
barges and dredgers in the river Thames, by ships at required by
anchor in the Mersey and its approaches, and by flats and local rules.
vessels without masts in the Mersey (*r*).  Private signal
and flash lights are authorised by 36 & 37 Vict. c. 85,
ss. 18—21.

In America coasting and inland steam-ships are required
to carry lights other than those described in Article 2 (*s*).
And in the Suez Canal ships not under way exhibit two
lights (*t*).

(*l*) *The Sea Nymph*, Holt, 34.
(*m*) *The Rona* and *The Ava*, 2 Asp.
Mar. Law Cas. 182.
(*n*) *The Ida* and *The Mary Ida*,
Ad. Court, Feb. 5th, 1878.
(*o*) *The Emperor* and *The Zephyr*,
Holt, 24.
(*p*) *The City of London*, Swab.
Ad. 245, 249.

(*q*) See *infra*, Art. 7.
(*r*) For the Thames, Mersey, and
other local Regulations as to lights,
see the Appendix, *infra*.
(*s*) Act of Congress of 28th Feb.,
1871, c. 100 ; *The Continental*, 14
Wall. 345.
(*t*) See App., p. 280, *infra*.

L 2

**Art. 2.**

**Consequences of not carrying lights to shipowner and master.**

A master or owner wilfully neglecting to carry lights in accordance with the Regulations is guilty of a misdemeanour, and punishable with a fine of £100 or imprisonment for six months (*u*). And a ship proceeding to sea may be stopped if she is not properly supplied with lights and screens, or if they are improperly placed (*x*).

ARTICLE 3.

**Art. 3.**

**Lights for steam-ships.**

*Seagoing steam-ships when under way shall carry:—*

(a) *On or in front of the fore-mast, at a height above the hull of not less than twenty feet, and if the breadth of the ship exceeds twenty feet, then at a height above the hull not less than such breadth (y), a bright white light so constructed as to show an uniform and unbroken light over an arc of the horizon of twenty points of the compass, so fixed (z) as to throw the light ten points on each side of the ship, viz., from right ahead to two points abaft the beam on either side; and of such a character as to be visible on a dark night, with a clear atmosphere, at a distance of at least five miles.*

(b) *On the starboard side a green light so constructed as to show an uniform and unbroken light over an arc of the horizon of ten points of the compass, so fixed as to throw the light from right ahead to two points abaft the beam on the starboard side, and of such a character as to be visible on a dark night, with a clear atmosphere, at a distance of at least two miles.*

(c) *On the port side a red light so constructed as to show an uniform unbroken light over an arc of the horizon*

---

(*u*) 25 & 26 Vict. c. 63, s. 27. It is said that lights are often not carried at sea.

(*x*) 25 & 26 Vict. c. 63, s. 30. See also 39 & 40 Vict. c. 80, ss. 1—15.

(*y*) The words from (a) were not

in Art. 3 of the Rules of 1863, which began "at the fore-mast head." The alteration removes a difficulty in the case of vessels having no distinguishable mast-head.

(*z*) In the Rules of 1863 these words were "so constructed."

*of ten points of the compass, so fixed as to throw the light* *from right ahead to two points abaft the beam on the port side, and of such a character as to be visible on a dark night, with a clear atmosphere, at a distance of at least two miles.*

(d) *The said green and red side lights shall be fitted with inboard screens projecting at least three feet forward from the light, so as to prevent these lights from being seen across the bow.*

This Article corresponds with Article 3 of the Regulations of 1863. It differs, as noted above, from that Article merely verbally.

Every ship not actually brought up is "under way" "Under way." within the meaning of this Article. She is under way though not making any way through the water (a) if her anchor is not down. A ship getting her anchor is "under way" so soon as she ceases to be holden by and under the control of her anchor (b). A steam-tug lying-to under canvas with her fires banked up has been held to be under way (c).

It seems to have been held by Dr. Lushington that a ship dropping or dredging with her anchor stern foremost with the tide was not required to carry side lights (d). But such a vessel would seem to be "under way" within the meaning of Article 3, and, it is submitted, that Article requires her to carry side lights. Under a former Act it

---

(a) Cf. the concluding paragraph of Art. 5.

(b) *The Esk* and *The Gitana*, L. R. 2 A. & E. 350. As to trawlers at work, and ships hove-to, see Art. 10.

(c) *The Jennie S. Barker*, 3 Asp. Mar. Law Cas. 42 ; and it has been so held in America : *The Sunnyside*, 1 Otto. 208. See, however, *The Helvetia*, 3 Asp. Mar. Law Cas. 43

(note), where it seems to have been held that the tug is not under way ; but the facts are not clear, and the case was not followed in *The Jennie S. Barker.*

(d) See *The Smyrna*, mentioned by Dr. Deane arguendo in *The George Arkle*, Lush. 382, 385, as to the meaning of "under way;" see also Art. 6.

Art. 3.

was held that a vessel driving about the sea in an unmanageable state was "under way," and required to carry her side lights (e). Such a case is now provided for by Article 5.

Lights of a steam-ship in tow.

The Regulations contain no special provision as to the lights to be carried by a steam-ship when in tow of another vessel. In a case where a steam-ship, with her engines broken down, while in tow carried her usual side lights, and no mast-head light, it does not appear to have been suggested that she was carrying improper lights (f).

The Regulations as to the fitting of ships' lights must be exactly observed.

It seems that a bright light carried elsewhere than in the position described in Article 3 is not in accordance with the law, although the light is visible in the required directions, and is in other respects sufficient (g). The side lights must be so fixed that their range is such as is described in the Article. If they are liable to be obscured by the sails, rigging, or other part of the ship, it would be held that the Regulations are not complied with (h). With regard to the necessity of a strict observance of the Regulations as to lights, Lord Chelmsford, in *The Emperor* and *The Lady of the Lake* (i), said: "It is not advisable to allow these important Regulations to be satisfied by equivalents, or by anything else than a close and literal adherence to what they prescribe."

Board of Trade instructions as to ships' lights.

Minute instructions are issued by the Board of Trade to their surveyors with regard to the fixing and construction of ships' lights. These instructions have not the force of law, so that a ship should be held in fault for a

---

(e) *The George Arkle, ubi supra,* decided under 17 & 18 Vict. c. 104.
(f) *The American* and *The Syria,* L. R. 4 A. & E. 226; on app., L. R. 6 P. C. 127.
(g) Upon the Regulations of 1863 the law officers of the Crown advised to this effect : see Parl. Pap. No.

353 of 1874.
(h) *The Tirzah,* 4 P. D. 33 ; *The Magnet; The Duke of Sutherland ; The Fanny M. Carvill,* L. R. 4 A. & E. 417 ; *The Fanny M. Carvill* (on app.), 2 Asp. Mar. Law Cas. 565.
(i) Holt, 37.

collision merely because her lights are not fitted in accord- **Art. 3.** ance with them (i).

A ship whose side lights were fixed on the top of a galley, or deck-house, seven feet high and six feet broad, so that each light was seven feet inboard from the ship's side, was held not to be in fault, the lights being properly screened and visible in the required directions (j).

Although the requirements of Article 3 are not exactly Slight in- complied with, the ship guilty of the infringement will not fringement of the Regula- be held to be in fault for a collision that could not possibly tions may be have been caused by the infringement of the law. In immaterial. *The Fanny M. Carvill* (k) it was held that, the lights of the other ship not having in fact been seen across her bow, she was not in fault for the collision. And in *The Duke of Sutherland* (l), one of two ships in collision was held not to be in fault, although her side lights were partially obscured, the obscuration not being such as would have prevented the other from seeing the former in time to avoid her if she had exercised proper skill.

Previous to the enactment of 36 & 37 Vict. c. 85, s. 17, a sailing-ship was held not to be in fault, even upon the assumption that her side lights were so fixed in the mizen rigging that they were not visible in the directions required by the Regulations, it being proved that the other vessel, a steam-ship, might, by slackening her speed and using proper care, have avoided her, notwithstanding the sug- gested insufficiency of her side lights (m). And in another case (n), where the screens of one ship were only a foot in length, and the side lights could be seen across the bow, it

(i) *The Magnet; The Duke of Sutherland; The Fanny M. Carvill, ubi supra.* See also observations of Dr. Lushington in *The Samphire* v. *The Fanny Beck*, Holt, 193, as to the value of the opinion of the Board of Trade upon ships' lights.

(j) *The City of Carlisle*, 2 Mar.

Law Cas. O. S. 91.

(k) L. R. 4 A. & E. 417 ; on app., 2 Asp. Mar. Law Cas. 565.

(l) L. R. 4 A. & E. 417.

(m) *The Bougainville* v. *The Jas. C. Stevenson*, L. R. 5 P. C. 316.

(n) *The Emperor* v. *The Lady of the Lake*, Holt, 37.

**Art. 3.** was held that she could recover against the other ship for a collision, it being proved that the lights were not in fact seen across the bow. Under the existing law, however, any infringement of the Regulations as to lights which might by possibility have contributed to the collision would be held to be negligence contributing to the collision (o).

Where the side lights were fixed to the pawl bitts, and the other ship alleged that she could not see them, it was held that the ship so carrying them was in fault for the collision (p). A ship having in tow a pilot boat, which carried a mast-head light and no side lights, was held in fault (q). So, where a steam-tug carried her mast-head and side lights in a line, lashed to a bar placed on the top of a cook-house on deck, four feet high and five wide, it was held (in Ireland) that they were improperly placed, and that the tug was in fault for a collision which occurred in consequence (r).

"Seagoing" steam-ships. It is not clear why Article 3 applies, in terms, to sea-going ships only (s). The following Articles as to tugs and sailing-ships appear to be applicable to all ships, whether seagoing or not. It would probably be held that it is the duty of every vessel propelled by steam, whether seagoing or not, to carry lights in accordance with the Regulations. In an Irish case it was said by the Court that, the collision having occurred at sea, there could be no question as to the duty of one of the vessels (a tug) to carry the Regulation lights of 1863 (t).

It is not clear whether the distance at which the lights are to be visible is stated in statute or nautical miles. In

(o) The Tirzah, 4 P. D. 33 ; see supra, p. 14.
(p) The New Ed v. The Gustar, 1 Mar. Law Cas. O. S. 407.
(q) The Mary Hounsell, 40 L. T. N. S. 368.
(r) The Louisa and The City of Paris, Holt, 15.

(s) The corresponding regulation in the American Act of Congress applies to "all steam-vessels : " see The U. S. Grant and The Tally Ho, 7 Bened. 195.
(t) The Louisa and The City of Paris, ubi supra.

the French regulations the distance is given as "deux   Art. 3.
milles."

## ARTICLE 4.

*A steam-ship when towing another ship shall, in ad-*   Art. 4.
*dition to her side lights, carry two bright white lights in a*  Lights for
*vertical line one over the other, not less than three feet*  steam-ships
*apart, so as to distinguish her from other steam-ships.*  towing other ships.
*Each of these lights shall be of the same construction*
*and character, and shall be carried in the same position*
*as the white light which other steam-ships are required*
*to carry.*

This Article differs verbally only from Article 4 of the
Regulations of 1863, except in the provision as to the distance between the lights, which is new.

The distinguishing lights required to be carried by a tug  Object of tug's
are "for the purpose of warning all approaching vessels  distinguishing
that she is not in all respects mistress of her move-  lights.
ments" (u), and to show that she is encumbered. There is
no provision in the Regulations as to distinguishing lights
for a sailing-ship towing another ship, or for a steam-ship
in tow.

## ARTICLE 5.

*A ship, whether a steam-ship or a sailing-ship, when*   Art. 5.
*employed either in laying or in picking up a telegraph*  Day and night
*cable, or which from any accident is not under command,*  signals for
*shall at night carry in the same position as the white light*  ships not
*which steam-ships are required to carry, and, if a steam-*  under command.
*ship, in place of that light, three red lights in globular*
*lanterns, each not less than ten inches in diameter, in a*
*vertical line one over the other, not less than three feet*
*apart; and shall by day carry in a vertical line, one over*
*the other, not less than three feet apart, in front of but not*

(u) *The American* and *The Syria,* L. R. 6 P. C. 127, 131.

*lower than her fore-mast head, three black balls or shapes, each two feet in diameter.*

*These shapes and lights are to be taken by approaching ships as signals that the ship using them is not under command, and cannot, therefore, get out of the way.*

*The above ships, when not making any way through the water, shall not carry the side lights, but when making way shall carry them.*

This is an entirely new Article (*x*). Under the new law it seems that it is necessary for a vessel to be always provided with these globular red lights and signal balls. If she fails to exhibit them when not under command through any accident, and a collision occurs, she will probably be held to have infringed the Regulations; and, coming within the penalty of 36 & 37 Vict. c. 85, s. **17**, she will probably be held in fault for the collision.

It is not clear what the effect of the words " through any accident " may be. Whether a ship hove-to through stress of weather, or for any other reason, would be required to exhibit the lights or balls of Article 5 seems doubtful. A vessel in such a condition is seldom " under command," and yet it can scarcely have been the intention of the Legislature that every time a ship is hove-to she should shift her lights.

Article 5 has no application to ships at anchor. Perhaps it would apply to a ship ashore in a fairway (*y*).

ARTICLE 6.

*A sailing-ship under way, or being towed, shall carry the same lights as are provided by Article 3 for a steam-ship under way, with the exception of the white light, which she shall never carry.*

(*x*) There has been in force for some years an Admiralty regulation similar to Art. 5, binding on Queen's ships engaged in telegraph work.

(*y*) Cf. *The Elizabeth* and *The Adalia*, 3 Mar. Law Cas. O. S. 345 ; *The Industrie*, L. R. 3 A. & E. 303.

Art. 6.

This Article corresponds with Article 5 of the Regulations of 1863.

"Under way:" meaning of the term.

There seems to be no doubt that a ship hove-to is under way within the meaning of Article 6. In a recent case it was so held under the Regulations of 1863 (*z*). And under a former Act there were decisions to the same effect (*a*). There was some doubt whether trawlers at work were "under way" within the meaning of the Regulations of 1863 (*b*); but under the Regulations of 1879 no such question can arise as to lights. A vessel coming to an anchor while hauling down her jibs, and having little or no way on her, was carrying her side lights; it does not appear to have been suggested that she was wrong in doing so (*c*).

## ARTICLE 7.

Art. 7.

Special lights for small vessels.

*Whenever, as in the case of small vessels during bad weather, the green and red side lights cannot be fixed, these lights shall be kept on deck on their respective sides of the vessel, ready for use; and shall, on the approach of or to other vessels, be exhibited on their respective sides in sufficient time to prevent collision, in such manner as to make them most visible, and so that the green light shall not be seen on the port side, nor the red light on the starboard side. To make the use of these portable lights more certain and easy, the lanterns containing them shall each be painted outside with the colour of the light they respectively contain, and shall be provided with proper screens.*

(*z*) *The Pennsylvania*, 3 Mar. Law Cas. O. S. 477; and the Supreme Court of the U. S. came to the same decision upon the same facts: *The Pennsylvania*, 19 Wall. 125.

(*a*) *The City of London*, Swab. Ad. 245; *The James*, *ibid.* 55. The words in the Act of 1854 are "under sail."

(*b*) See *The Robert and Ann* and *The Lloyds*, Holt, 55; *The Edith*, Ir. Rep. 10 Eq. 345; *The Englishman*, 3 P. D. 18.

(*c*) *The Adriatic*, 3 Asp. Mar. Law Cas. 16.

This Article is almost identical with Article 6 of the Regulations of 1863.

What vessels may carry their side lights on deck. It is not easy to see to what vessels the Article has any application. Article 10 provides for boats, and there are few craft other than boats in which side lights "cannot be fixed" and carried, even in the worst weather, if properly fitted. It was assumed in a case in Ireland that a full decked trawler of 41 tons cannot conveniently work her trawl with side lights fixed, and that such a vessel may carry them on deck, even in fine weather and when not at work (d). This can scarcely have been the intention of the framers of Article 7.

If a vessel seeks to excuse herself for not having her side lights fixed in their proper place and to bring herself within Article 7, the burden is on her to prove that the lights could not with safety be carried fixed. In the case of a brig of 255 tons, it was left by Dr. Lushington to the assessors to say whether it was practicable under the circumstances of the case to carry them fixed (e). In *The Tirzah*, Sir R. Phillimore appears to have considered that it was justifiable for a vessel of 239 register tons to shift her lights from their usual place in consequence of bad weather; although it was not contended that she came within the Article as to small vessels' lights (f).

## ARTICLE 8.

Art. 8. *A ship, whether a steam-ship or a sailing-ship, when at*
Riding lights. *anchor, shall carry, where it can best be seen, but at a height not exceeding twenty feet above the hull, a white light in a globular lantern of not less than eight inches in diameter, and so constructed as to show a clear uniform*

(d) *The Margaret* and *The Tuscar*, Holt, 44.
(e) *The Livingstone*, Swab. Adm.
519; see also *The Calla*, *ib.* 465.
(f) *The Tirzah*, 4 P. D. 33.

*and unbroken light visible all round the horizon, at a* **Art. 8.**
*distance of at least one mile.*

This Article corresponds with Article 7 of the Regulations
of 1863. The wording is slightly different, but the only
alteration of consequence is that the present Article 8
applies to ships at anchor anywhere, while the corresponding Article of the former rules applied only to ships
brought up in a roadstead or fairway.

A riding light should not be placed where it is obscured *Riding light*
in any direction by masts, spars, sails, or rigging. It *must not be obscured.*
is assumed that vessels at anchor are stationery (*h*), or
nearly so; ships, therefore, when at anchor, must not be
allowed to sheer about more than can be avoided. A
vessel ashore in a situation where other ships may run
into her, although probably she does not come within the
terms of Article 8, is required to exhibit a light to warn
other ships of her position (*i*).

In America it has been held that a ship moored to a *Ship moored*
wharf out of the regular track of ships is not required to *to a wharf.*
exhibit a light (*k*). But a tug moored to a boom anchored
in a fairway was held in fault for having no riding light
up (*l*).

As to special riding lights for ships in the Mersey, *Special riding*
dredgers in the Thames, and ships moored in the Suez *lights.*
Canal, see the Appendix. British drift net fishing boats at
anchor exhibit two horizontal lights: *infra*, p. 259.

### ARTICLE 9.

*A pilot vessel, when engaged on her station on pilotage* **Art. 9.**
*duty, shall not carry the lights required for other vessels,* *Lights for pilot vessels.*

(*h*) *The Esk* and *The Gitana*, L. R. 2 A. & E. 350.
(*i*) *The Industrie*, L. R. 3 A. & E. 303; *Kidson* v. *McArthur*, 5 Sess. Cas., 4th series, 936.
(*k*) *Culbertson* v. *Shaw*, 18 How. 584; *The Granite State*, 3 Wall. 310.
(*l*) *The Willard Saulsbury*, cited 1 Pars. on Ship., ed. 1869, 564.

**Art. 9.** *but shall carry a white light at the mast-head, visible all round the horizon, and shall also exhibit a flare-up light, or flare-up lights, at short intervals, which shall never exceed fifteen minutes. A pilot vessel, when not engaged on her station on pilotage duty, shall carry lights similar to those of other ships.*

There are considerable differences between this Article and the corresponding Article (No. 8) of the Regulations of 1863. Under the latter questions frequently arose as to the proper lights to be carried by pilot boats, when not serving vessels (*m*). The present Regulation will apply to steam, as well as sailing, pilot boats, should steam pilot boats be introduced. It has been held that a pilot boat in tow of another ship must not carry her mast-head light (*n*). A boat with pilots on board, and serving ships, would seem to be a pilot vessel within the scope of Article 9, whether the pilots were licensed pilots or not (*n*).

It has been held in America that a vessel running down a pilot boat from which she was taking a pilot was equally in fault, although the pilot boat was not carrying the Regulation light (*o*).

ARTICLE 10.

**Art. 10.**

Lights for open boats and fishing vessels.

(a) *Open fishing boats and other open boats when under way shall not be obliged to carry the side lights required for other vessels, but every such boat shall in lieu thereof have ready at hand a lantern with a green glass on the one side and a red glass on the other side; and on the approach of or to other vessels such lantern shall be exhibited in sufficient time to prevent collision,*

(m) *The Wanata*, 4 Bened. 310; 5 Otto. 600; *The Edinburgh*, before the Wreck Commissioner, March, 1879.

(n) *The Mary Hounsell*, 4 P. D. 204; 40 L. T. N. S. 368.
(o) *The City of Washington*, 2 Otto. 31.

*so that the green light shall not be seen on the port side,*   
*nor the red light on the starboard side.*

(b) *A fishing vessel and an open boat when at anchor shall exhibit a bright white light.*

(c) *A fishing vessel, when employed in drift net fishing, shall carry on one of her masts two red lights in a vertical line one over the other, not less than three feet apart.*

(d) *A trawler at work shall carry on one of her masts two lights in a vertical line one over the other, not less than three feet apart—the upper light red and the lower green —and shall also either carry the side lights required for other vessels, or, if the side lights cannot be carried, have ready at hand the coloured lights as provided in Article 7, or a lantern with a red and a green glass as described in paragraph* (a) *of this Article.*

(e) *Fishing vessels and open boats shall not be prevented from using a flare-up in addition if they desire to do so.*

(f) *The lights mentioned in this Article are substituted for those mentioned in the 12th, 13th and 14th Articles of the Convention between France and England scheduled to the British Sea Fisheries Act,* 1868 (p).

(g) *All lights required by this Article, except side lights, shall be in globular lanterns so constructed as to show all round the horizon.*

This Article corresponds with Article 9 of the Regulations of 1863, with some additions and alterations. It puts an end to a conflict which previously existed between the Sea Fisheries Act, 1868, and the International Regulations; and to many difficulties which arose under the former Regulations as to lights for trawlers and fishing boats (q).

---

(p) See Appendix for this Act;    *and Ann v. The Lloyds,* Holt, 55; and see also 38 & 39 Vict. c. 15, s. 3.    *The Englishman,* 3 P. D. 18; *The*
  (q) Such as arose in *The Robert*    *Edith,* Ir. Rep. 10 Eq. 345.

ARTICLE 11.

**Art. 11.**
**Light for overtaken ship.**

*A ship which is being overtaken by another shall show from her stern to such last-mentioned ship a white light, or a flare-up light.*

This Article is new. It is the duty of a ship being overtaken by another at night in such a direction that her side lights are not visible to the latter, and so that there is risk of collision, to keep the other ship in view, and, if necessary, warn her of her danger by showing a light over her stern (*r*). But under ordinary circumstances a ship is not bound to keep a look-out astern, and it is not her duty to, nor should she, carry a light permanently showing over her stern. If run down by an overtaking ship she will not be held in fault for not warning the latter, or for not showing her a light, unless it is proved that she saw the other in time, and deliberately neglected to warn her (*s*). Under the Regulations of 1863, when there was no Regulation in force corresponding to Article 11, a ship not having a bright light available was held not to be in fault for showing over her stern one of her side lights (*t*).

ARTICLE 12.

**Art. 12.**
**Sound signals for thick weather.**

*A steam-ship shall be provided with a steam-whistle or other efficient steam sound signal, so placed that the sound may not be intercepted by any obstructions, and with an efficient fog-horn to be sounded by a bellows or other mechanical means, and also with an efficient bell. A*

(r) *The City of Brooklyn*, 3 Asp. Mar. Law Cas. 230 ; *The Anglo-Indian, ibid.* 1 ; *The Hannah Park* v. *The Lena*, 2 Mar. Law Cas. 345; *The Earl Spencer*, L. R. 4 A. & E. 431. These cases were decided under the Regulations of 1863.
(s) *The Hannah Park* v. *The Lena, ubi supra.*
(t) *The Anglo Indian*, 3 Asp. Mar. Law Cas. 1.

*sailing-ship shall be provided with a similar fog-horn*
*and bell. In fog, mist, or falling snow, whether by day*
*or night, the signals described in this Article shall be used*
*as follows—that is to say,—*

(a) *A steam-ship under way shall make with her steam-*
*whistle, or other steam sound signal, at intervals of not*
*more than two minutes, a prolonged blast.*

(b) *A sailing-ship under way shall make with her fog-*
*horn, at intervals of not more than two minutes, when on*
*the starboard tack one blast, when on the port tack two*
*blasts in succession, and when with the wind abaft the*
*beam three blasts in succession.*

(c) *A steam-ship and a sailing-ship when not under*
*way shall, at intervals of not more than two minutes,*
*ring the bell.*

This Article goes into more detail, and is in some
respects different from the corresponding Regulation
(Article 9) of 1863. It contemplates sirens taking the place
of steam-whistles; it makes the blasts of the whistle and
horn more frequent; and the indication of the sailing-
ship's course by sound is entirely new (*u*). The fog
signal required of steam-ships appears to be modified by
Article 19 when another ship is in sight to which a vessel
wishes to indicate by whistling an alteration of her own
helm.

As to the meaning of "under way," see Article 3,
*supra*, p. 149. In a case under the Rules of 1863, Sir
R. Phillimore decided that a sailing-ship hove-to in a fog
should sound a fog-horn and not a bell (*x*). It would
appear that every ship not actually at anchor should sound
her whistle or horn. By the maritime law it was the
duty of a sailing-ship under way in a fog to sound a
horn (*y*). By local rules in force in different waters ships

(*u*) In America these signals have
been enforced by law for many
years.

(*x*) *The Pennsylvania*, 3 Mar. Law
Cas. 477; and see 19 Wall. 125.
(*y*) *The Carron*, 1 Sp. E. & A. 91.

M

**Art. 12.** are required to sound their horns at various intervals. In America it has been held gross negligence in a steam-ship not to be fitted with a whistle (z).

What is "fog" within the meaning of Art. 12. What amount, or density, of fog must exist so as to make the use of the fog signals necessary has not, so far as the writer is aware, been decided by the Courts of this country. A definition arrived at by an American Court is probably sufficiently accurate. It was there said that, to give the Article a reasonable meaning, we must suppose that its intent is to give to approaching vessels a warning of which the fog would otherwise deprive them, and that it applies where there is fog enough to shut out the view of the sails, or hull, by day, or of the lights by night, until the vessels are so close that there would be risk of collision (a).

## ARTICLE 13.

**Art. 13.** *Every ship, whether a sailing-ship or steam-ship, shall*

Speed in thick weather to be moderate. *in a fog, mist, or falling snow go at a moderate speed.*

This Article is entirely new, so far as it relates to sailing-ships, and to snow; as to steam-ships it corresponds (nearly) with part of Article 16 of the Regulations of 1863. It makes no alteration in the law, which, apart from the Regulations, has always required moderate speed in a fog (b).

As to what is "moderate" speed, see Article 18, *infra,* p. 185. Seven knots an hour was held by the Privy Council to be too high a rate of speed for an ocean steamship when in a fog in the track of ships 200 miles to the eastward of Sandy Hook (c).

(z) *The Electra,* 1 Bened. 282.
(a) *The Monticello,* Dist. Ct. of Mass., U. S.; 1 Parsons on Ship., 566 (ed. 1869).
(b) See *The Juliet Erskine,* 6 Not.

of Cas. 633 ; *The Lord Saumarez,* 6 Not. of Cas. 600.
(c) *The Pennsylvania,* 3 Mar. Law Cas. O. S. 477 ; see also *The City of Brooklyn, infra,* p. 166.

Where the fog was so dense that a steam-ship heard the Art. 13. whistle and hailing from another without being able to see her, it was held that her duty was to stop at once and hail the other vessel (*d*). In a fog so dense that it is not possible for a ship to see others in time to avoid them, she is not justified in being under way at all, except from necessity. Neither Article 13 nor Article 18 justifies her in being under way under such circumstances (*e*). In America it was said by the Supreme Court of the United States that a steam-ship must lie to if she is in a fog in a crowded part of the sea and cannot go ahead so as to have steerage way on her without danger to other vessels (*f*).

*The Lancashire* was a Liverpool and Birkenhead ferry Ferry boats running in a fog. steamer. She left her landing stage to cross the Mersey in a dense fog, and ran into *The Levant*, a vessel brought up in her track. It was contended for *The Lancashire* that it was the custom of the ferry boats to run in all weathers, and that it was necessary for the convenience of the public that they should do so. *The Lancashire* was held in fault for the collision on the ground that she had no right to be under way at all in such weather (*g*). In delivering judgment the learned Judge of the Admiralty Court (Sir R. Phillimore) said (*h*) : " The question arises in this case, whether it was proper and right in this ferry boat to go deliberately across the river in a fog of such a dense nature as here described, and with the knowledge of these vessels lying in her track, or one of them in her track and the others nearly so, and also with the knowledge that one of them had, as she contends, an insufficient

(*d*) The *Frankland* and *The Kestrel*, L. R. 4 P. C. 529 ; and see *The Teutonia*, 23 Wall. 77.

(*e*) *The Lancashire*, L. R. 4 A. & E. 198; *The Otter*, ibid. 203 ; *The Girolamo*, 3 Hag. Ad. 169 ; *The North American* and *The Wild Rose*, 2 Mar. Law Cas. O. S. 319 ; *Smith v. St. Lawrence Tow Boat Co.*, L. R.

5 P. C. 308 ; *The Orion*, 2 Mar. Law Cas. O. S. Dig. 822 ; *The Victoria*, 3 W. Rob. 49 ; and see cases cited *supra*, p. 162.

(*f*) *The Pennsylvania*, 19 Wall. 125.

(*g*) *The Lancashire*, L. R. 4 A. & E. 198.

(*h*) L. R. 4 A. & E. 201.

watch ?  It has been urged very strongly on the Court that, if this were not to be so, if the steam ferry boat was to be delayed on account of the fog, the greatest possible inconvenience would ensue to the public.  I have no doubt that it is very much for the convenience of the public that the ferry boat should go in all weathers, and at all times, but at the same time, I cannot myself think it right to set the convenience of the public in competition with the possibility, or rather the probability, of injuring human life and greatly damaging property.  At the same time, the custom appears to have been for this vessel to have gone across in foggy weather, as at other times, and regulations appear to have been made with a view to preventing accidents, surrounding her with every precaution that was possible. . . . . But one thing appears to me quite clear, that if this ferry steamer thinks herself justified in going across the river in such a dense fog as this, she takes upon herself all the responsibility incident to such a course.  She has the advantage if she goes over safely, and she must have the disadvantage if she injures life or property in the course of the passage."

Law in America as to ferry boats running in a fog. The law in America as to ferry steamers being under way in a fog seems to be more favourable to the ferry boats than that of this country, as laid down in *The Lancashire*.  In *The Exchange* (*i*) the U. S. Circuit Court held that while owners of ferry boats have not any exclusive privileges of navigation over owners of other vessels, nevertheless, while the public convenience requires the ferry boats to be running as constantly as possible, the rules which are applicable to the running of such a boat are, that while more than ordinary care, vigilance, and caution are required on the part of the ferry boat, she is entitled to more than ordinary diligence on the part of other vessels to avoid her.

(*i*)  10 Blatchf. 68.  See also  68 N. York Rep. 385.
*Huffman* v. *Union Ferry of Brooklyn*,

In another case (k) it was held that a ferry boat is not bound to stop running in a dense fog. There are other American cases to the effect that vessels are required to know the usual track of ferry boats, and to take precautions accordingly, and particularly not to anchor in their track (l).

*Art. 13.*

The duty of a steam-ship under way in a fog has been thus stated by the Supreme Court of the United States : " The best precautions are bright signal lights ; very low speed—just sufficient to subject the vessel to the command of her helm ; competent look-outs properly stationed and vigilant in the performance of their duties ; constant ringing of the bell or blowing of the fog-horn, as the case may be ; and sufficient force at the wheel to effect, if necessary, a prompt change in the course of the vessel " (m).

*Duty of steam-ship in a fog.*

A vessel going at too great a rate of speed on a dark night, or in thick weather, cannot be heard to say that a collision was the result of inevitable accident (n). Under such circumstances it is her duty to go at such a rate of speed as will enable her after discovering another vessel to avoid her by stopping and reversing her engines (o). If her speed is higher than this she will, almost certainly, be held in fault for any collision that may occur, although she does her best to avoid it when the other ship is seen (p).

*Inevitable accident cannot be pleaded where speed is excessive.*

Undue speed in a fog or thick weather is not more justifiable for sailing-ships than for steam-ships. Where a sailing-ship had her studding sails set in a thick fog and came into collision with another ship, Dr. Lushington said : " It is unquestionably the duty of a master in intense

*Speed of sailing-ships in a fog.*

(k) *The Lydia*, 11 Blatchf. 415.
(l) *The Hudson*, 5 Bened. 206; *The Relief*, Olcott, 104.
(m) *The Colorado*, 1 Otto. 692 ; and see *The Franconia*, 4 Bened. 181.
(n) *The Juliet Erskine*, 6 Not. of Cas. 633.
(o) *The Smyrna*, 2 Mar. Law Cas. O. S. 93.
(p) *The Samphire* v. *The Fanny Beck*, Holt, 193.

**Art. 13.** fog to exercise the utmost vigilance, and to put his vessel under command, so as to secure the best chance of avoiding all accidents, even though such precautions may occasion some delay in the prosecution of the voyage" (q). But in this, and in another case (r), the sailing-ship, though under a press of sail in a fog, was not therefore held in fault for the collision.

In *The City of Brooklyn* (s) Lush, J., said as to speed: "I think the rule of law, with regard to travelling at sea, is identical with the law of travelling on the high road. No one on a dark night has a right to go at such a rate of speed as not to be able to escape an accident if he happens to follow immediately in the wake of another, whether it be by sea or land."

In very thick weather, or great darkness, a vessel is not justified in running through a crowded roadstead, but should, if possible, bring up (t).

A sailing-ship going six and a-half knots over a fishing ground on a dark night, where vessels were visible only 100 or 200 yards off, was held in fault for a collision with a trawler (u).

American cases as to moderate speed in a fog. The necessity of moderate speed in thick weather has been insisted upon in numerous American cases. In a judgment of the District Court of New York it was said that in a dense fog a ship is bound to go as slow as possible, consistent with steerage way (x). Though not bound to lie to (y), ships are required to use extra caution, and to put themselves under moderate sail in a fog (z). A schooner carrying on at night, and racing with another vessel, was held in fault for a collision (a). The common

(q) *The Itinerant*, 2 W. Rob. 236.
(r) *The Ebenezer, ibid.* 206.
(s) 3 Asp. Mar. Law Cas. 230.
(t) *The Victoria*, 3 W. Rob. 49;
*The George*, 4 Not. of Cas. 161;
*The Lochibo*, 7 Moo. P. C. C. 427.
(u) *The Pepperell*, Swab. Ad. 12.

(x) *The Westphalia*, 4 Bened. 404.
(y) *The Morning Light*, 2 Wall. 550; *The Colorado*, 1 Otto. 692.
(z) *The Colorado, ubi supra.*
(a) *The Thomas Martin*, 3 Blatchf. 517.

excuse that a rate of speed greater than is consistent with Art. 13. safety to other ships is necessary for steerage way, is seldom listened to by the Courts; nor the suggestion that the ship was run at considerable speed in order to get out of the fog (b).

It was said by a Circuit Court of the United States **Pressure of steam when going slow.** that the meaning of the rule that a steam-ship shall in a fog go at a moderate speed is, not that she shall only have such a pressure of steam as will enable her to go slow, but that she shall have her full steam power, and still go slow, so that she may be able to bring herself to a stand still as soon as possible (c).

If a steam-ship has the wind aft, so that her own smoke **Steam-ship's smoke obscuring lights and view.** is blown ahead obscuring her lights or the view from her deck, it is her duty to go at a moderate speed, and so that she may see and be seen by other vessels in time to avoid collision (d).

## ARTICLE 14.

*When two sailing-ships are approaching one another* **Art. 14.** *so as to involve risk of collision, one of them shall keep out* **Two sailing-** *of the way of the other as follows, viz.:—* **ships.**

(a) *A ship which is running free shall keep out of the way of a ship which is close-hauled.*

(b) *A ship which is close-hauled on the port tack shall keep out of the way of a ship which is close-hauled on the starboard tack.*

(c) *When both are running free with the wind on different sides, the ship which has the wind on the port side shall keep out of the way of the other.*

(b) *The Hansa,* 5 Bened. 501, 521;    (d) *The Rona* and *The Ara,* 2 Asp.
*The Chancellor,* 4 Bened. 153, 164.    Mar. Law Cas. 182; *The Vivid,*
(c) *The Hansa,* 5 Bened. 501.    7 Not. of Cas. 127.

(d) *When both are running free with the wind on the same side, the ship which is to windward shall keep out of the way of the ship which is to leeward.*

(e) *A ship which has the wind aft shall keep out of the way of the other ship.*

This Article is new in form (e). Its effect is the same as that of the meeting and crossing rules (Articles 11 and 12) of the Regulations of 1863, except in one case—that of two sailing-ships meeting end on—that is to say, with their keels in a line, or nearly so. Such vessels were required by Article 11 of the Regulations of 1863 to put their helms to port, a manœuvre obviously dangerous for a vessel close-hauled on the starboard tack. The effect of putting the helm of a ship close-hauled on the starboard tack to port being, in many cases, to throw the ship out of command, and to cause imminent risk of collision, it was, under the port helm rule of former Acts, often a question of difficulty whether a ship close-hauled on the starboard tack broke the law by not porting (f).

As to what constitutes "risk of collision," see above, p. 136.

(e) Except, perhaps, as to paragraph (a), the rules of Article 14 embody the ancient practice of seamen, irrespective of legislation. But the practice seems to have been loose. Whether the ship on the port tack was always required to bear up and go under the stern of the other, or whether she was at liberty to keep out of the way by taking other steps, was uncertain : see *The Rose*, 2 W. Rob. 1 ; *The Dumfries*, Swab. Ad. 125 ; *The Gazelle*, 5 Not. of Cas. 101. The rule that the ship on the port tack must give way was applied to a ship with the wind a point or two free : *The Stranger*, 6 Not. of Cas. 36 ; and also where the course of the other ship was doubtful : *The Traveller*, 2 W.

Rob. 197 ; *The Anne and Mary*, *ibid.* 189 ; *The George*, 5 Not. of Cas. 368.

(f) See *The Norge* and *The Wolverine*, Holt's Rule of the Road, 89 ; *The Amalia* and *The Maria*, *ibid.* 87 ; *The Princessan Louisa* and *The Artemas, ibid.* 72. Under the former Acts see *The Betsy*, 1 Sp. E. & A. 34, note ; *The Clarence, ibid.* 206 ; *The Halcyon*, Lush. 100 ; *Chadwick* v. *City of Dublin Steam Packet Co.*, 6 Ell. & Bl. 771 ; *The Dumfries*, Swab. Ad. 125. American cases on the same point are *The Tracy J. Bronson*, 3 Bened. 341 ; *The Helen J. Holway* and *The Moore*, 6 Bened. 536 ; *The Annie Lindsay, ibid.* 290 ; *The Sylvester Hale, ibid.* 523.

A ship required by the Regulations to keep out of the way of another may do so in any way she thinks proper. She may go ahead or astern of the other, and she may put her helm to port or starboard, as she thinks best (g). But she has no right to embarrass the other, or to put her into a difficulty. Thus it has been held in America (h) that where two courses are open to a vessel required to keep out of the way, and she selects the more hazardous, she is responsible for a collision that would not have occurred if she had taken the safer course.

Article 14 is supplemented by, and must be read with, Articles 20 and 22. The difficulty which arose under the Rules of 1863 of drawing the line between "crossing" and "overtaking" ships is removed by the opening words of Article 20. It seems that under the Rules of 1880 every ship, whether steam-ship or sailing-ship, which is travelling faster than another ahead, or anywhere forward of her own beam, and coming up with her, must keep out of the way.

The duty of the ship close-hauled on the starboard tack under Article 14 is strictly to obey the rule requiring her to keep her course. She can excuse a departure from that rule only by showing that it was necessary to avoid immediate danger. "Keeping her course" under Article 22 means keeping her course by the wind. If in so doing she comes to or breaks off a little, she does not thereby infringe Article 22 (i). But a vessel would not be justified by Article 14 in standing on obstinately where it is clear that a collision may be avoided if she alters her helm, and in no other way (k).

The rule requiring a ship close-hauled on the starboard tack to stand on appears formerly not to have been so

*Art. 14.*
A ship required to keep out of the way may do so in any way she thinks proper.

Art. 14 is supplemented and modified by Art. 20 and Art. 22.

Duty of ship required to keep her course to stand on.

(g) The Nor, 2 Asp. Mar. Law Cas. 264; The Carroll, 8 Wall. 302; The Great Eastern, 2 Mar. Law Cas. O. S. 97.
(h) The Empire State, 1 Bened. 57.

(i) The Marmion, 1 Asp. Mar. Law Cas. 412; The Aimo and The Amelia, 2 Asp. Mar. Law Cas. 96.
(k) The Lake St. Clair and The Underwriter, 3 Asp. Mar. Law Cas. 361.

**Art. 14.**  strict as it is under the existing law. Formerly, where two
vessels on opposite tacks were approaching with risk of
collision, it was held to be the proper course for both to
put their helms to port (*l*). Such is not now the law.
Before altering her helm a ship must ascertain what course
the other ship is upon, and how she has the wind. Her
duty is to wait until she knows what the Regulations require
her to do. A wrong step taken by a ship in ignorance of
the other's course will cause her to be held in fault if a
collision ensues.

*A hard case.*  Hence arise cases of great perplexity to seamen. A ship,
A., close-hauled on the port tack, sees a red light of another,
B., ahead, and a point or two on his starboard bow. He
cannot make out on which side B. has the wind, or what is
his course. Not knowing which Article of the Regulations
applies to his case, A. stands on, and at the last moment
bears up, thinking, erroneously, that B. is close-hauled on
the starboard tack. At the same moment B., who has the
wind free, bears up. A collision follows, for which A. is
probably held in fault, because he did not keep his course.
The temptation for A. to take steps which he thinks will
ensure his keeping out of B.'s way on first seeing him,
without regard to the Regulations, is strong.

*Meaning of
"close-
hauled."*  A vessel may be close-hauled within the meaning of
Article 14, although she is not lying so close to the wind
that she cannot luff a trifle without throwing herself in
stays (*m*). A ship with the wind free must keep out of
the way of a ship hove-to (*n*), but whether by virtue of
Article 14 or not, is uncertain.

*Whether a
ship hove-to is
within Art. 14
and required*  It has been stated above that Article 14, relating to sailing-
ships not under command, probably does not apply to a
ship hove-to in the ordinary course of navigation. If that

(*l*) *The Seringapatam,* 5 Not. of
Cas. 61, 65.
(*m*) *The Singapore* v. *The Hebe,*
Holt, 124 ; see also *Chadwick* v.

*The City of Dublin Steam Packet Co.,*
6 Ell. & Bl. 771.
(*n*) *The Eleanor* v. *The Alma,* 2
Mar. Law Cas. O. S. 240.

be the law Article 14 would be held to apply to a ship Art. 14.
lying to, so as to require her to keep out of the way, not- to keep out of the way.
withstanding the fact that she was lying to and nearly
stationary. In a case(o) decided in 1847 the facts were as
follows:—*The Lavinia*, a schooner close-hauled on the
starboard tack, came into collision in broad daylight with
*The London*, a schooner hove-to on the port tack. The
crew of *The London* were engaged in reefing her topsail.
The helm of *The Lavinia*, which had been lashed a-lee,
was put over to port shortly before the collision. *The
Lavinia* kept her course up to the moment of collision,
and hailed *The London* to port. It was held that *1he
London* was solely in fault.

A schooner, with the wind free, was in collision with a
pilot boat lying to with her helm lashed a-lee. The pilot
boat was forging ahead at the rate of about a knot an hour,
as she kept coming to and falling off. Both vessels were (in
1866) held (p) by the District Court of the United States
to be in fault for the collision. The schooner for not keeping
out of the way of a vessel which was "close-hauled," and
the pilot boat for not keeping her course. The Court said
that the proper course for those on board the pilot boat to
have taken was to get way on her, so as to keep a steady
course.

The following cases, decided under the Regulations of
1863, illustrate the application of Article 14, and the
circumstances under which it may be departed from :—

Two ships were turning to windward in a narrow chan- Cases illus-
nel, both on the starboard tack, and one following in the trating Art. 14.
wake of the other. The leading ship, having stood as far
towards the side of the channel as prudent, went about.
There was risk of collision if the other ship stood on. It
was held that it was the duty of the following ship, although

---

(o) *The London*, 6 Not. of Cas. 29;  case.
*The Blenheim*, 1 Sp. E. & A. 285  (p) *The Transit*, 3 Bened. 192.
(decided in 1854), is a very similar

**Art. 14.** on the starboard tack, to go about when the leading ship did so (*q*).

In a case where the courses of the two ships were within a point of being directly opposite (W.N.W. and S.E. by E.), the Privy Council held that they were "crossing" and not "meeting" ships (*r*).

Where two vessels close-hauled on opposite tacks sighted each other at so short a distance that it was not possible for the ship on the port tack to avoid the other if the latter stood on, it was held that it was the duty of the latter to port and let go her head sheets (*s*).

Where a ship close-hauled on the port tack was unable to bear up owing to her head-gear being carried away, and the other ship, in ignorance of her disabled condition, kept her course, a collision which followed was held to be an inevitable accident (*t*).

The wind being somewhere from S. to S.S.E., the sloop *Constantine*, heading N.N.E., fell in with the cutter *Spring*, heading W. by S., and to leeward. It was held that it was the duty of *The Constantine* to keep out of the way, and that the duty of *The Spring* was to keep her course (*u*).

A full-rigged ship, with the wind free, crossing a brig and a schooner close-hauled on the same tack, was held in fault for approaching them so close that, upon the schooner going about, a collision with the brig was inevitable (*v*).

A ship just gathering way on the port tack, after going about, was held free from blame for a collision with another close-hauled on the starboard tack, which had approached her too near whilst in stays (*x*).

(*q*) *The Priscilla*, L. R. 3 A. & E. 125 ; and see *The Lake St. Clair* and *The Underwriter*, 3 Asp. Mar. Law Cas. 361.

(*r*) *The Constitution*, 2 Moo. P. C. C. 453.

(*s*) *The Lady Anne*, 15 Jur. 18.

(*t*) *The Aimo* and *The Amelia*, 2 Asp. Mar. Law Cas. 96.

(*u*) *The Spring*, L. R. 1 A. & E. 99.

(*v*) *The Mobile*, Swab. Adm. 67 ; on app., *ibid.* 127 ; this case was under a former Act.

(*x*) *The Charlotte Raab*, Brown Ad. 453.

Two ships close-hauled on opposite tacks were crossing each other. The ship on the starboard tack was held in fault for not keeping out of the way when the other, being a-head and to windward, could not bear up without risk of collision, and could not go about because of a shoal (*y*).

A sloop, with the wind free, was running through a narrow channel against a strong tide close to the shore. Two schooners, the combined length of which was equal to half the breadth of the channel, were beating to windward in the opposite direction. It was held that the sternmost of the schooners was in fault for standing on when under the stern of the leading schooner, so that when she was obliged to go about she ran into the sloop, which could not avoid her without going ashore (*z*).

Art. 14.

## ARTICLE 15.

*If two ships under steam are meeting end on, or nearly end on, so as to involve risk of collision, each shall alter her course to starboard, so that each may pass on the port side of the other.*

*This Article only applies to cases where ships are meeting end on, or nearly end on, in such a manner as to involve risk of collision, and does not apply to two ships which must, if both keep on their respective courses, pass clear of each other.*

*The only cases to which it does apply are when each of the two ships is end on, or nearly end on, to the other; in other words, to cases in which, by day, each ship sees the masts of the other in a line with her own; and by night to cases in which each ship is in such a position as to see both the side lights of the other.*

Art. 15.

Two ships under steam meeting.

(*y*) *The Ann Caroline*, 2 Mar. Law Cas. O. S. 208 (American case).

(*z*) *The Mark Ereline*, 16 Wall. 348.

Art. 15.    *It does not apply by day to cases in which a ship sees*
*another ahead crossing her own course; or by night to*
*cases where the red light of one ship is opposed to the red*
*light of the other, or where the green light of one ship is*
*opposed to the green light of the other, or where a red light*
*without a green light, or a green light without a red light,*
*is seen ahead, or where both green and red lights are seen*
*anywhere but ahead.*

This Article contains the substance of Article 13 of the
Regulations of 1863, and of the Order in Council of the
30th of July, 1868, explaining the meaning of " end on"(*a*).
The words " each shall alter her course to starboard " are
exactly equivalent to " the helms of both shall be put to
port " of the Regulations of 1863 (*b*). The words " so that
each may pass on the port side of the other " appear to be
merely explanatory. The vessels described in this Article
as " ships under steam " are probably the same as those
described elsewhere in the Regulations as " seagoing steam-
ships," or " steam-ships ;" and it is not clear why the same

(*a*) It is not clear that 25 & 26
Vict. c. 63 authorises an interpretation of the Regulations by Order in
Council. But any difficulty on this
point is removed by the enactment
of the Regulations in text in the
place of those of 1863.

(*b*) The alteration in the wording
of the new Regulations was probably
made with a view to a possible uni-
formity of system amongst the seamen of all nations as regards orders
to the helm. In English ships the
order which sends the ship's head to
starboard is " port !" In France the
equivalent order is " babord !"—the
literal translation of which is " starboard." Some nations, including
America, adopt the English system,
others the French. Since pilots of
one nation are frequently in charge
of ships of another nation, it is
manifest that a uniform system is

very desirable. The apparent para-
dox involved in the English system
originated with the use of the tiller,
the movements of which are opposite
to those of the ship's head. Most
vessels of any tonnage being now
steered by a wheel, and the tiller
being frequently aft of the rudder-
head, the orders to the helm are
altogether anomalous. With a
wheel, and a tiller aft of the rudder-
head, the order to send the ship's
head to starboard is still " port !"
whilst the wheel, the tiller, and the
ship's head all move together in the
same direction, to starboard. It
must be remembered that when
going astern the action of the rudder
is reversed, and that the order
" port !" and corresponding movement of the rudder to starboard
sends the ship's head to port.

term is not used throughout. As to the meaning of "so   **Art. 15.**
as to involve risk of collision," see above, p. 136.

In the Regulations of 1880 vessels approaching each Classification of ships into
other are described as "meeting" (c), "crossing," and meeting,
"overtaking," or being overtaken. It appears that this crossing, and overtaking
classification is intended to include all cases of ships ships.
approaching or being approached by others. It is a cross
classification, for although no ship that is a "crossing"
ship can at the same time come within the rule for
"meeting" ships, yet a "crossing" ship may at the same
time be an "overtaking" ship, and be bound by Article
20 (d).

The rule contained in Article 15 is not identical with Abolition of the rule of
the "port helm" rule of former Acts, and of the old mari- "port helm"
time law, with which seamen were familiar. The existing except in one case.
Regulations limit the application of the "port helm" to one
case only, namely, where both the ships are steam-ships,
and they are proceeding in directly opposite directions on
the same line, or nearly so. In every other case the "port
helm" rule is inapplicable, and the two ships must act as
required by the particular Article applicable to the case.
There is reason to think that the important alteration of
the law effected by the Regulations of 1863, and continued
by those of 1880, has not produced a corresponding change
in the practice of seamen. The proper application of the
"port helm" rule in its existing shape requires the careful
attention of seamen. Its indiscriminate application has
been a fruitful source of collision.

It appears from the explanatory part of Article 15 that Case of steam-ship making
the application of that Article is determined, not by the over the

(c) "Meets" in 17 & 18 Vict. c. 104, s. 296, had a wider meaning than "meeting" in the existing Regulations : see *The Cleopatra*, Swab. Ad. 135.
(d) See Articles 14, 16, and 20. As to the distinction between "meeting" and "crossing" ships

see *The Franconia*, 2 P. D. 8 ; *The Princessan Louisa* and *The Artemas*, Holt, 75 ; *The Eliza* and *The Orinoco*, ibid. 93 ; *The Superb* and *The Florence Bragington*, 2 Mar. Law Cas. O. S. 237 ; *The Peckforton Castle*, 3 P. D. 11 ; *The Columbia*, 10 Wall. 246.

Art. 15.

ground a
course dif-
ferent from
the direction
of her head.

directions in which two ships are approaching each other over the ground, but by the directions in which their heads are pointing. The case of a steam-ship crossing a tideway, or of a tug with a heavy ship in tow making considerable leeway, so that she is approaching another vessel upon a course over the ground directly opposite to that of the other, but in a direction different from that in which her head is pointing, does not seem to be expressly provided for. Such a case would probably be held to come within Article 23.

How much
the course
must be
altered; both
ships must
port; neither
need slacken
after risk is
determined.

"Altering her course to starboard" under Article 15 means altering sufficiently to take her clear, if the other ship does not starboard (e). The law is that both ships are to alter their helms, and the neglect by one to obey the rule will be no excuse to the other, although there would have been no collision if both had ported (f). Where a ship is in a position to which Article 15 applies, and she alters her course sufficiently to determine the risk of collision, she is not required at the same time to slacken under Article 18 (g).

If two steam-ships sight each other nearly right ahead, but so that each is a little on the starboard bow of the other, the law requires each to put her helm to port, although a collision would be avoided if each were to starboard, and that appears to be the safer and more convenient course. "It is essential that the law should be universally observed. If one obeys and the other does not, the utmost confusion and danger will be introduced. A vessel which obeys the law has a right to trust that the vessel which she meets . . . . . will obey it too, and she acts accordingly" (h).

(e) *The Jesmond* and *The Earl of Elgin*, L. R. 4 P. C. 1.
(f) See *The America*, 2 Otto. 432; *The Araxes* and *The Black Prince*, *infra*.
(g) *The Jesmond* and *The Earl of Elgin*, *supra*.

(h) *Per* Lord Kingsdown in *The Araxes* and *The Black Prince*, 15 Moo. P. C. C. 122 ; and see *The Cleopatra*, Swab. Ad. 135. These cases were under 17 & 18 Vict. c. 104, s. 296.

Art. 15.

The meaning of " nearly end on " has not been exactly
defined.  Vessels upon parallel courses, each with the other
nearly right ahead, and vessels upon courses making with
each other an angle of two, or even three, points have been
held to be meeting " nearly end on " (i).  These cases were,
however, decided before the interpretation of the term by
Order in Council of 30th July, 1868.

What is
"nearly end
on?"

## ARTICLE 16.

*If two ships under steam are crossing so as to involve
risk of collision, the ship which has the other on her own
starboard side shall keep out of the way of the other.*

Art. 16.

Two ships
under steam
crossing.

This Article is identical in terms with Article 14 of the
Regulations of 1863.  As to the meaning of " risk of collision," see above, p. 136 ; as to the distinction between
" meeting," " crossing," and " overtaking " ships, see p. 175 ;
as to how a ship is to " keep out of the way," see p. 198 ;
and as to the duty of the ship which has the other on her
port side, see Article 22, below.

There have been some important decisions as to the
application of the " crossing " rule in winding rivers.  The
steam-ship *Carbon*, coming up the Thames on the flood-tide,
and rounding a point where the river turns to starboard,
under a port helm, saw a little on her starboard bow the
masthead and red lights of *The Velocity*, a steam-ship
coming down the river.  In that part of the river it is
usual for ships bound down to keep near the north shore.
It was held that the ships were not " crossing " ships, and

Application of
Art. 16 in a
winding river.

(i) *The Fruiter* and *The Fingal*,
2 Mar. Law Cas. O. S. 291 ; *The
Kezia* and *The Victoria*, Holt, 70 ;
*The Princessan Lovisa* and *The Arte-*
mas, Holt, 75 ; *The Thames* and
*The Stork*, Holt, 151 ; *The St. Cyran*
and *The Henry*, Holt, 72.  But see
supra, p. 172, note (r).

N

Art. 16    that *The Carbon* was wrong in porting and attempting to
pass to the north of *The Velocity*. It was held by the
Privy Council that the duty of each ship was to continue
her course round the point in the usual track, in which
case they would have passed clear (*l*).

*The Velocity* was decided upon the general Regulations
of 1863, and before any special bye-laws for the Thames
were in force. According to this case, it appears that in
winding rivers, and channels where no special rules are in
force, two ships on opposite sides of a point, and rounding
the bend, are not always, or for that reason alone, "crossing"
ships. But it is not clear that this decision would be
followed where the "crossing" rule has been in terms
enacted for the regulation of navigation in a winding river.
In a recent case decided under the Thames Rules, which
contained an Article identical in terms with Article 16 of
the general Regulations, a steam-ship proceeding up the
river was crossing the channel obliquely in order to clear
a ship in her path. Whilst so doing, there was, on her
starboard side, and in the reach above her, which turned to
starboard, another steam-ship coming down. The collision
occurred about the meeting of the two reaches. It was
held by the Court of Appeal that the ships were crossing
ships, and that it was the duty of the vessel bound up the
river to keep out of the way (*m*).

A steam-ship, *The Cayuga*, after coming out of her dock
in New York harbour, and straightening herself down the
river, was heading S.S.W. At the same time *The James
Watt*, another steam-ship, was coming up on a S. by E.
course abaft the beam of *The Cayuga* on her starboard

(*l*) *The Velocity*, L. R. 3 P. C. 44.
See also *The Cologne* and *The Ranger*,
L. R. 4 P. C. 519; *The Esk* and *The
Niord*, L. R. 3 P. C. 436; and the
observations of James, L.J., on *The
Velocity* in *The Oceano* and *The*

*Virgo*, 3 P. D. 60.
(*m*) *The Oceano* and *The Virgo*, 3
P. D. 60. See also as to the duty of
two ships rounding a bend in a river,
one outside the other, *The Bywell
Castle*, 4 P. D. 219.

quarter, and overtaking her.   It was held by the Supreme   **Art. 16.**
Court of the United States that they were crossing ships,
and that *The Cayuga* was in fault for not keeping out of
the way of *The James Watt* under Article 14 of the
Regulations of 1863 (*n*).

ARTICLE 17.

*If two ships, one of which is a sailing-ship and the*   **Art. 17.**
*other a steam-ship, are proceeding in such directions as to* Sailing-ship
*involve risk of collision, the steam-ship shall keep out of* and ship under
*the way of the sailing-ship.*   steam.

This Article is identical with Article 15 of the Regulations of 1863.

As to "risk of collision," see above, p. 136; as to how
to "keep out of the way," see p. 198; and as to the duty
of the sailing-ship, see Article 23.

The reason of the rule of Article 17 is said to be that Reason of the
a steam-ship is more completely under command than a rule that a
sailing-ship.   She can go ahead in the teeth of the wind, and must keep out
she can stop or go astern, as she pleases (*o*).   This, how- of the way.
ever, is true only to a limited extent in the case of a tug plies to a tug.
with a ship in tow; and in approaching her, the other ship
must take her encumbered condition into consideration (*p*).
In America a schooner was held in fault for not holding
herself in stays to allow a tug with a fleet of barges in tow
to pass (*q*).   But the tug is a steam-ship within the meaning of Article 17, and must comply with that Article, so
far as she can (*r*).

(*n*) *The Cayuga*, 14 Wall. 270.
According to the definition proposed
by Brett, L.J., in *The Franconia*, 2
P. D. 8, *The James Watt* was an
"overtaking" ship. and bound to
keep out of the way of *The Cayuga*.
(*o*) *The Arthur Gordon* and *The
Independence*, Lush. 270.
(*p*) S. C.; *The Gala* and *The
Zenobia*, Holt, 112.   In narrow

waters it is frequently dangerous
for a long and heavy steam-ship to
keep out of the way, where the
sailing-ship can do so without difficulty.   But if it is possible, the
steam-ship must obey the law.
(*q*) *The W. C. Redfield*, 4 Bened.
227.
(*r*) See *supra*, pp. 79, 145.

N 2

**Art. 17.**

**Duty of a steam-ship meeting, crossing, and over-taking a sailing-ship.**

The duty of the steam-ship under Article 17 is the same whether the sailing-ship is close-hauled or free, and whether she is on the port or starboard tack. If the steam-ship is crossing the course of the sailing-ship, and at the same time overtaking her, she is required to keep out of the way by Article 20 as well as by Article 17. If she is meeting the sailing-ship end on, or nearly end on, she is not required by the Regulations to pass on one side rather than the other; she may " keep out of the way," under Article 17, as she thinks best. If she is being overtaken by the sailing-ship, it appears that by the operation of Article 20 and Article 22 she is required to keep her course (s).

**Difference between Art. 17 and the old rule of " port helm."**

The difference between the rule contained in Article 17 and the old rule of "port helm" should be observed. In the case of a sailing-ship with the wind free meeting a steam-ship end on, her duty is to keep her course, and not, as has been supposed, to put her helm to port (t).

**Heavy obligation of Art. 17 on steam-ships.**

The obligation which Article 17 throws upon a steam-ship in every case where there is risk of collision with a sailing-ship is heavy. "It is the duty of a steamer, where there is risk of collision, whatever may be the conduct of the sailing vessel, to do everything in her power that can be done, consistently with her own safety, in order to avoid collision" (u). At the same time, "When a steamer is condemned for having omitted to do something which she ought to have done, it seems just to require proof of three things : first, that the thing omitted to be done was clearly in the power of the steamer to do ; secondly, that, if done, it would in all probability have prevented collision ;

---

(s) Under the Regulations of 1863, there was a doubt as to the duty of a steam-ship being overtaken by a sailing-ship ; see *The Philotaxe*, 3 Asp. Mar. Law Cas. 512.

(t) *The Bougainville* and *The*

*Jas. C. Stevenson*, L. R. 5 P. C. 316.

(u) Per Westbury, C., in *Inman v. Beck, The City of Antwerp* and *The Friedrich*, L. R. 2 P. C. 25, 30, 34.

and, thirdly, that it was an act which would have occurred Art. 17. to any officer of competent skill and experience in command of the steamer " (x).

The duty of the steam-ship has been thus defined by the Duty of steam-ship: American case. Supreme Court of the United States : "The Rules require, when a steam-ship and sailing vessel are approaching from opposite directions or on intersecting lines, that the steamship, from the moment the sailing vessel is seen, shall watch with the highest diligence her course and movements, so as to be able to adopt such timely measures of precaution as will necessarily prevent the two boats coming in contact" (y). And in *The Falcon* (z), the same Court said : " It was the duty of the steamer to see the schooner as soon as she could be seen, to watch her progress and direction, to take into account all the circumstances of the situation, and so to govern herself as to guard against peril to either vessel."

Under Article 17 it is the duty of a steam-tug lying-to, Duty of steam-tug lying-to to keep out of the way. or drifting about waiting for employment, to keep out of the way of a sailing vessel (a).

The fact of a tug having a heavy ship in tow, and a And of a tug with a heavy ship in tow. strong head wind against her, does not justify the tug in departing from Article 17, and neglecting to keep out of the way of a sailing-ship (b). And a steam-ship of 1356 tons was held in fault for not keeping out of the way, although she had in tow a disabled vessel of 1495 tons, with a long scope of tow rope, so that the towage was a service of difficulty (c).

The duty of the sailing vessel is to keep her course, as if Duty of the sailing-ship under Art. 17. no other vessel were in sight ; but where a sailing-ship, when a considerable distance (two miles) off the steam-ship,

<hr/>

(x) *Ibid.*
(y) *The Carroll*, 8 Wall. 302, 306; *The Lucile*, 15 Wall. 676.
(z) *The Falcon*, 19 Wall. 75.
(a) *The Jennie S. Barker* and *The Spindrift*, 3 Asp. Mar. Law Cas.

44 ; see also *The Sunnyside*, 1 Otto, 208.
(b) *The Warrior*, L. R. 3 A. & E. 553.
(c) *The American* and *The Syria*, L. R. 6 P. C. 127.

**Art. 17.** altered her helm slightly, it was held that she was not therefore in fault for the collision (*d*).

**Cases illustrating Art. 17.** A sailing-ship, turning to windward in the Thames, went about when she got to the edge of the tide, without giving any notice to a steam-ship astern of her. The steam-ship was held solely in fault for a collision which followed (*e*).

A barque, rounding to before coming to an anchor, was held not to be in fault for a collision with a steam-ship, although the steam-ship alleged that she was baffled by the rapid change of the barque's lights, and that the collision was caused by the barque's departure from the rule requiring her to keep her course (*f*).

But a sailing-ship must not go about at an improper time or place, so as to embarrass the steam-ship (*g*).

Where a steam-ship was crossing the English Channel at twelve knots an hour, and ran down a sailing-ship with her lights burning and obeying the regulations, it was said by the court that she must be in fault. If it was thick, she was in fault for going so fast; and if it was fine, she was bound to see and avoid the other ship (*h*).

## ARTICLE 18.

**Art. 18.** *Every steam-ship, when approaching another ship, so as*
**Steam-ship to slow or reverse engines if necessary.** *to involve risk of collision, shall slacken her speed, or stop and reverse, if necessary.*

This Article is almost identical with Article 16 of the Regulations of 1863. The direction in the latter as to speed in a fog is omitted, and now forms part of Article 13.

---

(*d*) *The Norma*, 3 Asp. Mar. Law Cas. 272.

(*e*) *The Palatine*, 1 Asp. Mar. Law Cas. 468.

(*f*) *The Monsoon* v. *The Neptune*, 2 Mar. Law Cas. O. S. 289; Holt, 186.

(*g*) *The General Lee*, 3 Mar. Law Cas. O. S. 204 (Irish case); *The Potomac*, 8 Wall. 590; and see *infra*, p. 227, as to the duty of a sailing-ship to beat out her tack.

(*h*) *The Samphire* and *The Fanny Beck*, Holt, 193.

Apart from the Regulations, it would be held to be negligence if a steam-ship failed to stop and reverse, "if necessary" (i); and Article 18 appears to be little more than a declaration of the law in this respect.

*Art. 18.*

Article 18 applies only "where there is a continuous approaching of two ships." It does not apply in every case where Article 15, or Article 16, is applicable. To make it the duty of a steam-ship to slacken, or stop and reverse, under Article 18, it appears that the risk of collision must be more imminent than that mentioned in Articles 15 and 16 (k). Perhaps this is the meaning of the words "if necessary," which are peculiar to Article 18.

*Where Art. 18 applies.*

Where two steam-ships were approaching each other with risk of collision, and one of them ported so as to bring port light to port light, it was held by the Privy Council that risk of collision was then determined, and that the vessel that had ported was not required by the law to slacken, or to stop and reverse (l). But unless the alteration of the helm will determine the risk, the duty of the steam-ship is at once to stop and reverse (m). In America, it has been held by the Supreme Court that the rule requiring a steam-ship to slacken does not apply where, if both ships continue their courses, they will pass clear, although, if either deviates from her course, there will be risk of collision (n).

*It does not apply when risk is determined.*

A steam-ship being overtaken by another vessel is not "approaching" the overtaking ship within the meaning of Article 18. Her duty, therefore, is to keep her course under Article 22, and not to slacken under Article 18, for that Article does not apply to her (o).

(i) See *The Birkenhead*, 3 W. Rob. 75 ; *The James Watt*, 2 W. Rob. 270 ; *The Vivid*, 7 Not. of Cas. 127.

(k) *The Jesmond* and *The Earl of Elgin*, L. R. 4 P. C. 1 ; and see *The Milwaukee*, Brown Ad. 313.

(l) *The Jesmond* and *The Earl of Elgin, ubi supra.*

(m) *The Joseph Straker* v. *The Karla*, Holt, 203.

(n) *The Free State*, 1 Otto, 200 ; Brown Adm. 251.

(o) *The Franconia*, 2 P. D. 8.

Art. 18.

Engines not to be set on ahead until risk is over.

Stopping and reversing not always a prudent measure.

To comply with Article 18, a vessel must not only slacken or stop, but she must not set her engines ahead again until the risk of collision is past (p).

In applying Article 18, it must be borne in mind that reversing the screw whilst the ship has headway through the water always diminishes the turning power of the helm. In the case, therefore, of a screw steam-ship, stopping and reversing her engines is not always a necessary, or even a prudent, step for her to take when at close quarters with another ship.

Duty to stop or ease the engines where the other ship's lights or course cannot be made out.

If a steam-ship sights another ship or her lights, and cannot clearly make out what course she is upon, it is her duty at once to slacken until she can ascertain what the stranger's course is, so that she may be able to take the measures required by the Regulations (q); and she must do so before altering her helm, or taking any decisive step, for if she does not, and by altering her helm without knowing the other ship's position and course causes a collision, she will be held to be in fault (r).

Speed of a steam-ship approaching other craft.

Steamers navigating at a high rate of speed are required to slacken their speed when approaching other ships, when there is difficulty or danger in passing them. It was held by the Supreme Court in the United States that a large steamer approaching a tug with a number of barges in tow, and surrounded by other vessels, was bound to slacken, and not "hurl herself like a projectile in the midst of them" at the rate of seventeen miles an hour, taking the chance of clearing them (s). And in another case it was held by the same Court that a large steamer entering a harbour, or narrow channel, was bound to go at

(p) In Dowell v. General Steam Nav. Co., 5. Ell. & B. 195, under the old law, it was held that a ship was in fault if she did not continue to exhibit a light so long as danger of collision existed.

(q) The Rona and The Ava, 2

Asp. Mar. Law Cas. 182; The General Lee, 3 Mar. Law Cas. O. S. 204.

(r) The Bougainville and The Jas. C. Stevenson, L. R. 5 P. C. 316.

(s) The Syracuse, 9 Wall. 672.

such speed as was consistent with the safety of other
vessels (t).

"Moderate" speed is a relative term. It cannot be
defined so as to apply to all cases; what it should be in
each case depends on the circumstances of the particular
case. Four to five knots, or slow half-speed of a vessel
whose full speed was from seven to nine knots, seems to
have been held too great speed in a fog so dense that a
ship could not be seen more than seventy yards off (u).
In any case, speed such that another vessel cannot be seen
in time to avoid her is unlawful (x). Speed which is
justifiable in an unfrequented part of the ocean is unlawful, and even criminal, in a crowded roadstead or highway (y).

In the case of *The Europa* (z), it was said by the Privy
Council: "This may be safely laid down as a rule on all
occasions, fog or clear, light or dark, that no steamer has a
right to navigate at such a rate that it is impossible for her
to prevent damage, taking all precaution at the moment
she sees danger to be possible; and if she cannot do that
without going less than five knots an hour, then she is
bound to go at less than five knots an hour."

In *The Batavier* (a), it was said by Dr. Lushington:
" At whatever rate she (the steam-ship) was going, if going
at such a rate as made it dangerous to any craft which she
ought to have seen, and might have seen, she had no right
to go at that rate."

It has been held in America that it is not enough to
slacken until the speed is such as would enable the steam-
ship to avoid another vessel which is sounding her fog-
horn (b). And from the English decisions it appears that

(t) *The City of Paris*, 9 Wall.
634; and see *The Corsica*, 9 Wall.
630.
(u) *The Magna Charta*, 1 Asp.
Mar. Law Cas. 153.
(x) *The City of Brooklyn*, 3 Asp.
Mar. Law Cas. 280; 1 P. D. 276.
(y) *The Europa*, 14 Jur. 627.
(z) Cited in *The Pennsylvania*, 19
Wall. 125, 134.
(a) 1 Sp. E. & A. 378.
(b) *The Hansa*, 5 Bened. 501.

Art. 18.　the rate must be regulated by the thickness of the fog, rather than by the supposed distance at which a horn or bell would be audible.

Carrying mails no excuse for excessive speed.　It is no excuse for excessive speed that the ship is carrying mails, and under contract to deliver them by a certain date (*d*).

Excessive speed, if it could not possibly have contributed to the collision, does not prevent a ship from recovering.　But when a ship is shown to have been going at too great a rate of speed, it does, not follow, though it may have been an act of imprudence, that the ship is in fault for the collision. If the rate of speed could not by possibility have contributed to the collision, but was simply an act of imprudence, not connected with the collision, it must be left entirely out of the case (*e*).

## ARTICLE 19.

Art. 19.　*In taking any course authorised or required by these* Optional sound signals to indicate the course of ships under steam. *regulations, a steam-ship under way may indicate that course to any other ship which she has in sight by the following signals on her steam whistle, viz.:—*

*One short blast to mean " I am directing my course to starboard."*

*Two short blasts to mean " I am directing my course to port."*

*Three short blasts to mean " I am going full speed astern."*

*The use of these signals is optional; but if they are used, the course of the ship must be in accordance with the signal made.*

This article is entirely new. It applies only where a ship intends to comply with the Regulations, and is desirous to call the attention of the other ship to her intended

---

(*d*) *The Vivid*, Swab. Ad. 88 ; 10 Moo. P. C. C. 472 ; *The Northern Indiana*, 3 Blatchf. 92.

(*e*) *The Lord Saumarez*, 6 Not. of Cas. 600 ; but see 36 & 37 Vict. c. 85, s. 17, *supra*, pp. 14, *seq.*

course. Such signals have been in use in America for many years. It has been there held that a vessel cannot, by means of these signals, dictate to the other ship a departure from the Regulations (*f*). Care must be taken that the "short" blasts of Article 19 are not confounded with the "prolonged" fog-signal blasts of Article 12.

Art. 19.

## ARTICLE 20.

*Notwithstanding anything contained in any preceding Article, every ship, whether a sailing-ship or a steam-ship, overtaking any other, shall keep out of the way of the overtaken ship.*

Art. 20.

Ships overtaking other ships.

This Article corresponds with Article 17 of the Regulations of 1863, but its operation is larger. The opening words, "Notwithstanding, &c.," are intended to meet a difficulty, which existed under the Regulations of 1863, as to the duty of a sailing-ship overtaking a steam-ship, and as to the duty of a sailing-ship or a steam-ship overtaking another sailing- or steam-ship from abaft the beam of the latter, and crossing her course. In these cases there was an apparent conflict between Article 15 and Article 17 (*g*), and between Article 12 and Article 17 (*h*), of the Regulations of 1863.

Article 20 is express as to the duty of an overtaking sailing-ship to keep out of the way. And under the Regulations of 1880 it seems clear that a ship may be an "overtaking" ship within Article 20, when, if her speed were not greater than that of the other vessel, she would be a "crossing" ship coming under Article 14 or Article 16. As to how the other ship is to keep out of the way, see above, p. 180.

(*f*) *The Milwaukee*, Brown Ad. 313.
(*g*) See *The Philotaxe*, 3 Asp. Mar. Law Cas. 512 ; *The Wheatsheaf* and *The Intrepide*, 2 Mar. Law Cas.

O. S. 292.
(*h*) See *The Peckforton Castle*, 2 P. D. 222 ; 3 P. D. 11 ; *The Franconia*, 2 P. D. 8.

Art. 20.

What is an
"overtaking"
ship?

There is nothing in the Regulations to indicate how one ship must bear from another in order to be an "overtaking" ship. A ship dead astern of another, or on her quarter, is no doubt an "overtaking" ship if coming up with the other ahead. Whether a ship a point or two on the beam of another is "overtaking" the latter, if going at a greater speed, is not clear. Under the Regulations of 1863 a rule was suggested by Brett, L.J., in *The Franconia* (i), to the effect that a vessel approaching another from a direction in which, if it were night, the side lights of the ship ahead would not be visible to her, should be considered as an "overtaking" ship; and that a vessel approaching another from any other direction except directly ahead should be "crossing." In a subsequent case (k), however, doubts were expressed in the Court of Appeal as to the correctness of the rule suggested by Brett, L.J.

A ship coming up with another on a course differing from that of the latter by half a point was held to be "overtaking" her (l).

One of the Tyne bye-laws provides that, "when steam vessels are preceding in the same direction, but with unequal speed, the vessel which steams slowest shall, when overtaken," take certain steps to enable the other to pass. It was held by the Privy Council that this rule applied only to a vessel overtaking and passing another actually on the same course as herself (m).

In *The Cayuga* (n) the Supreme Court of the United States expressed an opinion that a vessel was "overtaking" another within the meaning of Article 17 of the Regulations of 1863 only when astern of the other and pursuing the same general direction. In that case it was held that two steam-ships on intersecting courses (S. by E. and S.S.W.)

(i) *The Franconia*, 2 P. D. 8, 12.    Law Cas. 569.
(k) *The Peckforton Castle*, 3 P. D.    (m) *The Henry Morton*, 2 Asp.
11.                                     Mar. Law Cas. 466.
(l) *The Chanonry*, 1 Asp. Mar.    (n) 14 Wall. 270, 277.

were "crossing" ships, although one was abaft the beam of, **Art. 20.**
and going faster than, the other.  It was said by the Court
that in such a case the relative speed of the two ships did
not affect the question as to what measures they are
required by the Regulations to take to avoid collision.
But in another American case it was held that a steam-
ship coming up on the quarter of another ahead is not
a "crossing" but an "overtaking" ship (o).

The rule, that an overtaking ship must keep out of the
way of a ship ahead, was a rule of the maritime law, and
was merely formulated by the Regulations of 1863 (p).  It
clashed, however, with the other equally well established
rule, that a ship with the wind free must keep out of the way
of another close-hauled.  In an American case, where a brig
and a schooner were upon converging courses, the schooner
overtaking the brig, it was held that the brig was in fault
for not keeping out of the way, she having the wind free.
It was said that, if she had been close-hauled, it would not
have been her duty to keep out of the way (q).  Under
the existing law a sailing-ship overtaking another must
keep out of the way, though she is close-hauled and the
other is free.

*The rule, that an overtaking ship must keep out of the way, is a rule of the maritime law.*

The Court of Appeal has said that a ship cannot be an
"overtaking" ship within the meaning of Article 20 unless
she is going faster than the ship ahead (r).

The duty of the ship ahead, under ordinary circumstances, is to keep her course under Article 22, and not to
slacken or stop.  Article 18 does not apply to her, as she
cannot be said to be approaching the overtaking ship
within the meaning of that Article (s).

*Duty of over-taken ship.*

(o) The Oceanus, 5 Bened. 545 ;
see also The Governor, Abbot Ad.
108 ; The Rhode Island, Olcott, 505 ;
1 Blatchf. 363.
(p) Whitridge v. Dill, 23 How.
448.

(q) The Clement, 1 Sprague, 257 ;
2 Curtis, 363.  The Supreme Court
was equally divided.
(r) The Franconia, 2 P. D. S.
(s) The Franconia, ubi supra.

**Art. 20.**     As to the duty of a ship which is being overtaken to show a light astern, see Article 11, *supra*, p. 160.

It is the duty of a steam-ship overtaking a sailing-ship to keep out of the way of the latter, both by virtue of Article 17 and Article 20.

Cases illustrating the application of Art. 20.     A steam-ship attempted to pass a sailing-ship turning up the Thames against a head wind. Owing to the latter going about when she got to the edge of the tide, the steamer ran into her. It was held that the sailing-ship was under no obligation to give notice that she was going about, and that the steamer in attempting to pass did so at her own risk (*t*).

Where a sailing-ship, A., with the wind free, was approaching another, B., hove-to, and driving to leeward in such a direction that her side lights were not for some time visible to A., it was held that it was the duty of A. to keep out of the way (*u*). It does not appear whether the decision was on the ground that A. was "overtaking" B., or that A. was "crossing" B. and to windward of her, with the wind on the same side, or whether it was A.'s duty to keep out of the way because she was going free and the other ship hove-to.

When two ships turning to windward in narrow waters are close-hauled on the same tack, one following in the wake of the other, if the leading ship goes about, and the following ship cannot stand on without risk of collision, it is the duty of the latter to keep out of the way of the ship ahead by going about (*x*).

If two ships are turning to windward, and the one ahead, instead of going about, wears, it seems that, while she is in the act of wearing and approaching the ship astern, the latter is not an "overtaking" ship, and that she is not required to keep out of the way (*y*).

(t) *The Palatine*, 1 Asp. Mar. Law Cas. 468.

(u) *The Eleanor* v. *The Alma*, 2 Mar. Law Cas. O. S. 240.

(x) *The Priscilla*, L. R. 3 A. & E.

125; *The Eclipse* v. *The Royal Consort*, Holt, 220.

(y) *The Falkland* and *The Navigator*, Br. & Lush. 204.

It was held in America that a vessel was in fault for attempting to pass another ahead in a channel so narrow that there was risk in making the attempt (z); and that the rule requiring the overtaking ship to keep out of the way does not cease to operate the moment the overtaking ship gets her nose in front of the other (a).

Art. 20.

## ARTICLE 21.

*In narrow channels every steam-ship shall, when it is safe and practicable, keep to that side of the fairway or midchannel which lies on the starboard side of such ship.*

Art. 21.<br>Ships under steam in narrow channels.

This Article is entirely new. It is substantially the re-enactment of a rule which existed from 1846 to 1862. During those years there were in force various Acts requiring ships to navigate on the starboard side of rivers and narrow channels. By 9 & 10 Vict. c. 100, s. 9, steam-ships were required to keep on the starboard side of midchannel, " due regard being had to the tide and the position of each vessel in such tide." In *The Leith* (b) this was interpreted to mean that a ship was to keep on the starboard side " provided it may be done with convenience and safety " to the other vessel. By subsequent Acts (14 & 15 Vict. c. 79, s. 27, and 17 & 18 Vict. c. 104, s. 297) the rule was re-enacted with the omission of the words as to having regard to the tide. In several cases (c) decided under these Acts it was held that no practice of the river as to ships keeping in or out of the strength of the tide, and no considerations of convenience, would justify a

History of the "starboard side" rule.

---

(z) *The City of Paris*, 1 Bened. 174 ; 9 Wall 634 ; *The Narragansett, infra.*

(a) *The Narragansett*, 10 Blatchf. 475.

(b) 7 Not. of Cas. 137.

(c) *The Duke of Sussex*, 1 W. Rob. 274 ; *The Sylph*, 2 Sp. E. & A. 75 ;

*The Panther*, 1 Sp. E. & A. 31 ; *The Malvina*, 1 Moo. P. C. C. N. S. 357 ; *The Mæander* and *The Florence Nightingale*, ibid. 63 ; *The Seine*, Swab. Ad. 411 ; *The Hand of Providence*, ibid. 107 ; *The Unity*, ibid. 101 ; are decisions under the starboard side rule of former Acts.

**Art. 21.** deviation from the express enactment as to keeping on the starboard side. By 25 & 26 Vict. c. 63 the "starboard side" rule was repealed, and from 1862 to the 1st of September, 1880, vessels have been free to navigate on either side of rivers, except in the Clyde and some other waters where the starboard side rule has been in force under local Acts.

*Consequence of navigating on the wrong side of a narrow channel.*   The re-enactment of the starboard side rule and its insertion in the Regulations are of the utmost consequence to seamen. Any person in charge of a ship who navigates her on the wrong side of a narrow channel, besides being guilty of a misdemeanour, will almost inevitably subject himself and his owners to liability for any collision occurring when he is on his wrong side, unless it is proved that his being on the wrong side was unavoidable (*d*).

*Meaning of terms "narrow channel," "midchannel," and "when it is safe and practicable."*   In *The Maunder* and *The Florence Nightingale* (*e*), it was held that the sea-channels at the entrance of the river Mersey were not within the provisions of a former Act relating to the navigation of "narrow channels." There has also been considerable discussion as to the meaning of "midchannel" under a former Act (*f*). The words, "when it is safe and practicable," appear to qualify the general operation of the rule; but it is doubtful whether they have any further effect than the general saving clause of Article 23 (*g*).

*Rules in American rivers.*   In America some of the States have passed laws as to the side on which vessels are to navigate; and in some rivers there is a customary track. Sometimes an ascending ship must keep on one side or the other of midchannel, leaving the middle of the river to descending ships. In the East River, at New York, it is the law that vessels going up or down shall keep in midchannel. Where a ship is

---

(*d*) See 36 & 37 Vict. c. 85, s. 17; *supra*, pp. 14, *seq.*
(*e*) 1 Moo. P. C. C. N. S. 63.
(*f*) *Smith* v. *Voss*, 2 H. & N. 97.

(*g*) As to the meaning of these words in former Acts, see *The Unity*, Swab. Ad. 101; *The Hand of Providence*, *ibid.* 107.

required by law or usage to keep on one side or the other, if she is on her wrong side, she is held to be in fault for a collision with another ship that is on her right side, and has done all that the law requires to keep clear (*h*).

There is great difficulty in determining the application of some of the Articles of the general Regulations to ships navigating a narrow and tortuous river. It appears to have been held by the Privy Council (*i*) in the case of two ships bound up and down a river, and first sighting each other on opposite sides of a point of land round which the river winds, that the ships are not "crossing" ships within the meaning of the Regulations; and that, if they are then on different sides of the river, the duty of each is to pursue her course as if the other were not in sight. If, when they first sight each other on opposite sides of a point of land, they are both in midchannel, or equidistant from the same shore, it is not clear how, and on which side, the law requires them to pass each other (*k*). It may happen, in such a case, that owing to the way of the ships through the water and the set of the tide it is possible for them to clear each other in one way, and in one way only.

In most tidal rivers there is a customary track for vessels going with the tide, and another for those going against it. Its course depends mainly on the practise for ships with a fair tide to keep in its strength, and for those with a foul tide to "cheat" it, or keep out of its strength. In a winding river, where there is an offset of the tide from

*Difficulty of applying the "crossing" and "meeting" rules in a winding river.*

*Customary course in rivers.*

---

(*h*) 1 Parsons on Shipping (ed. 1869), 582; *The Ivanhoe* and *The Martha M. Heath*, 7 Bened. 213 ; *The Vanderbilt*, 6 Wall. 225 ; *The Bay State*, 3 Blatchf. 48.

(*i*) See *The Velocity*, and cases cited below.

(*k*) In *The City of London* and *The Vesta* it appears to have been held by the Wreck Commissioner

(Sept. 1879) that two ships proceeding, the one down and the other up the Thames, each about midchannel, were "meeting" ships, though, owing to the winding of the river, they were not "end on." As to the duty of two ships rounding a bend in a river in opposite directions, one outside the other, see *The Byrell Castle*, 4 P. D. 219, *per* Brett, L.J.

194                      THE REGULATIONS.

**Art. 21.**

the points into the opposite bights, ships usually cross from one side of the river to the other at or about particular places in the different reaches. It has been held that such a practice, although not strictly a custom binding upon all ships, is one which a ship is justified in following and in assuming that other ships will follow (*l*). And it appears that this is so although her position with regard to another vessel is such that if she were in the open sea the Regulations would apply and require her to act differently. In determining, therefore, what are the proper steps for a ship to take in order to avoid another approaching her in a winding river, the sinuosities of the river, and also the usual course of vessels in the river, must be taken into consideration. In cases where, if each ship continues her course in the usual track, they will pass clear, although if either deviates from it there would be risk of collision, it appears that the Regulations do not apply, and that it is the duty of each vessel to continue her course in the usual track and as if the other were not in sight (*m*).

It appears, however, from a recent decision of the Court of Appeal, that the cases above cited as to the application of the general Regulations in a winding river do not necessarily apply in a river where there are in force special rules made under a local Act for the express purpose of regulating its navigation. Although the rules for the Thames are identical, as regards crossing ships, with the general Regulations, there seems some doubt whether the decision of the Privy Council in *The Velocity* and other cases following it, that two ships rounding a point are not within the " crossing " rule, would be followed in a similar case arising under the Thames rules (*n*). The true prin-

(*l*) *The Esk* and *The Niord*, L. R. 3 P. C. 436, 442.

(*m*) *The Velocity*, L. R. 3 P. C. 44; *The Cologne* and *The Ranger*, L. R. 4 P. C. 519; *The Esk* and *The Niord*, L. R. 3 P. C. 436; *The Col-*

*den Pledge*, Holt, 136; but see the observations of James, L.J., on these cases in *The Oceano*, 3 P. D. 60; see also *The Milwaukee*, Brown Ad. 313

(*n*) *The Oceano*, 3 P. D. The principle adopted in the above cases

ciple seems to be, that when two ships in a river first sight each other the "crossing" rule, or such other rule as may for the moment be literally applicable, should be applied, if it is possible to apply it safely and effectually, so as certainly to take the ships clear of each other; and further, that the Regulations should be so applied without regard to any practice of navigation in the particular river which is founded only on convenience.

The following cases illustrate the view taken by the American cases as to the application Supreme Court of the United States as to the application of the Regula- of the Regulations of 1863 in a winding river. tions in a winding river.

A sailing-ship descending a river on a southerly course sighted a steam-ship ascending it. In accordance with the practice of the river, the sailing-ship was on the west, and the steam-ship on the east, side of the channel. At a

---

by the Privy Council, that in determining the application of the Regulations in a winding river the customary track of ships is to be considered, does not appear to have been followed by Dr. Lushington. In *The Friends*, 1 W. Rob. 478, and *The Gazelle*, *ibid.* 471, he expressed a strong opinion that where, except for the practice of the river as to keeping in or out of the strength of the tide, the Rule of the Road (the Trinity Rule of 1840) would apply, the case was not taken out of the rule by the practice. In *The Friends* a steam-ship, going up the Thames against the ebb, sought to justify her not porting in compliance with the Trinity Rule upon the ground that the practice of the river required the other ship, which was going down with the ebb, to keep in the strength of the tide, and herself (*The Friends*) to keep out of it. Dr. Lushington refused to recognise the practice of the river in such a case. In addressing the Trinity masters, he said: "All I can say is this, if you are about to make an exception from your own rules, an exception not to be extracted from

anything to be found in the Rules themselves, but to be founded upon reasons which have been alleged for the sake of safe navigation of the river Thames, and the great interests which are daily and hourly there at stake, let your exception be clear and intelligible, in order that it may at the first glance be known to the mercantile and maritime world. If, instead of a clear and direct rule, there is to be any exception, let it be as distinct and definite as the rule itself. Unless it be so, it is obvious that persons in all cases will endeavour to form exceptions for themselves, and instead of security we shall have danger." And in *The Duke of Sussex*, 1 W. Rob. 274, it was held that the custom of the river as to vessels availing themselves of the strength of the tide was superseded by the Trinity Rule. The observations of Dr. Lushington as to the necessity of holding Regulations for preventing collision to be of almost universal application have lost none of their force, but there is some difficulty in reconciling them with the recent decisions of the Privy Council in the cases stated in the text.

point between the two vessels the river took a bend in a
south-easterly direction. On reaching this point, the sailing-ship's helm was put to starboard in order to round the
bend. Instead of porting, so as to resume her course in
the usual track along the west bank at a point where the
channel turned again to the west and ran in its original
southerly direction, the sailing-ship continued the course
she was on after her helm had been put to starboard.
Crossing the channel to the east shore, she ran into the
steam-ship, which had continued her original course along
that shore. It was held that the sailing-ship was in fault
for deviating from the customary track along the west
shore; that her duty under the rule (identical with Article
18 of the Regulations of 1863) requiring her to keep her
course was to keep her course along the west shore, deviating from a straight course only so far as the winding of
the river required (o). The judgment of the Supreme
Court in this case is to the effect that when a point of
land or other obstruction in the navigation interferes
with the literal application of the Regulations, they are,
nevertheless, to be complied with so far as possible; that a
vessel required by the law to keep her course, if she is
compelled by an obstruction or bend in the river to deviate
from it, must resume her original course as soon as possible.
And the Court expressly held that where two vessels will
pass clear if each adheres to the customary track, the
Regulations have no application; and a vessel deviating
from the customary track in supposed obedience to the
Regulations is in fault.

In the following case, where a sailing-ship was crossing
a river diagonally, for a temporary purpose, when she
sighted a steam-ship approaching with risk of collision, the
same Court held that the duty of the sailing-ship was to
keep on her course across the river. The sailing-ship

(o) *The John L. Hasbrouck*, 3 Otto, 405.

ascending a river on a northerly course and being over-   Art. 21.
taken by a steam-ship, starboarded until her head was
N.W. by N., in order to give the steam-ship more room to
pass on her starboard hand. While crossing the river on
the N.W. by N. course, she sighted another steam-ship
descending the river and preparing to pass the ascending
steam-ship port side to port side. After being passed by
the ascending steam-ship, the sailing vessel ported and
attempted to follow in her wake, so as to pass the descending steam-ship port side to port side. In doing so, she
came into collision with the latter, and it was held by the
Supreme Court that she was in fault for not keeping her
N.W. by N. course (p).

When two steam-ships proceeding in the same direction
were rounding a point or bend in a river nearly abreast, it
was held that it was the duty of each to keep in her own
water, and not attempt to cross the course of the other.
The outside boat was held in fault for a collision that
occurred while attempting to get in to the shore across
the bows of the other (q).

In *The Milwaukee* (r) it was held that the question
whether two ships were meeting "end on" in a river is to
be determined by their general course in the river, and
not by their compass course at a particular moment while
they are pursuing the windings of the channel.

## ARTICLE 22.

*Where by the above rules one of two ships is to keep out*   Art. 22.
*of the way the other shall keep her course.*

This Article corresponds with Article 18 of the Regulations of 1863. It supplements, and must be read with,

Ship not
required to
keep out of
the way must
keep her
course.

---

(p) *The Free State*, 1 Otto, 200.          (r) Brown Adm. 313.
(q) *The Oceanus*, 12 Blatchf. 430.

Art. 22.  Articles 14, 16, 17, and 20.  The concluding words of the old Article 18 were superfluous, and are omitted in the present Article 22.  The scope and application of the two Articles appears to be identical.

Art. 22 must be strictly observed.  Since a vessel, A., required by the Regulations to keep out of the way of another, B., may go ahead, or astern, or on either side of B., it is B.'s duty to do nothing that may embarrass A. or interfere with her right to keep clear of B. in any way she thinks fit.  The rule, therefore, requiring B. to keep her course must be observed strictly.  So long as B. can do so without immediate danger, and there is a possibility of A. clearing her, she must stand on.  With reference to the same rule under a previous Act, Dr. Lushington said : " I wholly deny that danger would be averted, or that infinitely greater danger would not occur, if a vessel close-hauled on the larboard tack, on descrying a steamer, were to take upon herself to deviate from her course for the purpose of getting out of the way ; because I am of opinion that by so doing it would lead to the chance of infinitely more collisions than at present" (s). The Supreme Court of the United States is equally strict in its interpretation of the rule, and for the same reasons. " The negligence of one (ship) is liable to baffle the vigilance of the other ; and if one of the vessels, under such circumstances, follows the rule, and the other omits to do so, or violates it, a collision is almost certain to follow " (t).

It has been held by the Privy Council that " if a ship bound to keep her course undertakes to justify her departure from that rule, she takes upon herself the obligation of showing both that her departure was, at the time it took place, necessary in order to avoid immediate danger, and also that the course adopted by her was reasonably calcu-

(s) The Vivid, 7 Not. of Cas. 127 : The Immaganda Sancta Clarissima, ibid. 582 ; The Test, 5 Not. of Cas. 276.

(t) New York and Liverpool U. S. Mail Co. v. Rumball, 21 How. 372, 384.

lated to avoid that danger" (u).  There are decisions of **Art. 22.** the Supreme Court of the United States to the same effect (x).

This rule is perhaps the most difficult of all the Regulations for seamen to adhere to.  The stringency with which it is applied by the Courts makes it necessary for an officer to take his ship into close proximity to another, where it may appear that risk of collision would be at once determined by directing her course away from the other ship.

In the case of a sailing-ship, A., close-hauled on the port tack, approaching another, B., having the wind free on the starboard tack within the "crossing" rule (Article 14), unless there are exceptional circumstances, and it is certain that B. will not keep out of the way, A. has no choice but to stand on (y).

The direction to "keep her course" does not mean that Meaning of "keep her course." the ship is to continue going ahead in the direction in which her head happens for the moment to be pointing, without regard to other circumstances.  It means that she is to continue the course she would pursue if the other vessel were not in sight (z).  Thus, a vessel rounding a point in a river, and approaching another under circumstances which require her to keep her course under Article 22, must continue her course round the point in the usual track (a).

Whether a ship required to keep her course is at liberty Whether an alteration of speed is an infringement of Art. 22. to alter her rate of speed, while risk of collision exists, seems doubtful.  If by doing so she increases the risk, or embarrasses the other ship, she would probably be held in fault.

(u) *The Agra* v. *The Elizabeth Jenkins*, L. R. 1 P. C. 501 ; see also *The Great Conquest* v. *The David Cannon*, Holt, 235 ; *The Uncus* v. *The Meander*, Holt, 243 ; and see the observations of Dr. Lushington in *The Test*, *ubi supra*.

(x) *The Scotia*, 14 Wall. 170; *The Potomac*, 8 Wall. 590.

(y) See *The Byfoged Christiansen*,

and *The William Frederick*, 41 L. T. N. S. 535, *infra*, p. 209.  See also, *supra*, p. 170, for a "hard case."

(z) *The Velocity*, L. R. 3 P. C. 44.

(a) *The Velocity*, *supra* ; *The Esk* and *The Niord*, L. R. 3 P. C. 436 ; *The Cologne* and *The Ranger*, L. R. 4 P. C. 519.  See *supra*, p. 177. See also *The John Taylor*, *infra*, p. 203.

**Art. 22.**

**How a ship hove-to is to "keep her course."**

Where the vessel required to keep her course is hove-to, it appears to be the duty of those on board to fill on her and get her under way without altering her course more than is necessary (b).

A vessel hove-to with her helm lashed to leeward, forging ahead as she comes to and falls off, does not fulfil the requirements of Article 22 (c).

**And a ship by the wind.**

A vessel close-hauled does not by luffing a little, and so that she does not lose her headway, break the rule requiring her to keep her course (d). If a close-hauled ship departs from the rule requiring her to keep her course, as a general rule she should luff rather than bear up, as she thereby lessens her way, and, if a collision takes place, its effect is likely to be less disastrous (e).

**A ship must not stand on obstinately.**

The rule that a ship is to keep her course does not mean that she is to do so obstinately when she sees that, under the particular circumstances of the case, she can, by departing from it, avoid a collision (f).

**Cases illustrating the application of Art. 22.**

The following cases illustrate the application of Article 22:—

A barque in Margate Roads in a strong wind was wearing preparatory to coming to an anchor. A steam-ship was held solely in fault for a collision with her, although the steam-ship alleged that she was baffled by the rapid change in the course and lights of the barque (g).

A sailing-ship with the wind aft, meeting a steam-ship nearly end on, was held in fault for porting (h). But a slight alteration in the helm of a sailing-ship, when an

---

(b) *The General Lee*, 3 Mar. Law Cas. O. S. 204.

(c) *The Transit*, 3 Bened. 192.

(d) *The Marmion*, 1 Asp. Mar. Law Cas. 412 ; *The Aimo* and *The Amelia*, 2 Asp. Mar. Law Cas. 96 ; *The Great Eastern*, 3 Moo. P. C. C. N. S. 31.

(e) *The Agra* and *The Elizabeth Jenkins*, L. R. 1 P. C. 501 ; *The Great Eastern*, *ubi supra*.

(f) *The Lake St. Clair* v. *The Underwriter*, 3 Asp. Mar. Law Cas. 361 ; *The Sunnyside*, 1 Otto, 208. See, however, *infra*, p. 200.

(g) *The Monsoon* and *The Neptune*, 2 Mar. Law Cas. O. S. 289 ; and see *The Falkland* and *The Navigator*, Br. & Lush. 204.

(h) *The Bougainville* and *The James C. Stevenson*, L. R. 5 P. C. 316.

approaching steam-ship was two miles distant, was held not Art. 22. to be an infringement of the rule requiring her to keep her course (*i*). And a steam-ship, with another a quarter of a mile astern on her port quarter and overtaking her, was held not to be in fault for porting half a point (*k*).

A sailing-ship must not go about close ahead of a steam-ship so as to make it difficult for the latter to keep out of her way (*l*). But a steam-ship, attempting to pass a sailing-ship turning to windward in a narrow channel, must be prepared for the sailing-ship going about, and the latter is under no obligation to give notice of her intention to go about (*m*).

In America there is a stringent rule, which has been American cases. frequently insisted upon by the Courts, requiring a sailing-ship working to windward in company with other ships, whose duty it is to keep out of her way, to "beat out her tack." If she goes about in a narrow channel before the shoaling of the water or other dangers of navigation require it, and comes into collision with another ship which would have cleared her if she had stood on, she is held to be in fault for the collision (*n*). In a case of collision between a sailing-ship turning to windward and a steam-ship the Circuit Court said : "What the law requires for a sailing vessel in a narrow channel is, to beat out her tack, and, having beat it out, to come about with all proper despatch upon the other, leaving to the steam vessel the responsibility of being in a position to enable her to do so without danger" (*o*).

In a case where it was proved that there was, at the time of the collision, a flat calm, it was held by the Supreme

<hr/>

(*i*) *The Norma,* 3 Asp. Mar. Law Cas. 272.

(*k*) *The Franconia,* 2 P. D. 8.

(*l*) *The Newburgh* v. *The Oscar,* Holt, 231 ; *The Saucy Lass* v. *The Bolderaa,* Holt, 205.

(*m*) *The Palatine,* 1 Asp. Mar.

Law Cas. 468 ; it is not quite clear in this case whether it was necessary for the sailing-ship to go about when she did.

(*n*) *The Empire State,* 1 Bened. 57 ; and see *infra,* p. 227.

(*o*) *The Empire State,* 1 Bened. 57.

**Art. 22**    Court that the sailing-ship, whose duty it was to keep her
course, could not be in fault (*p*).

The rule requiring a vessel to keep her course is strictly
enforced by the Courts in the United States. A sailing-
ship approaching a steam-ship admitted that so soon as
there was risk of collision she kept away two or three
points. She was held to be in fault. The Court said (*q*):
" A vessel whose duty it is to keep her course has no right
to change it as soon as she apprehends a collision. In this
case the duty of the tug to keep out of the way of the
lighter arose only when the two vessels were proceeding
in such directions as to involve risk of collision ; and it was
under the same circumstances that the duty arose on the
part of the lighter to keep her course. Therefore, under the
statute requiring the lighter to keep her course, her apprehension of a collision could not justify her in changing her
course. Moreover, it is the actual risk or danger of collision that determines the duty of both vessels, and not the
apprehension merely. The rule was made and is administered for the very purpose of preventing the vessel
charged with the duty of avoiding the other from being
embarrassed by a change of course on the part of the other
into danger, on the apprehension that such duty of avoid-
ance will not be fulfilled " (*r*).

A schooner, seeing the mast-head light of a steam-ship
and mistaking it for a light ashore, hove-to to get a cast of
the lead, thereby presenting her red light to the steam-ship.
The steam-ship ported. The schooner, on discovering her
mistake, got under way, and crossed the course of the
steam-ship, showing her green light. It was held that the
schooner was solely in fault for not keeping her course (*s*).

Where a ferry boat crossing a river was under a port
helm at the moment when she sighted another steam-ship

(*p*) *The Commerce*, 16 Wall. 33.    (*r*) See also *The Stephen Morgan*,
(*q*) *The General U. S. Grant*, 6    4 Otto, 599.
Bened. 465, 467.    (*s*) *The Virgo*, 7 Bened. 495.

Art. 22.

coming up the river, it was held that her duty, under the rule requiring her to keep her course, was to continue in her usual track (t).

The danger of departing from Article 22 is illustrated by an American case, where a vessel, A., starboarded in order to assist another, B., whose duty it was to keep out of her way, in an attempt to cross her bows. Finding that she could not cross A.'s bows, B., at the last moment, stopped. In consequence of B.'s stopping and A.'s starboarding, a collision occurred. A. was held to be solely in fault (u).

A steam-ship, just before reaching a point in New York harbour where the channel is narrow and the navigation difficult, sighted a schooner's red light. There were three channels open for the schooner, and only one for the steam-ship. The schooner selected the steam-ship channel, and a collision took place. The schooner was held in fault, because, although she kept her course, in the sense that she had from the first intended to make use of the steam-ship channel, she embarrassed the steam-ship by taking that course when she might have avoided any risk by taking one of the other channels (x).

It has been decided by the Supreme Court that a sailing-ship is not free from blame if, seeing the lights of a steam-ship ahead and not keeping out of the way, she pertinaciously keeps on her course and runs down the steam-ship (y).

## ARTICLE 23.

*In obeying and construing these rules due regard shall be had to all dangers of navigation, and to any special circumstances which may render a departure from the above rules necessary in order to avoid immediate danger.*

Art. 23.

Proviso saving special cases.

(t) *The John Taylor*, 6 Bened. 227.
(u) *The Corsica*, 9 Wall. 630.
(x) *The City of Hartford*, 7 Bened. 350.
(y) *The Sunnyside*, 1 Otto, 208.

Art. 23.    Article 23 corresponds and, with the exception of superfluous words, is identical with Article 19 of the Regulations
of 1863.

Regulations    It is sometimes attempted to urge this Article as an
never to be
departed from excuse for a departure from the Regulations where an
except for    adherence to them would have prevented a collision. In
necessity.
such a case Article 23 has no application; nor does it in
any way affect the universal application of the Regulations
where it is possible to apply them so as to avert collision.

Safety at-     A vessel is not justified in departing from the Regula-
tained by their
uniform and    tions because she fears that the other ship will not comply
exact observ-  with them. In a case decided under the Trinity Rules of
ance.
1840, Dr. Lushington, addressing the Trinity masters,
said:—

"I cannot conceive that anything would be more likely
to lead to mischievous consequences than to suppose that a
vessel whose duty it is to keep her course should anticipate
that another vessel will not give way, and so give way
herself. The consequence would be that there would be
no certainty; whereas the doctrine I have upheld, supported by your authority, is that in cases of this description
you ought always to follow the general rule. The certainty
which results from adherence to general rules is, in my
opinion, absolutely essential to the safety of navigation" (z).
In the same case he said that "the principle of law that
you are not to adhere to strict rules of navigation, but avoid
an accident if possible, is a doctrine to be very carefully
watched."

In another case (under the Trinity Rules) Dr. Lushington said:—

"All rules are framed for the benefit of ships navigating
the seas, and no doubt circumstances will arise in which it
would be perfect folly to attempt to carry into execution

(z) *The Test,* 5 Not. of Cas. 276 ; see also *The Superior,* 6 Not. of Cas. 607.

every rule, however wisely framed. It is, at the same time, Art. 23.
of the greatest possible importance to adhere as closely as
possible to established rules, and never to allow a deviation
from them unless the circumstances which are alleged to
have rendered such a deviation necessary are most distinctly proved and established ; otherwise vessels would
always be in doubt and doing wrong " (a).

The case of *The Superior* (b) is a strong one, as showing
the necessity of observing rules of navigation wherever it
is possible to do so. *The Superior* was a brig bound down
the Thames against the flood-tide, with the wind free.
*The Zior*, a brig bound up the river, was required by the
Trinity Rule (c) to pass to the northward of *The Superior*.
Close ahead of *The Superior* was a schooner, which, in
violation of the Trinity Rule, passed to the northward, or
inside *The Zior*. Expecting that *The Superior* would
follow in the wake of the schooner and pass inside, *The
Zior* starboarded, and in attempting to pass outside or to
the southward of *The Superior*, came into collision with
her. *The Zior* alleged that there was no room for her to
pass between the schooner and *The Superior*. It was held
that the fact of the schooner having safely passed *The Zior*
on the wrong side—of her having violated the rule with
impunity—was no justification to *The Zior* for herself
violating the rule in the expectation that *The Superior*
would not obey the rule but would follow the schooner
and pass inside.

It was to provide for cases where compliance with the Art. 23 pre-
preceding Articles would produce a collision that Article 23 vents the
Regulations
was enacted. Of the corresponding Article of the former being applied
so as to cause
law Dr. Lushington said that it was not a directory enact- collision.

---

(a) *The John Buddle*, 5 Not. of
Cas. 387 ; cf. *The Great Eastern*, 3
Moo. P. C. C. N. S. 31.
  (b) 6 Not. of Cas. 607.
  (c) It does not clearly appear

whether she had the wind free or
was close-hauled. In either case her
duty as to passing to the northward
of the other ship was the same.

Art. 23.

ment, telling persons to do this or that, but that it released them from the severe obligation of complying with the previous Articles under circumstances which would render obedience to them dangerous when by deviation they might escape danger (*d*). But its application is strictly limited to cases where the circumstances are such that " there is immediate danger perfectly clear to the apprehension of those present " (*e*). It " does not prescribe any particular measures that should be adopted in departing from the strict terms of any of the previous Regulations that it governs, but it merely states that in construing and obeying these Regulations as far as possible you may take into consideration urgent attendant circumstances. . . . . It is common sense, for if any rule were laid down by Act of Parliament, or any other authority, that could never be departed from in certain states of circumstances, such a rule would necessarily involve, on many occasions, the destruction of ships which it was intended to preserve" (*f*).

Duty to avoid collision, and for that purpose to depart from the Rule of the Road if necessary.

Not only is departure from the Rule of the Road excused by Article 23 where the rule cannot be obeyed without collision, but a literal observance of the Regulations cannot be set up as a defence where the collision might have been avoided by ordinary care. " You may depart and you must depart from a rule if you see with perfect clearness, almost amounting to certainty, that adhering to the rule will bring about a collision, and violating a rule will avoid it ; and indeed this is provided for by the 19th Article " (of the Regulations of 1863) (*g*).

(*d*) *The Eliza* and *The Orinoco*, Holt, 98.
(*e*) *The Allen* v. *The Flora*, Holt, 114 ; 2 Mar. Law Cas. O. S. 386.
(*f*) *Per* Dr. Lushington in *The Allan* and *The Flora, ubi supra;* and see *The Superior, ubi supra.* The Supreme Court of the United States used similar language with regard to the operation of Article 19 of the

Regulations of 1863 in *The Cayuga*, 14 Wall. 270 ; *The Sunnyside*, 1 Otto, 208.
(*g*) *Per* Dr. Lushington, in *The Boanerges* and *The Anglo-Indian*, 2 Mar. Law Cas. O. S. 239. See also *The Ida* and *The Wasa, infra; Handaysirle* v. *Wilson*, 3 Car. & P. 528.

Art. 23.

A barque close-hauled on the starboard tack was held to be solely in fault for a collision with a barque that had just been in stays, and had not gathered way on the port tack. The Court (in Ireland) said that if a ship insists on her right, under a rule of navigation, of not giving way, and makes no effort to prevent the collision when it is in her power to do so, she will be held not to have performed her duty, and to be in fault for the collision (h). So a ship on the port tack was (in 1850) held in fault for a collision with another having the wind free, which she had seen a mile and a half off and did not attempt to avoid (i). The same principle has been recognised in the Common Law Courts. In *Handayside* v. *Wilson* (k), Best, C.J., said :— " Although there may be a rule of the sea, yet a man who has the management of one ship is not to be allowed to follow that rule to the injury of the vessel of another, where he could avoid the injury by pursuing a different course."

As to the duty of a ship, under special circumstances, to depart from the Regulations, Dr. Lushington said : " You have no right to stand, in a difficulty, upon a right, though it may be a perfectly good right, obstinately, recklessly, and regardless of the safety of others. . . . . But in common justice, when charging a vessel with inactivity and not adopting measures to avoid a collision, we must be perfectly satisfied that the master of the vessel so charged was perfectly convinced of the imminent danger of a collision taking place, and had it in his power to adopt a safe measure to avoid the collision " (l). Again, in *The Lady Anne* (m): " If two vessels are approaching each other, it is the duty of both to prevent a collision, if possible. No

Reckless adherence to the Regulations.

(h) *The Ida* v. *The Wasa*, 2 Mar. Law Cas. O. S 414.
(i) *The Commerce*, 3 W. Rob. 287.
(k) 3 Car. & P. 528 ; and see *Mayhew* v. *Boyce*, 1 Stark. 423.

(l) *The Legatus* v. *The Emily*, Holt, 217.
(m) 15 Jur. 18, 19 ; this case was under the Trinity Rules of 1840.

doubt there are certain rules as to what they ought to do under particular circumstances, but the first and primary rule is to avoid a collision and the loss of property and life if it can be effected with safety." In that case *The Lady Anne*, close-hauled on the starboard tack, was meeting another ship, close-hauled on the port tack. It was held that *The Lady Anne* might have avoided the collision by putting her helm down at the last moment and easing off her head sheets, and she was held in fault for not doing so.

In *The Sunnyside* (*n*) the Supreme Court of the United States said : " Rules of navigation are adopted to save life and property; and they are required to be observed and are enforced to accomplish the same beneficent end, and not to promote collisions. Consequently, they have exceptions ; and no party ought ever to be permitted to defend or excuse a plain error by invoking a general rule of navigation, when it is clear that the case falls within an admitted exception."

Even a sailing-ship will be held in fault for a collision with a steam-ship if she makes no attempt to avoid a collision, where it is clearly in her power to do so. In such a case a mere adherence to Article 22 is no justification. In *The Sunnyside* a sailing-ship, with the wind free, saw the mast-head and green lights of a steam-ship half a point on her port bow, a considerable distance off. The lights were those of a tug, drifting before the wind at about a mile and a half an hour, and waiting for employment. The sailing-ship kept her course, and did not alter her helm until it was too late to avoid the tug. It was held in America by the Supreme Court that the sailing-ship was in fault, as well as the tug (*o*).

But great caution must be used in applying the principle

(*n*) 1 Otto, 208, 210; and see *Bentley* v. *Coyne*, 4 Wall. 509.
(*o*) *The Sunnyside*, 1 Otto, 208 ; but see *The Bougainville* v. *The*

*James C. Stevenson*, L. R. 5 P. C. 316, for a case of premature alteration of her course by the sailing-ship.

recognised in these cases, that under some circumstances **Art. 23.**
it is the duty of a ship to disobey the Regulations. It
may be applied only where the circumstances are very
exceptional. A ship, A., close-hauled on the port tack, and
another, B., on the starboard tack with the wind free, were
crossing within Article 12 of the Regulations of 1863. A.
stood on until immediately before the collision, when she
luffed. B. neglected to keep out of the way, as required by
the Regulations (p). It was held by the Gibraltar Court
that A. was in fault as well as B., because she pertinaciously
kept her course under Article 18 when she ought to have
seen that B. was not going to keep out of the way in compliance with the law; and in so deciding the learned judge
relied on *The Commerce* (q). The Privy Council reversed
the decision of the Court below, and held that A. was not
in fault. Sir J. W. Colvile, in delivering the judgment of
the Privy Council, said: " Their Lordships remark that,
though the principle involved in that case (*The Commerce*)
may be in itself a sound one, it is one which should be
applied very cautiously, and only when the circumstances
are clearly exceptional. They conceive that to leave to
masters of vessels a discretion as to obeying or departing
from the sailing rules is dangerous to the public; and
that, to require them to exercise such discretion, except
in a very clear case of necessity, is hard upon the
masters themselves, inasmuch as the slightest departure
from these rules is almost invariably relied on as contributory negligence."

Article 23 is not intended to apply to a case where the *If the Regula-*
Regulations cannot be complied with, nor to a case where *tions cannot*
non-compliance could not by possibility have caused the *with, or can-*
collision. In such a case non-compliance with the Regu- *plied with,*
lations is immaterial upon the question which ship is in *prevent the collision.*

(p) *The Byfoged Christiansen* and  N. S. 535; 4 App. Cas. 669.
*The William Frederick*, 41 L. T.  (q) 3 W. Rob. 287.

P

Art. 23.

Art. 23 does not apply. "Dangers of navigation."

"Special circumstances."

Disabled ship.

fault, but that is so by virtue of the general law, and not under Article 23 (r).

Nothing in the Regulations requires a ship to take a measure which is dangerous to her safety (s). A vessel is not bound to obey the rule requiring her to port if, by porting, she will go ashore (t). In such a case Article 23 may apply to both vessels, or to one of them It excuses non-compliance with the Article requiring her to port on the part of the one vessel because of the shoal; and if, in order to avoid a collision, it is necessary for the other vessel to depart from the Regulations, it is her duty to do so, and Article 23 excuses her departure.

So, where a ship required by the Regulations to keep out of the way is unable to do so, it is the duty of the other, not to keep her course, but herself to keep out of the way. Two vessels, close-hauled on opposite tacks, were crossing, and the ship on the port tack could not bear up for fear of collision, and could not go about because of a shoal. It was held (in America) that the ship on the starboard tack was in fault for not keeping out of the way (u).

If a vessel is partially disabled, or in a condition which prevents her answering her helm readily, she must take precautions in time, and do all she can to comply with the Regulations effectually (x). A brig hove-to, reefing topsails, was held in fault for not porting (y). Where a ship had no head sail on her, and the Regulations required her to bear up, it was held that it was the duty of those on board to take the after sail off her, so that she might be better able to bear up (z).

(r) See *Inman* v. *Beck*, *The City of Antwerp* and *The Friedrich*, L. R. 2 P. C. 25, 34; and *supra*, pp. 14–18.

(s) *The St. Cyran* v. *The Henry*, Holt, 72.

(t) *The Lucia Jantina* v. *The Mexican*, Holt, 130.

(u) *The Ann Caroline*, 2 Wall. 538.

(x) *The Test*, 5 Not. of Cas. 276.

(y) *The Blenheim*, 1 Sp. E. & A. 285.

(z) *The Calcutta*, 3 Mar. Law Cas. O. S. 336.

If it appears that a vessel is unable to comply with the Art. 23. Regulations owing to her being disabled, or in stays, or for other reasons, it is the duty of those on board the other to watch her closely. They have no right to speculate on the disabled ship being able to keep out of the way, but they should themselves at once take steps to make the collision impossible (a).

It was held in America that the fact of a schooner's flying-jib being carried away was no excuse for her not bearing up; and that the other ship was not in fault because she failed in the daytime to see that the schooner was partially disabled (b).

To justify a departure from the Regulations which is Necessity of alleged to have been necessary to avoid immediate danger, departure from the there must be clear proof that an adherence to them would Regulations have caused such danger, and also that the step taken was must be proved. the right step (c). Where it is possible to comply with the Regulations Article 23 would be no excuse for departing from them. In a case under the Trinity Rules of 1840 it was held that it was no excuse for not observing the rules that the night was very dark, and that the other ship was not seen until she was very close (d).

Where two steam-ships were meeting in the Thames end on, and one starboarded in order, as was alleged, to clear a barge, in the absence of proof that the starboarding was necessary, she was held in fault for a collision with the other steam-ship (e). The obligation on a ship which seeks to justify a departure from the Regulations is heavy. She takes upon herself the obligation of showing both that the departure was necessary in order to avoid imme-

(a) The Priscilla, L. R. 4 A. & E. 125; The Eclipse and The Royal Consort, Holt, 220; see also The Ch. Raab, Brown Adm. 453.

(b) The H. P. Baldwin, Brown Ad. 300.

(e) The Concordia v. The Esther,

infra; The Planet v. The Aura, Holt, 255; The Emperor v. The Zephyr, Holt, 24; and see The Corsica, 9 Wall. 630.

(d) The Flint, 6 Not. of Cas. 271.

(e) The Concordia and The Esther, L. R. 1 A. & E. 93.

Art. 23.

Cases where
departure
from the
Regulations
held not
justifiable.

diate danger, and also that the course adopted by her was
reasonably calculated to avoid that danger (ƒ).

The fact that a steam-tug had a heavy ship in tow, and
a strong wind and tide against her, was held not to justify
her departing from the rule requiring her to keep out of
the way of an approaching sailing-ship (g). And where
a large steam-ship of 1356 tons had a disabled steam-
ship of 1495 tons in tow, and was made fast to the latter
by a tow rope and chain cables of such length that from
the bow of the towing vessel to the stern of the other
was nearly a quarter of a mile, it was held by the Privy
Council that those circumstances did not justify them in
departing from the rule requiring steam-ships to keep out
of the way of a sailing-ship (h).

Two steam-ships on crossing courses (within Article 16),
both making for a pilot cutter, must keep clear of each
other by observing the Regulations. The mere fact that
they are both making for the cutter does not justify the
steam-ship with the other on her starboard hand in
neglecting to keep out of her way (i).

Convenience
no excuse for
departing
from the
Regulations.

Where a collision may be avoided by obeying the Regulations, it is not a sufficient excuse for departing from them
that the collision might with equal safety and more conveniently have been avoided by one or both ships departing
from the Regulations. Thus, where a steam-ship sighted
another at a considerable distance, approaching her nearly
end on and a little on her starboard bow, it was held that
the law required her to port, and that she was in fault for
starboarding, although by porting she would have had to
cross the bows of the other ship (k).

(ƒ) *The Agra* and *The Elizabeth
Jenkins*, L. R. 1 P. C. 501.
  (g) *The Warrior*, L. R. 3 A. & E.
553.
  (h) *The American* and *The Syria*,
L. R. 4 A. & E. 226 ; on appeal,
L. R. 6 P. C. 127.
  (i) *The Ada* v. *The Sappho*, 1 Asp.

Mar. Law Cas. 475 ; on app. 2 Asp.
Mar. Law Cas. 4.
  (k) *The Araxes* and *The Black
Prince*, 15 Moo. P. C. C. 122    This
case was decided under the Act of
1854 : but it is submitted that the
decision would have been the same
under the existing Regulations.

Art. 23.

In a case (*l*) which was decided under 17 & 18 Vict. c. 104, s. 296, where a collision with a sailing-ship close-hauled could have been avoided by a tug with a ship in tow, it was held that the sailing-ship was in fault for keeping her course, and for not keeping out of the way, on the ground that she had no right to depend on the tug being able to avoid her. It was said that it might be much less inconvenient for the sailing vessel to change her course than for the tug to do so. It is submitted that, under the existing law, a vessel would not be justified in departing from the Regulations in the belief that a collision could *more conveniently* be avoided by her so doing.

If a ship close-hauled must, in order to avoid a collision, either luff or bear up, the more prudent course for her is to luff, if possible, "so as thereby to stop her way, and mitigate as far as possible the effects of a collision, if a collision should take place" (*m*).

Although the steps which the Regulations require two vessels approaching with risk of collision to take are not necessary, in the sense that a collision would certainly be avoided by only one of the vessels obeying the Regulations, the law must be obeyed by both. A vessel departing from the Regulations will not be excused on the ground that the collision would have been avoided if the other vessel had not disobeyed the law. In such a case Article 23 is no justification for either ship in departing from the Regulations. Thus, where two steam-ships were meeting end on, and a collision would not have occurred if either had put her helm to port, both were held in fault by the Supreme Court of the United States (*n*).

*Neither ship may depart from the Regulations on the chance of the other obeying them.*

It remains to be decided what effect the new Article 19 has upon the application of Article 23. In America, where

*Combined operation of Art. 19 and Art. 23.*

(*l*) *The Arthur Gordon* and *The Independence*, Lush. 270.
(*m*) *The Agra* and *The Elizabeth,*
*Jenkins*, L. R. 1 P. C. 501.
(*n*) *The America*, 2 Otto. 432.

Art. 23.
a " whistling " rule similar to that of Article 19 has been in force for many years, it has been held that a steam-ship signalling to another that she intends to depart from the Regulations, and departing from them, is not in fault for such a departure if it was agreed to by the answering signal from the other ship. But strict proof was required that the assenting signal was given (o).

It would probably be held that where a ship is hailed by the other to take a particular course, if she does so and a collision occurs the other could not be heard to say that she was wrong for departing from the Regulations (p).

ARTICLE 24.

Art. 24.

Besides observing the Regulations proper precautions are to be taken in all cases.

*Nothing in these rules shall exonerate any ship, or the owner, or master, or crew thereof, from the consequences of any neglect to carry lights or signals, or of any neglect to keep a proper look-out, or of the neglect of any precaution which may be required by the ordinary practice of seamen, or by the special circumstances of the case.*

This Article is identical with Article 20 of the Regulations of 1863. It seems difficult to attribute to it any legal effect. It was inserted in the Regulations, probably, *ex abundante cautelâ,* and as a declaration, not to be overlooked by seamen, of the legal consequences of negligence.

The neglect of a vessel preparing to anchor to warn a ship astern of her position and intention was held neglect of a " precaution required by the special circumstances of the case " (q).

The duty of those in charge of a ship to navigate her with due regard to the ordinary rules of seamanship, and

---

(o) *The Milwaukee,* 1 Brown Adm. 313.
(p) See above, p. 7, and cases there cited.

(q) *The Philotaxe,* 3 Asp. Mar. Law Cas. 512. As to the duty of a ship in such a case, see *infra,* p. 221

under special circumstances to depart from the Regulations, has been already referred to (r). What is required of seamen is ordinary skill and ordinary intelligence. Neither Article 24, nor any other part of the Regulations, makes it their duty to foresee and provide against every accident. But where literal compliance with the Regulations is not enough to avoid a collision, all must be done that a seaman of ordinary skill and intelligence would do to keep clear of the other ship (s). Where, for example, an alteration of the helm is not enough, the helm must be assisted by lowering the peak or letting go the fore-sheets (t). So, a vessel has been held in fault for not backing her yards (u).

Art. 24.

The law as to what is proper care and skill in navigation, and what are precautions required by the ordinary practice of seamen, is illustrated by numerous decisions in the Courts, some of which are here collected.

Precautions required by the ordinary practice of seamen which have been recognised by the law.

First, as to look-out: If a ship is proved to have been negligent in not keeping a proper look-out she will be held answerable for all the reasonable consequences of her negligence. In an American case, where the look-out on board a schooner failed to report a steamer's light which could not be seen by the man at the wheel, the schooner was held partly in fault for the collision (v).

Look-out.

The look-out must be vigilant and sufficient according to the exigencies of the case. The denser the fog and the worse the weather the greater the cause for vigilance. A ship cannot be heard to say that a look-out was of no use because the weather was so thick that another ship could not be seen until actually in collision. In *The Mellona* (x) Dr. Lushington said: "It is no excuse to urge that from

(r) See pp. 203–214, above.
(s) *The Jesmond* and *The Earl of Elgin*, L. R. 4 P. C. 1 ; *The City of Antwerp* and *The Friedrich*, Inman v. *Beck*, L. R. 2 P. C. 25.
(t) *The Lady Anne*, 15 Jur. 18 ; *The Stranger*, 6 Not. of Cas. 36, 38 ;

*The Marpesia*, L. R. 4 P. C. 212 ; *The Ulster*, 1 Mar. Law Cas. O. S. 234.
(u) *The James*, Swab. Ad. 55.
(v) *The Fanita*, 14 Blatchf. 545.
(x) 3 W. Rob. 7, 13.

Art. 24.   the intensity of the darkness no vigilance, however great,
could have enabled *The Mellona* to have descried *The
George* in time to avoid a collision. In proportion to the
greatness of the necessity, the greater ought to have been
the care and vigilance employed."

One or more hands should be specially stationed on the
look-out by day as well as at night. They should not be
engaged upon any other duty; and they should be stationed in the bows, or in that part of the ship from which
other vessels can best be seen (*y*). On board a Mersey
ferry boat the proper place for the look-out was said to be
on the bridge between the paddle boxes (*z*). When passing
over a fishing ground a specially vigilant look-out must be
kept to avoid fishing boats (*a*). A vessel brought up in a
frequented channel should have an anchor watch ready to
sheer her clear of an approaching vessel, or to give her
chain (*b*). For a large steam-ship going 11 knots off
Dungeness, a crowded part of the English Channel, on a
hazy night, the Privy Council considered that one hand on
the look-out was not sufficient (*c*). It was held negligence
that an anchor watch was not kept on board a ship at
moorings in the river Tyne, the weather being bad and
threatening (*d*).

A vessel will not be held in fault for not keeping a look-
out astern on a clear night; although if she sees a vessel
approaching her astern it is her duty to warn her of her
danger (*e*).

Where a vessel going up a river ran into another coming

(*y*) *The Diana*, 1 W. Rob. 131 ;
4 Moo. P. C. C. 11 ; *The Batavier*, 9
Moo. P. C. C. 286 ; *The Bold Buc-
cleugh*, 1 Pr. Adm. Dig. 144 ; *The
Giannibanta*, 1 P. D. 283 ; see *The
Morning Light*, 2 Wall. 550.

(*z*) *The Wirral*, 3 W. Rob. 56.

(*a*) *The Robert and Ann* v. *The
Lloyds*, Holt, 55.

(*b*) See *Luck* v. *Seward*, 4 Car. &
P. 106 ; *Vanderplank* v. *Miller*, M.

& M. 169 ; and *The Masters* and
*The Raynor*, Brown Adm. 342; *The
Marcia Tribou*, 2 Sprague, 17 (Ame-
rican cases).

(*c*) *The Germania*, 3 Mar. Law
Cas. O. S. 269.

(*d*) *The Pladda*, 2 P. D. 34.

(*e*) *The Earl Spencer*, L. R. 4
A. & E. 431 ; *The City of Brooklyn*,
1 P. D. 276.

Art. 24.

out of dock, it was held that the duty of the look-out was to see that the channel was clear, and that it was not negligence on his part not to have reported the vessel coming out of dock (*f*).

Where to keep a good look-out glasses are necessary, it would probably be held negligence not to use them (*g*). In an American case the use of a night-glass on board a steamer coming into harbour was held to be necessary (*h*).

The requirements of the law in America as to look-out have been stated in many cases in stringent terms. In *The Sunnyside* (*i*) the Supreme Court held that it is the duty of a sailing-ship to watch the movements of an approaching steam-ship in order that, if the steam-ship fails to comply with the law and keep out of the way, she may herself be able to avoid a collision.

*American cases as to look-out.*

In another case it was held that the absence of a look-out on board a vessel will cause her to be held in fault for a collision, unless it is proved that the other ship was seen as soon as it was possible to see her, and that the proper steps to avoid her were taken, and as soon as it was possible to take them (*k*).

The Supreme Court has held that the officer in charge of the deck is not a sufficient look-out. For a first-class ocean steam-ship two men with no other duty to perform constitute a proper look-out. They should be stationed forward in the ship's bows *l*), or in the part of the ship from which other vessels can best be seen (*m*). The rule that there must be one or more men specially stationed on the look-out, and that the officer in charge or the man at the wheel is not sufficient, has been established by numerous cases (*n*).

(*f*) *The Calabar*, L. R. 2 P. C. 238.

(*g*) See *The Hibernia*, 2 Asp. Mar. Law Cas. 454.

(*h*) *The Ville du Havre*, 7 Bened. 328.

(*i*) 1 Otto. 208.

(*k*) *The Atlas*, 10 Blatchf. 459.

(*l*) *Chamberlain v. Ward*, 21 How. 548, 570.

(*m*) *The Morning Light*, 2 Wall. 550.

(*n*) *The Northern Indiana*, 3 Blatchf. 92 ; *The Comet*, 9 Blatchf.

In *The Ariadne* (*o*) the Supreme Court said that the rigour of the requirement as to an efficient look-out rises according to the speed and power of the vessel, and the chance of meeting other ships. So that a vessel entering a harbour at night should have all the crew on deck, and keep as sharp a look-out as is possible (*p*).

It has been held by the Supreme Court that the absence of a look-out was not excused by the fact that it was day-time, and all hands were engaged in reefing (*q*); or that they were repairing damage caused by an accident (*r*). The duty of ferry boats, and of vessels crossing the track of ferry boats, to keep a specially good look-out has been insisted upon in many cases (*s*).

A vessel under way must have on board a sufficient crew to work her for the voyage on which she is engaged. When in dock or harbour she should be provided with sufficient hands to tend her, having regard to her position, the character of the dock or harbour, and to ordinary changes of the weather (*t*). Where a new ship was in collision on her trial trip, when she had not on board her full complement of officers and crew, she was not therefore held in fault, there being on board a sufficient crew to work her (*u*). It is negligence for the captain of a ship at moorings in a river to be ashore when the weather is bad and threatening (*v*). The officer in charge should be always on deck (*x*). In a fog there should be strength at

323 ; *The Parkersburg*, 5 Blatchf. 247; *The Douglass*, Brown Ad. 105; *The Nabob*, ibid. 115 ; *The Blossom*, Olcott, 188.

(*o*) 13 Wall. 475.

(*p*) *The Scioto*, Davies, 359.

(*q*) *The Catharine* v. *Dickinson*, 17 How. 170 ; *Thorp* v. *Hammond*, 12 Wall. 408 ; see also *The H. P. Baldwin*, Brown Adm. 300.

(*r*) *Whitridge* v. *Dill*, 23 How. 448.

(*s*) *The America*, 10 Blatchf. 155; *Ince* v. *East Boston Ferry Co.*, 106 Massach. Rep. 149 ; and see *supra*, p. 164.

(*t*) *The Excelsior*, L. R. 2 A. & E. 268 ; *The Patriotto* and *The Rival*, 2 L. T. N. S. 301.

(*u*) *The Clyde Navigation Co.* v. *Barclay*, 1 Ap. Cas. 790.

(*v*) *The Kepler*, 2 P. D. 40.

(*x*) *The Arthur Gordon* and *The Independence*, Lush. 270.

Art. 24.

the helm to alter the ship's course as quickly as possible on the order being given (*y*).

A vessel under way is bound to keep clear of another at anchor. The rule seems to be the same in all cases where one of the ships is under way and the other, though not at anchor, is for any other reason unable to keep out of the way; as where she is fishing and fast to her nets, in stays, hove-to, or disabled (*z*). And it applies though the ship at anchor is brought up in the fair-way, or elsewhere in an improper berth. "It is the bounden duty of a vessel under way, whether the vessel at anchor be properly or improperly anchored, to avoid, if it be possible with safety to herself, any collision whatever" (*a*). If one ship is fast to the shore, or lying at established moorings, it can scarcely happen that the other would not be held in fault for a collision (*b*). Where a steam-ship in the daytime ran into a sailing-ship brought up in a river 500 yards wide, it was held by an American Court that the steam-ship was solely in fault, although the sailing-ship was riding with her sails up, sheering about, and with no anchor watch (*c*).

*Keeping clear of ship at anchor.*

The following cases illustrate the requirements of the law as to the duty of a ship when coming to an anchor, when brought up, and when getting under way:—

*Precautions to be taken when at anchor, bringing up, or getting under way.*

A ship in bringing up must not give another a foul berth. "If one vessel anchors there, and another here, there should be that space left for swinging to the anchor that in ordinary circumstances the two vessels cannot come together. If that space is not left, I apprehend it is a foul berth" (*d*). In an American case it was held that a

*Foul berth.*

(*y*) *The Europa*, 14 Jur. 627.
(*z*) See above, p. 211.
(*a*) *Per* Dr. Lushington in *The Batavier*, 2 W. Rob. 407; and see *The Dura*, 1 Pritch. Adm. Dig. 174; *The Marcia Tribou*, 2 Sprague, 17.
(*b*) See *The Secret*, 26 L. T. N. S. 670; and (American cases) *Culbertson* v. *Shaw*, 18 How. 584; *Portevant* v.

*The Bella Donna*, Newb. Adm. 510; *The Bridgeport*, 7 Blatchf. 361; 14 Wall. 116; *The Granite State*, 3 Wall. 310; *The Helen Cooper* and *The R. L. Mabey*, 7 Blatchf. 378.
(*c*) *The Planet*, Brown Adm. 124.
(*d*) *Per* Dr. Lushington in *The Northampton*, 1 Spinks, E. & A. 152, 160.

ship at anchor is entitled to have room to swing not only
with the scope of cable which she has out at the time
when the other ship takes up her berth, but with as long a
scope as may be necessary to enable her to ride in safety (e).

If a ship gives another a foul berth she cannot require
the latter to take extraordinary precautions to avoid a
collision (f). And not only must a vessel not bring up so
close to another as not to give her room to swing, but she
must not bring up in such a place that she endangers the
other ship. She should not bring up directly ahead, or in
the stream, of another ship, having regard to the current
and also to prevailing winds. If she brings up directly in
the hawse of another ship, or elsewhere in the neighbourhood of another ship, there should be such a distance between them that if either of them drives or parts from
her anchors she may have the opportunity to keep clear (g).
Where a ship, in bad weather, took up a berth two cables'
length to windward of another, in an anchorage where
there was plenty of room, and then rode with only one
anchor down and that not her best, she was held in fault
for a collision with the ship to leeward, against which she
was driven when her cable parted in a heavy squall (h).
Where a vessel gave another a foul berth, and subsequently
drove against her in a hurricane, it was held to be an
inevitable accident (i).

If a vessel takes up a berth alongside another where
she takes the ground and falls over and injures the other
she will be held in fault (k). A vessel voluntarily taking
up such a berth in a dock does so at her own risk (l).

(e) The Queen of the East and The
Calypso, 4 Bened. 103.
(f) The Virid, 1 Asp. Mar. Law
Cas. 601.
(g) The Cumberland (Vice-Ad.
Court, Lower Canada), Stuart's Rep.
(1858), p. 75; The Egyptian, 1 Mar.
Law Cas. O. S. 358.
(h) The Volcano. 2 W. Rob. 337;
The Maggie Armstrong and The Blu-

Bell, 2 Mar. Law Cas. O. S. 318.
(i) The Innisfail and The Secret,
35 L. T. N. S. 819.
(k) The Indian and The Jessie, 2
Mar. Law Cas. O. S. 217; The
George and The Lidskjalf, Swab.
Adm. 117.
(l) The Patriotto and The Rival,
2 L. T. N. S. 301.

So in coming to an anchor caution must be used not to injure or embarrass other ships. A vessel rounding to, so as to bring her head upon tide, should, before altering her helm, look round and see that all is clear, and that her manœuvre will not endanger other ships (*m*).

In coming to an anchor in a crowded roadstead or harbour, proper care must be used to shorten sail in time, and not to run in at too great speed. A vessel running into Stangate Creek, in the Medway, was held in fault for a collision caused by her running in under too great a press of sail (*n*).

Where a ship delayed taking up her berth until night, and in consequence of the darkness injured another, she was held in fault for not having brought up by daylight, when she might have done so in safety (*o*).

After coming to an anchor those on board must show proper skill and seamanship in keeping their vessel from driving and endangering other craft. If a ship parts from her anchor, when with proper care she might have ridden in safety, and drives against another vessel, the collision will be held to have been caused by the negligence of the former, although after parting from her anchor the collision was inevitable, and all was done that could be done to avoid it. If she drives from her anchor in consequence of her yards not having been sent down, or because she was not tended or made properly snug, she will be held in fault (*p*). Where it is customary and prudent to moor, a vessel neglecting to do so will be held in fault (*q*). The duty to keep an anchor watch has been already referred to (*r*).

(right margin) Precautions to be taken when at anchor.

(*m*) *The Ceres*, Swab. Adm. 250; *The Shannon*, 1 W. Rob. 463; *The Philotaxe*, 37 L. T. N. S. 540.

(*n*) *The Neptune the Second*, 1 Dod. 467; *The Secret*, 26 L. T. N. S. 670; *The Earl Spencer*, L. R. 4 A. & E. 431; *The Masten*, Brown Ad. 436.

(*o*) *The Egyptian*, 2 Mar. Law.

Cas. O. S. 56; 1 Moo. P. C. C. N. S. 373.

(*p*) *The Excelsior*, L. R. 2 A. & E. 268; *The Christiana*, 7 Moo. P. C. C. 160.

(*q*) *The Gipscy King*, 2 W. Rob. 537.

(*r*) *Supra*, p. 216.

Where a ship gave another a foul berth in the Downs, and drove against her in a gale of wind while riding at single anchor with forty-five fathoms of chain, it was held that although the other vessel drove also, she was herself solely to blame (*q*).

Insufficient ground tackle, or riding by a single anchor when there should have been two down, will make a ship liable for a collision so caused (*r*). The ship must be duly tended while at anchor. A ship which goes foul of another through improperly breaking her sheer, will be held in fault (*s*). Where a ship was riding in an open and crowded roadstead in blowing weather, without having sent down her top-gallant and main-royal yards, she was held in fault for a collision caused by her driving (*t*). If a ship in a dock or harbour, subject to the Harbours, Dock, and Piers Clauses Act, 1847, is insufficiently moored, after notice from the harbour-master to provide proper fasts, she incurs a penalty of £10 (*u*). It has been held negligence not to increase moorings where the state of the weather required it (*v*).

It was held by the Supreme Court of the United States that a vessel in a gale of wind with another brought up near her was in fault for not taking timely precautions for avoiding a collision caused by the other driving on her (*w*). In another American case (*x*) it was held that where a ship at anchor drives and comes into collision with another at anchor, the burden is on the former, alleging inevitable accident, to prove that she had a proper watch on deck, that she discovered the dragging at once, that she

(*q*) *The Maggie Armstrong* v. *The Blue Bell*, 2 Mar. Law. Cas. O. S. 318, 319.

(*r*) *The Massachussetts*, 1 W. Rob. 371 ; *The Despatch*, 3 L. T. N. S. 219 ; *The Volcano*, 2 W. Rob. 337.

(*s*) See *The Peerless*, Lush. 30.

(*t*) *The Christiana*, 7 Moo. P. C. C. 160 ; and see *The Ruby Queen*,

Lush. 266 ; *The Excelsior*, L. R. 2 A. & E. 268.

(*u*) 10 & 11 Vict. c. 27, s. 61.

(*v*) *The John Harley* and *The William Tell*, 2 Mar. Law Cas. O. S. 290 ; *The Louisiana*, 3 Wall. 164.

(*w*) *The Sapphire*, 11 Wall. 164.

(*x*) *The Dutchess*, 6 Bened. 48.

took proper measures to prevent it, and that her ground tackle was sufficient.

If a ship is brought up by her own people, or by a compulsory pilot, in an improper berth, so as to endanger other ships, she must be shifted and taken to a proper berth as soon as possible (y). Where a ship was compelled to shift her berth in bad weather owing to her having only one anchor down, and in doing so, although proper precautions were taken, she came into collision, it was held that she was in fault for the collision because of her original neglect in riding to a single anchor (z).

It was held negligence in a ship in threatening weather to ride to a buoy in a river with her chain cables unbent and with no anchor ready to let go in case of parting from the buoy. Even in such situations, if the weather is threatening or there is cause for special precautions, an anchor watch must be kept and hands enough must remain on board to tend the ship (a).

A ship cannot take up or keep a berth by mooring a buoy at a particular spot; although it seems that in particular localities there may be a custom enabling her to do so (b).

The parting of a cable, the giving way of a buoy to which the ship was moored, and the jamming of the cable on the windlass on letting go the anchor, have been held to be inevitable accidents (c).

Making fast to another vessel in harbour instead of to the shore has been held to be negligence (d).

Where a ship, A., was made fast to another, B., and B., in getting under way, injured A., it was held in America

<hr/>

(y) The *Woburn Abbey*, 3 Mar. Law. Cas. O. S. 240. As to the duty of the master to shift, although the pilot is on board, if he is no longer in charge, see S. C. Ch. V.

(z) The *Despatch*, 3 L. T. N. S. 219.

(a) The *Pladda*, 2 P. D. 34 ; The *Kepler*, 2 P. D. 40.

(b) The *Vivid*, 1 Asp. Mar. Law Cas. 601.

(c) See *supra*, p. 23.

(d) The *Atlas*, 2 Mar. Law Cas. O. S. Dig. 1480.

Art. 24.

that B. was in fault, although the accident might have been caused partly by the lines by which A. was made fast to B., and which A. had not let go when desired to do so by B. It was held to be negligence in B. to have got under way without seeing that the lines were let go (e).

Bringing up in a fair-way or improper place.

In harbours and waters where there are local rules, or an established custom, as to the proper anchorage ground, a vessel would be held in fault for a collision caused by her bringing up elsewhere. But if she were compelled to bring up in the fair-way it would be otherwise (f). If there is no rule or custom requiring her to bring up out of the fairway she may anchor there, although directly in the track of ships. Thus, a vessel brought up in the Mersey directly in the track of the ferry steamers was held not to be in fault for lying there (g). In America it is held that if a vessel does bring up in the track of ferry boats, as she is at liberty to do, she must keep a vigilant look out and warn the ferry boat of her position (h).

The obligation on a ship under way to keep clear of another at anchor, as before stated (i), applies although the ship at anchor is in an improper berth. And a vessel brought up in a berth which is improper only in the sense that it is an exposed and dangerous position, does not thereby contribute to a collision caused by another ship negligently driving into her (k). But when a barge in the Thames was brought up in an exposed position, and was sunk partly by the swell of a passing steamer, it was held that the negligence in bringing up where she was exposed to the steamer's wash partly caused the loss, and the suit against the steam-ship was dismissed (l).

(e) The Thornton, 2 Bened. 429.
(f) The Kjobenhavn, 2 Asp. Mar. Law Cas. 213 ; and see The Clarita and The Clara, 23 Wall. 1.
(g) The Lancashire. L. R. 4 A. & E. 198.
(h) The D. S. Gregory, 6 Blatchf. 528 ; The Hudson, 5 Bened. 206 ;

The Exchange, 10 Blatchf. 168 ; and see supra, pp. 164, 215.
(i) Supra. p. 219.
(k) The Despatch, 3 L. T. N. S. 219.
(l) The Duke of Cornwall, 1 Pr. Adm. Dig. p. 135.

It seems that a vessel at anchor is not justified under all **Art. 24.** circumstances in holding on when by slipping she could Slipping to avoid a collision. A vessel in Falmouth harbour was driv- avoid a collision. ing in a gale of wind towards the breakwater. She could have avoided the breakwater by slipping from her anchor, and getting under way. She did not slip in time, went ashore, and did injury to the breakwater. It was held that she was liable for the damage because of her neglect in not slipping in time (m).

A vessel getting under way unnecessarily in bad weather Getting under with a number of other ships about her would probably be way. held in fault for a collision which would not have occurred if she had lain fast (n). The duty of a large ship to exercise caution in getting under way, and of other ships to keep clear of her, has been insisted upon by the American Courts (o).

A vessel which was moved from one dock to another by a tug at night was held in fault for a collision with a ship at anchor. It was held she had no right to be under way at all at night under such circumstances (p).

In an American case it was held that a ferry steamer getting under way when there was another vessel in her way which she ought to have seen, and which it was impossible to clear, was solely in fault for the collision. But it was said that she was not required to wait for the arrival of another boat running on the same ferry, and which was due (q).

If a vessel rides by, or makes fast to, or runs foul of, any Riding by a light-ship or buoy, in addition to the obligation to make light-ship. good all damage she incurs a penalty of fifty pounds (r).

(m) *The Uhla*, 3 Mar. Law Cas. O. S. 148; Cf. *The Sapphire*, 11 Wall. 164.

(n) *The Carrier Dove*, Br. & Lush. 113; *The Julia M. Hallock*, 1 Sprague, 539; *O'Neil* v. *Sears*, 2 Sprague, 52; *The Thornton*, 2 Bened. 429. The last three are American

decisions.

(o) *The City of Paris*, 14 Blatchf. 531.

(p) *The Borussia*, Swab. Adm. 94.

(q) *The Columbus*, Abbot Adm. 384.

(r) Merchant Shipping Act, 1854 (17 & 18 Vict. c. 104), s. 111.

Q

**Art. 24.**

**Ship in stays; precautions before going about.**

A vessel in stays—" in irons "—is almost as helpless for the purpose of keeping out of the way of another as a ship at anchor. It is the duty of other ships to keep clear of her. Before going about it is the duty of those on board " to take a due look round beforehand to ascertain that no ship is in the neighbourhood likely to come upon them " (s).

If weather permits a ship must have such canvas on her that she can be kept under command, and be able to stay (t). It has been held by the Privy Council that a ship should not wear without reason when she can stay; and a ship has been held in fault for a collision with a ship astern when she wore unnecessarily (u). In America a schooner wearing so close ahead of another ship that the latter could not clear her was held in fault (x).

**Missing stays.**

If a vessel misses stays the duty of those on board is to get her under command again as quickly as possible (y).

**Ships working to windward in company.**

Where it is the duty of a ship under the Regulations to keep out of the way, she should not stand so close to the other ship, before going about, that if she misses stays a collision must take place. It will be no excuse that she was struck by a squall while in the act of going about (z). A full-rigged ship, with the wind aft, meeting a brig and a schooner, both close-hauled on the starboard tack, came into collision with the brig, owing to the sudden and unexpected going about of the schooner. It was held that she ought not to have stood so close to the other ships as to make a collision inevitable if either of them went about (a).

---

(s) *The Sea Nymph*, Lush. 23 ; see also *The Ida* and *The Wasa*, 2 Mar. Law Cas. O. S. 414 ; *The Allan* and *The Flora*, ibid. 386 ; *The Eleanor* and *The Ahaa*, ibid, 240 ; *The Bolderaa*, Holt, 205 ; *The Newburgh* and *The Oscar*, Holt, 231.

. (t) *The Stirlingshire* and *The Africa*, 2 Mar. Law Cas. O. S. Dig. 672 ; *The Falkland* and *The Navigator*, Br. & Lush. 204.

(u) *The Falkland* and *The Naviga-*

tor, ubi supra.

(x) *The Saxonia*, 2 Mar. Law Cas. O. S. 417.

(y) *The Kingston by-Sea*, 3 W. Rob. 152 ; *The Lake St. Clair* and *The Underwriter*, 3 Asp. Mar. Law Cas. 361.

(z) *The Kingston-by-Sea, ubi supra;* *The Plato* and *The Perseverance*, Holt, 262.

(a) *The Mobile*, Swab. Adm. 69 ; ibid. 127.

Where two ships are turning through a narrow channel, one astern of the other and on the same tack, the duty of the sternmost ship is to keep a good look-out, and be ready to go about, if necessary, the instant the other goes about; so as not to risk a collision by standing on while the other is in stays, or has not gathered way on the other tack (b). It seems to have been considered by the Privy Council that a ship in stays, or just gathering way on the port tack, should apprise another ship approaching her on the starboard tack of her inability to keep out of the way (c). But a sailing-ship turning up the Thames was held not to blame for giving no notice to a steam-ship astern of her intention to go about (d).

The rule in America as to ships working to windward in narrow channels is that they must "beat out their tacks," and not go about before the depth of water or exigencies of the navigation require it (e). Vessels are expected to know the channel and the point at which other ships will be compelled to go about (f). A ship going about before she gets to the edge of the channel, and thereby causing a collision with a passing steam-ship, was held in fault (g). But the rule as "to beating out tacks" does not apply so as to preclude a ship from going about before she reaches the shoal water in order that she may be able to weather a point of land, or other object, on the next tack (h). The rule does not appear to have been expressly recognised in any Court in this country. In *The Palatine* (i), where there seems to have been room for its application, it was not referred to.

(b) *The Priscilla*, L. R. 4 A. & E. 125 ; *The Eclipse* and *The Royal Consort*, Holt, 220.

(c) *The Lake St. Clair* and *The Underwriter*, 3 Asp. Mar. Law Cas. 361 ; and see *The Leonidas*, Stuart's Vice Ad. Rep., Lower Canada (1858), p. 226.

(d) *The Palatine*, 1 Asp. Mar. Law Cas. 468.

(e) *Thorp* v. *Hammond*, 12 Wall. 408 ; *The Empire State*, 1 Bened. 57 ; *The Bridgeport*, 6 Blatchf. 3 ; *The Charlotte Raab*, Brown Adm. 453.

(f) *The Nellie D.*, 5 Blatchf. 245.

(g) *The Nereus*, 3 Bened. 238.

(h) *The Vicksbury*, 7 Blatchf. 216 ; *The Empire State*, supra.

(i) 1 Asp. Mar. Law Cas. 468.

**Art. 24.**

Whether a
ship should
hold herself
in stays for
another.

Whether a ship, being in stays, is required to hold
herself in stays to allow another vessel to pass, is not clear.
Two American cases are contradictory on the point. In
*The Empire State* (j) the Court said that it is the duty of
a ship to beat out her tack and come about on the other
tack with proper despatch ; and that " she is not obliged
to remain in the wind for a steamer to pass her." On the
other hand, in *The W. C. Redfield* (k), it was held that a
sailing-ship was in fault for not holding herself in stays to
allow a tug and her tow to pass clear.

There are decisions of the American Courts to the effect
that it cannot be imputed to a ship as a fault that she is
sluggish in going about (l) ; and that she is not wrong in
fore-reaching or shooting ahead in the wind's eye whilst
going about (m).

Extra care
required in
passing over
fishing
grounds.

Fishing boats have a right to fish on the high sea, and
to be fast to their nets, whether their fishing ground is in
the track of ships or not. It is the duty of other ships to
take greater precautions when passing over a fishing ground,
so as to keep clear of the fishing boats, and not make them
cast off from their nets (n).

Vessels navi-
gating in an
unusual
manner or
course do so
at their own
risk.

Vessels navigating in an unusual manner or by an
improper course do so at their own risk. By the bye-laws
in force in the Tyne (clause 17), all vessels proceeding to
sea are required to keep on the south side of midchannel ;
and (clause 20) vessels crossing the river take upon themselves the responsibility of doing so with safety to the
passing traffic. A vessel outward bound, coming out of the
Tyne dock on the south side of the river, and either inten-
tionally, or under the influence of the tide, crossing over to

( j ) 1 Bened. 57.
(k) 4 Bened. 227 ; see also *The
Arthur Gordon* and *The Independence*, Lush. 270 ; *The Lake St.
Clair* and *The Underwriter*, ubi
supra.
(l) *The Charlotte Raab*, Brown
Adm. 453.

(m) 1 Parsons on Shipping (2nd
ed.), 578, note.
(n) *The Columbus*, 2 Mar. Law
Cas. O. S. Dig. 730 ; *Murphy v.
Palgrave*, 3 Mar. Law Cas. O. S.
284 (Irish case) ; *The Margaret* and
*The Tuscar*, Holt, 44.

the north side of the river, came into collision on the north side with two steam-ships also going down the river. She was held in fault for the collision as she should not have attempted to cross when there was risk of collision (o).

It was held in *The Smyrna* (p) that a usual and proper precaution for vessels to take when navigating a winding river against a strong stream is to keep under the points in the slack of the tide, so as to avoid descending vessels which are swept across the river into the opposite bight by the stream setting off the point. But the rule would seem to be different under the present law of " starboard side " in narrow channels (q).

In New York harbour, where ferry boats are constantly coming out from their slips or docks at right angles to the course of vessels navigating the river, the law requires vessels navigating the river to keep in midchannel, or if they go along the shore to go very slowly (r).

Where two steam-ships were meeting in a narrow channel, one going with and the other against the tide, and it was necessary for one of them to stop, it was held by the Supreme Court in America that the vessel going against the tide should have stopped at once, as she could do so the more readily (s).

A vessel warping down the Thames against the flood tide was held in fault for a collision thereby occasioned (t) ; and in America it was held that a vessel with a warp across a river fair-way is bound to slack it to allow another vessel to cross (u). A steam-ship proceeding down the Thames at night against a flood tide is required to exercise the greatest caution (x).

(o) *The Henry Morton*, 2 Asp. Mar. Law Cas. 466. As to the duty of ships to keep on their proper side and in the usual track in rivers, see *supra*, pp. 193—197; and *The Java*, 14 Wall. 189.

(p) 2 Mar. Law Cas. O. S. 93.

(q) See Article 21.

(r) *The Favorita*, 18 Wall. 598.

(s) *The Galatea*, 2 Otto. 439; as to the Thames, see *infra*, p. 278.

(t) *The Hope*, 2 W. Rob. 8.

(u) *The Maverick*, 1 Sprague, 23.

(x) *The Trident*, 1 Sp. E. & A. 217.

**Art. 24.**

**Eddy tide.**

If a vessel enters an eddy tide and is thereby prevented from answering her helm and goes into collision with another ship, it is no excuse that the eddy prevented her from answering her helm (*y*) ; and the effect of the tide on other ships must be known and allowed for (*z*),

**Being under way in thick weather ; stress of weather.**

If the weather is such that an object cannot be seen in time to avoid it, a vessel has no right to be under way at all. In such weather she should bring up on the first opportunity, and not get under way unless obliged to do so (*a*). In thick and bad weather generally it is the duty of a vessel under way to exercise more than ordinary care to avoid doing damage to other ships (*b*). "Stress of weather" is an excuse frequently put forward for omitting to exercise ordinary care, but it is one which the Court is very unwilling to accept (*c*).

**Standing too close to other craft.**

In squally weather it is the duty of a ship not to approach another so near that if a squall strikes her she will go in collision with the other. A vessel will be held in fault if she navigates so close to another that her view is obstructed and she cannot see a third ship in time to avoid her (*d*) ; or that she is affected by the wash or suction of the ship ahead, and will not answer her helm (*e*).

A brig on the starboard tack endeavouring to pass a collier driving up the Thames with the tide was caught by a heavy squall which split her foretopsail and did other damage. The brig came up into the wind and drove against the collier. She was held solely in fault for the collision, because, having reason to expect squalls, she should have given the other vessel a wider berth ( *f* ).

(*y*) *The La Plata*, Swab. Adm. 220, 223 ; *The Russia*, 3 Bened. 471.

(*z*) *The Frantz Sigel*, 14 Blatchf. 480.

(*a*) *The Lancashire*, L. R. 4 A. & E. 198 ; *The Otter*, L. R. 4 A. & E. 203. And see *supra*, p. 163.

(*b*) *The Flint*, 6 Not. of Cas. 271 ; *The John Harley* and *The William*

Tell, 2 Mar. Law Cas. O. S. 290.

(*c*) *The Uhla*, 3 Mar. Law Cas. O. S. 148 ; *The Flint, ubi supra*.

(*d*) *The Zollverein*, Swab. Adm. 96 ; and see *Mayhew* v. *Boyce*, 1 Stark. 423, *supra*, p. 4.

(*e*) *The General McCandlass*, 6 Bened. 223, 226.

( *f* ) *The Globe*, 6 Not. of Cas. 275.

A barge turning down the Thames on a squally night stood so close to a ship at anchor that, upon her missing stays owing to a squall, she ran into her. The barge was held solely in fault (*g*).

In America, a steam-ship passing so close to a sloop at anchor that the boom of the latter was driven against her by a sudden gust of wind, was held solely in fault (*h*). And where a steam-ship at sea sighted a schooner seven miles off, and shaped her course so as to pass within a cable's length of her, it was held by the Circuit Court that for two ships approaching each other at the rate of eighteen miles an hour such a course was "very far from an exercise of reasonable prudence" (*i*).

Where a ship, which had been ashore, came off unexpectedly and received damage in a collision with another ship which was near her, it was held that the latter was not bound to take such precautions that, at whatever time the ship ashore floated, she would not come against her (*k*).

A ship driving over a sand on which she had been ashore came into collision with another brought up just clear of the sand. It was held that the former was not in fault for the collision, and that it was the result of inevitable accident. The ship that had been ashore could not have let go her anchor whilst driving over the sand without risk to herself, and if she had let go when clear of the sand, the collision would not have been avoided (*l*).

If a ship steers a course to take her alongside another ship to speak her or for any other purpose, she does so at her own risk (*m*). The Supreme Court of the United States held a steam-ship solely in fault for a collision with

(*g*) The *Plato* and The *Persever-ance*, Holt, 262.

(*h*) The *George Law*, 3 Bened. 396.

(*i*) The *Benefactor*, 14 Blatchf, 254.

(*k*) The *Coxon*, 2 Mar. Law Cas. O. S. Dig. 549.

(*l*) The *Thornley*, 7 Jur. 659.

(*m*) The *Thames*, 5 C. Rob. 345. See The *Bellerophon*, 3 Asp. Mar. Law Cas. 58,

Art. 24.  a pilot boat from which she was taking a pilot and which was plainly visible to her, although the pilot boat had no mast-head light and crossed the bows of the steamship (*n*).

In another case (*o*) before the same Court two tugs making for the same vessel in order to get the contract to tow came into collision. It was held that the proper and usual way for tugs to come alongside was to come up on the quarter heading the same way as the vessel, and that the tug which was ahead of the vessel was in fault for not rounding to and coming up under the ship's stern.

A steam-tug unnecessarily entering a narrow cut leading to the Bute Docks, after a signal had been made by the harbour authority for sailing-ships to enter, was held in fault for a collision (*p*).

The Supreme Court in America has held that a vessel undertaking to pass another in a narrow channel (*q*), or navigating such a channel in weather that makes it dangerous (*r*), does so at her own risk. Where a ship was ashore in such a place, it was held that whether she went ashore by her own negligence or not, another vessel attempting to pass her was in fault for running into her (*s*).

Where the leading vessel of two steamers proceeding down a river with the stream, and bound to the same place on its bands, rounded to at a proper place to land her passengers, and the following vessel, instead of stopping and rounding to under her stern, attempted to turn ahead of her and a collision occurred, the following vessel was (in Canada) held solely in fault (*t*).

(*n*) *The City of Washington*, 2 Otto. 31.
(*o*) *Sturgis* v. *Clough*, 21 How. 451.
(*p*) *The Effort*, 5 Not. of Cas. 279.
(*q*) *The Merrimac*, 14 Wall. 199.

(*r*) *The Mohler*, 21 Wall. 231.
(*s*) *The Ellen S. Terry*, 7 Bened. 401.
(*t*) *The Crescent* v. *The Rowland Hill*, Stuart's Rep. (1858) (Vice-Adm. Ct., Lower Canada), 289.

If a vessel is of a construction or is in a condition which is specially dangerous to other vessels, it is her duty to warn approaching vessels of the fact. Where a ship of war carried on her stem under water a projecting ram or spur, it was held that it was her duty to apprise a vessel coming alongside of the danger she ran in approaching her (u).

Art. 24.
Vessel, owing to peculiar construction or otherwise, dangerous to others.

Special precautions are required of a ship in a disabled condition, of a ship hove-to and unable to keep clear of other ships, as well as of other ships approaching the disabled vessel (x); of a tug with a ship in tow, and of both the tug and her tow, so as not to damage each other when taking the tow line on board, and during the performance of the towage (y). It is the duty of a ship unable to keep out of the way in compliance with the Regulations to hail the other ship, and of the latter herself to keep out of the way (z).

Where a vessel is coming out of dock, or executing a manœuvre in the course of which an alteration of her helm is necessary, another ship approaching her is justified in acting upon the assumption that the necessary measures will be taken by the former vessel with proper skill and despatch, and that her course will be that which is obviously intended. A schooner coming out of St. George's Dock in the Mersey, the tide being flood and the wind southerly, saw a tug with a ship in tow coming down the river towards her. She put her helm hard-a-port and scandalized her mainsail in order to get her head to point down the river. Owing to the flood tide catching her under the starboard bow she did not answer her helm readily, and came into collision with the tug. If she had

Coming out of dock.

(u) The Bellerophon, 3 Asp. Mar. Law Cas. 58; and see The Batavier. 1 Sp. E. & A. 378.
(x) The Arthur Gordon and The Independence, Lush. 270; and see

supra, p. 210.
(y) See supra, p. 82, seq.
(z) The Lake St. Clair and The Underwriter, 3 Asp. Mar. Law Cas. 361.

**Art. 24.** run up her outer jib, which she did not do, she would have answered her helm better and would have kept clear of the tug. The latter had kept her course in the expectation that the schooner would set her jib and straighten herself in the river, as she was intending to do. It was held that the schooner was solely in fault for the collision, and that the tug did right in acting upon the assumption that the schooner's jib would have been run up, and that she would have straightened herself and kept on the tug's starboard side (*a*).

**Dumb barges.** A dumb barge, or lighter, that drives with the tide has little or no control over her own movements, and cannot keep out of the way of other craft. It is therefore the duty of other vessels, and particularly of steam-ships, to keep out of her way. In order to do this they must know the set of the tide and probable course of the lighter (*b*).

**Speed in narrow channels.** In a river or narrow channel steam-ships must go at such a rate of speed as will not raise a swell to endanger barges and other craft. In the Thames, and some other rivers, there are bye-laws to this effect. Whatever the rate of speed required by local bye-laws, if a ship, though not exceeding that rate, endangers other craft, she will be held in fault (*c*). But to recover against another ship for sinking her by her swell it must be clearly proved that the sunken craft was not mismanaged or overladen (*d*). In the Suez Canal the local rules specify five and a-half knots as the maximum speed.

**Special pre-** When a vessel is launched, the law casts upon the

---

(*a*) *The Ulster*, 1 Mar. Law Cas. O. S. 234.

(*b*) *The Swallow*, 3 Asp. Mar. Law Cas. 371 ; *The Owen Wallis*, L. R. 4 A. & E. 175. For American decisions to the same effect, see *Fretz* v. *Bull*, 12 How. 466 ; *Pearce* v. *Page*, 24 How. 228 ; *Butterfield* v. *Boyd*, 4 Blatchf. 356.

(*c*) *The Batavier*, 1 Sp. E. & A. 378 ; 9 Moo. P. C. C. 286 ; see *The Duke of Cornwall*, 1 Pr. Adm. Dig. 135 ; *Smith* v. *Dobson*, 3 M. & G. 59.

(*d*) *Luxford* v. *Large*, 5 C. & P. 421. The rule of equal division of loss only applies in case of *collision*, 36 & 37 Vict. c. 66, s. 25, sub-s. 9.

persons in charge of the launch the obligation of conduct-
ing it with the utmost precaution, and of giving such
notice as is reasonable and sufficient to prevent injury to
passing vessels.

In the case of *The Andalusian* (e), although notice of
the intended launch was posted up in a conspicuous place,
flags were flying on the ship to be launched, and two tugs
with boats were employed to warn passing vessels, a vessel
that was passing was not warned, and those in charge of
the launch were held responsible for a collision with her.

In *The Blenheim* (f) Dr. Lushington said with regard
to the duty of those in charge of the launch :—

" Such reasonable notice of a launch shall be given as
shall prevent danger or reasonable chance of danger to
other vessels navigating in the river. That is the first
great principle and rule in these cases. As all other
vessels have a right to navigate in a river, no person shall
interfere with that navigation without such reasonable
notice of a launch as may prevent the chance of an injury
to them. What is reasonable notice depends on local
circumstances, the breadth of the river, the number of
vessels passing, and other circumstances of that kind. It
must be not a mere general notice of a launch on a
particular day : the notice must so specify the time of the
launch that vessels navigating up and down the river
may not be damaged or incur danger."

Similar language was used by Sir R. Phillimore as to
the duty of those launching a vessel in *The Glengarry* (g) ;
in which case it was held that the burden of showing
that proper precautions were taken lies on those launching
the ship. In *The Glengarry* it was held that all proper
precautions were taken, and that the vessel under way (a
tug with barges in tow) was solely in fault for steaming

(e) 2 P. D. 231 ; see also *The Vianna*, Swab. Adm. 405.    (f) 4 Not. of Cas. 393.
(g) 2 P. D. 235.

**Art. 24.**

across the path of *The Glengarry* at the moment she was being started.

Even after proper notice of a launch has been given it must not take place so long as other vessels are in the way. If it is customary for the harbour-master to superintend or be present, it should not take place in his absence (*h*).

As to the duty of a vessel coming out of dock into the fair-way of a river, see above, p. 233.

**Small craft not required by law to keep out of the way of heavy ships.**

There is no rule in law requiring small vessels to keep out of the way of larger ones, though it may be much easier for them to do so than for the larger ship to take the steps required by the Regulations. A large ship going at a slow speed in a narrow channel may be unable to alter her course rapidly, but, so far as she can do so, she must comply with the Regulations. In such a case it will be the duty of the smaller vessel to take such precautions as are rendered necessary by the comparatively helpless condition of the larger ship (*i*).

## ARTICLE 25.

**Art. 25.**

**Local rules not affected by the general rules.**

*Nothing in these rules shall interfere with the operation of a special rule, duly made by local authority, relative to the navigation of any harbour, river, or inland navigation.*

This Article is new. It does not appear to make any alteration in the law, the effect of local rules being saved by 25 & 26 Vict. c. 63, s. 31.

Local rules have not, in all cases, been recognised by the Courts as of equally binding effect with the general Regu-

---

(*h*) *The United States*, 2 Mar. Law Cas. O. S. 166.

(*i*) See *The La Plata*, Swab.

Adm. 220 ; on app., *ibid*. 298 ; and see *The Arthur Gordon* and *The Independence*, Lush. 270.

lations; but there is no doubt that a material infringe- Art. 25.
ment of them will, unless excused by special circumstances,
be held to be negligence contributing to a collision. A
bye-law made under a local Act required ships coming
into the Tyne to keep on the north side of the river. *The
Raithwaite Hall*, coming in from the sea in a thick fog,
was in collision, on the south side of the river, with a vessel
bound out. In the absence of proof of negligence on the
part of the latter, *The Raithwaite Hall* was held to be in
fault for the collision (*k*). In this case Sir R. Phillimore
said, with regard to the effect of local rules : " There should,
however, be no misunderstanding as to the effect of these
and similar bye-laws governing the navigation of a river.
It cannot be held that, because they or any of them are
disobeyed, the vessel disobeying them is therefore to be
held to blame. They are only evidence of what it is the
duty of a vessel to do under the circumstances named in
the particular bye-law. As such evidence, however, they
are an important element in every case that comes within
their provisions; and if it should appear that by the breach
of one of them a ship has occasioned or contributed to a
collision, the existence of such a bye-law would afford the
very strongest reason for holding that the ship had been
guilty of a breach of duty and was to blame for the collision " (*l*).

The words of Article 25 are very wide, and appear to Effect of local
negative the operation of the general Regulations in all rules in foreign<br>waters.
waters at home or abroad where they conflict with rules
" duly made by local authority." But it seems that, under
the Regulations of 1863, local rules as to ships' lights in
foreign waters were not binding on British ships (*m*).

(*k*) *The Raithwaite Hall*, 2 Asp.
Mar. Law Cas. 210.
(*l*) As to the obligation to obey
local rules, see *The Henry Morton*, 2
Asp. Mar. Law Cas. 466 ; *The Iron
Duke*, Holt, 227 ; *The Peerless*, Lush.

30; 13 Moo. P. C. C. 484 : *The
Smyrna*, 2 Mar. Law Cas. O. S. 93.
(*m*) *The William Hutt*, cited in
Lowndes on Collision, 187 ; *The
Michelimo* and *The Dacca*, P. C.,
May, 1877.

Local rules are in force in the Thames, the Mersey, the Clyde, the Tees, the Tyne, and at Belfast, Dublin, and Cork. In the case of the Thames and some other waters the local rules are nearly identical with the general Regulations. The rules will be found in the Appendix, *infra*.

Difficulties arise in some cases where the local rules are not consistent with the general Regulations; but it appears that in the waters in which they are in force the local rules must be obeyed without regard to the general Regulations, if the latter conflict with them. Previous to enactment of the existing bye-laws there was no bye-law in force in the Thames requiring sailing-ships to carry lights. A Trinity sailing ballast lighter having been run down in the river when carrying no lights, it was held that, not being a sea-going vessel, she was not required by the general Regulations to carry lights, and that she was not required to carry them under the local rules, there being no bye-law on the subject (*n*). Sir R. Phillimore expressed an opinion that the power of the Conservators did not enable them to make bye-laws for seagoing ships, and their powers applied to river craft only. It seems, however, that the existing bye-laws are binding on all ships in the Thames.

Vessels navigating the sea channels at the mouth of the Mersey are required to keep on the starboard side of the channel; and vessels at anchor in those channels are required to exhibit a second riding light at the mizen-peak(*o*).

By 25 & 26 Vict. c. 63, s. 32, Her Majesty has power to make regulations for rivers and inland waters where they cannot be made under any local Act. Under this power rules have been made for the Mersey (*p*) and for some of the Lancashire inland navigations (*q*).

---

(*n*) *The C. S. Butler*, L. R. 4 A. & E. 238. In America there are in force special rules as to steam-ships' lights, some of which appear to be inconsistent with the international Regulations.

(*o*) 37 & 38 Vict. c. 52. See Appendix.

(*p*) See Order in Council of 27th June, 1866.

(*q*) See two Orders in Council of 18th May, 1870.

By 10 & 11 Vict. c. 27, dock and harbour authorities **Art. 25.**
have power to make such regulations; and by 28 & 29
Vict. c. 125, in dockyard ports the Queen's harbour-master
has a similar power. Under the last-mentioned Act regulations have been made for Queenstown, Deptford, Wool-
wich, Portsmouth, Plymouth, Pembroke, and Portland (*r*).

There are special rules for the navigation of the Danube (*s*)
and for the Suez Canal (*t*).

It appears that where the local rules do not conflict with
the general rules the latter are supplementary to the local
rules. Local rules, though not made by any competent
authority, may, by long usage and well-recognised practice,
obtain the force of law. The obligation to obey such a
custom of the river was upheld by the Privy Council in
*The Fyenoord.* That case was decided under s. 297 of
17 & 18 Vict. c. 104, by which it was enacted, in effect,
that vessels going up the Thames should keep on the north
or starboard side. *The Fyenoord*, a foreign ship, was navigating on the south side and came into collision with a
vessel bound down. It was held that, even if the statute
was not binding on foreign ships, a custom had emanated
from the statute that ships should navigate in accordance
with it, and that *The Fyenoord* was to blame for trans-
gressing the custom (*u*).

ARTICLE 26.

*Nothing in these rules shall interfere with the operation* **Art. 26.**
*of any special rules made by the Government of any nation* Special lights
*with respect to additional station and signal lights for* for squadrons
and convoys.

(*r*) See Orders in Council of 29th Feb. 1868, and 29th June, 1878.
(*s*) See Parl. Pap., No. 29, of 1878 (Turkey); as to former rules for the Danube, see *The Smyrna*, 2 Mar. Law. Cas. O. S. 93; Orders in Council of 6th January, 1862; 21st

March, 1863.
(*t*) The substance of these rules will be found in the Appendix.
(*u*) *The Fyenoord*, Swab. Adm. 374; see also, as to local custom, *The Smyrna*, 2 Mar. Law Cas. O. S. 93.

**Art. 26.** *two or more ships of war, or for ships sailing under convoy.*

This Article is entirely new. Her Majesty's ships were not technically bound by the Regulations of 1863, nor, probably, are they by those of 1880. But Regulations exactly in accordance with them being issued by the Lords of the Admiralty, Her Majesty's ships are practically, in case of collision, before the law, in the same position as other ships (x).

(x) H.M.S. *Topaze*, 2 Mar. Law Cas. O. S. 38; H.M.S. *Supply*, *ibid.* 262. And see Art. 1001 of the Queen's Regulations for the Navy, of 1879.

# APPENDIX.

*25 & 26 Vict. c. 63, ss. 25—33, and 54—60.*

S. 25. On and after the 1st day of June, 1863 (*a*), or such later day as may be fixed for the purpose by Order in Council, the Regulations contained in the Table marked (C) in the Schedule hereto shall come into operation and be of the same force as if they were enacted in the body of this Act ; but Her

*Enactment of Regulations concerning Lights, Fog-Signals, and Sailing Rules in Schedule, Table (C).*

*Legislation as to the Rule of the Road previous to 1862.*

(*a*) The following were the Regulations and Acts of Parliament relating to the Rule of the Road which were successively in force previous to the year 1862. The London Trinity House issued the following order on the 30th of Oct. 1840 :—

" Whereas the recognised rule for sailing-vessels is that those having the wind fair shall give way to those on a wind ; that when both are going by the wind the vessel on the starboard tack shall keep her wind, and the one on the larboard tack bear up, thereby passing each other on the larboard hand ; when both vessels have the wind large or abeam and meet, they shall pass each other in the same way on the larboard hand ; to effect which, these two last-mentioned objects, the helm must be put to port ; and as steam-vessels may be considered in the light of vessels navigating with a fair wind, and should give way to sailing-vessels on a wind on either side, it becomes only necessary to provide a rule for their observance when meeting other steamers or sailing-vessels going large. When steam-vessels on different courses

must unavoidably or necessarily cross so near that by continuing their courses there would be a risk of coming in collision, each vessel shall put her helm to port so as always to pass on the larboard side of each other."

By 9 & 10 Vict. c. 100, s. 9, it was enacted that :—

" Every steam-vessel, when meeting or passing any other steam-vessel, shall pass as far as may be safe on the port side of such other vessel, and every steam-vessel navigating any river or narrow channel shall keep, as far as practicable, to that side of the fairway or mid-channel of such river or channel which lies on the starboard side of such vessel, due regard being had to the tide, as to the position of each vessel in such tide ; and the master or other person having charge of such vessel and neglecting to observe these Regulations, or either of them, shall for each and every instance of neglect forfeit and pay a sum not exceeding fifty pounds."

The next Act, 14 & 15 Vict. c. 79, s. 27, was as follows :—

" Whenever any vessel proceeding in one direction meets a vessel pro-

R

**25 & 26 Vict. c. 63.** Majesty may from time to time, on the joint recommendation of the Admiralty and the Board of Trade, by Order in Council, annual or modify any of the said Regulations, or make new Regulations in addition thereto or in substitution therefor; and any alterations in or additions to such Regulations made in manner aforesaid shall be of the same force as the Regulations in the said Schedule.

**Regulations to be published.** S. 26. The Board of Trade shall cause the said Regulations, and any alterations therein or additions thereto hereafter to be made, to be printed, and shall furnish a copy thereof to any owner or master of a ship who applies for the same; and production of the *Gazette* in which any Order in Council containing such Regulations, or any alterations therein, or additions thereto is published, or of a copy of such Regulations, alterations, or additions signed, or purporting to be signed by one of the Secretaries or Assistant-Secretaries of the Board of Trade, or sealed, or purporting to be sealed with the Seal of the Board of Trade, shall be sufficient evidence of the due making and purport of such Regulations, alterations, or additions.

**Owners and masters bound to obey them.** S. 27. All owners and masters of ships shall be bound to take notice of all such Regulations as aforesaid, and shall, so long as

ceeding in another direction, and the master or other person having charge of either such vessel perceives that if both vessels continue their respective courses they will pass so near as to involve any risk of a collision, he shall put the helm of his vessel to port, so as to pass on the port side of the other vessel, due regard being had to the tide and to the position of each vessel with respect to the dangers of the channel, and, as regards sailing-vessels, to the keeping of each vessel under command; and the master of any steam-vessel navigating any river or narrow channel shall keep as far as is practicable to that side of the fairway or mid-channel thereof which lies on the starboard side of such vessel; and if the master or other person having charge of any steam-vessel neglect to observe these Regulations or either of them, he shall for every such offence be liable to a penalty not exceeding fifty pounds "

The next Act, 17 & 18 Vict. c. 104, contained the following enactments :—

S. 296. Whenever any ship, whether a steam or sailing-ship, proceeding in one direction, meets another ship, whether a steam or sailing-ship, proceeding in another direction, so that if both ships were to continue their respective courses they would pass so near as to involve any risk of a collision, the helms of both ships shall be put to port so as to pass on the port side of each other, and this rule shall be obeyed by all steam-ships and by all sailing-ships, whether on the port or starboard tack, and whether close hauled or not, unless the circumstances of the case are such as to render a departure from the rule necessary in order to avoid immediate danger, and subject also to proviso that due regard shall be had to the dangers of navigation, and, as regards sailing-ships on the starboard tack, close hauled, to the keeping of ships under command.

S. 297. Every steam-ship when navigating any narrow channel shall, whenever it is safe and practicable, keep to that side of the fairway or mid-channel which lies on the starboard side of such steam-ship.

the same continue in force, be bound to obey them, and to carry and exhibit no other lights, and to use no other fog signals than such as are required by the said Regulations; and in case of wilful default the master or the owner of the ship, if it appear that he was in such fault, shall, for each occasion upon which such Regulations are infringed, be deemed to be guilty of a misdemeanour. *25 & 26 Vict. c. 63.*

S. 28. In case any damage to person or property arises from the non-observance by any ship of any Regulation made by or in pursuance of this Act, such damage shall be deemed to have been occasioned by the wilful default of the person in charge of the deck of such ship at the time, unless it is shown to the satisfaction of the Court that the circumstances of the case made a departure from the Regulation necessary. *Breaches of Regulations to imply wilful default of person in charge.*

*S. 29. If in any case of collision it appears to the Court before which the case is tried, that such collision was occasioned by the non-observance of any Regulation made by or in pursuance of this Act, the ship by which such Regulation has been infringed shall be deemed to be in fault, unless it is shown to the satisfaction of the Court, that the circumstances of the case made a departure from the Regulation necessary.* (Repealed 36 & 37 Vict. c. 85, s. 33. The same Act containing (s. 17) a corresponding proviso. See *infra*, p. 260.) *If collision ensues from breach of the Regulations, ship to be deemed in fault.*

S. 30. The following steps may be taken to enforce compliance with the said Regulations; that is to say, *Inspection for enforcing Regulations.*

(1.) The surveyors appointed under the third part of the Principal Act (*b*), or such other persons as the Board of Trade may appoint for the purpose, may inspect any ships for the purpose of seeing that such ships are properly provided with lights and with the means of making fog signals in pursuance of the said Regulations, and shall for that purpose have the powers given to inspectors by the 14th section of the Principal Act.

(2.) If any such surveyor or person finds that any ship is not so provided he shall give to the master or owner notice in writing, pointing out the deficiency, and also what is, in his opinion, requisite in order to remedy the same.

(3.) Every notice so given shall be communicated in such manner as the Board of Trade may direct to the collector or collectors of customs at any port or ports from which such ship may seek to clear, or at which her *transire* is to be obtained; and no collector to whom such communication is made shall clear such ship outwards, or grant her a *transire*, or allow her to proceed to sea without a certificate under the hand of one of the said surveyors, or other persons appointed by the Board of

(*b*) 17 & 18 Vict. c. 104.

25 & 26 Vict.
c. 63.

Trade as aforesaid, to the effect that the said ship is properly provided with lights, and with the means of making fog signals in pursuance of the said Regulations (c).

Rules for harbours under local Acts to continue in force.

S. 31. Any rules concerning the lights or signals to be carried by vessels navigating the waters of any harbour, river, or other inland navigation, or concerning the steps for avoiding collisions to be taken by such vessels, which have been or are hereafter made by or under the authority of any Local Act, shall continue and be of full force and effect, notwithstanding anything in this Act or in the Schedule thereto contained.

In harbours and rivers where no such rules exist they may be made.

S. 32. In case of any harbour, river, or other inland navigation, for which such Acts are not and cannot be made under the authority of any Local Act, it shall be lawful for Her Majesty in Council, upon application from the harbour, trust, or body corporate, if any, owning or exercising jurisdiction upon the waters of such harbour, river, or inland navigation, or, if there is no such harbour, trust, or body corporate, upon application from persons interested in the navigation of such waters, to make rules concerning the lights or signals to be carried, and concerning the steps for avoiding collision to be taken by vessels navigating such waters, and such rules when so made shall, so far as regards vessels navigating such waters, have the same effect as if they were regulations contained in Table (C) in the Schedule to this Act, notwithstanding anything in this Act or in the Schedule thereto contained.

In case of collision one ship shall assist the other.

*S. 33. In every case of collision between two ships it shall be the duty of the person in charge of each ship, if and so far as he can do so without danger to his own ship and crew, to render to the other ship, her master, crew, and passengers (if any) such assistance as may be practicable, and as may be necessary in order to save them from any danger caused by the collision;*

*In case he fails so to do, and no reasonable excuse for such failure is shown, the collision shall, in absence of proof to the contrary, be deemed to have been caused by his wrongful act, neglect, or default; and such failure shall also, if proved upon any investigation held under the third or eighth part of the Principal Act, be deemed to be an act of misconduct or a default for which his certificate (if any) may be cancelled or suspended.* (Repealed by 36 & 37 Vict. c. 85, s. 33. The same Act contains (s. 16) a similar provision ; see *infra*, p. 260.)

\*       \*       \*       \*       \*       \*

Ship-owners' liability limited.

S. 54. The owners of any ship, whether British or foreign, shall not, in cases where all or any of the following events occur without their actual fault or privity, that is to say :

(c) The M. S. Act, 1876 (39 & 40 Vict. c. 80), s. 14, gives an appeal to a Court of Survey against a surveyor's refusal of a certificate.

(1) where any loss of life or personal injury is caused to 25 & 26 Vict. any person being carried in such ship; c. 63.

(2) where any damage or loss is caused to any goods, merchandise, or other things whatsoever on board any such ship;

(3) where any loss of life or personal injury is, by reason of the improper navigation of such ship as aforesaid, caused to any other ship or boat, or to any goods, merchandise, or other things whatsoever on board any other ship or boat;

be answerable in damages in respect of loss of life or personal injury, either alone or together with loss or damage to ships, boats, goods, merchandise, or other things, to an aggregate amount exceeding fifteen pounds for each ton of their ship's tonnage; nor in respect of loss or damage to ships, goods, merchandise, or other things, whether there be in addition loss of life or personal injury or not, to an aggregate amount exceeding eight pounds for each ton of the ship's tonnage; such tonnage to be the registered tonnage in the case of sailing-ships, and in the case of steam-ships the gross tonnage, without deduction on account of engine room.

In the case of any foreign ship which has been or can be measured according to British law, the tonnage as ascertained by such measurement shall, for the purposes of this section, be deemed to be the tonnage of such ship.

In case of any foreign ship which has not been and cannot be measured under British law, the surveyor-general of tonnage in the United Kingdom, and the chief measuring officer in any British possession abroad, shall, on receiving from or by direction of the Court hearing the case such evidence concerning the dimensions of the ship as it may be found practicable to furnish, give a certificate under his hand, stating what would, in his opinion, have been the tonnage of such ship if she had been duly measured according to British law; and the tonnage so stated in such certificate shall, for the purposes of this section, be deemed to be the tonnage of such ship.

S. 55. Insurances effected against any or all of the events Limitation of enumerated in the section last preceding, and occurring without invalidity of such actual fault or privity as therein mentioned, shall not be insurances. invalid by reason of the nature of the risk.

S. 57. Whenever foreign ships are within British jurisdic- Foreign ships tion, the Regulations for preventing collision contained in Table in British (C) in the Schedule to this Act, or such other Regulations for be subject to preventing collision as are for the time being in force under regulations in this Act, and all provisions of this Act relating to such Regula- Table (C) in Schedule.

25 & 26 Vict. c. 63.

tions, or otherwise relating to collisions, shall apply to such foreign ships; and in any cases arising in any British Court of justice concerning matters happening within British jurisdiction, foreign ships shall, so far as regards such Regulations and provisions, be treated as if they were British ships.

Regulations when adopted by a foreign country, may be applied to its ships on the high seas.

S. 58. Whenever it is made to appear to Her Majesty that the Government of any foreign country is willing that the Regulations for preventing collision contained in Table (C) in the Schedule to this Act, or such other Regulations for preventing collision as are for the time being in force under this Act, or any of the said Regulations, or any provisions of this Act relating to collisions, should apply to the ships of such country when beyond the limits of British jurisdiction, Her Majesty may, by Order in Council, direct that such Regulations, and all provisions of this Act which relate to such Regulations, and all such other provisions as aforesaid, shall apply to the ships of the said foreign country, whether within British jurisdiction or not.

Ships of foreign countries adopting the rules for measurement of tonnage need not be re-measured in this country.

S. 60. Whenever it is made to appear to Her Majesty that the rules concerning the measurement of tonnage of merchant ships for the time being in force under the Principal Act (d) have been adopted by the Government of any foreign country, and are in force in that country, it shall be lawful for Her Majesty, by Order in Council, to direct that the ships of such foreign country shall be deemed to be of the tonnage denoted in their certificates of registry or other national papers; and thereupon it shall no longer be necessary for such ships to be remeasured in any port or place in Her Majesty's dominions, but such ships shall be deemed to be of the tonnage denoted in the certificates of registry or other papers, in the same manner, to the same extent, and for the same purposes in, to, and for which the tonnage denoted in the certificates of registry of British ships is deemed to be the tonnage of such ships.

The Schedule referred to in this Act—Table (C) :—

(The Regulations contained in this Schedule, which, with the exception of some verbal errors, were identical with those of January, 1863, were modified by an Order in Council of the 9th January, 1863, and by the same Order in Council the following Regulations were substituted in their place. The Regulations of 1863 remain in force until the 1st of September, 1880, on which day the Regulations enacted by Order in Council of the 14th of August, 1879, come into force. By the same Order the Regulations of 1863 are repealed as from that day. For convenience of reference the Regulations of 1863 and 1880 are here set out in parallel columns.)

(d) 17 & 18 Vict. c. 104.

(THE REGULATIONS OF 1863.)

REGULATIONS FOR PREVENTING
   COLLISIONS AT SEA.

*Contents.*

Art. 1. Preliminary.

RULES CONCERNING LIGHTS
   AND SIGNALS.

RULES CONCERNING FOG
   SIGNALS.

STEERING AND SAILING RULES.

The Regula-
tions of 1863
and 1880.

(THE REGULATIONS OF 1880.)

REGULATIONS FOR PREVENTING
   COLLISIONS AT SEA.

*(See next page.)*

The Regulations of 1863 and 1880.

*Preliminary.*

Article 1. In the following rules every steam-ship which is under sail and not under steam is to be considered a sailing-ship; and every steamship which is under steam, whether under sail, or not, is to be considered a ship under steam.

*Rules concerning Lights.*

Article 2. The lights mentioned in the following articles, and no others, shall be carried in all weathers from sunset to sunrise.

Article 3. Seagoing steamships when under weigh shall carry :

(*a.*) At the foremast head, a bright white light, so fixed as to show an uniform and unbroken light over an arc of the horizon of 20 points of the compass, so fixed as to throw the light 10 points on each side of the ship, viz., from right ahead to 2 points abaft the beam on either side, and of such a character as to be visible on a dark night, with a clear atmosphere, a distance of at least five miles :

(*b.*) On the starboard side, a green light, so constructed as to show an uniform and unbroken light over an arc of the horizon of 10 points of the

*Preliminary.*

Article 1. In the following rules every steam-ship which is under sail and not under steam is to be considered a sailing-ship; and every steam-ship which is under steam, whether under sail or not, is to be considered a ship under steam.

*Rules concerning Lights.*

Article 2. The lights mentioned in the following articles, numbered 3, 4, 5, 6, 7, 8, 9, 10, and 11, and no others, shall be carried in all weathers, from sunset to sunrise.

Article 3. A seagoing steamship when under way shall carry :

(*a.*) At, or in front of, the foremast, at a height above the hull of not less than 20 feet, and if the breadth of the ship exceeds 20 feet then at a height above the hull not less than such breadth, a bright white light, so constructed as to show an uniform and unbroken light over an arc of the horizon of 20 points of the compass ; so fixed as to throw the light 10 points on each side of the ship, viz., from right ahead to 2 points abaft the beam on either side ; and of such a character as to be visible on a dark night, with a clear atmosphere, at a distance of at least five miles :

(*b.*) On the starboard side, a green light, so constructed as to show an uniform and unbroken light over an arc of the horizon of 10 points of the compass; so fixed as to throw the light from right ahead to two points abaft the beam on the starboard side; and of such a character as to be visible on a dark night, with a clear atmosphere, at a distance of at least two miles:

(c.) *On the port side,* a red light, so constructed as to show an uniform and unbroken light over an arc of the horizon of 10 points of the compass; so fixed as to throw a light from right ahead to 2 points abaft the beam on the port side; and of such a character as to be visible on a dark night, with a clear atmosphere, at a distance of at least two miles:

(d.) The said green and red side lights shall be fitted with inboard screens, projecting at least three feet forward from the light, so as to prevent these lights from being seen across the bow.

*Lights for Steam-tugs.*

Article 4. Steam-ships when towing other ships shall carry two bright white masthead lights vertically, in addition to their side lights, so as to distinguish them from other steamships. Each of these masthead lights shall be of the same construction and character as the masthead lights which other steam-ships are required to carry.

compass; so fixed as to throw the light from right ahead to 2 points abaft the beam on the starboard side; and of such a character as to be visible on a dark night, with a clear atmosphere, at a distance of at least two miles:

(c.) On the port side, a red light, so constructed as to show an uniform and unbroken light over an arc of the horizon of 10 points of the compass; so fixed as to throw the light from right ahead to 2 points abaft the beam on the port side; and of such a character as to be visible on a dark night, with a clear atmosphere, at a distance of at least two miles:

(d.) The said green and red side lights shall be fitted with inboard screens projecting at least three feet forward from the light, so as to prevent these lights from being seen across the bow.

The Regulations of 1863 and 1880.

Article 4. A steam-ship, when towing another ship shall, in addition to her side lights, carry two bright white lights in a vertical line one over the other, not less than three feet apart, so as to distinguish her from other steamships. Each of these lights shall be of the same construction and character, and shall be carried in the same position as the light which other steamships are required to carry.

Article 5. A ship, whether a steam-ship or a sailing-ship, when employed either in lay-

## 250 APPENDIX.

ing

vessel, ready for instant exhibition; and shall, on the approach of or to other vessels, be exhibited on their respective sides in sufficient time to prevent collision, in such manner as to make them most visible, and so that the green light shall not be seen on the port side, nor the red light on the starboard side.

To make the use of these portable lights more certain and easy, they shall each be painted outside with the colour of the light they respectively contain, and shall be provided with suitable screens.

*Lights for Ships at Anchor.*

Article 7. Ships, whether steam-ships or sailing-ships, when at anchor in roadsteads or fairways, shall exhibit, where it can best be seen, but at a height not exceeding 20 feet above the hull, a white light in a globular lantern of eight inches in diameter, and so constructed as to show a clear, uniform and unbroken light visible all round the horizon, and at a distance of at least one mile.

*Lights for Pilot Vessels.*

Article 8. Sailing pilot vessels shall not carry the lights required for other sailing-vessels, but shall carry a white light at the masthead visible all round the horizon, and shall also exhibit a flare-up light every fifteen minutes.

vessel, ready for use; and shall, on the approach of or to other vessels, be exhibited on their respective sides in sufficient time to prevent collision, in such manner as to make them most visible, and so that the green light shall not be seen on the port side, nor the red light on the starboard side.

To make the use of these portable lights more certain and easy, the lanterns containing them shall each be painted outside with the colour of the light they respectively contain, and shall be provided with proper screens.

Article 8. A ship, whether a steam-ship or a sailing-ship, when at anchor shall carry, where it can best be seen, but at a height not exceeding 20 feet above the hull, a white light, in a globular lantern of not less than eight inches in diameter, and so constructed as to show a clear, uniform and unbroken light visible all round the horizon, at a distance of at least one mile.

Article 9. A pilot vessel, when engaged on her station on pilotage duty, shall not carry the lights required for other sailing-vessels, but shall carry a white light at the mast-head, visible all round the horizon, and shall also exhibit a flare-up light or flare-up lights at short intervals, which shall never exceed fifteen minutes.

The Regulations of 1863 and 1880.

*Lights for Fishing Vessels and Boats.*

Article 9. Open fishing boats and other open boats shall not be required to carry the side lights required for other vessels; but shall, if they do not carry such lights, carry a lantern having a green slide on the one side and a red slide on the other side; and on the approach of or to other vessels, such lantern shall be exhibited in sufficient time to prevent collision, so that the green light shall not be seen on the port side, nor the red light on the starboard side.

Fishing vessels and open boats when at anchor, or attached to their nets and stationary, shall exhibit a bright white light.

Fishing vessels and open boats shall, however, not be prevented from using a flare-up in addition, if considered expedient.

A pilot vessel, when on her station on pilotage duty, shall carry lights similar to those of other ships.

Article 10. (*a.*) Open fishing boats and other open boats when under way shall not be obliged to carry the side lights required for other vessels; but every such boat shall in lieu thereof have ready at hand a lantern with a green glass on the one side, and a red glass on the other side; and on the approach of or to other vessels, such lantern shall be exhibited in sufficient time to prevent collision, so that the green light shall not be seen on the port side, nor the red light on the starboard side.

(*b.*) A fishing vessel and an open boat when at anchor shall exhibit a bright white light.

(*c.*) A fishing vessel, when employed in drift net fishing, shall carry on one of her masts two red lights in a vertical line one over the other, not less than three feet apart.

(*d.*) A trawler at work shall carry on one of her masts two lights in a vertical line one over the other, not less than three feet apart, the upper light red, and the lower green, and shall also either carry the side lights required for other vessels, or if the side lights cannot be carried, have ready at hand the coloured lights as provided in Article 7, or a lantern with a red and a green glass as described in paragraph (*a.*) of this Article.

(*e.*) Fishing vessels and open

boats shall not be prevented The Regulations of 1863 and 1880. from using a flare-up in addition, if they desire to do so.

(*f.*) The lights mentioned in this Article are substituted for those mentioned in the 12th, 13th, and 14th Articles of the Convention scheduled to the British Sea Fisheries Act, 1868 (*e*).

Article 11. A ship which is being overtaken by another shall show from her stern to such last-mentioned ship a white light or a flare-up light.

RULES CONCERNING FOG SIGNALS.

*Fog Signals.*

Article 10. Whenever there is fog, whether by day or night, the fog-signals described below shall be carried and used, and shall be sounded at least every five minutes, viz. :—

(*a.*) Steam-ships under weigh shall use a steam-whistle placed before the funnel, not less than eight feet from the deck :

(*b.*) Sailing-ships under weigh shall use a fog-horn :

(*c.*) Steam-ships and sailing-ships when not under weigh shall use a bell.

*Sound Signals for Fog, &c.*

Article 12. A steam-ship shall be provided with a steam-whistle or other efficient steam sound signal, so placed that the sound may not be intercepted by any obstructions, and with an efficient fog-horn, to be sounded by a bellows or other mechanical means, and also with an efficient bell. A sailing ship shall be provided with a similar fog-horn and bell.

In fog, mist, or falling snow, whether by day or night, the signals described in this Article shall be used as follows; that is to say,

(*a.*) A steam-ship under way shall make with her steam-whistle, or other steam sound signal, at intervals of not more than two minutes, a prolonged blast :

(*e*) The Regulations are not expressed to be made in exercise of the powers of the Sea Fisheries Act, 1868; and it seems doubtful whether they are for all purposes equivalent to rules of that Act. The Board of Trade are considering memorials praying for an alteration of this article.

The Regula-
tions of 1863
and 1880.

(*b.*) A sailing-ship under way shall make with her fog-horn, at intervals of not more than two minutes, when on the starboard tack one blast, when on the port tack two blasts in succession, and when with the wind abaft the beam three blasts in succession:

(*c.*) A steam-ship and a sailing-ship when not under way shall, at intervals of not more than two minutes, ring the bell.

*Speed of Ships to be Moderate in Fog, &c.*

[*See Art.* 16, *infra.*]

Article 13. Every ship, whether a sailing-ship or steam-ship, shall, in a fog, mist, or falling snow, go at a moderate speed.

STEERING AND SAILING RULES.

*Two Sailing-ships meeting.*

Article 11. If two sailing-ships are meeting end on, or nearly end on, so as to involve risk of collision, the helms of both shall be put to port, so that each may pass on the port side of each other.

*Two Sailing-ships crossing.*

Article 12. When two sailing-ships are crossing so as to involve risk of collision, then if they have the wind on different sides, the ship with the wind on the port side shall keep out of the way of the ship with the wind on the starboard side; except in the case in which the ship with the wind on the port side is close-hauled and the other ship free, in which case the latter ship shall keep out

*Steering and Sailing Rules.*

Article 14. When two sailing-ships are approaching one another, so as to involve risk of collision, one of them shall keep out of the way of the other, as follows, viz. :—

(*a.*) A ship which is running free shall keep out of the way of a ship which is close-hauled :

(*b.*) A ship which is close-hauled on the port tack shall keep out of the way of a ship which is close-hauled on the starboard tack :

(*c.*) When both are running free with the wind on different sides, the ship which has the wind on the port side shall keep out of the way of the other :

(*d.*) When both are running free with the wind on the same

of the way; but if they have the wind on the same side, or if one of them has the wind aft, the ship which is to windward shall keep out of the way of the ship which is to leeward.

side, the ship which is to windward shall keep out of the way of the ship which is to leeward:

(*c.*) A ship which has the wind aft shall keep out of the way of the other ship.

*Two Ships under Steam meeting.*

Article 13. If two ships under steam are meeting end on, or nearly end on, so as to involve risk of collision, the helms of both shall be put to port, so that each may pass on the port side of the other.

[*And see Order in Council of 30th July*, 1868, *infra, p.* 258.]

Article 15. If two ships under steam are meeting end on, or nearly end on, so as to involve risk of collision, each shall alter her course to starboard, so that each may pass on the port side of the other.

This Article only applies to cases where ships are meeting end on, or nearly end on, in such a manner as to involve risk of collision, and does not apply to two ships which must, if both keep on their respective courses, pass clear of each other.

The only cases to which it does apply are when each of the two ships is end on, or nearly end on, to the other; in other words, to cases in which, by day, each ship sees the masts of the other in a line, or nearly in a line, with her own; and, by night, to cases in which each ship is in such a position as to see both the side lights of the other.

It does not apply by day to cases in which a ship sees another ahead crossing her own course; or by night to cases where the red light of one ship is opposed to the red light of the other, or where the green light of one ship is opposed to the green light of the other, or

*Ships under Steam crossing.*

Article 14. If two ships under steam are crossing so as to involve risk of collision, the ship which has the other on her own starboard side shall keep out of the way of the other.

*Sailing-ship and Ship under Steam.*

Article 15. If two ships, one of which is a sailing-ship and the other a steam-ship, are proceeding in such directions as to involve risk of collision, the steam-ship shall keep out of the way of the sailing-ship.

*Ships under Steam to slacken Speed.*

Article 16. Every steam-ship, when approaching another ship so as to involve risk of collision, shall slacken her speed, or, if necessary, stop and reverse ; and every steam-ship shall, when in a fog, go at a moderate speed.

where a red light without a green light, or a green light without a red light, is seen a-head, or where both green and red lights are seen anywhere but a-head.

Article 16. If two ships under steam are crossing so as to involve risk of collision, the ship which has the other on her own starboard side shall keep out of the way of the other.

Article 17. If two ships, one of which is a sailing-ship and the other a steam-ship, are proceeding in such directions as to involve risk of collision, the steam-ship shall keep out of the way of the sailing-ship.

Article 18. Every steam-ship, when approaching another ship so as to involve risk of collision, shall slacken her speed, or stop and reverse, if necessary.

Article 19. In taking any course authorised or required by these Regulations a steamship under way may indicate that course to any other ship which she has in sight by the following signals on her steamwhistle, viz. :—

One short blast to mean " I am directing my course to starboard."

Two short blasts to mean "I am directing my course to port."

Three short blasts to mean " I am going full speed astern."

The use of these signals is

*Vessels overtaking other Vessels.*

Article 17. Every vessel overtaking any other vessel, shall keep out of the way of the said last-mentioned vessel.

*Construction of Articles 12, 14, 15, and 17.*

Article 18. Where by the above rules one of two ships is required to keep out of the way, the other shall keep her course, subject to the qualifications contained in the following Article.

*Proviso to save Special Cases.*

Article 19. In obeying and construing these rules, due regard must be had to all dangers of navigation; and due regard must also be had to any special circumstances which may exist in any particular case rendering a departure from the above rules necessary in order to avoid immediate danger.

*No Ship under any Circumstances to neglect Proper Precautions.*

Article 20. Nothing in these rules shall exonerate any ship, or the owner, or master, or crew thereof, from the consequences of any neglect to carry lights or signals, or of any neglect to keep a proper look-

optional; but if they are used, the course of the ship must be in accordance with the signal made.

Article 20. Notwithstanding anything contained in any preceding Article, every ship, whether a sailing-ship or a steam-ship, shall keep out of the way of the overtaken ship.

Article 21. In narrow channels every steam-ship shall, when it is safe and practicable, keep to that side of the fairway or midchannel which lies on the starboard side of such ship.

Article 22. Where by the above rules one of two ships is to keep out of the way, the other shall keep her course.

Article 23. In obeying and construing these rules, due regard shall be had to all dangers of navigation; and to any special circumstances which may render a departure from the above rules necessary in order to avoid immediate danger.

*No Ship under any Circumstances to neglect Proper Precautions.*

Article 19. Nothing in these rules shall exonerate any ship, or the owner, master, or crew thereof, from the consequences of any neglect to carry lights or signals, or of any neglect to keep a proper look-out, or of

The Regulations of 1863 and 1880.

out, or of the neglect of any precaution which may be required by the ordinary practice of seamen, or by the special circumstances of the case.

The following addition to, or explanation of, the above Articles 11 and 13 was made by Order in Council of the 30th of July, 1868.

The two Articles numbered 11 and 13 respectively only apply to cases where ships are meeting end on, or nearly end on, *in such a manner as to involve risk of collision.* They, consequently, do not apply to two ships which must, if both keep on their respective courses, pass clear of each other.

The only cases in which the said two Articles apply are when each of the two ships is end on, or nearly end on, to the other ; in other words, to cases in which, *by day,* each ship sees the masts of the other in a line, or nearly in a line, with her own ; and *by night,* to cases in which each ship is in such a position as to see both the side lights of the other.

The said two Articles do not apply *by day,* to cases in which a ship sees another *ahead* crossing her own course ; or *by night,* to cases where the red light of one ship is opposed to the red light of the other ; or where the green light of one ship is opposed to the green light of the other ; or where a red light without a green light, or a green light without a red light, is seen ahead ; or where both green and red lights are seen anywhere but ahead.

the neglect of any precaution which may be required by the ordinary practice of seamen, or by the special circumstances of the case.

Reservation of Rules for Harbour and Inland Navigation.

Article 25. Nothing in these rules shall interfere with the operation of a special rule, duly made by local authority, relative to the navigation of any harbour, river, or inland navigation.

**Special Lights for Squadrons and Convoys.**

Article 26. Nothing in these rules shall interfere with the operation of any special rules made by the government of any nation with respect to additional station and signal lights for two or more ships of war, or for ships sailing under convoy.

## 31 & 32 VICT. c. 45.

Sect. 20. Articles 13 and 14 of the First Schedule to this Act shall, as to all sea-fishing boats within the exclusive fishery limits of the British Islands, and as to British sea-fishing boats outside of these limits, have the same force as if they were Regulations respecting lights within the meaning of the Acts relating to merchant shipping, with this addition, that any sea-fishery officer shall have the same powers of enforcing such Regulations as are given to any officer by such Acts, and any infringement of the Regulations contained in Articles 13 and 14 shall be deemed an offence within the meaning of the portion of this Act which gives power to sea-fishery officers. *Sea Fisheries Act, 1868; s. 20, as to lights.*

(Articles 12, 13 and 14 of the Convention contained in the Schedule and referred to in the above section are as follows.)

### Article 12.

No boat shall anchor between sunset and sunrise on grounds where drift-net fishing is actually going on.

This prohibition shall not apply to anchorings which may take place in consequence of accidents, or any other compulsory circumstances; but in such case the master of the boat thus obliged to anchor shall hoist, so that they shall be seen from a distance, two lights, placed horizontally, about three feet (one metre, French) apart, and shall keep those lights up all the time the boat shall remain at anchor.

### Article 13.

Boats fishing with drift-nets shall carry on one of their masts two lights, one over the other, three feet (one metre, French) apart. These lights shall be kept up during all the time their nets shall be in the sea between sunset and sunrise.

### Article 14.

Subject to the exceptions or additions mentioned in the two preceding Articles, the fishing-boats of the two countries shall conform to the general rules respecting lights which have been adopted by the two countries (*a*).

(*a*) See as to these lights Article 10 of the International Regulations of 1880, *supra*, p. 253. As to the limits within which this Act applies, see s. 70. The Act came into force on 1st Feb. 1869, as to British boats; see notice of 6th Feb. 1869, Lond. Gazette. As to French boats, see 40 & 41 Vict. c. 42, s. 15, and the Act there referred to, 6 & 7 Vict. c. 79.

## 36 & 37 Vict. c. 85.

Duties of masters in case of collision.

Sect. 16. In every case of collision between two vessels it shall be the duty of the master or person in charge of each vessel, if and so far as he can do so without danger to his own vessel, crew, and passengers (if any), to stay by the other vessel until he has ascertained that she has no need of further assistance, and to render to the other vessel, her master, crew, and passengers (if any), such assistance as may be practicable, and as may be necessary in order to save them from any danger caused by the collision; and also to give to the master or person in charge of the other vessel the name of his own vessel, and of her port of registry, or of the port or place to which she belongs, and also of the names of the ports and places from which and to which she is bound.

If he fails so to do, and no reasonable cause for such failure is shown, the collision shall, in the absence of proof to the contrary, be deemed to have been caused by his wrongful act, neglect, or default.

Every master or person in charge of a British vessel who fails, without reasonable cause, to render such assistance, or give such information as aforesaid, shall be deemed guilty of a misdemeanor, and if he is a certificated officer an inquiry into his conduct may be held and his certificate may be cancelled or suspended.

Liability for infringement of Regulations in case of collision.

Sect. 17. If in any case of collision it is proved to the Court before which the case is tried that any of the Regulations for preventing collision contained in, or made under, the Merchant Shipping Acts, 1854 to 1873, has been infringed, the ship by which such Regulations has been infringed shall be deemed to be in fault, unless it is shown to the satisfaction of the Court that the circumstances of the case made departure from the Regulation necessary.

## 38 Vict. c. 15.

Sea Fisheries Act, 1875; s. 3, as to ships' lights.

Sect. 3. Nothing in the Sea Fisheries Act, 1868, or in the Schedule thereto, shall be deemed to repeal or alter any of the Regulations for preventing collisions at sea contained in the Schedule to the Merchant Shipping Amendment Act, 1862, or to take away or diminish the power to annul or modify any of the said Regulations, and to make new Regulations in addition thereto, or in substitution therefor, which by the said last-mentioned Act is given to Her Majesty in Council.

---

## 37 & 38 Vict. c. 52.

An Act to make Regulations for preventing collisions in the sea channels leading to the River Mersey.

*Mersey sea channels (a).*

Whereas it is expedient to make special regulations for preventing collisions between vessels in the sea channels leading to the River Mersey:

Be it enacted by the Queen's Most Excellent Majesty, by and with the advice and consent of the Lords Spiritual and Temporal and Commons in this present Parliament assembled, and by the authority of the same, as follows :—

Sect. 1. Any general regulations for preventing collisions at sea for the time being in force under the provisions of the Merchant Shipping Acts shall be construed as if the following Regulations were added thereto, that is to say—

(1) Every steam-ship, and every vessel in tow of any steam-ship, when navigating in the sea channels or approaches to the River Mersey, between the Rock Lighthouse and the furthest point seawards to which such sea channels or approaches respectively are for the time being buoyed on both sides, shall, whenever it is safe and practicable, keep to that side of the fairway or midchannel which lies on the starboard side of such steam-ship or vessel in tow.

(2) Every ship at anchor in the said sea channels or approaches, within the limits aforesaid, shall carry the single white light prescribed by Article 7 of the General Regulations (b) for preventing collisions at sea, made under the authority of the "Merchant Shipping Acts Amendment Act, 1862," at a height not exceeding twenty feet above the hull, suspended from the forestay, or otherwise near the bow of the ship where it can be best seen ; and, in addition to the said light, all ships having two or more masts shall exhibit another similar white light, at double the height of the bow light, at the main or mizzen peak, or at the boom topping lift, or other position near the stern where it can be best seen.

(a) For Mersey river rules, see *infra*, p. 279.   (b) Of 1863.

Sect. 2. This Act shall not come into operation until the first day of November, 1874.

## LOCAL REGULATIONS.

### BELFAST.

Belfast.

The bye-laws and regulations in force at Belfast, made, it seems, under 10 & 11 Vict. c. 52 (Local), are as follows :—

Sect. 67. That, when steam-vessels on different courses must unavoidably or necessarily pass so near that by continuing their respective courses there would be a risk of coming in collision, the helm of each vessel shall be put to port, so that the one shall always pass on the larboard or port side of the other. Penalty for breach of this bye-law, a sum not exceeding five pounds for each offence.

Sect. 68. That a steam-vessel passing another in the Channel and going in same direction shall always leave the vessel she is passing on the larboard or port hand, under a penalty of a sum not exceeding five pounds for each offence.

Sect. 69. That, when two such vessels are proceeding in the same direction, either coming up or going down, the vessel astern shall on no account attempt to pass, when there is so little room from vessels being in the way, or other causes, as to occasion a risk of damage ; and that the vessel ahead shall, when the other is passing, keep well over on the larboard or port side, and in no part of the channel or harbour must she be allowed to cross the course of the vessel passing. Penalty for breach of any part of this bye-law, a sum not exceeding five pounds for each offence.

Sect. 70. That no tug-steamer shall take more than four vessels in tow at one time, nor have more than two abreast, under a penalty of a sum not exceeding five pounds for each offence.

Sect. 71. That no tug-steamer shall attempt to bring up any vessel whose draft of water is so great that the rise of tide will not admit of so doing, under a penalty not exceeding five pounds.

Sect. 72. That masters or persons in charge of steamers coming up or going down the channel shall slow their engines to half-speed between the entrance to the channel and the quays, so as to prevent danger or risk of injury to other vessels, Local rules or to the harbour works—that is to say, if coming up, slow (Belfast). their engines to a *safe rate*, not exceeding half-speed, when abreast of the beacon, buoy, or lighthouse, at the entrance to the new channel; and, if going down, keep their engines at a *safe rate*, not exceeding half-speed, until after passing that point, under a penalty of a sum not exceeding five pounds.

Sect. **73.** (*Steamers to slow their engines when passing dredgers.*)

### ADDITIONAL RULES.

1st. That, when steamers are likely to meet at, or near the Holywood Lighthouse, the *outgoing steamer* ("being the one which has the other on her own starboard side") shall wait until the *incoming steamer* has come round far enough to give her a clear course.

2nd. That no steamer shall swing in the harbour at such a time as to interfere with the arrival or departure of any other steamer.

3rd. That no irregular or casual trading steamer shall *leave* at a time that will interfere with or cause delay to an advertised steamer.

4th. That when two or more steamers are advertised to sail *at the same time,* the steamer which lies furthest down the harbour, or seawards, is expected to sail first, and in no case is the steamer which lies further up the harbour to leave her berth before the other further down, unless ordered to do so by the harbour-master or his deputy, or until the master has ascertained by sounding his steam-whistle that the other steamer is not ready to leave (*a*).

(*a*) When a steam-whistle is sounded by a steamer lying further up the harbour to ascertain whether the river be clear, it will be the duty of the steamer further down to sound her whistle in reply, *if she is ready to start,* but to remain silent if not ready, in which case the upper steamer may leave.

---

## THE CLYDE.

Bye-laws of 3rd January, 1860, made under 21 & 22 Vict. c. 149 (Local). Clyde.

1. (*Vessels over sixty tons to have pilots.*)

2. Every vessel shall, during the daytime, have one person, and from sunset to sunrise, or in time of fogs, two persons,

Local rules (Clyde).

properly qualified, stationed at the bow as a look-out, to give notice in due time of any obstruction or danger, who shall be furnished with a trumpet or whistle, to be used when there is reason to believe another vessel is near.

3. When vessels proceeding in opposite directions approach each other, they shall put their helms to port in sufficient time, and keep to the right or starboard side of the river; and when within thirty yards of each other shall, if necessary, haul in their main booms and leave sufficient room for each to pass; and all steamers or vessels sailing with a fair wind, and falling in with vessels beating to windward, shall alter their course in sufficient time to pass astern of the vessel so beating.

4. (*Vessels to have their yards peaked or braced, booms rigged in, and anchor ready to let go. Vessels to make fast to buoys and not ride to their own anchors; to slack down moorings when required, and be berthed by harbour-master.*)

5. Every vessel lying aground or at anchor in the river shall lower the boom to and make it fast upon the taffrail by the main sheet being brought hard home and belayed, and shall not lay the anchor in the deepened channel so as to interrupt or interfere with the free passage; the buoy ropes exceeding at no time four fathoms. And if any vessel grounds across the channel, the bowsprit, if running, and jib-boom shall be rigged in.

6. Every vessel, of whatever description, moored to the buoys, or at anchor in the stream, or moving in the harbour, shall, between sunset or sunrise, exhibit a white light in a globular or octagonal lantern of not less than eight inches in diameter, and placed in a conspicuous situation, and raised at least twelve feet above the deck so as to show a clear, uniform, and unbroken light all round the horizon.

7. (*Vessels to come to at the buoys and be berthed by the harbour-master.*)

12 and 13. (*Small boats prohibited in certain parts of the river; scows to have sufficient coamings.*)

30. When steamers, proceeding in opposite directions, approach each other, they shall, at a proper distance, put their helms to port, and when within thirty yards shall slow their engines sufficiently, and keep as near as possible to the right or starboard side of the river, so as to afford all possible facility for passing each other.

31. When steamers are proceeding in the same direction, but with unequal speed, the vessel which steams slowest shall, when overtaken, keep sufficiently to the left or port side, and shall offer no obstruction whatever, by crossing the channel or otherwise, to the free passage of the faster vessel, and shall slow,

and, if necessary, stop the engines as soon as a faster vessel comes within thirty yards; and in like manner the master of the faster vessel shall slow his engines when he comes within thirty yards of the slower vessel, until he has passed the vessel so overtaken; and that ignorance of the approach of the faster vessel may not be pretended by the master of the slower vessel, it shall be sufficient intimation of such approach if the bell of the faster vessel be three times rung. Local rules of (Clyde).

32. The master of every steamer (steamers when employed in tugging vessels, and steam lighters excepted) meeting or overtaking any sailing-vessels, or steam-tug with sailing-vessels in tow, shall slow the engines of his vessel when within thirty yards, until he shall have passed the sailing-vessel or steam-tug and train. He shall likewise slow his engines at least one hundred yards from any vessel aground or at anchor in the river. Steam-tugs and train, when meeting other vessels, shall, in proper time, put their helms to port, and, when overtaken, shall put their helms to starboard, and keep sufficiently to the proper side of the river.

33. The master of any steamer, either putting out or taking in passengers or goods, by small boats, shall keep as near as can with safety be done to the shore upon which he is putting out, or from which he is receiving passengers or goods, so as to allow ample room for other vessels to pass in safety on the off-side.

34. (*Passenger steamers to stop their engines before and when boats are alongside: precautions to be used in picking up or putting out passengers.*)

35. (*Ferry steamers arriving at landing place at the same time; the last to arrive to stop fifty yards off.*)

44. (*Steamers not to try their engines when at berths.*)

45. *Steamers to have lanterns for the convenience of passengers;* "and all vessels when on the river shall conform to the Admiralty Rules with regard to lights."

46. (*Steamers to go at reduced speed.*)

47. (*Passenger steamers not to take up passengers in certain parts of the river.*)

---

## CORK.

The bye-laws and regulations of 9th June, 1869, for preventing collisions, in force at Cork (under 1 Geo. IV. c. 52, and the Cork Harbour Amendment Act, 1866), are substantially the same as the General Regulations. There are, however, some variations and additions, the principal of which are as follows:—The local rules are expressly made applicable to steam and sailing lighters; the fog-horn or bell is to be sounded once every minute; Cork.

Local rules
(Cork).

and there are special provisions for speed when passing dredgers and other craft, and for the navigation of rafts of timber. Rules 85, 89, 90 and 91 are as follows :—

85. When any steam-vessels moving in opposite directions shall approach each other, the masters shall respectively slow engines as soon as such vessels shall come within one hundred yards of each other, and shall cause the respective vessels to keep as near as they can towards the side of the river to the right or starboard, so as to afford all possible facility to each other to pass.

89. Every steam-vessel, when navigating any narrow channel, shall, whenever it is safe and practicable, keep to that side of the fairway or midchannel which lies on the starboard side of such steam-vessel.

90. No steam-vessel shall race, or attempt to strive or race, the one against the other ; nor shall any steam-vessel attempt to come in the wake of another steam-vessel between Horsehead and the sea, nor pass one proceeding in the same direction, except at a safe distance ; and the slower-moving vessel shall allow the faster-moving vessel freely to pass.

91. The master, or other person in charge of steam-vessels, shall not proceed at any greater speed than quarter-speed in any part of the river west of the east end of Myrtle Hill Terrace.

## DUBLIN.

Dublin.

The bye-laws made under the Dublin Port and Docks Act, 1869, provide for the regulation of the navigation of the Port by the Harbour and Dock Masters ; vessels on an outside tier are to exhibit a conspicuous bright light ; if ashore in the fairway, they are to exhibit a similar light, and in foggy and thick weather sound a fog-horn or bell ; when a vessel has a warp out, other vessels are not to run foul of it ; vessels are not to swing or warp while there is risk of collision to others ; ropes and moorings are to be slacked when necessary ; the General Regulations are specially made applicable to vessels navigating the port ; between Poolbeg Lighthouse and the Royal Canal Dock no more than two vessels are to be towed abreast or three in a length, west of the Royal Canal Dock only two vessels in length and not abreast, and at a speed of not more than two miles an hour ; slow speed is enjoined on tugs when bringing their tows to a berth, and on steam-ships generally, so as not to endanger dredgers and other craft at work.

# HOLYHEAD.

At Holyhead, by Regulations of the 1st December, 1877, issued by order Holyhead. of the Board of Trade, and signed by the Harbour-master, ships are warned against bringing up outside the breakwater, or in the fairway, where they are in the track of packets ; if unavoidably brought up in the fairway, masters are particularly requested to exhibit two riding lights, one at the peak and one forward ; when navigating the fairway at night, vessels should burn a flare-up or bright light ; small vessels should come into the harbour of refuge and leave the outer anchorage for large ships ; vessels riding in the harbours or roadsteads are to exhibit the Regulation riding light ; vessels are not to enter the inner harbour at a high rate of speed, or endanger the packets alongside the jetties ; in bad weather vessels are to be securely anchored and made snug ; coming round the breakwater vessels are to go at reduced speed, as they are coming round a blind corner ; the mail packets burn a red flashing light when rounding the breakwater ; and when swinging and blocking the entrance, the red flash light is burnt and fog-bell sounded ; when the harbour is clear, a green flash light is burnt.

---

# HUMBER.

Rules for the River Humber are under consideration.

---

# MERSEY.

See pages 261, 279.

---

# THE TEES.

Bye-laws of 5th September, 1870, made under the Tees Conservancy Tees. Acts and the Harbours, Docks and Piers Clauses Act, 1847, provide for the proper mooring of ships under the direction of the Harbour-master ; vessels in the harbour are to have at least one responsible person on board ; anchors are to be in clear of the gunwale or with the stock awash ; no more than two ships are to be alongside the wharves' staiths or spouts at the same time, and when so lying are not to have their anchors in the channel ; ships are to carry the lights required by the General Regulations, except that steam-ships in tow are to carry side lights only ; fog-horns and steam-whistles are to be sounded during fog once in every minute ; masters of passenger steam-ships are to remain on the paddle-box ; tugs are to attend on their tows till moored ; steam-wherries are to be provided with whistles ; other rules (17—31) are as follows:—

17. Every ship navigating the river shall keep the starboard side, so that the port-helm may always be applied to clear vessels proceeding in the opposite direction.

18. Every steam-ship when approaching another ship on an opposite course or from an opposite direction shall, before

approaching within thirty yards, slacken her speed, and keep as near as possible to the starboard side of the river, so as to afford the greatest facility for passing the approaching ship.

19. All steam-vessels and ships towed by steam-ships must so approach the river from sea as to enter on that side of the channel reserved for their navigation.

20. All ships, when under way, requiring to pass over a part of the channel which is not within that portion reserved for their navigation, for the purpose of proceeding to or from landings, moorings, or other places, must take upon themselves the responsibility of doing so in safety with reference to the passing traffic; and any ship continuing its navigation after reaching such landing, mooring, or other place, must again proceed to the side of the river specified as the proper side for its navigation, so soon as practicable, and take upon itself the responsibility of doing so in safety with respect to the passing traffic.

21. Ships crossing the river, and ships turning, must take upon themselves the responsibility of doing so safely with reference to the passing traffic.

22. No steam-ship shall at any time be navigated in any part of the river at a higher rate of speed than a maximum rate of six miles per hour.

23. Whenever there is a fog, no steam-ship shall be navigated in any part of the river at a higher rate of speed than three miles per hour.

25. When steam-ships are proceeding in the same direction, but with unequal speed, the ship which steams slowest shall, when overtaken, keep sufficiently to that bank of the river which is on her own starboard side, and shall offer no obstruction whatever, by crossing the channel or otherwise, to the free passage of the faster ship, and shall ease and, if necessary, stop the engine as soon as a faster ship comes within thirty yards, and in like manner the faster ship shall ease its engine when it comes within thirty yards of the slower ship, until it has passed the ship so overtaken; and, that ignorance of the approach of the faster ship may not be pleaded by the master of the slower ship, it shall be sufficient intimation of such approach if the steam-whistle of the faster ship be three times sounded; but no ship overtaking any other ship will be justified in passing such ship at any of the points or other dangerous turnings of the river, or at any dock entrance.

26. Every steam-ship, other than a steam-ship employed in towing, meeting or overtaking any sailing-ship or steam-tug with sailing-ships in tow, shall ease its engines before arriving within thirty yards of, and until it shall have passed, the sailing-ship

or steam-tug and train.  Every steam-tug and train, when meet- ing another vessel, shall, in proper time, put their helms to port, and, when overtaken, shall keep sufficiently to the proper side of the river to allow the ship overtaking them to pass.

27.  All ships towing in from sea with a long scope of tow-line must shorten the same on getting inside the river, and before reaching the Cleveland Railway jetty, near Cargo Fleet. The tow-line, when so shortened, must not exceed twenty-five fathoms in length.

28.  Every steam-tug or other steam-ship towing a ship into the port which shall not already have a pilot on board, and whether showing a signal for a pilot or not, shall be bound to ease, or stop if necessary, to enable a pilot to board the ship, unless the master thereof shall have previously informed the master of the steam-ship that he did not intend to take a pilot.

29.  No ship shall be allowed to drift in any part of the river or harbour.  Every ship must be properly navigated, or moored clear of the navigable channel.  Ships proceeding to any dock, and arriving off the entrance of such dock before the signal for admission is hoisted, must keep on either side of the navigable channel, and out of the fairway of the river or dock traffic, until the signal is hoisted for their reception.

30.  No steam-tug or other steam-ship shall tow two or more ships alongside each other, nor shall tow more than one raft of timber when such rafts exceed 150 feet in length or 30 feet in breadth.

31 and 32. (*Steam-ships to be properly manned; one man to be on the look-out by day and two at night; steam-ship's bell or whistle to be sounded in fog once a minute.*)

---

# TYNE.

The bye-laws of December 12th, 1867, made under the River Tyne Improvement Acts of 1850, 1857, 1861, 1865, and the Harbours, Docks and Piers Clauses Act, 1847, provide (cl. 1—3) for the mooring and dis-mantling of vessels under the Harbour-master's directions; vessels at anchor or at moorings are to rig in booms, bowsprits, and davits, peak their yards, and have their anchors awash or on deck, as required by the Harbour-master.  The Regulations as to ships' lights (cl. 11—16) are substantially the same as the General Regulations of 1863; express provision being made for steam-ships in tow, which are required to carry side lights and no mast-head light, and for keels, open boats not exceeding fifty feet in length, and rafts of timber, which are required to carry only a lantern with red and green slide.  There are special rules (29—33) as to keeping clear of dredgers and their gear; as to manning of ships and keeping two hands after sunset or in fog on the look-out (35) ; as to steam-ships and steam-wherries, bells and whistles, which are to be sounded in fog once every minute (36) ; as to steam-ships going half-speed during fog (38) ; as to the master of passenger steam-ships remaining on the paddle-box (42) ; and various other minute regulations for the safe navigation of the river and docks.

Other special rules as to navigation are as follows :—

9. Vessels shall not be allowed to lie at anchor between Whitehill Point and the Low Lighthouse. All vessels within the above limits must make fast to the moorings provided for the purpose.

10. (*Steam-ships, when moored, not to move their engines.*)

&ast; &ast; &ast; &ast; &ast;

17. All vessels navigating the river, when proceeding towards sea, shall keep to the south of midchannel ; and, when coming from seaward, shall keep to the north of midchannel, so that the port-helm may always be applied to clear vessels proceeding in opposite directions.

18. All steam-vessels, and vessels towed by steam-vessels, must so approach the river from the sea as to enter on that side of the channel reserved for their navigation.

19, 20, 21, 23, 24, 27 and 28 are identical, except verbally in one or two instances, with clauses 19, 20, 21, 25, 26 and 28 of the Tees Regulations (above, p. 267).

22. When steam-vessels, proceeding in opposite directions, approach each other, they shall, at a proper distance, put their helms to port, and, when within thirty yards, shall ease their engines sufficiently, and keep as near as possible to the right or starboard side of the river, so as to afford all possible facility for passing each other.

25. All vessels towing in from sea with a long scope of tow-line must shorten the same before entering the Narrows, and in all parts of the river extending upwards from the Low Light-house. The length of the tow-line must not exceed fifteen . fathoms in length.

26. No steam-tug, or other steam-vessel, shall, within the port, take or have in tow at one time more than one ship or other seagoing vessel of a register tonnage exceeding one hundred tons (100 tons), but this rule shall not apply to vessels or craft used by or belonging to the commissioners (*a*).

(*a*) See the cases cited *supra*, pp. 188, 237, as to the effect of the Tyne rules.

---

## THAMES.

Rules and bye-laws for the navigation of the River Thames, made under Thames. the Thames Conservancy Acts, 1857 and 1864, the Thames Navigation Act, 1866, the Thames Conservancy Act, 1867, and the Thames Navigation Act, 1870, and approved by Order in Council of February 5th, 1872, provide (3 – 13) for the mooring and berthing of vessels at the tiers and public moorings; (14) vessels in certain parts of the river are to navigate singly; 15 is as follows :—

15. All vessels navigating Gravesend Reach are to keep to the northward of a line defined by a skeleton beacon erected upon the India Arms Wharf on with the high chimney of the Cement Works at Northfleet; and all vessels intending to anchor in the reach are to bring up to the southward of that line. A lantern is placed on the above beacon which shows (at night) a bright light to the northward of the same line, and a red light to the southward of it, over the anchorage ground. All vessels so anchoring and remaining beyond a period of twenty-four hours are to be moored.

Barges are to be sufficiently manned (16); anchors are to be buoyed; they may not be laid in the fairway, or carried a-cock-bill (17—20); there are various regulations as to vessels lying at the tiers and their moorings (21—27); 28 provides that vessels are to be navigated with due care for the safety of others; engines are not to be moved when at moorings (31); the master of every steam-ship is required to remain on the paddle-box when under way (36); barges are to have fifteen inches free board to the top of their coamings (41). The rules as to navigation and ships' lights are as follows :—

29. The following steering and sailing rules shall be observed by vessels navigating the River Thames :—

(The Rules distinguished by the letters a, b, c, and j are, with the exception of immaterial verbal differences, identical with the General Regulations of 1863, Articles 19, 11, 12, 13, 14, 15, 16, 17, 18 and 20 respectively : see supra, pp. 247—258).

32. Every steam-vessel navigating the River Thames (except as hereinafter provided) shall, between sunset and sunrise, while under way, exhibit the three following lights of sufficient power to be distinctly visible with a clear atmosphere, on a dark night, at a distance of at least one mile, namely—

(a) At the fore-mast, or if there be no fore-mast at the funnel, a bright white light suspended at the height of not less than ten feet from the deck, and so fixed as to throw the light from right ahead to two points abaft the beam on either side.

(*b*) On the starboard side, a green light so fixed and fitted with an inboard screen as to throw the light from direct ahead to two points abaft the beam on the starboard side.

(*c*) On the port side, a red light so fixed and fitted with an inboard screen as to throw the light from direct ahead to two points abaft the beam on the port side.

(*d*) Provided, however, that no passenger steam-vessel whilst navigating the said river above London Bridge, and when under way, shall be bound to exhibit between sunset and sunrise any other lights than two bright white lights, one at her mast-head and one at her stem.

33. Steamers towing vessels shall, between sunset and sunrise, exhibit, in addition to the above-mentioned three lights, a white light on the fore-mast or funnel not less than four feet vertically above the first-mentioned white light, of the like power and similar to it in every respect.

34. Every steam dredger moored in the River Thames shall, between sunset and sunrise, exhibit three bright lights from globular lanterns of not less than eight inches in diameter, the said three lights to be placed in a triangular form, and to be of sufficient power to be distinctly visible with a clear atmosphere, on a dark night, at a distance of at least one mile, and to be placed not less than six feet apart on the highest part of the framework athwart ships.

35. Every steam-vessel, when the steam is up, and when under way, shall, in all cases of fog, use as a signal a steam-whistle, which shall be sounded at least every three minutes.

(*a*) Sailing-vessels, when under way, shall in like manner use a fog-horn.

(*b*) When at anchor, all vessels shall in like manner use a bell.

46. No steam-vessel shall be worked or navigated upon the said river between Teddington Lock, in the parish of Ham, in the county of Surrey, and Cricklade, in the county of Wilts, at such speed as shall endanger or cause damage to other vessels, or cause any injury to the banks of the river.

(The following was approved by Order in Council of 20th November, 1873.)

All barges on the River Thames above Putney Bridge, whether navigated by sail or towed by steam or horses, shall, between sunset and sunrise, while under way, exhibit in their bows or on their masts a red light of sufficient power to be distinctly visible with a clear atmosphere, on a dark night, at a distance of at least one mile.

(The following were approved by Order in Council of 17th March, 1875.)

1. All vessels under sail east of London Bridge shall exhibit,

between sunset and sunrise, two lights, namely, a green light on the starboard side, so fixed and fitted with an inboard screen as to throw the light from direct ahead to two points abaft the beam on the starboard side ; and a red light on the port side, so fixed and fitted with an inboard screen as to throw a light from direct ahead to two points abaft the beam on the port side, such lights to be visible on a dark night, with a clear atmosphere, at a distance of at least one mile.

2. Every person in charge of a dumb-barge, when under way and not in tow, shall, between sunset and sunrise, when below or to the eastward of a line drawn from the upper part of Silvertown, in the county of Essex, to Charlton Pier, in the county of Kent, have a white light always ready, and exhibit the same on the approach of any vessel.

3. The person in charge of the sternmost or last of a line of barges, when being towed, shall exhibit, between sunset and sunrise, a white light from the stern of his barge.

4. All vessels and barges, when at anchor in the fairway of the river, shall exhibit the usual riding light.

5. All vessels, when employed to mark the positions of wrecks or other obstructions, shall exhibit two bright lights placed horizontally not less than six feet apart.

(The following were approved by Order in Council of 11th July, 1877.)

2. All vessels navigating the river between the Albert Bridge, at Chelsea, and Charlton Pier, shall be navigated singly and separately, except small boats fastened together, or towed alongside, or astern of other vessels, and except vessels towed by steam.

3. Vessels towed by steam shall be placed two abreast, if more than four in number, and not more than six shall be towed together at one time.

4. Above and to the westward of the Albert Bridge, at Chelsea, six vessels and no more may be towed together in a single line, at one time, and the distance between any two of the vessels, so towed, shall not exceed fifty feet.

5. Every steam-vessel, before passing any vessel employed in dredging or in lifting any sunken vessel or in removing any obstruction from the river, shall ease her engines so as to reduce her speed while passing. In construing this bye-law the word "vessel" shall have the same interpretation as is assigned to it by Bye-law 2 of the Bye-laws of 1872.

T

# PROPOSED NEW RULES FOR THE THAMES.

Proposed new rules for the Thames.

The Conservators of the River Thames have published a notice that they propose, in exercise of their statutory powers, and with the consent of Her Majesty in Council, to repeal the bye-laws stated in the text, Nos. 28, 29, 32, 33, 34, 35 and 46 of the 5th of February, 1872, that of the 20th of November, 1873, Nos. 1, 4 and 17 of the 17th of March, 1875, and No. 5 of the 11th of July, 1877, and to enact the following new rules, dated 16th January, 1880, in their place :—

*The word "vessel" shall mean any ship, lighter, barge, boat, wherry, punt, canoe, and any kind of craft whatever, whether navigated by steam or otherwise.*

*The word "river" shall mean that part of the River Thames which is within the jurisdiction of the Conservators between Cricklade, in the county of Wilts, and Yantlet Creek, in the county of Kent.*

*1. In obeying and construing the following rules due regard shall be had to all dangers of navigation, and to any special circumstances which may render a departure from the rules necessary in order to avoid immediate danger.*

*2. Nothing in the following rules shall exonerate any vessel, or the owner, or master, or crew thereof, from the consequences of any neglect to carry lights or signals, or of any neglect to keep a proper look-out, or of the neglect of any precaution which may be required by the ordinary practice of seamen, or by the special circumstances of the case.*

*Bye-law for the Regulation of the Navigation of the River.*

*3. Every steam-vessel navigating the river shall be navigated with care and caution, and at a speed and in a manner which shall not endanger the safety of other vessels or moorings, or cause damage thereto, or to the banks of the river. Special care and caution shall be used in navigating such steam-vessels when passing vessels employed in dredging or removing sunken vessels or other obstructions.*

*If the safety of any vessel or moorings is endangered, or damage is caused thereto or to the banks of the river by a passing steam-vessel, the onus shall lie upon the owner of such steam-vessel to show that she was navigated with care and caution, at such speed and in such manner as directed by this rule.*

*Bye-laws and Rules for the Regulation of the Navigation of the* Proposed rules
*River between Yantlet Creek and Teddington Lock.* (Thames).

*Rules concerning Lights.*

4. *The lights mentioned in the following rules, numbered 5 to
10, and no others, shall be carried in all weathers from sunset to
sunrise.*

5. *A steam-vessel, when under way, shall carry*

(a.) *On or before the foremast, or if there be no foremast, on a
staff at the forepart of the vessel at a height above the hull of not
less than twenty feet, and if the breadth of the vessel exceeds twenty
feet then at a height above the hull not less than such breadth, a
bright white light, so constructed as to show a uniform and unbroken light over an arc of the horizon of twenty points of the compass, so fixed as to throw the light ten points on each side of the
vessel—viz., from right ahead to two points abaft the beam on
either side, and of such a character as to be visible on a dark
night, with a clear atmosphere, at a distance of at least two
miles. Provided that steam-vessels which navigate both above and
below London Bridge shall not be required to carry their lights at
a greater height than twelve feet above the hull.*

*Steam-vessels navigating only above London Bridge may carry
the white light at any convenient height above the stem.*

(b.) *On the starboard side, a green light so constructed as to
show a uniform and unbroken light over an arc of the horizon of
ten points of the compass, so fixed as to throw the light from right
ahead to two points abaft the beam on the starboard side; and of
such a character as to be visible on a dark night, with a clear
atmosphere, at a distance of at least one mile.*

(c.) *On the port side, a red light so constructed as to show a
uniform and unbroken light over an arc of the horizon of ten points
of the compass, so fixed as to throw the light from right ahead to
two points abaft the beam on the port side; and of such a character as to be visible on a dark night, with a clear atmosphere, at a
distance of at least one mile.*

(d.) *The said green and red side lights shall be fitted in such a
manner as to prevent these lights from being seen across the bow.*

(e.) *A steam-vessel, when towing another vessel, shall, in addition
to her side lights, carry two bright white lights in a vertical line
one over the other, not less than four feet apart. Each of these lights
shall be of the same construction and character, and shall be
carried in the same position, as the white light which other steam-
vessels are required to carry.*

T 2

(f.) *A steam-vessel towing may also carry a light showing
astern as a guiding light to the vessel or vessels towed, but this
light must be so screened as not to be visible further forward than
four points abaft her beam.*

6. *A sailing-vessel under way, or being towed, shall only carry
the side lights provided by* (b.) *and* (c.) *of Rule 5 for a steam-vessel
under way.*

7. *A steam-vessel, a sailing-vessel, or a barge when at anchor in
the river, shall carry where it can best be seen, at a height not exceeding twenty feet above the hull, a white light, in a globular lantern
of not less than eight inches in diameter, and so constructed as to
show a clear, uniform, and unbroken light, visible all round the
horizon, at a distance of at least one mile; provided always that
where masted vessels are lying in tiers, the outermost off-shore
masted vessels only of each tier shall each carry a light similar
to that required for vessels at anchor; but barges lying at the
usual barge-moorings in the river above Barking Creek shall not
be required to exhibit such riding light.*

8. *A vessel which is being overtaken by another vessel below
Barking Creek shall show from her stern to such last-mentioned
vessel a white light, or a flare-up light.*

*This rule shall not apply to boats, wherries, punts, or canoes.*

9. *All vessels, when employed to mark the positions of wrecks or
other obstructions, shall exhibit two bright lights placed horizontally not less than six nor more than twelve feet apart.*

10. *Every steam dredger moored in the river shall, between sunset and sunrise, exhibit three bright lights from globular lanterns
of not less than eight inches in diameter, the said three lights to
be placed in a triangular form, and to be of sufficient power
to be distinctly visible with a clear atmosphere, on a dark night,
at a distance of at least one mile, and to be placed not less than
six feet apart on the highest part of the framework athwart
ships.*

### Rules concerning Fog, &c., Signals.

11. *All vessels entering or being overtaken by a fog shall be
navigated with the greatest caution, and at a very moderate speed.*

12. *Every steam-vessel navigating the river shall be provided
with a steam-whistle or other efficient steam sound signal, so
placed that the sound may not be intercepted by any obstruction,
and also with an efficient bell. Every sailing-vessel navigating
the river shall be provided with an efficient fog-horn, and also
with an efficient bell.*

13. *In fog, whether by day or night, the signals described in
this Rule shall be used, that is to say:*

(a.) *A steam-vessel under way shall make with her steam-* Proposed rules
*whistle, or other steam sound signal, at intervals of not more than* (Thames).
*two minutes, a prolonged blast.*

(b.) *A sailing-vessel under way shall sound her fog-horn, at intervals of not more than two minutes.*

(c.) *All steam-vessels and all sailing-vessels, when in the fairway of the river, and not under way, shall at intervals of not more than two minutes ring the bell.*

### *Rules as to Speed and Mode of Navigation.*

**14.** *Every steam-vessel, when approaching another vessel, so as to involve risk of collision, shall slacken her speed, and shall stop and reverse if necessary.*

**15.** *Steam-vessels navigating the river between Barking Creek and London Bridge other than river passenger steamers certified to carry passengers in smooth water only shall never exceed a speed of seven statute miles per hour over the ground, whether with or against the tide.*

**16.** *Every sailing-vessel or steam-vessel, overtaking any other vessel, shall keep out of the way of the overtaken vessel, which latter vessel shall keep her course.*

### *Bye-laws and Rules regulating the Navigation of the River between Yantlet Creek and a Line drawn from Blackwall Point to Bow Creek.*

#### *Steam-whistle Signals.*

**17.** *When two steam-vessels are in sight of one another, and are approaching, with risk of collision, the following steam signals shall be intimations of the course they intend to take:—*

(a.) *One short blast of the steam-whistle of about three seconds' duration to mean " I am directing my course to starboard, and intend to pass you port side to port side." The use of this signal shall be optional.*

(b.) *Two short blasts of the steam-whistle, each of about three seconds' duration, to mean " I am directing my course to port, and intend to pass you starboard side to starboard side."*
*This latter signal shall not be used in the case provided by Rule (22) where that rule can be obeyed ; but it shall be compulsory to use this signal when a departure from that rule is necessary to avoid immediate danger.*

**18.** *When it is unsafe or impracticable for a steam-vessel to keep out of the way of a sailing-vessel, she shall signify the same to the sailing-vessel by four or more blasts of the steam-whistle in rapid succession, the blasts to be of about two seconds' duration.*

19. *The signals by whistle mentioned in the preceding rules shall not be used on any occasion or for any purpose except those mentioned in the rules; and no other signal by whistle shall be made by any steam-vessel unless it be by a prolonged blast of not less than five seconds' duration.*

*Steering and Sailing Rules.*

20. *When two sailing-vessels are approaching one another, so as to involve risk of collision, one of them shall keep out of the way of the other, as follows, viz. :—*

*(a.) A vessel which is running free shall keep out of the way of a vessel which is close-hauled.*

*(b.) A vessel which is close-hauled on the port tack shall keep out of the way of a vessel which is close-hauled on the starboard tack.*

*(c.) When both are running free with the wind on different sides, the vessel which has the wind on the port side shall keep out of the way of the other.*

*(d.) When both are running free with the wind on the same side, the vessel which is to windward shall keep out of the way of the vessel which is to leeward.*

*(e.) A vessel which has the wind aft shall keep out of the way of the other vessel.*

21. *If a sailing-vessel and a steam-vessel are proceeding in such a direction as to involve risk of collision, the steam-vessel shall keep out of the way of the sailing-vessel.*

*If, owing to causes beyond the control of those navigating the steam-vessel, it is unsafe or impracticable for the steam-vessel to keep out of the way of the sailing-vessel, she shall signify the same to the sailing-vessel by four or more blasts of the steam-whistle in rapid succession, as mentioned in Rule* 18; *the sailing-vessel shall then keep out of the way.*

22. *When two steam-vessels proceeding in opposite directions, the one up and the other down the river, are approaching one another so as to involve risk of collision, they shall pass one another port side to port side.*

23. *Steam-vessels navigating against the tide shall, before rounding the following points, viz., Coalhouse Point, Tilburyness, Broadness, Stoneness, Crayfordness, Cold Harbour Point, Jenningtree Point, Halfway-house Point or Crossness, Margaretness or Tripcock Point, Bull Point or Gallionsness, Hookness, and Blackwall Point, ease their engines and wait until any other vessels rounding the point with the tide have passed clear.*

24. *Steam-vessels crossing from one side of the river towards*

*the other side shall keep out of the way of vessels navigating up* Proposed rules (Thames).
*and down the river.*

25. *Where by the above rules one of two vessels is to keep out of the way, the other shall keep her course.*

### *Bye-laws and Rules regulating the Navigation of the River above Teddington.*

26. *When two steam-vessels proceeding in opposite directions, the one up and the other down the river, are approaching one another so as to involve risk of collision, they shall pass one another port side to port side.*

27. *Steam-vessels navigating against the stream shall ease, and, if necessary, stop, to allow vessels coming down with the stream to pass clear.*

28. *Every steam-vessel shall, when under way after sunset and before sunrise, either carry the lights required for steam-vessels by Rule 5 or exhibit a bright white light on or above the stem, or on the funnel.*

29. *The name of every steam-vessel navigating the river shall be painted or marked and kept in plainly legible characters not less than two inches in length on the outside of both bows and on the outside of the stern; and such name and the residence of the owner shall be registered with the Conservators.*

## MERSEY (*a*). Local rules.

An Order in Council, of the 27th of June, 1866, contains the following Mersey. rules, made under 25 & 26 Vict. c. 63, s. 31:—

*Rules concerning the Lights or Signals to be carried and concerning the Steps for avoiding Collision to be taken by Vessels navigating the River Mersey.*

1. All vessels, as well sailing vessels as steamers, including river craft exceeding ten tons measurement, while navigating or anchoring in any part of the river Mersey below Warrington Bridge, shall, save as mentioned in the third rule, observe and obey the "Regulations for preventing Collisions at Sea," set out in Table C (*b*) in the schedule to the Act 25 & 26 Vict. cap. 63,

(*a*) For rules relating to the sea channels leading to the Mersey, see above, p. 261.

(*b*) The regulations require the riding light to be exhibited from "sunrise to sunset."

Local rules (Mersey).

the short title of which is "The Merchant Shipping Act Amendment Act, 1862," together with the additional regulations following:—

2. Canal flats, or vessels without masts, being towed, shall carry the lights prescribed for sailing vessels by Articles 5 and 6 of the said Table C.

3. The single bright light, prescribed by Article 7 of the same table, is to be carried by all vessels when at anchor in the Mersey or the sea channels or approaches thereto, at a height not exceeding twenty feet above the hull, suspended from the forestay, or otherwise near the bow of the vessel where it can be best seen; and in addition to the said light all ships or vessels having two or more masts shall exhibit another bright light, at double the height of the bow light, at the main, or mizen peak, or the boom topping lift, or other position near the stern where it can be best seen.

---

## SUEZ CANAL.

Suez Canal.

The substance of the Regulations for the navigation of the Suez Canal (of 1st July, 1878) is as follows (*a*):—The maximum speed is to be five and a half knots. All ships over 100 tons are to take pilots; "but the responsibility as regards the management of the ship devolves solely on the captain;" yards are to be braced forward; jib-booms to be in; and a kedge ready to let go astern; a boat is to be towed astern; watch to be kept by day and night; hands are to be stationed ready to let go hawsers; navigation at night is at the captain's risk.

Ships moored are to show a light forward and another aft; otherwise the usual lights to be carried, except that on the approach of another ship two white lights are to be shown over the side on which the other is to pass; whistles are to be blown on ships approaching and passing; steamships are to stop when the passage is not clear, and to reduce speed when passing craft. "Whenever a collision appears probable, no ship must hesitate to take the ground, and thus avoid collision. The expenses consequent upon a grounding under these circumstances shall be defrayed by the ship in fault." Vessels approaching are to reduce speed and hug the starboard side, if required to do so by the pilot; vessels are not to overtake and pass others, except when necessary, and then only at sidings and by the direction of the canal authorities.

(*a*) See "Nautical Magazine," 1878, p. 572.

# INDEX.

U

THE END.

STEVENS AND RICHARDSON, PRINTERS, 5, GREAT QUEEN STREET, W.C.

*May*, 1880.

A CATALOGUE
OF
# L A W   W O R K S,
PUBLISHED BY
# STEVENS AND SONS,
119, CHANCERY LANE, LONDON, W.C.
(*Formerly of Bell Yard, Lincoln's Inn*).

Law Books Purchased or Valued.

**Acts of Parliament.**—*Public and Local Acts from an early date, may be had of the Publishers of this Catalogue, who have also on sale the largest collection of Private Acts, relating to Estates, Enclosures, Railways, Roads, &c., &c.*

**ACTION AT LAW.**—Foulkes' Elementary View of the Proceedings in an Action.—Founded on "SMITH's ACTION AT LAW." By W. D. I. FOULKES, Esq., Barrister-at-Law. Second Edition. 12mo. 1879. 10s. 6d.

" The student will find in ' Smith's Action' a manual, by the study of which he may easily acquire a general knowledge of the mode of procedure in the various stages of an action in the several divisions of the High Court of Justice."—*Law Times.*

Peel.—*Vide* " Chancery."

Prentice's Proceedings in an Action in the Queen's Bench, Common Pleas, and Exchequer Divisions of the High Court of Justice. Second Edition (including the New Rules, April, 1880). By SAMUEL PRENTICE, Esq., one of Her Majesty's Counsel. Royal 12mo. 1880. 12s.

"The book can be safely recommended to students and practitioners"—*Law Times.*

Smith's Action.—*Vide* " Foulkes."

**ADMIRALTY.**—Boyd.—*Vide* " Shipping."

Lowndes.—Marsden.—*Vide* " Collisions."

Pritchard's Admiralty Digest.—With Notes from Text Writers, and the Scotch, Irish, and American Reports. Second Edition. By ROBERT A. PRITCHARD, D.C.L., Barrister-at-Law, and WILLIAM TARN PRITCHARD. With Notes of Cases from French Maritime Law. By ALGERNON JONES, Avocat à la Cour Impériale de Paris. 2 vols. Royal 8vo. 1865. 3l.

Roscoe's Treatise on the Jurisdiction and Practice of the Admiralty Division of the High Court of Justice, and on Appeals therefrom, &c. With an Appendix containing Statutes, Rules as to Fees and Costs, Forms, Precedents of Pleadings and Bills of Costs. By EDWARD STANLEY ROSCOE, Esq., Barrister-at-Law, and Northern Circuit. Demy 8vo. 1878. 1l.

" Mr. Roscoe has performed his task well, supplying in the most convenient shape a clear digest of the law and practice of the Admiralty Courts."—*Liverpool Courier.*

\*\* *All standard Law Works are kept in Stock, in law calf and other bindings.*
[No. 4.] A

**AGENCY.—Petgrave's Principal and Agent.**—A Manual
of the Law of Principal and Agent. By E. C. PETGRAVE,
Solicitor. 12mo. 1857.                                    *7s. 6d.*

**Petgrave's Code of the Law of Principal and
Agent,** with a Preface. By E. C. PETGRAVE, Solicitor.
Demy 12mo. 1876.                                        *Net, 2s.*

**Rogers.**—*Vide* "Elections."

**Russell's Treatise on Mercantile Agency.**—Second
Edition. 8vo. 1873.                                        *14s.*

**AGRICULTURAL LAW.—Addison's Practical Guide to
the Agricultural Holdings (England) Act, 1875**
(38 & 39 Vic. c. 92), and Treatise thereon, showing the Alterations
in the Law, and containing many useful Hints and Suggestions as
to the carrying out of the Provisions of the Act; with Handy Forms
and a Carefully Prepared Index. Designed chiefly for the use of
Agricultural Landlords and Tenants. By ALBERT ADDISON,
Solicitor of the Supreme Court of Judicature. 12mo. 1876. *Net, 2s. 6d.*

**Cooke on Agricultural Law.**—The Law and Practice
of Agricultural Tenancies, with Numerous Precedents of Tenancy
Agreements and Farming Leases, &c., &c. By G. WINGROVE
COOKE, Esq., Barrister-at-Law. 8vo. 1851.                *18s.*

**Dixon's Farm.**—*Vide* "Farm."

**ARBITRATION.—Russell's Treatise on the Duty and
Power of an Arbitrator, and the Law of
Submissions and Awards;** with an Appendix of
Forms, and of the Statutes relating to Arbitration. By FRANCIS
RUSSELL, Esq., M.A., Barrister-at-Law. Fifth Edition. Royal
8vo. 1878.                                              *1l. 16s.*

**ARTICLED CLERKS.—Butlin's New and Complete
Examination Guide and Introduction to the
Law**; for the use of Articled Clerks and those who contemplate
entering the legal profession, comprising Courses of Reading for the
Preliminary and Intermediate Examinations and for Honours, or a
Pass at the Final, with Statute, Case, and Judicature (Time) Tables,
Sets of Examination Papers, &c., &c. By JOHN FRANCIS
BUTLIN, Solicitor, &c. 8vo. 1877.                         *18s.*
" A sensible and useful guide for the legal tyro."—*Solicitors' Journal.*
"In supplying law students with materials for preparing themselves for examination,
Mr. Butlin, we think, has distanced all competitors. The volume before us contains
hints on reading, a very neat summary of law, which the best read practitioner need
not despise. There are time tables under the Judicature Act, and an excellent tabular
arrangement of leading cases, which will be found of great service . . . . Tuition
of this kind will do much to remove obstacles which present themselves to commencing
students, and when examinations are over the book is one which may be usefully kept
close at hand, and will well repay 'noting up.'"—*Law Times.*

**Rubinstein and Ward's Articled Clerks' Hand-
book.**—Being a Concise and Practical Guide to all the Steps
Necessary for Entering into Articles of Clerkship, passing the
Preliminary, Intermediate and Final Examinations, obtaining
Admission and Certificate to Practise, with Notes of Cases affecting
Articled Clerks, Suggestions as to Mode of Reading and Books to
be read during Articles. Second Edition. By J. S. RUBINSTEIN
and S. WARD, Solicitors. 12mo. 1878.                       *3s.*
"No articled clerk should be without it."—*Law Times.*
'We think it omits nothing which it ought to contain."—*Law Journal.*

**Wharton's Articled Clerk's Manual.**—A Manual
for Articled Clerks: being a comprehensive Guide to their successful
Examination, Admission, and Practice as Attorneys and Solicitors
of the Superior Courts. Ninth Edition. Greatly enlarged. By
C. H. ANDERSON. Royal 12mo. 1864.                          *18s.*

*.* *All standard Law Works are kept in Stock, in law calf and other bindings*

**ARTICLES OF ASSOCIATION.**—Palmer.—*Vide* "Conveyancing."

**ATTORNEYS.**—Cordery.—*Vide* "Solicitors."

**Pulling's Law of Attorneys,** General and Special, Attorneys-at-Law, Solicitors, Notaries, Proctors, Conveyancers, Scriveners, Land Agents, House Agents, &c., and the Offices and Appointments usually held by them, &c. By ALEXANDER PULLING, Serjeant-at-Law. Third Edition. 8vo. 1862. 18s.

"It is a laborious work, a careful work, the work of a lawyer, and, beyond comparison the best that has ever been produced npon this subject."—*Law Times.*

**Smith.**—The Lawyer and his Profession.—A Series of Letters to a Solicitor commencing Business. By J. ORTON SMITH. 12mo. 1860.                4s.

**AVERAGE.**—Hopkins' Hand-Book on Average.—Third Edition. 8vo. 1868.                18s.

**Lowndes' Law of General Average.**—English and Foreign. Third Edition. By RICHARD LOWNDES, Author of "The Admiralty Law of Collisions at Sea." Royal 8vo. 1878. 21s.

**BALLOT.**—FitzGerald's Ballot Act.—With an INTRODUCTION. Forming a Guide to the Procedure at Parliamentary and Municipal Elections. Second Edition. Enlarged, and containing the Municipal Elections Act, 1875, and the Parliamentary Elections (Returning Officers) Act, 1875. By GERALD A. R. FITZGERALD, M.A., of Lincoln's Inn, Esq., Barrister-at-Law. Fcap. 8vo. 1876. 5s. 6d.

"A useful guide to all concerned in Parliamentary and Municipal Elections."—*Law Magazine.*

"We should strongly advise any person connected with elections, whether acting as candidate, agent, or in any other capacity, to become possessed of this manual."

**BANKING.**—Walker's Treatise on Banking Law. Including the Crossed Checks Act, 1876, with dissertations thereon, also references to some American Cases, and full Index. By J. DOUGLAS WALKER, Esq., Barrister-at-Law. Demy 8vo. 1877.                14s.

"The work has been carefully written, and will supply the want of a compact summary of Banking Law."—*Solicitors' Journal.*

"Persons who are interested in banking law may be guided out of many a difficulty by consulting Mr. Walker's volume."—*Law Times.*

**BANKRUPTCY.**—Bedford's Final Examination Guide to Bankruptcy.—Third Edition. 12mo. 1877.                6s.

**Haynes.**—*Vide* "Leading Cases."

**Lynch's Tabular Analysis of Proceedings in Bankruptcy,** for the use of Students for the Incorporated Law Society's Examinations. Second Edition. 8vo. 1874.                *Net*, 1s.

**Scott's Costs in Bankruptcy.**—*Vide* "Costs."

**Smith's Manual of Bankruptcy.**—A Manual relating to Bankruptcy, Insolvency, and Imprisonment for Debt ; comprising the New Statute Law verbatim, in a consolidated and readable form. With the Rules, a Copious Index, and a Supplement of Decisions. By JOSIAH W. SMITH, B.C.L., Q.C. 12mo. 1873.                10s.

*₊* The Supplement may be had separately, *net*, 2s. 6d.

**Williams' Law and Practice in Bankruptcy:** comprising the Bankruptcy Act, the Debtors Act, and the Bankruptcy Repeal and Insolvent Court Act of 1869, and the Rules and Forms made under these Acts. Second Edition. By ROLAND VAUGHAN WILLIAMS, of Lincoln's Inn, Esq., and WALTER VAUGHAN WILLIAMS, of the Inner Temple, Esq., assisted by FRANCIS HALLETT HARDCASTLE, of the Inner Temple, Esq., Barristers-at-Law. 8vo. 1876.                1l. 8s.

"'Williams on Bankruptcy' is quite satisfactory."—*Law Magazine.*

"It would be difficult to speak in terms of undue praise of the present work."

*₊* *All standard Law Works are kept in Stock, in law calf and other bindings.*

A 2

**BAR, GUIDE TO THE.**—Shearwood.—*Vide* "Examination Guides."

**BILLS OF EXCHANGE.**—Chalmers' Digest of the Law of Bills of Exchange, Promissory Notes, and Cheques. By M. D. CHALMERS, of the Inner Temple, Esq. Barrister-at-Law. Demy 8vo. 1878.  12s. 6d.

*₊* This work is n the form of the Indian Codes, besides the English Cases it is noted up with reference to the French Law and the German Code, and on doubtful points to the more recent American Decisions; it also contains a table of overruled or doubted cases.
  "Mr. Chalmers has done wisely in casting his book into its present form, and the plan, thus well conceived, has been most effectually carried out. As a handy book of reference on a difficult and important branch of the law, it is most valuable, and it is perfectly plain that no pains have been spared to render it complete in every respect. The index is copious and well arranged."—*Saturday Review*.
  "The book is not only well planned, but well executed . . . . . for the rising generations and for men of business this digest will be a gift of no small value."—*Pall Mall Gazette*.

Chitty on Bills of Exchange and Promissory Notes, with references to the law of Scotland, France and America.—Eleventh Edition. By JOHN A. RUSSELL, Esq., LL.B., one of Her Majesty's Counsel, and Judge of County Courts. Demy 8vo. 1878.  1l. 8s.

Eddis' Rule of Ex parte Waring. By A. C. EDDIS, B.A., of Lincoln's Inn, Barrister-at-Law. Post 8vo. 1876. *Net*, 2s. 6d.

**BILLS OF SALE.**—Cavanagh.—*Vide* "Money Securities."
Millar's Bills of Sale.—A Treatise on Bills of Sale, with an Appendix containing the Acts for the Registration of Bills of Sale Precedents, &c. (being the Fourth Edition of Millar and Collier's Treatise on Bills of Sale). By F. C. J. MILLAR, of the Inner Temple, Esq., Barrister-at-Law. 12mo. 1877.  12s
  "The original work is brought down to date, and the latest cases are referred to and considered. The value of the work is enhanced throughout by careful annotation."—*Law Magazine*.

**BOOK-KEEPING.**—Bedford's Intermediate Examination Guide to Book-keeping.—Second Edition. 12mo. 1875.  *Net*, 2s. 6d.

**CANAL TRAFFIC ACT.**—Lely's Railway and Canal Traffic Act, 1873.—And other Railway and Canal Statutes ; with the General Orders, Forms, and Table of Fees. Post 8vo. 1873.  8s.

**CARRIERS.**—Browne on Carriers.—A Treatise on the Law of Carriers of Goods and Passengers by Land and Water. With References to the most recent American Decisions. By J. H. BALFOUR BROWNE, of the Middle Temple, Esq., Barrister-at-Law, Registrar to the Railway Commission. 8vo. 1873.  18s.

**CHANCERY,** and *Vide* "EQUITY."
Daniell's Chancery Practice. — Sixth Edition, by LEONARD FIELD and EDWARD CLENNELL DUNN, Barristers-at-Law; assisted by W. H. UPJOHN, Student and Holt Scholar of Gray's Inn, &c., &c., Editor of "Daniell's Forms, Third Edition." 2 vols. 8vo.  (*In preparation.*)

Daniell's Forms and Precedents of Proceedings in the Chancery Division of the High Court of Justice and on Appeal therefrom ; with Dissertations and Notes, forming a complete guide to the practice of the Chancery Division of the High Court and of the Courts of Appeal. Being the Third Edition of "Daniell's Chancery Forms." By WILLIAM HENRY UPJOHN, Esq., Student and Holt Scholar of Gray's Inn, Exhibitioner in Jurisprudence and Roman

*₊* *All standard Law Works are kept in Stock, in law calf and other bindings.*

**CHANCERY.**—*Continued.*

Law in the University of London, Holder of the First Senior Studentship in Jurisprudence, Roman Law and International Law awarded by the Council of Legal Education in Hilary Term, 1870. In one thick vol. Demy 8vo. 1879. *2l. 2s.*

"Mr. Upjohn has restored the volume of Chancery Forms to the place it held before the recent changes, as a trustworthy and complete collection of precedents. It has all the old merits ; nothing is omitted as too trivial or commonplace ; the solicitor's clerk finds how to indorse a brief, and how, when necessary, to give notice of action ; and the index to the forms is full and perspicuous."—*Solicitors' Journal.*

"It will be as useful a work to practitioners at Westminster as it will be to those in Lincoln's Inn."—*Law Times.*

**Haynes' Chancery Practice.**—The Practice of the Chancery Division of the High Court of Justice and on Appeal therefrom, for the use of Practitioners and Students.— By JOHN F. HAYNES, LL.D. Author of the "Student's Leading Cases," &c. Demy 8vo. 1879. *1l. 5s.*

"Materials for enabling the practitioner himself to obtain the information he may require are placed before him in a convenient and accessible form. The arrangement o the work appears to be good."—*Law Magazine and Review,* February, 1880.

**Morgan's Chancery Acts and Orders.**—The Statutes, General Orders, and Rules of Court relating to the Practice, Pleading, and Jurisdiction of the Supreme Court of Judicature, particularly with reference to the Chancery Division, and the Actions assigned thereto. With copious Notes. Fifth Edition. Carefully revised and adapted to the new Practice by GEORGE OSBORNE MORGAN, M.P., one of Her Majesty's Counsel, and CHALONER W. CHUTE, of Lincoln's Inn, Barrister-at-Law, and late Fellow of Magdalen College, Oxford. Demy 8vo. 1876. *1l. 10s.*

"This edition of Mr. Morgan's treatise must, we believe, be the most popular with the profession."—*Law Times.*

**Morgan and Davey's Chancery Costs.**— *Vide* "Costs."

**Peel's Chancery Actions.**—A Concise Treatise on the Practice and Procedure in Chancery Actions.—By SYDNEY PEEL, of the Middle Temple, Esq., Barrister-at-Law. Demy 8vo. 1878. *7s. 6d.*

"To Chancery practitioners of both branches the volume will doubtless prove very useful."—*Law Times.*

**CHANCERY PALATINE OF LANCASTER.**—Snow and Winstanley's Chancery Practice.—The Statutes, Consolidated and General Orders and Rules of Court relating to the Practice, Pleading and Jurisdiction of the Court of Chancery, of the County Palatine of Lancaster. With Copious Notes of all practice cases to the end of the year 1879, Time Table and Tables of Costs and Forms. By THOMAS SNOW, M.A., and HERBERT WINSTANLEY, Esqrs., Barristers-at-Law. Royal 8vo. 1880. *1l. 10s.*

**CIVIL LAW.**—Bowyer's Commentaries on the Modern Civil Law.—By Sir GEORGE BOWYER, D.C.L., Royal 8vo. 1848. *18s.*

**Bowyer's Introduction to the Study and Use of the Civil Law.**—By Sir GEORGE BOWYER, D.C.L. Royal 8vo. 1874. *5s.*

**Cumin's Manual of Civil Law,** containing a Translation of, and Commentary on, the Fragments of the XII. Tables, and the Institutes of Justinian ; the Text of the Institutes of Gaius and Justinian arranged in parallel columns ; and the Text of the Fragments of Ulpian, &c. By P. CUMIN, M.A., Barrister-at-Law Second Edition. Medium 8vo. 1865. *18s.*

*⁎* *All standard Law Works are kept in Stock, in law calf and other bindings.*

**COLLISIONS.**—Lowndes'Admiralty Law of Collisions at Sea.—8vo. 1867.                     7s. 6d.

Marsden on Maritime Collision.—A Treatise on the Law of Collisions at Sea. With an Appendix containing Extracts from the Merchant Shipping Acts, the International Regulations (of 1863 and 1880) for preventing Collisions at Sea; and local Rules for the same purpose in force in the Thames, the Mersey, and elsewhere. By REGINALD G. MARSDEN, Esq., Barrister-at-Law. Demy 8vo. 1880.                     12s.

**COLONIAL LAW.**—Clark's Colonial Law.—A Summary of Colonial Law and Practice of Appeals from the Plantations. 8vo. 1834.                     1l. 4s.

**COMMENTARIES ON THE LAWS OF ENGLAND.**—Bedford.—*Vide* "Examination Guides."

Broom and Hadley's Commentaries on the Laws of England.—By HERBERT BROOM, LL.D., of the Inner Temple, Barrister-at-Law; and EDWARD A. HADLEY, M.A., of Lincoln's Inn, Barrister-at-Law; late Fellow of Trinity Coll., Cambridge. 4 vols. 8vo. 1869.     3l. 3s.
"Nothing that could be done to make the work useful and handy has been left undone."—*Law Journal.*

**COMMERCIAL LAW.**—Goirand's French Code of Commerce and most usual Commercial Laws. With a Theoretical and Practical Commentary, and a Compendium of the judicial organization and of the course of procedure before the Tribunals of Commerce; together with the text of the law; the most recent decisions of the Courts, and a glossary of French judicial terms. By LEOPOLD GOIRAND, Licencié en droit. In 1 vol. (850 pp.). Demy 8vo. 1880.                     2l. 2s.

Levi.—*Vide* "International Law."

**COMMON LAW.**—Archbold's Practice of the Queen's Bench, Common Pleas and Exchequer Divisions of the High Court of Justice in Actions, etc., in which they have a common jurisdiction.—Thirteenth Edition. By SAMUEL PRENTICE, Esq., one of Her Majesty's Counsel. 2 vols. Demy 8vo. 1879. 3l. 3s.

Ball's Short Digest of the Common Law; being the Principles of Torts and Contracts. Chiefly founded upon the works of Addison, with Illustrative Cases, for the use of Students. By W. EDMUND BALL, LL.B., late "Holt Scholar" of Gray's Inn, Barrister-at-Law and Midland Circuit.     (*Nearly ready.*)

Chitty.—*Vide* "Forms."          Foulkes.—*Vide* "Action."
Fisher.—*Vide* "Digests."        Prentice.—*Vide* "Action."
Shirley.—*Vide* "Leading Cases."

Smith's Manual of Common Law.—For Practitioners and Students. A Manual of Common Law, comprising the fundamental principles and the points most usually occurring in daily life and practice. By JOSIAH W. SMITH, B.C.L., Q.C. Eighth Edition. 12mo. 1878.                     14s.

**COMMONS AND INCLOSURES.**—Chambers' Digest of the Law relating to Commons and Open Spaces, including Public Parks and Recreation Grounds, with various official documents; precedents of by-laws and regulations. The Statutes in full and brief notes of leading cases. By GEORGE F. CHAMBERS, of the Inner Temple, Esq., Barrister-at-Law. Imperial 8vo. 1877.                     6s. 6d.

Cooke on Inclosures.—With Forms as settled by the Inclosure Commissioners. By G. WINGROVE COOKE, Esq., Barrister-at-Law. Fourth Edition. 12mo. 1864.     16s.

*⁎* *All standard Law Works are kept in Stock, in law calf and other bindings.*

**COMPANY LAW.—Finlason's Report of the Case of Twycross v. Grant.** 8vo. 1877. *Net, 2s. 6d.*

**Palmer.**—*Vide* "Conveyancing."

**Palmer's Shareholders' and Directors' Companion.**—A Manual of every-day Law and Practice for Promoters, Shareholders, Directors, Secretaries, Creditors and Solicitors of Companies, under the Companies' Acts, 1862, 1867, and 1877. Second Edition. By FRANCIS B. PALMER, Esq., Barrister-at-Law, Author of "Company Precedents." 12mo. 1880. *Net, 2s. 6d.*

**Thring.**—*Vide* "Joint Stocks."

**CONTINGENT REMAINDERS.—An Epitome of Fearne on Contingent Remainders and Executory Devises.** Intended for the Use of Students. By W. M. C. Post 8vo. 1878. *6s. 6d.*

"An acquaintance with Fearne is indispensable to a student who desires to be thoroughly grounded in the common law relating to real property. Such student will find a perusal of this epitome of great value to him."—*Law Journal.*

**CONSTITUTIONAL LAW.—Bowyer's Commentaries on the Constitutional Law of England.**—By Sir GEO. BOWYER, D.C.L. Second Edition. Royal 8vo. 1846. *1l. 2s.*

**Haynes.**—*Vide* "Leading Cases."

**CONTRACTS.—Addison on Contracts.**—Being a Treatise on the Law of Contracts. By C. G. ADDISON, Esq., Author of the "Law of Torts." Seventh Edition. By L. W. CAVE, Esq., one of Her Majesty's Counsel, Recorder of Lincoln. Royal 8vo. 1875. *1l. 18s.*

"At present this is by far the best book upon the Law of Contract possessed by the Profession, and it is a thoroughly practical book."—*Law Times.*

**Leake on Contracts.**—An Elementary Digest of the Law of Contracts (being a new edition of "The Elements of the Law of Contracts"). By STEPHEN MARTIN LEAKE, Barrister-at-Law. 1 vol. Demy 8vo. 1878. *1l. 18s.*

**Pollock's Principles of Contract** at Law and in Equity ; being a Treatise on the General Principles relating to the Validity of Agreements, with a special view to the comparison of Law and Equity, and with references to the Indian Contract Act, and occasionally to American and Foreign Law. Second Edition. By FREDERICK POLLOCK, of Lincoln's Inn, Esq., Barrister-at-Law. Demy 8vo. 1878. *1l. 6s.*

The Lord Chief Justice in his judgment in *Metropolitan Railway Company v. Brogden and others*, said, "The Law is well put by Mr. Frederick Pollock in his very able and learned work on Contracts."—*The Times.*

"For the purposes of the student there is no book equal to Mr. Pollock's."—*The Economist.*

"He has succeeded in writing a book on Contracts which the working lawyer will find as useful for reference as any of its predecessors, and which at the same time will give the student what he will seek for in vain elsewhere, a complete *rationale* of the law. — *Law Magazine and Review.*

"We see nothing to qualify in the praise we bestowed on the first edition. The chapters on unlawful and impossible agreements are models of full and clear treatment."—*Solicitors' Journal.*

**Smith's Law of Contracts.**—By the late J. W. SMITH, Esq., Author of "Leading Cases," &c. Seventh Edition. By VINCENT T. THOMPSON, Esq., Barrister-at-Law. Demy 8vo. 1878. *1l. 1s.*

"We know of few books equally likely to benefit the student, or marked by such distinguished qualities of lucidity, order, and accuracy as the work before us."—*Solicitors' Journal*, December 28, 1878.

*₊* *All standard Law Works are kept in Stock, in law calf and other bindings.*

**CONVICTIONS.—Paley's Law and Practice of Summary Convictions under the Summary Jurisdiction Acts, 1848 and 1879;** including Proceedings preliminary and subsequent to Convictions, and the responsibility of convicting Magistrates and their Officers, with Forms. Sixth Edition. By W. H. MACNAMARA, Esq., Barrister-at-Law. Demy 8vo. 1879. 1*l*. 4*s*

**Stone.**—*Vide* " Petty Sessions."

**Templer.**—*Vide* " Summary Convictions."

**Wigram.**—*Vide* " Justice of the Peace."

**CONVEYANCING.—Dart.**—*Vide* " Vendors and Purchasers."

**Greenwood's Manual of Conveyancing.—A** Manua of the Practice of Conveyancing, showing the present Practice relating to the daily routine of Conveyancing in Solicitors' Offices To which are added Concise Common Forms and Precedents in Conveyancing; Conditions of Sale, Conveyances, and all other Assurances in constant use. Fifth Edition. By H. N. CAPEL, B.A., LL.B., Solicitor. Demy 8vo. 1877. 15*s*.

" A careful study of these pages would probably arm a diligent clerk with a much useful knowledge as he might otherwise take years of desultory questioning and observing to acquire."—*Solicitors' Journal.*

The young solicitor will find this work almost invaluable, while the members of the higher branch of the profession may refer to it with advantage. We have not met with any book that furnishes so simple a guide to the management of business entrusted to articled clerks."

**Haynes.**—*Vide* " Leading Cases."

**Martin's Student's Conveyancer.—A** Manual on the Principles of Modern Conveyancing, illustrated and enforced by a Collection of Precedents, accompanied by detailed Remarks. Part I. Purchase Deeds. By THOMAS FREDERIC MARTIN, Solicitor. Demy 8vo. 1877. 5*s*. 6*d*.

" It should be placed in the hands of every student."

**Palmer's Company Precedents.—**Conveyancing and other Forms and Precedents relating to Companies' incorporated under the Companies' Acts, 1862 and 1867. Arranged as follows :— Agreements, Memoranda of Association, Articles of Association, Resolutions, Notices, Certificates, Provisional Orders of Board of Trade, Debentures, Reconstruction, Amalgamation, Petitions, Orders. With Copious Notes. By FRANCIS BEAUFORT PALMER, of the Inner Temple, Esq., Barrister-at-Law. Demy 8vo. 1877. 1*l*. 5*s*.

" There had never, to our knowledge, been any attempt to collect and edit a body of Forms and Precedents exclusivelyr elating to the formation, working and winding-up of companies. This task Mr. Palmer has taken in hand, and we are glad to say with much success . . . . The information contained in the 650 pages of the volume is rendered easily accessible by a good and full index. The author has evidently not been sparing of labour, and the fruits of his exertions are now before the legal profession in a work of great practical utility."—*Law Magazine.*

" To those concerned in getting up companies, the assistance given by Mr. Palmer must be very valuable, because he does not confine himself to bare precedents, but by intelligent and learned commentary lights up, as it were, each step that he takes. The volume before us is not, therefore a book of precedents merely, but, in a greater or less degree, a treatise on certain portions of the Companies' Acts of 1862 and 1867. There is an elaborate index, and the work is one which must commend itself to the profession."—*Law Times.*

"The precedents are as a rule exceedingly well drafted, and adapted to companies for almost every conceivable object. So especially are the forms of memoranda and articles of association; and these will be found extremely serviceable to the conveyancer. . . All the notes have been elaborated with a thoroughly scientific knowledge of the principles of company law, as well as with copious references to the cases substantiating the principles. . . We venture to predict that his notes will be found of great utility in guiding opinions on many complicated questions of law and practice."—*Law Journal.*

\*\*\* *All standard Law Works are kept in Stock, in law calf and other bindings.*

**CONVEYANCING.**—*Continued.*

### Prideaux's Precedents in Conveyancing.—With

Dissertations on its Law and Practice. Ninth Edition. By
FREDERICK PRIDEAUX, late Professor of the Law of Real and
Personal Property to the Inns of Court, and JOHN WHITCOMBE,
Esqrs., Barristers-at-Law. 2 vols. Royal 8vo. 1879.    *3l. 10s.*

" We have been always accustomed to view 'Prideaux' as **the most useful work
out on conveyancing.** It combines conciseness and clearness in its precedents
with aptness and comprehensiveness in its dissertations and notes, to a degree superior
to that of any other work of its kind."—*Law Journal,* February 8, 1879.

" Prideaux has become an indispensable part of the Conveyancer's library. . . . .
The new edition has been edited with a care and accuracy of which we can hardly speak
oo highly. . . . . . The care and completeness with which the dissertation has
been revised leaves us hardly any room for criticism."—*Solicitors' Journal.*

" The volumes are now something more than a mere collection of precedents; they
contain most valuable dissertations on the law and practice with reference to conveyancing.
These dissertations are followed by the precedents on each subject dealt with, and are in
themselves condensed treatises, embodying all the latest case and statute law . . . Having
regard to the wide general knowledge required of all lawyers in the present day, such a
work as this must prove highly acceptable to the whole Profession."—*Law Times.*

### COPYRIGHT.—Phillips' Law of Copyright.—The Law of

Copyright in Works of Literature and Art, and in the Appli-
cation of Designs. With the Statutes relating thereto. By
CHARLES PALMER PHILLIPS, of Lincoln's Inn, Esq.,
Barrister-at-Law. 8vo. 1863.    12s.

### CORONERS.—Jervis on the Office and Duties of

Coroners.—With Forms and Precedents. Fourth Edition.
*(In preparation.)*

### COSTS.—Morgan and Davey's Treatise on Costs in

Chancery.—By GEORGE OSBORNE MORGAN, M.P.,
one of Her Majesty's Counsel, late Stowell Fellow of University
College, Oxford, and Eldon Scholar ; and HORACE DAVEY,
M.A., one of Her Majesty's Counsel, late Fellow of University
College, Oxford, and Eldon Scholar. With an Appendix, containing
Forms and Precedents of Bills of Costs. 8vo. 1865.    1l. 1s.

### Scott's Costs in the High Court of Justice

and other Courts. Fourth Edition. By JOHN SCOTT,
of the Inner Temple, Esq., Barrister-at-Law, Reporter of the Common Pleas Division. Demy 8vo. 1880.    1l. 6s.

" Mr. Scott's introductory notes are very useful, and the work is now a compendium
on the law and practice regarding costs, as well as a book of precedents."—*Law Times,*
January 3, 1880

### Scott's Costs in Bankruptcy and Liquidation

under the Bankruptcy Act, 1869. Royal 12mo.
1873.    *net 3s.*

### Summerhays and Toogood's Precedents of

Bills of Costs in the Chancery, Queen's
Bench, Common Pleas, Exchequer, Probate
and Divorce Divisions of the High Court of
Justice, in Conveyancing, Bankruptcy, the Crown Office, Lunacy,
Arbitration under the Lands Clauses Consolidation Act, the Mayor's
Court, London ; the County Courts, the Privy Council, and on
Passing Residuary and Succession Accounts ; with Scales of Allow-
ances and Court Fees, the Law Society's Scale of Commission in
Conveyancing ; Forms of Affidavits of Increase, and Objections to
Taxation. By WM. FRANK SUMMERHAYS, Solicitor, and
THORNTON TOOGOOD. Third Edition, Enlarged. Royal 8vo.
1879.    1l. 1s.

"In the volume before us we have a very complete manual of taxation. The work is
beautifully printed and arranged, and each item catches the eye instantly."—*Law
Journal.*

\*\* *All standard Law Works are kept in Stock, in law calf and other bindings.*

A 3

**COSTS.**—*Continued.*

**Webster's Parliamentary Costs.**—Private Bills, Election Petitions, Appeals, House of Lords. By EDWARD WEBSTER, Esq., of the Taxing and Examiners' Office. Third Edition. Post 8vo. 1867. 20s.

**COUNTY COURTS.—Pitt-Lewis' County Court Practice.**—A Complete Practice of the County Courts, including Admiralty and Bankruptcy, embodying the Acts, Rules, Forms and Costs, with Additional Forms and a Full Index. By G. PITT-LEWIS, of the Middle Temple and Western Circuit, Esq., Barrister-at-Law, sometime Holder of the Studentship of the Four Inns of Court, assisted by H. A. DE COLYAR, of the Middle Temple, Esq., Barrister-at-Law, Author of "A Treatise on the Law of Guarantees." In Two parts. 2 vols. (2028 pp.). Demy 8vo. 1880. 2l. 2s.

*The parts, each complete in itself, sold separately.*

Part I. History, Constitution, and Jurisdiction (including Prohibition and Mandamus), Practice in all ordinary Actions (including Actions under the Bills of Exchange Acts, in Ejectment, in Remitted Actions, and in Replevin), with Appendices, Index, &c. (1184 pp.). 30s.
Part II. Practice in Admiralty, Probate, the Practice under Special Statutes, and in Bankruptcy, with Appendices, Index, &c. (1004 pp.). 25s.

**CRIMINAL LAW.—Archbold's Pleading and Evidence in Criminal Cases.**—With the Statutes, Precedents of Indictments, &c., and the Evidence necessary to support them. By JOHN JERVIS, Esq. (late Lord Chief Justice of Her Majesty's Court of Common Pleas). Nineteenth Edition, including the Practice in Criminal Proceedings by Indictment. By WILLIAM BRUCE, of the Middle Temple, Esq., Barrister-at-Law, and Stipendiary Magistrate for the Borough of Leeds. Royal 12mo. 1878. 1l. 11s. 6d.

**Cole on Criminal Informations and Quo Warranto.**—By W. R. COLE, Esq., Barrister-at-Law. 12mo. 1843. 12s.

**Greaves' Criminal Law Consolidation and Amendment Acts of the 24 & 25 Vict.**—With Notes, Observations, and Forms for Summary Proceedings. By CHARLES SPRENGEL GREAVES, Esq., one of Her Majesty's Counsel. Second Edition. Post 8vo. 1862. 16s.

**Haynes.**—*Vide* "Leading Cases."

**Roscoe's Digest of the Law of Evidence in Criminal Cases.**—Ninth Edition. By HORACE SMITH, Esq., Barrister-at-Law. Royal 12mo. 1878. 1l. 11s. 6d.

**Russell's Treatise on Crimes and Misdemeanors.**—Fifth Edition. By SAMUEL PRENTICE, Esq., one of Her Majesty's Counsel. 3 vols. Royal 8vo. 1877. 5l. 15s. 6d.

This treatise is so much more copious than any other upon all the subjects contained in it, that it affords by far the best means of acquiring a knowledge of the Criminal Law in general, or of any offence in particular ; so that it will be found peculiarly useful as well to those who wish to obtain a complete knowledge of that law, as to those who desire to be informed on any portion of it as occasion may require.
"What better Digest of Criminal Law could we possibly hope for than 'Russell on Crime?' "—*Sir James Fitzjames Stephen's Speech on Codification.*
"No more trustworthy authority, or more exhaustive expositor than 'Russell' can be consulted."—*Law Magazine and Review.*
"Alterations have been made in the arrangement of the work which without interfering with the general plan are sufficient to show that great care and thought have been bestowed. . . . . We are amazed at the patience, industry and skill which are exhibited in the collection and arrangement of all this mass of learning."—*The Times.*

*⁎* *All standard Law Works are kept in Stock, in law calf and other bindings.*

**CROSSED CHEQUES ACT.**—Cavanagh.—*Vide* "Money Securities."

**Walker.**—*Vide* "Banking."

**DECREES.**—Seton.—*Vide* "Equity."

**DIARY.**—Lawyer's Companion (The), Diary, and Law Directory for 1880.—For the use of the Legal Profession, Public Companies, Justices, Merchants, Estate Agents, Auctioneers, &c., &c. Edited by JOHN THOMPSON, of the Inner Temple, Esq., Barrister-at-Law; and contains a Digest of Recent Cases on Costs; Monthly Diary of County, Local Government, and Parish Business; Oaths in Supreme Court; Summary of Legislation of 1878; Alphabetical Index to the Practical Statutes; a Copious Table of Stamp Duties; Legal Time, Interest, Discount, Income, Wages and other Tables; Probate, Legacy and Succession Duties; and a variety of matters of practical utility. PUBLISHED ANNUALLY. Thirty-fourth Issue.

The work also contains the most complete List published of Town and Country Solicitors, with date of admission and appointments, and is issued in the following forms, octavo size, strongly bound in cloth:—

|  |  | s. | d. |
|---|---|---|---|
| 1. | Two days on a page, plain | 5 | 0 |
| 2. | The above, INTERLEAVED for ATTENDANCES | 7 | 0 |
| 3. | Two days on a page, ruled, with or without money columns | 5 | 6 |
| 4. | The above, INTERLEAVED for ATTENDANCES | 8 | 0 |
| 5. | Whole page for each day, plain | 7 | 6 |
| 6. | The above, INTERLEAVED for ATTENDANCES | 9 | 6 |
| 7. | Whole page for each day, ruled, with or without money columns | 8 | 6 |
| 8. | The above, INTERLEAVED for ATTENDANCES | 10 | 6 |
| 9. | Three days on a page, ruled blue lines, without money columns | 5 | 0 |

*The Diary contains memoranda of Legal Business throughout the Year.*

"An excellent work."—*The Times.*

"A publication which has long ago secured to itself the favour of the profession, and which, as heretofore, justifies by its contents the title assumed by it."—*Law Journal.*

"Contains all the information which could be looked for in such a work, and gives it in a most convenient form and very completely. We may unhesitatingly recommend the work to our readers."—*Solicitors' Journal.*

"The 'Lawyer's Companion and Diary' is a book that ought to be in the possession of every lawyer, and of every man of business."

"The 'Lawyer's Companion' is, indeed, what it is called, for it combines everything required for reference in the lawyer's office."—*Law Times.*

"It is a book without which no lawyer's library or office can be complete."—*Irish Law Times.*

"This work has attained to a completeness which is beyond all praise."—*Morning Post.*

**DICTIONARY.**—Wharton's Law Lexicon.—A Dictionary of Jurisprudence, explaining the Technical Words and Phrases employed in the several Departments of English Law; including the various Legal Terms used in Commercial Transactions. Together with an Explanatory as well as Literal Translation of the Latin Maxims contained in the Writings of the Ancient and Modern Commentators. Sixth Edition. Enlarged and revised in accordance with the Judicature Acts, by J. SHIRESS WILL, of the Middle Temple, Esq., Barrister-at-Law. Super royal 8vo. 1876.     2*l.* 2*s.*

'As a work of reference for the library, the handsome and elaborate edition of Wharton's Law Lexicon' which Mr. Shiress Will has produced, must supersede all former issues of that well-known work."—*Law Magazine and Review.*

"No law library is complete without a law dictionary or law lexicon. To the practitioner it is always useful to have at hand a book where, in a small compass, he can find an explanation of terms of infrequent occurrence, or obtain a reference to statutes on most subjects, or to books wherein particular subjects are treated of at full length. To the student it is almost indispensable."—*Law Times.*

\*\*\* *All standard Law Works are kept in Stock, in law calf and other bindings.*

A 4

12 STEVENS AND SONS' LAW PUBLICATIONS.

**DIGESTS.**—Bedford.— *Vide* "Examination Guides."

**Chamber's**— *Vide* "Public Health."

**Chitty's Equity Index.**—Chitty's Index to all the Reported Cases, and Statutes, in or relating to the Principles, Pleading, and Practice of Equity and Bankruptcy, in the several Courts of Equity in England and Ireland, the Privy Council, and the House of Lords, from the earliest period. Third Edition. By J. MACAULAY, Esq., Barrister-at-Law. 4 vols. Royal 8vo. 1853. *7l. 7s.*

**Fisher's Digest of the Reported Cases** determined in the House of Lords and Privy Council, and in the Courts of Common Law, Divorce, Probate, Admiralty and Bankruptcy, from Michaelmas Term, 1756, to Hilary Term, 1870; with References to the Statutes and Rules of Court. Founded on the Analytical Digest by Harrison, and adapted to the present practice of the Law. By R. A. FISHER, Esq., Judge of the County Courts of Bristol and of Wells. Five large volumes, royal 8vo. 1870. *12l. 12s.*

*(Continued Annually.)*

"Mr. Fisher's Digest is a wonderful work. It is a miracle of human industry."—*Mr. Justice Willes.*

"I think it would be very difficult to improve upon Mr. Fisher's 'Common Law Digest.'"—*Sir James Fitzjames Stephen, on Codification.*

**Leake.**— *Vide* "Real Property" and "Contracts."

**Notanda Digest in Law, Equity, Bankruptcy, Admiralty, Divorce, and Probate Cases.**—By H. TUDOR BODDAM, of the Inner Temple, and HARRY GREENWOOD, of Lincoln's Inn, Esqrs., Barristers-at-Law. The NOTANDA DIGEST, from the commencement, October, 1862, to December, 1876. In 2 volumes, half-bound. *Net, 3l. 10s*

Ditto, Third Series, 1873 to 1876 inclusive, half-bound. *Net, 1l. 11s. 6d.*

Ditto, Fourth Series, for the years 1877, 1878, and 1879, with Index. *Each, net, 1l. 1s.*

Ditto, ditto, for 1880, Plain Copy and Two Indexes, or Adhesive Copy for insertion in Text-Books (without Index). Annual Subscription, payable in advance. *Net, 21s.*

\*\* The numbers are issued regularly every alternate month. Each number will contain a concise analysis of every case reported in the *Law Reports, Law Journal, Weekly Reporter, Law Times,* and the *Irish Law Reports,* up to and including the cases contained in the parts for the current month, with references to Text-books, Statutes, and the Law Reports Consolidated Digest. An ALPHABETICAL INDEX of the subjects contained IN EACH NUMBER will form a new feature in this series.

**Pollock.**— *Vide* "Partnership."

**Roscoe's.**— *Vide* "Criminal Law" and "Nisi Prius."

**DISCOVERY.**—Hare's Treatise on the Discovery of Evidence.—Second Edition. Adapted to the Procedure in the High Court of Justice, with Addenda, containing all the Reported Cases to the end of 1876. By SHERLOCK HARE, Barrister-at-Law. Post 8vo. 1877. *12s.*

"The book is a useful contribution to our text-books on practice."—*Solicitors' Journal.*

"We have read his work with considerable attention and interest, and we can speak in terms of cordial praise of the manner in which the new procedure has been worked into the old material. . . . All the sections and orders of the new legislation are referred to in the text, a synopsis of recent cases is given, and a good index completes the volume."—*Law Times.*

**Seton.**— *Vide* "Equity."

\*\* *All standard Law Works are kept in Stock, in law calf and other bindings.*

**DISTRICT REGISTRIES.**—Archibald.—*Vide* "Judges' Chambers Practice."

**DIVORCE.**—Browne's Treatise on the Principles and Practice of the Court for Divorce and Matrimonial Causes:—With the Statutes, Rules. Fees and Forms relating thereto. Fourth Edition. By GEORGE BROWNE, Esq., B.A., of the Inner Temple, Barrister-at-Law, Recorder of Ludlow. Demy 8vo. 1880.      1*l.* 4*s.*

Haynes.—*Vide* "Leading Cases."

**DOMICIL.**—Dicey on the Law of Domicil as a branch of the Law of England, stated in the form of Rules.—By A. V. DICEY, B.C.L., Barrister-at-Law. Author of "Rules for the Selection of Parties to an Action." Demy 8vo. 1879.      18*s.*
"The practitioner will find the book a thoroughly exact and trustworthy summary of the present state of the law."—*The Spectator,* August 9th, 1879.

Phillimore's (Sir R.) Law of Domicil.—8vo. 1847.   9*s.*

**DUTCH LAW.**—Vanderlinden's Institutes of the Laws of Holland.—8vo. 1828.      1*l.* 18*s.*

**EASEMENTS.**—Goddard's Treatise on the Law of Easements.—By JOHN LEYBOURN GODDARD, of the Middle Temple, Esq., Barrister-at-Law. Second Edition. Demy 8vo. 1877.      16*s.*

"The book is invaluable : where the cases are silent the author has taken pains to ascertain what the law would be if brought into question."—*Law Journal.*
"Nowhere has the subject been treated so exhaustively, and, we may add, so scientifically, as by Mr. Goddard. We recommend it to the most careful study of the law student as well as to the library of the practitioner."—*Law Times.*

**ECCLESIASTICAL.** — Finlason's Folkestone Ritual Case.—The Judgment of the Judicial Committee in the Folkestone Ritual Case, with an Historical Introduction and brief Notes. By W. F. FINLASON, of the Middle Temple, Esq., Barrister-at-Law. 8vo. 1877.      *Net,* 2*s.* 6*d.*

Phillimore's (Sir R.) Ecclesiastical Law.—The Ecclesiastical Law of the Church of England. With Supplement, containing the Statutes and Decisions to end of 1875. By SIR ROBERT PHILLIMORE, D.C.L., Official Principal of the Arches Court of Canterbury ; Member of Her Majesty's Most Honourable Privy Council. 2 vols. 8vo. 1873-76.      3*l.* 7*s.* 6*d.*
\*.\* The Supplement may be had separately, price 4*s.* 6*d.*, sewed.

**ELECTIONS.**—Browne (G. Lathom.)—*Vide* "Registration."

FitzGerald.—*Vide* "Ballot."

Rogers on Elections, Registration, and Election Agency.—Thirteenth Edition, including PETITIONS and Municipal Elections and Registration. With an Appendix of Statutes and Forms. By JOHN CORRIE CARTER, of the Inner Temple, Esq., and Midland Circuit, Barrister-at-Law. 12mo. 1880.   1*l.* 12*s.*

"Petition has been added, setting forth the procedure and the decisions on that subject; and the statutes passed since the last edition are explained down to the Parliamentary Elections and Corrupt Practices Act (1880)."—*The Times,* March 27th, 1880.
"We have no hesitation in commending the book to our readers as a useful and adequate treatise upon election law."—*Solicitors' Journal,* April 3rd, 1880.

**ENGLAND, LAWS OF,**—Bowyer.—*Vide* "Constitutional Law."

Broom and Hadley.—*Vide* "Commentaries."

\*.\* *All standard Law Works are kept in Stock, in law calf and other bindings.*

**EQUITY, and *Vide* CHANCERY.**

## Seton's Forms of Decrees, Judgments, and Orders in the High Court of Justice and Courts of Appeal, having especial reference to the Chancery Division, with Practical Notes. Fourth Edition. By R. H. LEACH, Esq., Senior Registrar of the Chancery Division ; F. G. A. WILLIAMS, of the Inner Temple, Esq. ; and the late H. W. MAY, Esq. ; succeeded by JAMES EASTWICK, of Lincoln's Inn, Esq., Barristers-at-Law. 2 vols. in 3 parts. Royal 8vo. 1877—79. *4l. 10s.*

\*\*\* Vol. II., Parts 1 and 2, may be had separately, to complete sets, price each 1*l.* 10*s.*

" Of all the editions of ' Seton ' this is the best.—*Solicitors' Journal.*

" We can hardly speak too highly of the industry and intelligence which have been bestowed on the preparation of the notes."—*Solicitors' Journal.*

" Now the book is before us complete ; and we advisedly say complete, because it has scarcely ever been our fortune to see a more complete law book than this. Extensive in sphere and exhaustive in treatise, comprehensive in matter, yet apposite in details, it presents all the features of an excellent work . . . The index, extending over 278 pages, is a model of comprehensiveness and accuracy."—*Law Journal*

## Smith's Manual of Equity Jurisprudence.— A Manual of Equity Jurisprudence for Practitioners and Students, founded on the Works of Story, Spence, and other writers, and on more than a thousand subsequent cases, comprising the Fundamental Principles and the points of Equity usually occurring in General Practice. By JOSIAH W. SMITH, B.C.L., Q.C. Twelfth Edition. 12mo. 1878. *12s. 6d.*

"There is no disguising the truth ; the proper mode to use this book is to learn its pages by heart."—*Law Magazine and Review.*

" It will be found as useful to the practitioner as to the student."—*Solicitors' Journal.*

**EXAMINATION GUIDES.—Bedford's Guide to the Preliminary Examination for Solicitors.—Fourth Edition. 12mo. 1874.** *Net, 3s.*

## Bedford's Preliminary.—Containing the Questions and Answers of the Preliminary Examinations. Edited by E. H. BEDFORD, Solicitor (No. 15, May, 1871, to No. 48, July, 1879). *(Discontinued).* *Sewed, net, each, 1s.*

## Bedford's Digest of the Preliminary Examination Questions on English and Latin, Grammar, Geography, History, French Grammar, and Arithmetic, with the Answers. 8vo. 1875. *18s.*

## Bedford's Preliminary Guide to Latin Grammar.—12mo. 1872. *Net, 3s.*

## Bedford's Intermediate Examination Guide to Bookkeeping.—Second Edition. 12mo. 1875. *Net, 2s. 6d.*

## Bedford's Intermediate.—Containing the Questions and Answers at the Intermediate Examinations. Edited by E. H. BEDFORD. Nos. 1 (Hilary, 1869) to 34 (Hilary, 1877). 6*d.* each. Nos. 35 (Easter, 1877) to 43 (Trinity, 1879). *(Discontinued).* 1*s.* each, *Net.*

## Bedford's Student's Guide to Stephen's New Commentaries on the Laws of England. Demy 8vo. 1879. *12s.*

" Here is a book which will be of the greatest service o students. It reduces the ' Commentaries ' to the form of question and answer . . . We must also give the author credit, not only for his selection of questions, but for his answers thereto. These are models of fulness and conciseness, and lucky will be the candidate who can hand in a paper of answers bearing a close resemblance to those in the work before us."—*Law Journal.*

## Bedford's Student's Guide to Smith on Contracts. Demy 8vo. 1879. *3s. 6d.*

\*\*\* *All standard Law Works are kept in Stock, in law calf and other bindings.*

**EXAMINATION GUIDES.**—*Continued.*

**Bedford's Final.**—Containing the Questions and Answers at the Final Examinations. Edited by E. H. BEDFORD. Nos. 1 (Easter, 1869) to 33 (Easter, 1877). 6d. each. Nos. 34 (Trinity, 1877) to 42 (Trinity, 1879). 1s. each, *Net.* (*Discontinued.*)

**Bedford's Final Examination Digest**: containing a Digest of the Final Examination Questions in matters of Law and Procedure determined by the Chancery, Queen's Bench, Common Pleas, and Exchequer Divisions of the High Court of Justice, and on the Law of Real and Personal Property and the Practice of Conveyancing. In 1 vol. 8vo. 1879. 16s.

"Will furnish students with a large armoury of weapons with which to meet the attacks of the examiners of the Incorporated Law Society.'—*Law Times, Nov. 8, 1879.*

**Bedford's Final Examination Guide to Bankruptcy.**—Third Edition. 12mo. 1877. 6s.

**Bedford's Outline of an Action in the Chancery Division.** 12mo. 1878. *Net,* 2s. 6d.

**Butlin.**—*Vide* "Articled Clerks."

**Dickson's Analysis of Blackstone's Commentaries.**—In Charts for the use of Students. By FREDERICK S. DICKSON. 4to. 10s. 6d.

**Haynes.**—*Vide* "Leading Cases."

**Rubinstein and Ward.**—*Vide* "Articled Clerks."

**Shearwood's Student's Guide to the Bar, the Solicitor's Intermediate and Final and the Universities Law Examinations.**—With Suggestions as to the books usually read, and the passages therein to which attention should be paid. By JOSEPH A. SHEARWOOD, B.A., Esq., Barrister-at-law, Author of "A Concise Abridgment of the Law of Real Property," &c. Demy 8vo. 1879. 5s. 6d.

"A work which will be very acceptable to candidates for the various examinations, any student of average intelligence who conscientiously follows the path and obeys the instructions given him by the author, need not fear to present himself as a candidate for any of the examinations to which this book is intended as a guide."—*Law Journal.*

**EXECUTORS.**—**Williams' Law of Executors and Administrators.**—By the Rt. Hon. Sir EDWARD VAUGHAN WILLIAMS, late one of the Judges of Her Majesty's Court of Common Pleas. Eighth Edition. By WALTER VAUGHAN WILLIAMS and ROLAND VAUGHAN WILLIAMS, Esqrs., Barristers at-Law. 2 vols. Royal 8vo. 1879. 3l. 16s.

"A treatise which occupies a unique position and which is recognised by the Bench and the profession as having paramount authority in the domain of law with which it deals."—*Law Journal.*

**EXECUTORY DEVISES.**—**Fearne.**—*Vide* "Contingent Remainders."

**FACTORY ACTS.**—**Notcutt's Law relating to Factories and Workshops, with Introduction and Explanatory Notes.** Second Edition. Comprising the Factory and Workshop Act, 1878, and the Orders of the Secretary of State made thereunder. By GEO. JARVIS NOTCUTT, Solicitor, formerly of the Middle Temple, Esq., Barrister-at-Law. 12mo. 1879. 9s.

"The task of elucidating the provisions of the statute is done in a manner that leaves nothing to be desired."—*Birmingham Daily Gazette.*

**FARM, LAW OF.**—**Addison ; Cooke.**—*Vide* "Agricultural Law."

**Dixon's Law of the Farm**—A Digest of Cases connected with the Law of the Farm, and including the Agricultural Customs of England and Wales. Fourth Edition. By HENRY PERKINS, Esq., Barrister-at-Law and Midland Circuit. Demy 8vo. 1879. 1l. 6s.

"It is impossible not to be struck with the extraordinary research that must have been used in the compilation of such a book as this."—*Law Journal.*

\*\*\* *All standard Law Works are kept in Stock, in law calf and other bindings.*

**FINAL EXAMINATION DIGEST.**—Bedford.—*Vide* "Examination Guides."

**FIXTURES.**—Amos and Ferard on Fixtures.—Second Edition. Royal 8vo. 1847. *16s.*

**FOREIGN JUDGMENTS.**—Piggott's Foreign Judgments, their effect in the English Courts, the English Doctrine, Defences, Judgments in Rem, Status.—By F. T. PIGGOTT, M.A., LL.M., of the Middle Royal 8vo. 1879. *15s.*

" A useful and well-timed volume."—*Law Magazine*, August, 1879.

" Mr. Piggott writes under strong conviction, but he is always careful to rest his arguments on authority, and thereby adds considerably to the value of his handy volume." *Law Magazine and Review*, November, 1879.

" M. Piggott donne à l'étude de l'une des questions les plus complexes du droit international privé une forme tout nouvelle ; il applique dans toute sa rigueur la méthode des sciences exactes, et ne recule pas devant l'emploi des formules algébriques. C'était là une tentative périlleuse dont le succès pouvait sembler douteux ; mais il suffit d'indiquer la marche suivie et les résultats obtenus par l'auteur pour comprendre l'importance et le mérite de cette publication."—*Journal du Droit International Privé*, 1879.

**FORMS.**—Archibald.—*Vide* "Judges' Chambers Practice."

Chitty's Forms of Practical Proceedings in the Queen's Bench, Common Pleas and Exchequer Divisions of the High Court of Justice: with Notes containing the Statutes, Rules and Practice relating thereto. Eleventh Edition. By THOS. WILLES CHITTY, Esqr. Demy 8vo. 1879. *1l. 18s.*

Daniell's Forms and Precedents of Proceedings in the Chancery Division of the High Court of Justice and on Appeal therefrom ; with Dissertations and Notes, forming a complete guide to the Practice of the Chancery Division of the High Court and of the Courts of Appeal. Being the Third Edition of " Daniell's Chancery Forms." By WILLIAM HENRY UPJOHN, Esq., Student and Holt Scholar of Gray's Inn, Exhibitioner in Jurisprudence and Roman Law in the University of London, Holder of the First Senior Studentship in Jurisprudence, Roman Law and International Law, awarded by the Council of Legal Education in Hilary Term 1879. In one thick vol. Demy 8vo. 1879. *2l. 2s.*

" Mr. Upjohn has restored the volume of Chancery Forms to the place it held before the recent changes, as a trustworthy and complete collection of precedents."—*Solicitors' Journal.*

" We have had this work in practical use for some weeks, and so careful is the noting up of the authorities. so clearly and concisely are the notes expressed, that we have found it of as much value as the ordinary text books on the Judicature Acts. It will be as useful a work to, practitioners at Westminster as it will be to those in Lincoln s Inn."—*Law Times.*

**FRENCH COMMERCIAL LAW.**—Goirand.—*Vide* "Commercial Law."

**HIGHWAYS**—Baker's Law of Highways. By THOMAS BAKER, of the Inner Temple, Esq., Barrister-at-Law. (*In the press.*)

Chambers' Law relating to Highways and Bridges, being the Statutes in full and brief Notes of 700 Leading Cases; to which is added the Law relating to the Lighting of Rural Parishes under the Lighting Act, 1833. By GEO. F. CHAMBERS, Esq., Barrister-at-Law. Imperial 8vo. 1878. *18s.*

Shelford's Law of Highways.—The Law of Highways ; including the General Highway Acts for England and Wales, and other Statutes, with copious Notes of the Decisions thereon ; with Forms. Third Edition. With Supplement by C. MANLEY SMITH, Esq., one of the Masters of the Queen's Bench. 12mo. 1865. *15s.*

\*\*\* *All standard Law Works are kept in Stock, in law calf and other bindings.*

**INCLOSURES.**— *Vide* "Commons."

**INDIAN LAW.**—Norton's Leading Cases on the Hindu Law of Inheritance.—2 vols. Royal 8vo. 1870-71.
*Net, 2l. 10s.*

**INJUNCTIONS.**—Seton.— *Vide* "Equity."

**INSURANCE.**—Arnould on the Law of Marine Insurance.—Fifth Edition. By DAVID MACLACHLAN, Esq., Barrister-at-Law. 2 vols. Royal 8vo. 1877.     *3l.*

"As a text book, 'Arnould' is now all the practitioner can want, and we congratulate the editor upon the skill with which he has incorporated the new decisions."—*Law Times.*

Hopkins' Manual of Marine Insurance.—8vo. 1867.     *18s.*

**INTERNATIONAL LAW.**—Amos' Lectures on International Law.—Delivered in the Middle Temple Hall to the Students of the Inns of Court, by SHELDON AMOS, M.A., Professor of Jurisprudence (including International Law) to the Inns of Court, &c. Royal 8vo. 1874.     *10s. 6d.*

Dicey.— *Vide* "Domicil."

Kent's International Law.— Kent's Commentary on International Law. Edited by J. T. ABDY, LL.D., Judge of County Courts. Second Edition. Revised and brought down to the present time. Crown 8vo. 1878.     *10s. 6d.*

"Altogether Dr. Abdy has performed his task in a manner worthy of his reputation. His book will be useful not only to Lawyers and Law Students, for whom it was primarily intended, but also for laymen. It is well worth the study of every member of an enlightened and civilized community."—*Solicitors' Journal.*

Levi's International Commercial Law.—Being the Principles of Mercantile Law of the following and other Countries —viz. : England, Ireland, Scotland, British India, British Colonies, Austria, Belgium, Brazil, Buenos Ayres, Denmark, France, Germany, Greece, Hans Towns, Italy, Netherlands, Norway, Portugal, Prussia, Russia, Spain, Sweden, Switzerland, United States, and Würtemberg. By LEONE LEVI, Esq., F.S.A., F.S.S., Barrister-at-Law, &c. Second Edition. 2 vols. Royal 8vo. 1863.     *1l. 15s.*

Vattel's Law of Nations.—By JOSEPH CHITTY, Esq. Royal 8vo. 1834.     *1l. 1s.*

Wheaton's Elements of International Law; Second English Edition. Edited with Notes and Appendix of Statutes and Treaties, bringing the work down to the present time. By A. C. BOYD, Esq., LL.B., J.P., Barrister-at-Law. Author of "The Merchant Shipping Laws." Demy 8vo. 1880.     *1l. 10s.*

"Mr. Boyd, the latest editor, has added many useful notes ; he has inserted in the Appendix public documents of permanent value, and there is the prospect that, as edited by Mr. Boyd, Mr Wheaton's volume will enter on a new lease of life. . . . . It is all the more important that their works (*Kent and Wheaton*) should be edited by intelligent and impartial Englishmen, such as Dr. Abdy, the editor of *Kent*, and Mr. Boyd."—*The Times.*
" Both the plan and execution of the work before us deserves commendation. Mr. Boyd gives prominence to the labours of others. The text of Wheaton is presented without alteration, and Mr. Dana's numbering of the sections is preserved. Mr. Boyd's notes, which are numerous, original, and copious, are conveniently interspersed throughout the text; but they are in a distinct type, and therefore the reader always knows whether he is reading Wheaton or Boyd. The Index, which could not have been compiled without much thought and labour makes the book handy for reference, and, consequently, valuable to public writers, who in these days have frequently to refer to International Law."—*Law Journal.*
"Students who require a knowledge of Wheaton's text will find Mr. Boyd's volume very convenient."—*Law Magazine.*

Wildman's International Law.—Institutes of International Law, in Time of Peace and Time of War. By RICHARD WILDMAN, Barrister-at-Law. 2 vols. 8vo. 1849-50.     *1l. 2s. 6d.*

**JOINT OWNERSHIP.**—Foster.— *Vide* "Real Estate."

\*\* *All standard Law Works are kept in Stock, in law calf and other bindings.*

**JOINT STOCKS.**—Palmer.—*Vide* "Conveyancing" and "Company Law."

Thring's (Sir H.) Joint Stock Companies' Law.—
The Law and Practice of Joint Stock and other Public Companies, including the Statutes, with Notes, a Collection of Precedents of Memoranda and Articles of Association, and all the other Forms required in Making, Administering, and Winding-up a Company. By SIR HENRY THRING, K.C.B., The Parliamentary Counsel. Third Edition. By G. A. R. FITZGERALD, Esq., Barrister-at-Law, and Fellow of St. John's College, Oxford. 12mo. 1875. 1*l.*

"This, as the work of the original draughtsman of the Companies' Act of 1862, and well-known Parliamentary counsel, Sir Henry Thring is naturally the highest authority on the subject."—*The Times.*

Jordan's Joint Stock Companies.—A Handy Book of Practical Instructions for the Formation and Management of Joint Stock Companies. Sixth Edition. 12mo. 1878.    *Net,* 2*s.* 6*d.*

**JUDGES' CHAMBERS PRACTICE.**—Archibald's Forms of Summonses and Orders, with Notes for use at Judges' Chambers and in the District Registries. By W. F. A. ARCHIBALD, M.A., of the Inner Temple, Barrister-at-Law. Royal 12mo. 1879.    12*s.* 6*d.*

"The work is done most thoroughly and yet concisely. The practitioner will find plain directions how to proceed in all the matters connected with a common law action, interpleader, attachment of debts, *mandamus,* injunction—indeed, the whole jurisdiction of the common law divisions, in the district registries, and at Judges' chambers."—*Law Times,* July 26, 1879.

"A clear and well-digested *vade mecum,* which will no doubt be widely used by the profession."—*Law Magazine,* November, 1879.

**JUDGMENTS.**—Piggott.—*Vide* "Foreign Judgments."

Walker's Practice on Signing Judgment in the High Court of Justice. With Forms. By H. H. WALKER, Esq., of the Judgment Department, Exchequer Division. Crown 8vo. 1879.    4*s.* 6*d.*

"The book undoubtedly meets a want, and furnishes information available for almost every branch of practice."

"We think that solicitors and their clerks will find it extremely useful."—*Law Journal.*

**JUDICATURE ACTS.**—Ilbert's Supreme Court of Judicature (Officers) Act, 1879; with the Rules of Court and Forms, December, 1879, and April, 1880. With Notes. By COURTENAY P. ILBERT, Esq., Barrister-at-Law. Royal 12mo. 1880.    6*s.*

(*In limp leather,* 9*s.* 6*d.*)

\*\* A LARGE PAPER EDITION (for marginal notes). Royal 8vo.    8*s.*

(*In limp leather,* 12*s.*)

*Forming a Supplement to "Wilson's Judicature Acts."*

Leys' Complete Time-Table to the Rules under the Supreme Court of Judicature Act, 1875. Showing all the periods fixed by the Rules within or after which any proceedings may be taken. By JOHN KIRKWOOD LEYS, M.A., of the Middle Temple, Esq., Barrister-at-Law. Royal 8vo. 1875.

*Net,* 1*s.* 6*d.*

Lynch's Epitome of Practice in the Supreme Court of Judicature in England. With References to Acts, Rules, and Orders. For the Use of Students. Fourth Edition. Royal 8vo. 1878.    *Net,* 1*s.*

Morgan.—*Vide* "Chancery."

Stephen's Judicature Acts 1873, 1874, and 1875, consolidated. With Notes and an Index. By Sir JAMES FITZJAMES STEPHEN, one of Her Majesty's Judges. 12mo. 1875.    4*s.* 6*d.*

\*\* *All standard Law Works are kept in Stock, in law calf and other bindings.*

**JUDICATURE ACTS.**—*Continued.*

**Swain's Complete Index to the Rules of the Supreme Court,** April, 1880, and to the Forms (uniform with the Official Rules and Forms). By EDWARD SWAIN. Imperial 8vo. 1880. *Net.* 1s.

**Wilson's Supreme Court of Judicature Acts, Appellate Jurisdiction Act, 1876, Rules of Court and Forms.** With other Acts, Orders, Rules and Regulations relating to the Supreme Court of Justice. With Practical Notes and a Copious Index, forming a COMPLETE GUIDE TO THE NEW PRACTICE. Second Edition. By ARTHUR WILSON, of the Inner Temple, Barrister-at-Law. (Assisted by HARRY GREENWOOD, of Lincoln's Inn, Barrister-at-Law, and JOHN BIDDLE, of the Master of the Rolls Chambers.) Royal 12mo. 1878. (*pp.* 726.) 18s.

(*In limp leather for the pocket,* 22s. 6d.)

\*\*\* A LARGE PAPER EDITION OF THE ABOVE (for marginal notes). Royal 8vo. 1878. (*In limp leather or calf,* 30s.) 1l. 5s.

"As regards Mr. Wilson's notes, we can only say that they are indispensable to the proper understanding of the new system of procedure. They treat the principles upon which the alterations are based with a clearness and breadth of view which have never been equalled or even approached by any other commentator."—*Solicitors' Journal.*

"Mr. Wilson has bestowed upon this edition an amount of industry and care which the Bench and the Profession will, we are sure, gratefully acknowledge. . . . . A conspicuous and important feature in this second edition is a table of cases prepared by Mr. Biddle, in which not only are cases given with references to two or three reports, but every place in which the cases are reported. . . . . Wilson's 'Judicature Acts,' is now the latest, and we think it is the most convenient of the works of the same class. . . . . . The practitioner will find that it supplies all his wants."—*Law Times.*

**JURISPRUDENCE.**—**Amos, Law as a Science and as an Art.**—An Introductory Lecture delivered at University College at the commencement of the session 1874-5. By SHELDON AMOS, Esq., M.A., Barrister-at-Law. 8vo. 1874. *Net,* 1s. 6d.

**Phillimore's (J. G.) Jurisprudence.**—An Inaugural Lecture on Jurisprudence, and a Lecture on Canon Law, delivered at the Hall of the Inner Temple, Hilary Term, 1851. By J. G. PHILLIMORE, Esq., Q.C. 8vo. 1851. Sewed. 3s. 6d.

**Piggott.**—*Vide* "Foreign Judgments."

**JUSTINIAN, INSTITUTES OF.**—**Cumin.**—*Vide* "Civil Law."

**Greene.**—*Vide* "Roman Law."

**Mears.**—*Vide* "Roman Law."

**Ruegg's Student's "Auxilium" to the Institutes of Justinian.**—Being a complete synopsis thereof in the form of Question and Answer. By ALFRED HENRY RUEGG, of the Middle Temple, Barrister-at-Law. Post 8vo. 1879. 5s.

"The student will be greatly assisted in clearing and arranging his knowledge by a work of this kind."—*Law Journal.*

**JUSTICE OF THE PEACE.**—**Burn's Justice of the Peace and Parish Officer.**—Edited by the following Barristers, under the General Superintendence of JOHN BLOSSETT MAULE, Esq., Q.C. The Thirtieth Edition. Vol. I. containing titles "Abatement" to "Dwellings for Artisans;" by THOS. S. PRITCHARD, Esq., Recorder of Wenlock. Vol. II. containing titles "Easter Offering" to "Hundred ;" by SAML. B. BRISTOWE, Esq., Q.C., M.P. Vol. III. containing titles "Indictment" to "Promissory Notes ;" by L. W. CAVE, Esq., Q.C., Recorder of Lincoln. Vol. IV. containing the whole title "Poor ;" by J. E. DAVIS, Esq., Stipendiary Magistrate for Stoke-upon-Trent. Vol. V. containing titles "Quo Warranto" to "Wreck;" by J. B. MAULE, Esq., Q.C., Recorder of Leeds. Five vols. 8vo. 1869. 7l. 7s.

\*\*\* *All standard Law Works are kept in Stock, in law calf and other bindings.*

**JUSTICE OF THE PEACE.**—*Continued.*
**Paley.**—*Vide* "Convictions."

**Stone's Practice for Justices of the Peace,** Justices' Clerks and Solicitors at Petty and Special Sessions, in Summary Matters and Indictable Offences, with a List of Summary Convictions and of Matters not Criminal. With Forms. Eighth Edition. By THOMAS SIRRELL PRITCHARD, Esq., Barrister-at-Law, Recorder of Wenlock. Demy 8vo. 1877.    1*l*. 10*s*.

**Wigram's The Justices' Note Book.** By W. KNOX WIGRAM, Esq., Barrister-at-Law, J.P. Middlesex. Royal 12mo., 1880.    10*s*. 6*d*.

In the first portion, or 'Preliminary Notes,' the constitution of courts of Summary Jurisdiction, together with the whole course of ordinary procedure, as modified by the recent Act, are explained in a series of short chapters, under the following heads:— I. Justices—Jurisdiction—Divisions—Petty and Special Sessions. II. Summary Jurisdiction upon Information—Preliminary Proceedings. III. Summary Jurisdiction upon Information—the Hearing and Punishment. IV. Indictable Offences—Committal for Trial. V. Summary Jurisdiction as regards Indictable Offences; (children - young persons - and adults). VI. Summary Jurisdiction upon Complaint. VII. Quarter Sessions and Appeal. VIII. Note on the Summary Jurisdiction Act, 1879.

In the second part, entitled 'Notes of Matters and Offences alphabetically arranged,' will be found an account of most subjects which from time to time occupy the attention of Justices, either in Petty or Special Sessions.

" We have nothing but praise for the book, which is a justices' royal road to knowledge, and ought to lead them to a more accurate acquaintance with their duties than many of them have hitherto possessed."—*Solicitors' Journal.*

"This is altogether a capital book. Mr. Wigram is a good lawyer and a good justices' lawyer."—*Law Journal.*

" We can thoroughly recommend the volume to magistrates."—*Law Times.*

**LAND TAX** —**Bourdin's Land Tax.**—An Exposition of the Land Tax ; its Assessment and Collection, with a statement of the rights conferred by the Redemption Acts. By MARK A. BOUR-DIN, of the Inland Revenue Office, Somerset House (late Registrar of Land Tax). Second Edition. Crown 8vo. 1870.    4*s*.

**LANDLORD AND TENANT.**—**Woodfall's Law of Landlord and Tenant.**—A Practical Treatise on the Law of Landlord and Tenant, with a full Collection of Precedents and Forms of Procedure. Eleventh Edition. Containing an Abstract of Leading Propositions, and Tables of certain Customs of the Country. By J. M. LELY, of the Inner Temple, Esq., Barrister-at-Law. Royal 8vo. 1877.    1*l*. 16*s*.

"The editor has expended elaborate industry and systematic ability in making the work as perfect as possible ; and we doubt not that this eleventh edition will be a greater success than any of its predecessors."—*Solicitors' Journal.*

**LAW LIST.**—**Law List (The).**—Comprising the Judges and Officers of the different Courts of Justice, Counsel, Special Pleaders, Draftsmen, Conveyancers, Solicitors, Notaries, &c., in England and Wales ; the Circuits, Judges, Treasurers. Registrars, and High Bailiffs of the County Courts, District Registries and Registrars under the Probate Act, Lords Lieutenant of Counties, Recorders, Clerks of the Peace, Town Clerks, Coroners, Colonial Judges, and Colonial Lawyers having English Agents, Metropolitan and Stipendiary Magistrates, Law Agents, Law and Public Officers, Circuits of the Judges and Counsel attending Circuit and Sessions, List of Sheriffs and Agents, London Commissioners to Administer Oaths in the Supreme Court of Judicature in England, Conveyancers Practising in England under Certificates obtained in Scotland, &c., &c., and a variety of other useful matters so far as relates to Special Pleaders, Draftsmen, Conveyancers, Solicitors, Proctors and Notaries. Compiled by WILLIAM HENRY COUSINS, of the Inland Revenue Office, Somerset House, Registrar of Stamped Certificates, and of Joint Stock Companies. Published annually. By Authority. 1880.    (*Net cash* 9*s*.)    10*s*. 6*d*.

\*\* *All standard Law Works are kept in Stock, in law calf and other bindings.*

**LAW REPORTS.**—A large Stock of second-hand Reports. Estimates on application.

**LAWYER'S COMPANION.**— *Vide* "Diary."

**LEADING CASES.**—Haynes' Student's Leading Cases. Being some of the Principal Decisions of the Courts in Constitutional Law, Common Law, Conveyancing and Equity, Probate, Divorce, Bankruptcy, and Criminal Law. With Notes for the use of Students. By JOHN F. HAYNES, LL.D., Author of "The Practice of the Chancery Division of the High Court of Justice," "The Student's Statutes," &c. Demy 8vo. 1878.     16s.

"We consider Mr. Haynes' book to be one of a very praiseworthy class; and we may say also that its editor appears to be a competent man. He can express himself with clearness, precision, and terseness."—*Solicitors' Journal.*

"Will prove of great utility, not only t Students, but Practitioners. The Notes are clear, pointed and concise."—*Law Times.*

"We think that this book will supply a want . . . . the book is singularly well arranged for reference."—*Law Journal.*

Shirley's Leading Cases made Easy. A Selection of Leading Cases in the Common Law. By W. SHIRLEY SHIRLEY, M.A., Esq., Barrister-at-Law, North-Eastern Circuit. Demy 8vo. 1880.     14s.

"Mr. Shirley writes well and clearly, and evidently understands what he is writing about."—*Law Times,* April 10, 1880.

**LEXICON.**— *Vide* "Dictionary."

**LIBRARIES AND MUSEUMS.**—Chambers' Public Libraries and Museums and Literary and Scientific Institutions generally, a Digest of the Law relating to. Second Edition. By G. F. CHAMBERS, of the Inner Temple, Barrister-at-Law. Imperial 8vo. 1879.     8s. 6d.

**LICENSING.**—Lely and Foulkes' Licensing Acts, 1828, 1869, 1872, and 1874; Containing the Law of the Sale of Liquors by Retail and the Management of Licensed Houses ; with Notes to the Acts, a Summary of the Law, and an Appendix of Forms. Second Edition. By J. M. LELY and W. D. I. FOULKES, Esqrs., Barristers-at-Law. Royal 12mo. 1874.     8s.

"The notes are sensible and to the point, and give evidence both of care and knowledge of the subject."—*Solicitors' Journal.*

**LIENS.**—Cavanagh.— *Vide* "Money Securities."

**LIFE ASSURANCE.**—Scratchley's Decisions in Life Assurance Law, collated alphabetically according to the point involved ; with the Statutes. Revised Edition. By ARTHUR SCRATCHLEY, M.A., Barrister-at-Law. Demy 8vo. 1878.     5s.

**LIGHTS.**—Woolrych's Practical Treatise on the Law of Window Lights.—Second Edition. 12mo. 1864.     6s.

**LOCKE KING'S ACTS.**—Cavanagh.— *Vide* "Money Securities."

**LORD MAYOR'S COURT PRACTICE.**—Candy.— *Vide* "Mayor's Court Practice."

**LUNACY.**—Elmer's Practice in Lunacy.—The Practice in Lunacy under Commissions and Inquisitions, with Notes of Cases and Recent Decisions, the Statutes and General Orders, Forms and Costs of Proceedings in Lunacy, an Index and Schedule of Cases. Sixth Edition. By JOSEPH ELMER, of the Office of the Masters in Lunacy. 8vo. 1877.     21s.

**MAGISTERIAL LAW.**—Burn.— *Vide* "Justice of the Peace."

Leeming and Cross.— *Vide* "Quarter Sessions."

Pritchard.— *Vide* "Quarter Sessions."

Stone.— *Vide* "Petty Sessions."

Wigram.— *Vide* "Justice of the Peace."

\*\*\* *All standard Law Works are kept in Stock, in law calf and other bindings.*

**MANDAMUS.**—Tapping on Mandamus.—The Law and
Practice of the High Prerogative Writ of Mandamus as it obtains
both in England and Ireland. Royal 8vo. 1848.    *Net*, 1*l*. 1*s*.

**MARITIME COLLISION.**—Lowndes.—Marsden.—*Vide* "Collision."

**MAYOR'S COURT PRACTICE.**—Candy's Mayor's Court
Practice.—The Jurisdiction, Process, Practice, and Mode of Pleading in Ordinary Actions in the Mayor's Court, London (commonly called
the "Lord Mayor's Court"). **Founded on Brandon.** By GEORGE
CANDY, Esq., Barrister-at-Law. Demy 8vo. 1879.    14*s*.
"The 'ordinary' practice of the Court is dealt with in its natural order, and is
simply and clearly stated."—*Law Journal*.

**MERCANTILE LAW.**—Boyd.—*Vide* "Shipping."

Russell.—*Vide* "Agency."

Smith's Compendium of Mercantile Law.—Ninth
Edition. By G. M. DOWDESWELL, of the Inner Temple, Esq.,
one of Her Majesty's Counsel. Royal 8vo. 1877.    1*l*. 18*s*.
"We can safely say that, to the practising Solicitor, few books will be found more
useful than the ninth edition of 'Smith's Mercantile Law.'"—*Law Magazine*.

Tudor's Selection of Leading Cases on Mercantile and Maritime Law.—With Notes. By O. D. TUDOR,
Esq., Barrister-at-Law. Second Edition. Royal 8vo. 1868. 1*l*. 18*s*.

**METROPOLIS BUILDING ACTS.**—Woolrych's Metropolis
Building Acts, with Notes, Explanatory of the Sections and
of the Architectural Terms contained therein. Second Edition. By
NOEL H. PATERSON, M.A., Esq., Barrister-at-Law. 12mo.
1877.    8*s*. 6*d*.

**MINES.**—Rogers' Law relating to Mines, Minerals,
and Quarries in Great Britain and Ireland;
with a Summary of the Laws of Foreign States and Practical
Directions for obtaining Government Grants to work Foreign Mines.
Second Edition Enlarged. By ARUNDEL ROGERS, Esq.,
Judge of County Courts. 8vo. 1876.    1*l*. 11*s*. 6*d*.
"The volume will prove invaluable as a work of legal reference."—*The Mining Journal*.

**MONEY SECURITIES.**—Cavanagh's Law of Money Securities.—In Three Books. I. Personal Securities. II. Securities
on Property. III. Miscellaneous; with an Appendix containing the
Crossed Cheques Act, 1876, The Factors Acts, 1823 to 1877, Locke
King's, and its Amending Acts, and the Bills of Sale Act, 1878. By
CHRISTOPHER CAVANAGH, B.A., LL.B. (Lond.), of the Middle
Temple, Esq., Barrister-at-Law. In 1 vol. Demy 8vo. 1879. 21*s*.
"We know of no work which embraces so much that is of every-day importance, nor
do we know of any author who shows more familiarity with his subject. The book is
one which we shall certainly keep near at hand, and we believe that it will prove a
decided acquisition to the practitioner."—*Law Times*.
"The author has the gift of a pleasant style; there are abundant and correct
references to decisions of a recent date; and, in the matter of newly-enacted statutes;
attempts are made, and, as we think, not without success, to grapple with points of
practice and interpretation which as yet remain judicially unsolved. An appendix,
in which is embodied the full text of several important statutes, adds to the utility
of the work as a book of reference; and there is a good index."—*Solicitors' Journal*.
"In the second book bills of sale extend over some sixty-three pages; and the
treatise on them seems on the whole well written, especially with reference to the
alterations made by 41 & 42 Vict. c. 31."—*Law Journal*.
"May be the means of saving enormous labour to thousands of readers."—*Bullionist*.

**MORTGAGE.**—Coote's Treatise on the Law of Mortgage.—Third Edition. Royal 8vo. 1850.    *Net*, 1*l*.

**MORTMAIN.**—Rawlinson's Notes on the Mortmain
Acts; shewing their operation on Gifts, Devises and Bequests for
Charitable Uses. By JAMES RAWLINSON, Solicitor. Demy 8vo.
1877. Interleaved.    *Net*, 2*s*. 6*d*.

\*\* *All standard Law Works are kept in Stock, in law calf and other bindings.*

**NAVY.—Thring's Criminal Law of the Navy,** with an Introductory Chapter on the Early State and Discipline of the Navy, the Rules of Evidence, and an Appendix comprising the Naval Discipline Act and Practical Forms. Second Edition. By THEODORE THRING, of the Middle Temple, Barrister-at-Law, late Commissioner of Bankruptcy at Liverpool, and C. E. GIFFORD, Assistant-Paymaster, Royal Navy. 12mo. 1877. 12s. 6d.

"A full series of forms of warrants, minutes, charges, &c., and a good Index, complete the utility of a work which should be in the hands of all who have to deal with the regulating and governing of the Fleet."—*Law Magazine.*

"In the new edition, the procedure, naval regulations, forms, and all matters connected with the practical administration of the law have been classified and arranged by Mr. Gifford, so that the work is in every way useful, complete, and up to date."—*Naval and Military Gazette.*

**NISI PRIUS.—Roscoe's Digest of the Law of Evidence on the Trial of Actions at Nisi Prius.—**Fourteenth Edition. By JOHN DAY, one of Her Majesty's Counsel, and MAURICE POWELL, Barrister-at-Law. Royal 12mo. 1879. 2l.

(*Bound in one thick volume calf or circuit, 5s., or in two convenient vols. calf or circuit, 9s. net, extra.*)

"The task of adapting the old text to the new procedure was one requiring much patient labour, careful accuracy, and conciseness, as well as discretion in the omission of matter obsolete or unnecessary. An examination of the bulky volume before us affords good evidence of the possession of these qualities by the present editors, and we feel sure that the popularity of the work will continue unabated under their conscientious care."—*Law Magazine.*

**Selwyn's Abridgment of the Law of Nisi Prius.—**Thirteenth Edition. By DAVID KEANE, Q.C., Recorder of Bedford, and CHARLES T. SMITH, M.A., one of the Judges of the Supreme Court of the Cape of Good Hope. 2 vols. Royal 8vo. 1869. (*Published at 2l. 16s.*) *Net, 1l.*

**NOTANDA.—***Vide* "Digests."

**NOTARY.—Brooke's Treatise on the Office and Practice of a Notary of England.—**With a full collection of Precedents. Fourth Edition. By LEONE LEVI, Esq., F.S.A., of Lincoln's Inn, Barrister-at-Law. 8vo. 1876. 1l. 4s.

**NUISANCES.—FitzGerald.—***Vide* "Public Health."

**OATHS.—Braithwaite's Oaths in the Supreme Court of Judicature.—**A Manual for the use of Commissioners to Administer Oaths in the Supreme Court of Judicature in England. Part I. containing practical information respecting their Appointment, Designation, Jurisdiction, and Powers; Part II. comprising a collection of officially recognised Forms of Jurats and Oaths, with Explanatory Observations. By T. W. BRAITHWAITE, of the Record and Writ Clerks' Office. Fcap. 8vo. 1876. 4s. 6d.

"Specially useful to Commissioners."—*Law Magazine.*

"The work will, we doubt not, become the recognised guide of commissioners to administer oaths."—*Solicitors' Journal.*

**PARTITION.—Foster.—***Vide* "Real Estate."

**PARTNERSHIP.—Pollock's Digest of the Law of Partnership.** By FREDERICK POLLOCK, of Lincoln's Inn, Esq., Barrister-at-Law. Author of "Principles of Contract at Law and in Equity." Demy 8vo. 1877. 8s. 6d.

\*\* The object of this work is to give the substance of the Law of Partnership (excluding Companies) in a concise and definite form,

"Of the execution of the work, we can speak in terms of the highest praise. The language is simple, concise, and clear; and the general propositions may bear comparison with those of Sir James Stephen."—*Law Magazine.*

"Mr. Pollock's work appears eminently satisfactory . . . the book is praiseworthy in design, scholarly and complete in execution."—*Saturday Review.*

"A few more books written as carefully as the 'Digest of the Law of Partnership,' will, perhaps, remove some drawbacks, and render English law a pleasanter and easier subject to study than it is at present."—*The Examiner.*

\*\* *All standard Law Works are kept in Stock, in law calf and other bindings.*

**PATENTS.**—Hindmarch's Treatise on the Law relating to Patents.—8vo. 1846.    1*l.* 1*s.*

Johnson's Patentees' Manual; being a Treatise on the Law and Practice of Letters Patent, especially intended for the use of Patentees and Inventors.—By JAMES JOHNSON, Barrister-at-Law. and J. H. JOHNSON, Solicitor and Patent Agent. Fourth Edition. Thoroughly revised and much enlarged. Demy 8vo. 1879.   10*s.* 6*d.*

" A very excellent manual."—*Law Times,* February 8, 1879.
" The authors have not only a knowledge of the law, but of the working of the law. Besides th*e* table of cases there is a copious index to subjects.,'—*Law Journal,* March 1, 1879.

Thompson's Handbook of Patent Law of all Countries.—Third Edition, revised. By WM. P. THOMPSON, C.E., Head of the International Patent Office, Liverpool. 12mo. 1878.    *Net* 2*s.* 6*d.*

**PERSONAL PROPERTY.**—Smith.— *Vide* " Real Property."

**PETITIONS.**—Palmer.—*Vide* " Conveyancing."

Rogers.— *Vide* " Elections."

**PETTY SESSIONS.**—Stone's Practice for Justices of the Peace, Justices' Clerks and Solicitors at Petty and Special Sessions, in Summary Matters and Indictable Offences, with a List of Summary Convictions and of Matters not Criminal. With Forms. Eighth Edition. By THOMAS SIRRELL PRITCHARD, of the Inner Temple, Esq., Barrister-at-Law, Recorder of Wenlock. In 1 vol. Demy 8vo. 1877.    1*l.* 10*s.*

"The book, as a whole, is thoroughly satisfactory, and, having gone carefully through it, we can recommend it with confidence to the numerous body of our readers who are daily interested in the subjects to which it relates."—*Solicitors' Journal.*

**POOR LAW.**—Davis' Treatise on the Poor Laws.—Being Vol. IV. of Burns' Justice of the Peace. 8vo. 1869.    1*l.* 11*s.* 6*d.*

**POWERS.**—Farwell on Powers.—A Concise Treatise on Powers. By GEORGE FARWELL, B.A., of Lincoln's Inn, Esq., Barrister-at-Law. 8vo. 1874.    1*l.* 1*s.*

" We recommend Mr. Farwell's book as containing within a small compass what would otherwise have to be sought out in the pages of hundreds of confusing reports."—*The Law.*

**PRECEDENTS.**— *Vide* " Conveyancing."

**PRINCIPAL AND AGENT.**—Petgrave's Principal and Agent.—A Manual of the Law of Principal and Agent. By E. C. PETGRAVE, Solicitor. 12mo. 1857.    7*s.* 6*d.*

Petgrave's Code of the Law of Principal and Agent, with a Preface. By E. C. PETGRAVE, Solicitor. Demy 12mo. 1876.    *Net, sewed,* 2*s.*

**PRIVY COUNCIL.** — Finlason's History, Constitution, and Character of the Judicial Committee of the Privy Council, considered as a Judicial Tribunal, especially in Ecclesiastical Cases, with special reference to the right and duty of its members to declare their opinions. By W. F. FINLASON, Barrister-at-Law. Demy 8vo. 1878.    4*s.* 6*d.*

Lattey's Handy Book on the Practice and Procedure before the Privy Council.—By ROBERT THOMAS LATTEY, Attorney of the Court of Queen's Bench, and of the High Court of Bengal. 12mo. 1869.    6*s.*

**PROBATE.**—Browne's Probate Practice: a Treatise on the Principles and Practice of the Court of Probate, in Contentious and Non-Contentious Business, with the Statutes, Rules, Fees, and Forms relating thereto. By GEORGE BROWNE, Esq., Barrister-at-Law, Recorder of Ludlow. 8vo. 1873.    1*l.* 1*s.*

" A cursory glance through Mr. Browne's work shows that it has been compiled with more than ordinary care and intelligence. We should consult it with every confidence."—*Law Times.*

Haynes.— *Vide* " Leading Cases."

\*\* *All standard Law Works are kept in Stock, in law calf and other bindings.*

**PUBLIC HEALTH.**—Chambers' Digest of the Law relating to Public Health and Local Government.—With Notes of 1073 leading Cases. Various official documents ; precedents of By-laws and Regulations. The Statutes in full. A Table of Offences and Punishments, and a Copious Index. Seventh Edition, enlarged and revised, with SUPPLEMENT containing new Local Government Board By-Laws in full. Imperial 8vo. 1875-7. 1*l.* 8*s.*

\*\* The SUPPLEMENT may be had separately, price 9*s.*

FitzGerald's Public Health and Rivers Pollution Prevention Acts.—The Law relating to Public Health and Local Government, as contained in the Public Health Act, 1875, with Introduction and Notes, showing all the alterations in the Existing Law, with reference to the Cases, &c.; together with a Supplement containing " The Rivers Pollution Prevention Act, 1876." With Explanatory Introduction, Notes, Cases, and Index. By G. A. R. FITZGERALD, Esq., Barrister-at-Law. Royal 8vo. 1876. 1*l.* 1*s.*

" A copious and well-executed analytical index completes the work which we can confidently recommend to the officers and members of sanitary authorities, and all interested in the subject matter of the new Act."—*Law Magazine and Review.*

" Mr. FitzGerald comes forward with a special qualification for the task, for he was employed by the Government in the preparation of the Act of 1875; and, as he himself says, has necessarily, for some time past, devoted attention to the law relating to public health and local government."—*Law Journal.*

**PUBLIC MEETINGS.**—Chambers' Handbook for Public Meetings, including Hints as to the Summoning and Management of them ; and as to the Duties of Chairmen, Clerks, Secretaries, and other Officials; Rules of Debate, &c., to which is added a Digest of Reported Cases. By GEORGE F. CHAMBERS, Esq., Barrister-at-Law. 12mo. 1878. *Net,* 2*s.* 6*d.*

**QUARTER SESSIONS.**—Leeming & Cross's General and Quarter Sessions of the Peace.—Their Jurisdiction and Practice in other than Criminal matters. Second Edition. By HORATIO LLOYD, Esq., Recorder of Chester, Judge of County Courts, and Deputy-Chairman of Quarter Sessions, and H. F. THURLOW, of the Inner Temple, Esq., Barrister-at-Law. 8vo. 1876. 1*l.* 1*s.*

" The present editors appear to have taken the utmost pains to make the volume complete, and, from our examination of it, we can thoroughly recommend it to all interested in the practice of quarter sessions."—*Law Times*

Pritchard's Quarter Sessions.—The Jurisdiction, Practice and Procedure of the Quarter Sessions in Criminal, Civil, and Appellate Matters. By THOS. SIRRELL PRITCHARD, of the Inner Temple, Esq., Barrister-at-Law, Recorder of Wenlock. 8vo. 1875. 2*l.* 2*s.*

" We can confidently say that it is written throughout with clearness and intelligence, and that both in legislation and in case law it is carefully brought down to the most recent date."—*Solicitors' Journal.*

**RAILWAYS.**—Browne and Theobald's Law of Railways. By J. H. BALFOUR BROWNE, of the Middle Temple, Registrar of the Railway Commissioners, and H. S. THEOBALD, of the Inner Temple, Esqrs., Barristers-at-Law. (*In preparation.*)

Lely's Railway and Canal Traffic Act, 1873.—And other Railway and Canal Statutes; with the General Orders, Forms, and Table of Fees. By J. M. LELY, Esq. Post 8vo. 1873. 8*s.*

\*\* *All standard Law Works are kept in Stock, in law calf and other binding*

**RATES AND RATING.—Castle's Practical Treatise on the Law of Rating.** By EDWARD JAMES CASTLE, of the Inner Temple, Barrister-at-Law. Demy 8vo. 1879. 1*l.* 1*s.*

"Mr. Castle's book is a correct, exhaustive, clear and concise view of the law."—*Law Times.*

"The book is a useful assistant in a perplexed branch of Law."—*Law Journal.*

**Chamber's Law relating to Rates and Rating:** with especial reference to the Powers and Duties of Rate-levying Local Authorities, and their Officers. Being the Statutes in full and brief Notes of 550 Cases. By G. F. CHAMBERS, Esq., Barrister-at-Law. Imp. 8vo. 1878. 12*s.*

**REAL ESTATE.—Foster's Law of Joint Ownership and Partition of Real Estate.** By EDWARD JOHN FOSTER, M.A., late of Lincoln's Inn, Barrister-at-Law. 8vo. 1878. 10*s.* 6*d.*

"Mr. Foster may be congratulated on having produced a very satisfactory *vade mecum* on the Law of Joint Ownership and Partition. He has taken considerable pains to make his treatise practically useful, and has combined within the fifteen chapters into which the book is divided, brevity of statement with completeness of treatment."—*Law Magazine.*

**REAL PROPERTY.— Greenwood's Recent Real Property Statutes.** Comprising those passed during the years 1874-1877 inclusive. Consolidated with the Earlier Statutes thereby Amended. With Copious Notes, and a Supplement containing the Orders under the Settled Estates Act, 1878. By HARRY GREENWOOD, M.A., Esq., Barrister-at-Law. 8vo. 1878. 10*s.*

"To students particularly this collection, with the careful notes and references to previous legislation, will be of considerable value."—*Law Times.*

"The author has added notes which, especially on the Vendor and Purchaser Act, and the Settled Estates Act, are likely to be useful to the practitioner . . . so far as we have tested them, the st·tements appear to be generally accurate and careful, and the work will be found exceedingly handy for reference."—*Solicitors' Journal.*

"Mr. Greenwood's book gives such of the provisions of the amended statutes as are still in force, as well as the provisions of the new statutes, in order to show more clearly the effect of the recent legislation."—*Law Journal.*

**Leake's Elementary Digest of the Law of Property in Land.**—Containing: Introduction. Part I. The Sources of the Law.—Part II. Estates in Land. By STEPHEN MARTIN LEAKE, Barrister-at-Law. 8vo. 1874. 1*l.* 2*s.*

*.* The above forms a complete Introduction to the Study of the Law of Real Property.

**Shearwood's Real Property.—A Concise Abridgment** of the Law of Real Property and an Introduction to Conveyancing. Designed to facilitate the subject for Students preparing for Examination. By JOSEPH A. SHEARWOOD, of Lincoln's Inn, Esq., Barrister-at-Law. Demy 8vo. 1878. 6*s.* 6*d.*

"The present law is expounded paragraphically, so that it could be actually *learned* without understanding the origin from which it has sprung, or the principles on which it is based."—*Law Journal.*

**Shelford's Real Property Statutes.—Eighth Edition.** By T. H. CARSON, Esq., Barrister-at-Law. 8vo. 1874. 1*l.* 10*s.*

**Smith's Real and Personal Property.—A Compendium** of the Law of Real and Personal Property, primarily connected with Conveyancing. Designed as a second book for Students, and as a digest of the most useful learning for Practitioners. By JOSIAH W. SMITH, B.C.L., Q.C. Fifth Edition. 2 vols. Demy 8vo. 1877. 2*l.* 2*s.*

"He has given to the student a book which he may read over and over again with profit and pleasure."—*Law Times.*

"The work before us will, we think, be found of very great service to the practitioner."—*Solicitors' Journal.*

*.* *All standard Law Works are kept in Stock, in law calf and other bindings.*

**REGISTRATION.—Browne's(G.Lathom)Parliamentary and Municipal Registration Act, 1878** (41 & 42 Vict. cap. 26); with an Introduction, Notes, and Additional Forms. By G. LATHOM BROWNE, of the Middle Temple, Esq., Barrister-at-Law. 12mo. 1878.                    5s. 6d.

Rogers—*Vide* "Elections."

**REGISTRATION CASES.—Hopwood and Coltman's Registration Cases.**—Vol. I. (1868-1872). *Net*, 2l. 18s. Calf. Vol. II. (1873-1878). *Net*, 2l. 10s. Calf.

**RIVERS POLLUTION PREVENTION.—FitzGerald's Rivers Pollution Prevention Act, 1875.**—With Explanatory Introduction, Notes, Cases, and Index. Royal 8vo. 1876.   3s. 6d.

**ROMAN LAW.—Cumin.—***Vide* "Civil."

**Greene's Outlines of Roman Law.**—Consisting chiefly of an Analysis and Summary of the Institutes. For the use of Students. By T. WHITCOMBE GREENE, B.C.L., of Lincoln's Inn, Barrister-at-Law. Third Edition. Foolscap 8vo. 1875.   7s. 6d.

**Mears' Student's Ortolan.**—An Analysis of M. Ortolan's **Institutes of Justinian,** including the History and Generalization of ROMAN LAW. By T. LAMBERT MEARS, M.A., LL.D. Lond., of the Inner Temple, Barrister-at-Law. *Published by permission of the late M. Ortolan.* Post 8vo. 1876. 12s. 6d.

Ruegg.—*Vide* "Justinian."

**SAUNDERS' REPORTS.—Williams' (Sir E. V.) Notes to Saunders' Reports.**—By the late Serjeant WILLIAMS. Continued to the present time by the Right Hon. Sir EDWARD VAUGHAN WILLIAMS. 2 vols. Royal 8vo. 1871.   2l. 10s.

**SETTLED ESTATES.—Middleton's Settled Estates Act, 1877, and the Settled Estates Act Orders, 1878,** with Introduction, Notes and Forms, and Summary of Practice. Second Edition. By JAMES W. MIDDLETON, B.A., of Lincoln's Inn, Barrister-at-Law. 12mo. 1879.            4s. 6d.

"A complete work as a practical edition of the Settled Estates Act, 1877, and will be found exceedingly useful to legal practitioners."—*Law Journal.*

"The book is a well-timed and useful manual of the Act."—*Solicitors' Journal.*

"The book is excellently arranged, particularly in the summary of practice."—*Saturday Review.*

**SHERIFF LAW.—Churchill's Law of the Office and Duties of the Sheriff,** with the Writs and Forms relating to the Office. By CAMERON CHURCHILL, B.A., of the Inner Temple, Barrister-at-Law, assisted by A. CARMICHAEL BRUCE, B.A., of Lincoln's Inn, Barrister-at-Law. Demy 8vo. 1879.   18s.

"This is a work upon a subject of large practical importance, and seems to have been compiled with exceptional care. . . . . There is an appendix of forms which will be found useful."—*Law Times.*

"Under-Sheriffs, and lawyers generally, will find this a useful book to have by them, both for perusal and reference."—*Law Magazine.*

**SHIPPING,** and *vide* "Admiralty."

**Boyd's Merchant Shipping Laws;** being a Consolidation of all the Merchant Shipping and Passenger Acts from 1854 to 1876, inclusive; with Notes of all the leading English and American Cases on the subjects affected by Legislation, and an Appendix containing the New Rules issued in October, 1876; forming a complete Treatise on Maritime Law. By A. C. BOYD, LLB., of the Inner Temple, Esq., Barrister-at-Law, and Midland Circuit. 8vo. 1876.            1l. 5s.

"We can recommend the work as a very useful compendium of shipping law."—*Law Times.*

**SIGNING JUDGMENTS.—Walker.—***Vide* "Judgments."

\*\*\* *All standard Law Works are kept in Stock, in law calf and other bindings.*

**SOLICITORS.**—Cordery's Law relating to Solicitors of the Supreme Court of Judicature.—With an Appendix of Statutes and Rules. By A. CORDERY, of the Inner Temple, Esq., Barrister-at-Law. Demy 8vo. 1878.    14s.

"Mr. Cordery writes tersley and clearly, and displays in general great industry and care in the collection of cases."—*Solicitors' Journal.*

"The chapters on liability of solicitors and on lien may be selected as two of the best in the book."—*Law Journal.*

**SOLICITORS' GUIDES.**—*Vide* "Examination Guides."

**STAMP LAWS.**—Tilsley's Treatise on the Stamp Laws.—Being an Analytical Digest of all the Statutes and Cases relating to Stamp Duties, with practical remarks thereon. Third Edition. With Tables of all the Stamp Duties payable in the United Kingdom after the 1st January, 1871, and of Former Duties, &c., &c. By E. H. TILSLEY, of the Inland Revenue Office. 8vo. 1871.    18s.

**STATUTES**, and *vide* "Acts of Parliament."

Biddle's Table of Statutes.—A Table of References to unrepealed Public General Acts, arranged in the Alphabetical Order of their Short or Popular Titles. Second Edition, including References to all the Acts in Chitty's Collection of Statutes. Royal 8vo. 1870. *(Published at 9s. 6d.)*    *Net,* 2s. 6d.

Chitty's Collection of Statutes.—A Collection of Statutes of Practical Utility ; with Notes thereon. The Third Edition, containing all the Statutes of Practical Utility in the Civil and Criminal Administration of Justice to the Present Time. By W. N. WELSBY and EDWARD BEAVAN, Esqrs., Barristers-at-Law. In 4 very thick vols. Royal 8vo. 1865. *(Published at 12l. 12s.)*
Reduced to, net, 6l. 6s.

Supplements to the above. By HORATIO LLOYD, Esq., Judge of County Courts, and Deputy-Chairman of Quarter Sessions for Cheshire. Royal 8vo. Part I., comprising the Statutes for 1873, 7s. 6d. Part II., 1874, 6s. Part III., 1875, 16s. Part IV., 1876, 6s. 6d. Part V., 1877, 4s. 6d. Part VI., 1878, 10s. Part VII., 1879, 7s. 6d., sewed.
\*\*\* Continued Annually.

" When he (Lord Campbell) was upon the Bench he always had this work by him, and no statutes were ever referred to by the Bar which he could not find in it."

\*The Revised Edition of the Statutes, A.D. 1235-1868, prepared under the direction of the Statute Law Committee, published by the authority of Her Majesty's Government. In 15 vols. Imperial 8vo. 1870-1878.    19l. 9s.

| | | |
|---|---|---|
| Vol. 1.—Henry III. to James II., | 1235-1685 | . 1l. 1s. 0d. |
| „ 2.—Will. & Mary to 10 Geo. III., | 1688-1770 | . 1 0 0 |
| „ 3.—11 Geo. III. to 41 Geo. III., | 1770-1800 | . 0 17 0 |
| „ 4.—41 Geo. III. to 51 Geo. III., | 1801-1811 | . 0 18 0 |
| „ 5.—52 Geo. III. to 4 Geo. IV., | 1812-1823 | . 1 5 0 |
| „ 6.—5 Geo. IV. to 1 & 2 Will. IV., | 1824-1831 | . 1 6 0 |
| „ 7.—2 & 3 Will. IV. to 6 & 7 Will. IV., | 1831-1836 | . 1 10 0 |
| „ 8.—7 Will. IV. & 1 Vict. to 5 & 6 Vict., | 1837-1842 | . 1 12 6 |
| 9.—6 & 7 Vict. to 9 & 10 Vict., | 1843-1846 | . 1 11 6 |
| „ 10.—10 & 11 Vict. to 13 & 14 Vict., | 1847-1850 | . 1 7 6 |
| „ 11.—14 & 15 Vict. to 16 & 17 Vict., | 1851-1853 | . 1 4 0 |
| „ 12.—17 & 18 Vict. to 19 & 20 Vict., | 1854-1856 | . 1 6 0 |
| „ 13.—20 Vict. to 24 & 25 Vict., | 1857-1861 | . 1 10 0 |
| „ 14.—25 & 26 Vict. to 28 & 29 Vict., | 1862-1865 | . 1 10 0 |
| „ 15.—29 & 30 Vict. to 31 & 32 Vict., and Supplement, | 1866-1867-8 | 1 10 6 |

\*\*\* The above Work is now completed.

\*\*\* *All standard Law Works are kept in Stock in low calf and other bindings.*

**STATUTES.**—*Continued.*

**\*Chronological Table of and Index to the Statutes** to the end of the Session of 1878. Fifth Edition, imperial 8vo. 1879. 14s.

**\*Public General Statutes**, royal 8vo, issued in parts and in complete volumes, and supplied immediately on publication.

\* Printed by Her Majesty's Printers, and Sold by STEVENS & SONS.

**Head's Statutes by Heart**; being a System of Memoria Technica, applied to Statutes, and embracing Common Law, Chancery, Bankruptcy, Criminal Law, Probate and Divorce, and Conveyancing. By FREDERICK WILLIAM HEAD, of the Inner Temple, Student-at-Law. Demy 8vo. 1877. *Net*, 1s. 6d.

**SUMMARY CONVICTIONS.**—**Paley's Law and Practice of Summary Convictions under the Summary Jurisdiction Acts, 1848 and 1879**; including Proceedings preliminary and subsequent to Convictions, and the responsibility of convicting Magistrates and their Officers, with Forms. Sixth Edition. By W. H. MACNAMARA, Esq., Barrister-at-Law. Demy 8vo. 1879. 1l. 4s.

" We gladly welcome this good edition of a good book."—*Solicitors' Journal.*

**Templer's Summary Jurisdiction Act, 1879.**— Rules and Schedules of Forms. With Notes. By FREDERIC GORDON TEMPLER, of the Inner Templer, Esq., Barrister-at-Law. Demy 8vo. 1880. 5s.

" We think this edition everything that could be desired."—*Sheffield Post*, Feb. 7, 1880.

**Wigram.**—*Vide* "Justice of the Peace."

**SUMMONSES AND ORDERS.**—**Archibald.**— *Vide* " Judges' Chambers Practice."

**TORTS.**—**Addison on Wrongs and their Remedies.**— Being a Treatise on the Law of Torts. By C. G. ADDISON, Esq., Author of " The Law of Contracts." Fifth Edition. Re-written. By L. W. CAVE, Esq., M.A., one of Her Majesty's Counsel, Recorder of Lincoln. Royal 8vo. 1879. 1l. 18s.

"Since the last edition of this work was published, by the operation of the Judicature Acts, great changes have been effected in practice and pleading. . . . In the present edition the nature of the right infringed has been taken as the basis of the arrangement throughout. . . . Every effort has been made, while assimilating this edition in form to the companion treatise *On Contracts*, to maintain the reputation which the work has already acquired."— *Extract from Preface.*

" As now presented, this valuable treatise must prove highly acceptable to judges and the profession."—*Law Times*, February 7th, 1880.

"Cave's 'Addison on Torts' will be recognized as an indispensable addition to every lawyer's library."—*Law Magazine and Review*, February, 1880.

**TRADE MARKS.**—**Rules under the Trade Marks' Registration Act, 1875 (by Authority).** Sewed. *Net*, 1s.

**Sebastian on the Law of Trade Marks.**—The Law of Trade Marks and their Registration, and matters connected therewith, including a chapter on Goodwill. Together with Appendices containing Precedents of Injunctions, &c.; The Trade Marks Registration Acts, 1875—7, the Rules and Instructions thereunder; The Merchandise Marks Act, 1862, and other Statutory enactments; and The United States Statute, 1870 and 1875, and the Treaty with the United States, 1877 ; and the New Rules and Instructions issued in February, 1878. With a copious Index. By LEWIS BOYD SEBASTIAN, B.C.L., M.A., of Lincoln's Inn, Esq., Barrister-at-Law. 8vo. 1878. 14s.

" The book cannot fail to be of service to a large class of lawyers."—*Solicitors' Journal.*

" Mr. Sebastian has written the fullest and most methodical book on trade marks which has appeared in England since the passing of the Trade Marks Registration Acts."—*Trade Marks.*

" Viewed as a compilation, the book leaves little to be desired. Viewed as a treatise on a subject of growing importance, it also strikes us as being well, and at any rate carefully executed."—*Law Journal.*

"Mr. Sebastian's book is a careful statement of the law,"—*Law Times.*

\*\* *All Standard Law Works are kept in Stock, in law calf and other bindings.*

**TRADE MARKS.**—*Continued.*

Sebastian's Digest of Cases of Trade Mark, Trade Name, Trade Secret, Goodwill, &c., decided in the Courts of the United Kingdom, India, the Colonies, and the United States of America. By LEWIS BOYD SEBASTIAN, B.C.L., M.A., of Lincoln's Inn, Esq., Barrister-at-Law, Author of "The Law of Trade Marks." Demy 8vo. 1879.    1*l*. 1*s*.

"A digest which will be of very great value to all practitioners who have to advise on matters connected with trade marks."—*Solicitors' Journal*, July 26, 1879.

Trade Marks' Journal.—4to. Sewed. (*Issued fortnightly.*)
Nos. 1 to 192 are now ready.                     *Net, each* 1*s*.
Index to Vol. I. (Nos. 1—47.)                    *Net,* 3*s*.
Ditto, „ Vol. II. (Nos. 48—97.)                  *Net,* 3*s*.
Ditto, „ Vol. III. (Nos. 98—123.)                *Net,* 3*s*.
Ditto, „ Vol. IV. (Nos. 124—156.)                *Net,* 3*s*.
Ditto, „ Vol. V. (Nos. 157—183.)                 *Net,* 3*s*.

Wood's Law of Trade Marks.—Containing the Merchandise Marks' Act, 1862, and the Trade Marks' Registration Act, 1875 ; with the Rules thereunder, and Practical Directions for obtaining Registration ; with Notes, full Table of Cases and Index. By J. BIGLAND WOOD, Esq., Barrister-at-Law. 12mo. 1876. 5*s*.

**TRAMWAYS.**—Palmer.—*Vide* "Conveyancing."

Sutton's Tramway Acts.—The Tramway Acts of the United Kingdom, with Notes on the Law and Practice, and an Appendix containing the Standing Orders of Parliament, Rules of the Board of Trade relating to Tramways, and Decisions of the Referees with respect to Locus Standi. By HENRY SUTTON, B.A., of Lincoln's Inn, Barrister-at-Law. Post 8vo. 1874. 12*s*.

**TRUSTS AND TRUSTEES.**—Godefroi's Digest of the Principles of the Law of Trusts and Trustees.—By HENRY GODEFROI, of Lincoln's Inn, Esq., Barrister-at-Law. Joint Author of "Godefroi and Shortt's Law of Railway Companies." Demy 8vo. 1879. 1*l*. 1*s*.

"No one who refers to this book for information on a question within its range is, we think, likely to go away unsatisfied."—*Saturday Review*, September 6, 1879.
"Is a work of great utility to the practitioner."—*Law Magazine*.
"As a digest of the law, Mr. Godefroi's work merits commendation, for the author's statements are brief and clear, and for his statements he refers to a goodly array of authorities. In the table of cases the references to the several contemporaneous reports are given, and there is a very copious index to subjects."—*Law Journal*.

**USES.**—Jones (W. Hanbury) on Uses.—8vo. 1862. 7*s*.

**VENDORS AND PURCHASERS.**—Dart's Vendors and Purchasers.—A Treatise on the Law and Practice relating to Vendors and Purchasers of Real Estate. By J. HENRY DART, of Lincoln's Inn, Esq.. one of the Six Conveyancing Counsel of the High Court of Justice, Chancery Division. Fifth Edition. By the AUTHOR and WILLIAM BARBER, of Lincoln's Inn, Esq., Barrister-at-Law. 2 vols. Royal 8vo. 1876. 3*l*. 13*s*. 6*d*.

"A standard work like Mr. Dart's is beyond all praise."—*The Law Journal*.

**WATERS.**—Woolrych on the Law of Waters.—Including Rights in the Sea, Rivers, Canals, &c. Second Edition. 8vo. 1851.
Goddard.—*Vide* "Easements."    *Net,* 10*s*.

**WATERWORKS.**—Palmer.—*Vide* "Conveyancing."

**WILLS.**—Rawlinson's Guide to Solicitors on taking Instructions for Wills.—8vo. 1874. 4*s*.

**WILLS.**—*Continued.*

### Theobald's Concise Treatise on the Construction of Wills.—With Table of Cases and Full Index. By H. S. THEOBALD, of the Inner Temple, Esq., Barrister-at-Law, and Fellow of Wadham College, Oxford. 8vo. 1876. 1*l.*

"Mr. Theobald has certainly given evidence of extensive investigation, conscientious labour, and clear exposition."—*Law Magazine.*

"We desire to record our decided impression, after a somewhat careful examination, that this is a book of great ability and value. It bears on every page traces of care and sound judgment. It is certain to prove of great practical usefulness, for it supplies a want which was beginning to be distinctly felt."—*Solicitors' Journal.*

"His arrangement being good, and his statement ot the effect of the decisions being clear, his work cannot fail to be of practical utility, and as such we can commend it to the attention of the profession."—*Law Times.*

"It is remarkably well arranged, and its contents embrace all the principal heads on the subject."—*Law Journal.*

**WRONGS.**—*Vide* "Torts."

---

REPORTS.—*A large stock new and second-hand. Estimates on application.*

BINDING.—*Executed in the best manner at moderate prices and with dispatch.*

---

### The Law Reports, Law Journal, and all other Reports, bound to Office Patterns, at Office Prices.

PRIVATE ACTS.—*The Publishers of this Catalogue possess the largest known collection of Private Acts of Parliament (including Public and Local), and can supply single copies commencing from a very early period.*

VALUATIONS.—*For Probate, Partnership, or other purposes.*

---

## STEVENS AND SONS,

### Law Publishers, Booksellers, Exporters and Licensed Valuers,

#### 119, CHANCERY LANE, LONDON, W.C.

# NEW WORKS AND NEW EDITIONS.

## IN PREPARATION.

**Archibald's Handbook of the Practice in the Common Law Divisions of the High Court of Justice;** with Forms for the use of Country Solicitors. By *W. F. A. Archibald*, Esq., Barrister-at-Law, Author of " Forms of Summonses and Orders, with Notes for use at Judges' Chambers, &c. (*In the press*).

**Baker's Law of Highways in England and Wales,** including Bridges and Locomotives. Comprising a succinct code of the several provisions under each head, the statutes at length in an Appendix; with Notes, Forms, and complete Index. By *Thomas Baker*, of the Inner Temple, Esq., Barrister-at-Law. (*Nearly ready.*)

**Ball's Short Digest of the Common Law;** being the Principles of Torts and Contracts, chiefly founded upon the works of Addison, **with Illustrative Cases,** for the use of Students. By *W. Edmund Ball*, LL.B., late " Holt Scholar " of Gray's Inn, Barrister-at-Law and Midland Circuit. (*Nearly ready.*)

**Browne and Theobald's Law of Railways.** By *J. H. Balfour Browne*, of the Middle Temple, Esq., Barrister-at-Law, Registrar to the Railway Commissioners, and *H. S. Theobald*, of the Inner Temple, Esq., Barrister-at-Law.

**Bullen and Leake's Precedents of Pleading.** Fourth Edition. By *T. J. Bullen*, Esq., Special Pleader, and *Cyril Dodd*, of the Inner Temple, Esq , Barrister-at-Law. (*In the press.*)

**Coote's Treatise on the Law of Mortgage.** Fourth Edition, thoroughly revised. By *William Wyllys Mackeson*, Esq., one of Her Majesty's Counsel. (*In the press.*)

**Daniell's Chancery Practice.—Sixth Edition.—By *L. Field* and *E. C. Dunn*, Esqrs., Barristers-at-Law. Assisted by *W. H. Upjohn*, Esq., Student and Holt Scholar of Gray's Inn, &c., Editor of the Third Edition of "Daniell's Forms."

**Jepson's Lands Clauses Consolidation Acts;** with Decisions, Forms, and Table of Costs. By *Arthur Jepson*, of Lincoln's Inn, Esq., Barrister-at-Law. (*In the press.*)

**Jervis on the Office and Duties of Coroners;** with Forms and Precedents. Fourth Edition. By *R. E. Melshcimer*, of the Inner Temple, Esq., Barrister-at-Law. (*In the press.*)

**Morgan and Davey's Treatise on Costs in Chancery.** Second Edition. By *George Osborne Morgan*, of Lincoln's Inn, Esq., one of Her Majesty's Counsel; assisted by *E. A. Wurtzburg*, of Lincoln's Inn, Esq., Barrister-at-Law. With an Appendix, containing Forms and Precedents of Bills of Costs.

**Smith's Treatise on the Law of Negligence.** By *Horace Smith*, B.A., of the Inner Temple, Esq., Barrister-at-Law, Author of "The Law of Landlord and Tenant," Editor of "Roscoe's Criminal Evidence." (*Nearly ready.*)

**Stone's Practice for Justices of the Peace, Justices' Clerks, and Solicitors at Petty and Special Sessions, &c.** Ninth Edition. By *F. G. Templer*, of the Inner Temple, Esq., Barrister-at-Law, Editor of "The Summary Jurisdiction Act, 1879."

STEVENS AND SONS, 119, CHANCERY LANE, LONDON, W.C.

www.ingramcontent.com/pod-product-compliance
Lightning Source LLC
Chambersburg PA
CBHW030911270326
41929CB00008B/660